KU-712-869

W.T. GRAHAM

AA

Explorer Scotland

Gilbert Summers

Front cover
Top: Highland dancing at the Edinburgh Military Tattoo (Jim Carnie and Jonathon Smith); Middle (left to right) (a) *the Superfast ferry passing under the Forth Rail Bridge (Jonathon Smith);* (b) *Edinburgh's Scottish Whisky Heritage Centre (Ken Paterson);* (c) *a symbol of Scotland: the thistle (Eric Ellington); (d) Scottish piper (Chris Coe); (e) Glasgow Science Centre (Stephen Whitehorne)*
Spine
Tartan rugs at the Edinburgh Woollen Mill (Stephen Whitehorne)
Back cover
Left: Kilchurn Castle, Loch Awe (Stephen Whitehorne); Right: Highland cow (Stephen Whitehorne)
Page 3: Brodick Castle, Arran, Islands of the Clyde

All pictures from the AA World Travel Library

Written by Gilbert Summers

Published by AA Publishing, a trading name of Automobile Association Developments Limited, whose registered office is Fanum House, Basing View, Basingstoke, Hampshire RG21 4EA. Registered number 1878835.

ISBN 978-0-7495-4382-5

The contents of this publication are believed correct at the time of printing. Nevertheless, AA Publishing accepts no responsibility for errors, omissions, or changes in the details given, or for the consequences of readers' reliance on this information. This does not affect your statutory rights. Assessments of the attractions, hotels and restaurants are based upon the author's own experience, and contain subjective opinions that may not reflect the publisher's own opinion or a reader's experience. We have tried to ensure accuracy, but things do change, so please let us know if you have any comments or corrections.

A CIP catalogue record for this book is available from the British Library.

Colour separation by Fotographics Ltd
Printed and bound in Italy by Printer Trento Srl

Find out more about AA Publishing and the wide range of travel publications and services the AA provides by visiting our website at www.theAA.com/travel.

Reprinted 2007. Information verified and updated.
Reprinted June 2005, Feb 2006
Revised sixth edition 2005
First published 1995

Titles in the Explorer series:
Australia • Boston & New England • Britain • Brittany
California • Canada • Caribbean • China • Costa Rica • Crete
Cuba • Cyprus • Egypt • Florence & Tuscany • Florida
France • Germany • Greek Islands • Hawaii • India • Ireland
Italy • Japan • London • Mallorca • Mexico • New York
New Zealand • Paris • Portugal • Provence • Rome
San Francisco • Scotland • South Africa • Spain • Thailand
Tunisia • Turkey • Venice • Vietnam

A02985

How to use this book

ORGANIZATION

Scotland Is, Scotland Was
Discusses aspects of life and culture in modern Scotland and explores significant periods in its history.

A–Z
An alphabetical listing of places to visit. The book begins with sections on Edinburgh and Glasgow, and is subsequently divided into regions. Places of interest are listed alphabetically within each section. Suggested walks, drives, and Focus On articles, which provide an insight into aspects of life in Scotland, are included in each section.

Travel Facts
Contains the practical information that is vital for a successful trip.

Hotels and Restaurants
Lists places to stay and places to eat alphabetically by region. The entries are graded budget, moderate, or expensive.

Admission Charges
Inexpensive is under £4
Moderate is between £4 and £8
Expensive is £8 and over

ABOUT THE RATINGS
Most places described in this book have been given a separate rating. These are as follows:

- ▶▶▶ **Do not miss**
- ▶▶ **Highly recommended**
- ▶ **Worth seeing**

MAP REFERENCES
To make the location of a particular place easier to find, every main entry in this book is given a map reference, such as 176B3. The first number (176) indicates the page on which the map can be found, the letter (B) and the second number (3) pinpoint the square in which the main entry is located. The maps on the inside front cover and inside back cover are referred to as IFC and IBC respectively.

Contents

Gilbert Summers is a Scot who has spent many years living in Scotland and earning his living writing about his native land, working closely with the tourism industry. He has produced a variety of material for many international publishers.

Above: Walking by Rest and Be Thankful, Arrochar

My Scotland

Growing up in the northern part of a pre-motorway Scotland brought its own pleasingly skewed perceptions of the shape and form of the nation. Aberdeen was a dramatic granite city in the south, Edinburgh was an age away and only really existed as an illustration on a tin of shortbread. Skye and the west coast were fantastically exotic. Orkney and Shetland were definitely abroad. Yet all were encompassed by "Scottishness." Since then, distances have "shrunk," both in my perception and because of improved road and rail networks. Now, travel in Scotland is measured in more manageable statistics: over five hours to the Moray Firth coast from the border near Carlisle; just an hour from Inverness to Ullapool and the ferry to the Western Isles; and less than one hour by train from Edinburgh to Glasgow. But the vague feeling of many Scotlands still clings on.

It is remarkable how little time it takes to reach widely contrasting places, and for me this is one of the best things about Scotland. If the Edinburgh Festival crowds begin to wear you down, there are high brackeny green hills close at hand in the Pentlands. Or you can lose yourself in native Scots pinewoods that lie within easy distance of, say, Inverness airport.

As a native, I have always wondered why Scotland, with all its diversity in ancestry, landscape, and culture, drapes itself in tartan finery as an instantly recognizable symbol of Scottishness. The humble cloth of the Celt—once despised, even outlawed—has become a powerful marketing tool. Yet, this convenient stereotype hides a complex character. I have always exhorted any traveller to pull aside the tartan curtain and discover other threads of the nation's complex story, such as Picts and Vikings, or the close links with France and the Low Countries, or even why more Scots took the government side at the Battle of Culloden than joined to fight with Bonnie Prince Charlie.

Scotland is certainly fertile ground for romantics. Hills that make the heart ache, city skylines with castles and spires, tales of heroism in the glen—you can find them all. Maybe delving too deep isn't necessary. Just sit back and enjoy the sheer variety of it all.

Gilbert Summers

Scotland Is

9

Misty glens, lochs, mountains, tartan, bagpipes, and kilts: these are the most familiar images of Scotland. How these essentially Highland aspects came to represent the whole of Scotland—Highland, Lowland, urban, and rural—is one of the oddities of the nation's history.

TARTAN Today, you can cross the Border and hear bagpipes in a Southern Uplands town, eat shortbread from a tartan wrapper in the middle of Glasgow, and take in a Highland Games within easy reach of Edinburgh. All this is well before you reach the real Highlands. Scotland, at least those aspects of it dealing with tourism, embraces its kilted image wholeheartedly: tartan sells.

The glorious paradox is that if a tartan-clad Highlander had appeared in a Lowland town a few centuries ago, he would have been locked up, if not shot on sight. The Highlanders were regarded as barbarous thieves by Lowland Scots. After the crushing of the final rebellion against the Hanoverian dynasty on Culloden Moor near Inverness, the tartan was even banned by Act of Parliament. Tartan was associated with revolt and lawlessness. Now, thoroughly rehabilitated, the kilt and its associated paraphernalia represent the whole of Scotland, Highland or Lowland, Gaelic-speaking or otherwise, to many of today's visitors.

The new face of Scottish tradition?

BAGPIPES The unmistakable tones of the bagpipe or Highland war pipe form the soundtrack to the romantic image of Scotland. Perhaps originally a device for signalling across long Highland distances, the bagpipe survived partly through its use in Highland regiments, and now plays its role in many pipe bands. Most Scottish towns have at least one band, and the pipes create instant Highland atmosphere at all kinds of gatherings from protest marches to weddings.

SCENERY As for the misty glens and bens (high hills), a love for this kind of landscape grew out of the cult of the picturesque embraced by the Romantic poets (William Wordsworth, strongly associated with the English Lake District, made several tours of the Scottish Highlands). Today, a taste for wild scenery is for many people the main reason for visiting Scotland.

The scenery is certainly splendid, and it is perfectly possible to see some of Scotland's most rugged places without leaving a main road. This is why Glencoe appears on the headboard of many a coach. It provides a matchless combination of awesome scenery and chilling tale of the Highlands of old: A massacre of the local clan by a perfidious clan militia took place there in 1692. Farther west, the island of Skye makes a startling impact when the Cuillin Hills etch themselves against a blue sky.

Morning mist over Flanders Moss, from the edge of the Trossachs

With scenic grandeur like this, and the romance of kilts and other Highland paraphernalia, it is all too easy to forget the other aspects of Scotland. The country has some of the finest stretches of unspoilt coastline in Europe: On the east coast, both sheer cliffs and sandy beaches provide superb scenery. The Border towns, with their textile traditions and strong sense of community, are full of character and do not need any dressing up in Highland guise. The Northern Isles, notably Shetland, are a world away from "Highlandry" and have a vivid Scandinavian heritage. Then there is the modern Scotland, as expressed in style-conscious Glasgow or cosmopolitan Edinburgh. Scotland can offer you *ceilidhs* (Highland-style evenings of song and dance) if you want them, but make the most of its wealth of other attributes as well.

❑ After the Battle of Culloden in 1746, many rebels were condemned to death by the authorities. One of these unfortunates was a Highland piper. He pleaded for mercy on the grounds that he was a musician, but the judge defined his pipes as a weapon of war and the sentence was duly carried out. ❑

Many Scottish postcards tend to perpetuate the tartan cliché

Perhaps the best-known Scottish festivity is Hogmanay—the last night of the year and its hung-over aftermath. Until recent years it was far more important than Christmas north of the Border.

HOGMANAY Though none can agree on the word's origins (possibly dialect French *"au geux menez"* "bring [gifts] to the beggars"), Hogmanay is still strong in Scotland. Until recent times the night of 31 December, Hogmanay Night, was the most important in the Scots calendar. Other deep-winter festivals, derived from early pagan fire rituals, survive in places, for example the swinging of fire-balls, with the combustible material held in place by wire, in Stonehaven, or the "burning of the clavie," a kind of portable bonfire in a basket, at Burghead in Moray. Most famous of all is Up-Helly-Aa, a Viking celebration in Shetland, when people go guising (dressing up in costume) and enjoy various shows, including the spectacular burning of a Viking longship. Hallowe'en and Beltane or May Day festivities can also be found in a few places in modern Scotland.

Other types of event are those comparatively modern ones such as Highland Games and agricultural shows. Highland Games are popular in many towns and have spread beyond the Highlands. A combination of musical, dancing, and athletic skills all happening in the same arena, often simultaneously, they are held in towns and villages throughout the Highlands and beyond.

HIGHLAND GAMES Clan societies and other promoters of Scotland's romantic martial image give the Games an ancient history, arguing that they were originally held so that clan chiefs could select the most talented people for their retinues. However, most seem to have originated in early Victorian times, when a resurgence of interest in things Scottish resulted in the formation of various Caledonian Clubs. Games gave the members an excuse to cavort in tartan finery. Yet another explanation is that the Games were trials of strength devised by bored lumberjacks cutting down the Highland forests. No matter what their origins, be prepared to enjoy parachute jumps and guest appearances by TV characters as part of the Games "tradition" as well.

RURAL EVENTS Agricultural shows are as entertaining as Highland

Fringe Sunday in Edinburgh's Holyrood Park—truly cosmopolitan

On the festival cavalcade

Games and serve as a showcase for Scottish agriculture. They take place throughout the Lowlands. They are great meeting places for the rural communities, embracing not just the business of selling agricultural machinery and livestock, but also displaying just about anything else from trick cycling to terrier racing.

❑ The Gaels, that is the Gaelic speakers of Celtic origin whose linguistic stronghold is in the far northwest of Scotland, have their own big cultural event for Gaeldom, the autumn National Mod, which is sometimes rather unkindly and unjustifiably described in the press as the "Whisky Olympics." ❑

❑ Unlike Highland Games, the Borders Common Ridings are definitely not held for the benefit of visitors. These ancient celebrations of horsemanship in the Border towns owe their origins in part to a need to reaffirm town boundaries in the face of frequent cross-border raiding over the centuries. ❑

CULTURAL FESTIVALS The Edinburgh International Festival is the spectacular flagship of the main-stream cultural events in Scotland. In fact, the capital suffers from Festival "overkill" in late August, partly due to the size of the Fringe, the less formal and more unruly younger brother of the "official" Festival. This huge lucky dip spreads out of the halls and theatres on to the streets of the capital. Nobody could visit Edinburgh during the Fringe and possibly miss it! Also adding to the throng is the Edinburgh Military Tattoo and a whole range of smaller events such as the Book Festival and the Jazz Festival. In January, rival Glasgow holds the Celtic Connections festival, a homage to Celtic music, with performers from all over the world playing and tutoring hands-on workshops for prospective players or instrument makers. Folk festivals are also held in many places at various times of the year, two of the most notable being in Shetland: the Folk Festival in April and the Accordion and Fiddle Festival in October.

Highland events—the hammer thrower at the Pitlochry Games

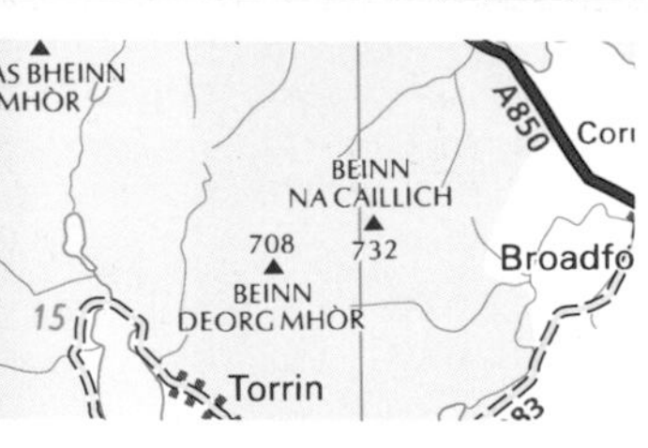

Three languages are spoken in Scotland: Gaelic, (Lowland) Scots, and English. All Gaels are bilingual. Some Lowlanders still tend to undervalue their native tongue, while the use of a broad Scots vowel by a child of English parents living in Scotland can sometimes be greeted with near horror.

THE FIRST LANGUAGE Gaelic was once the principal language over much of Scotland, but has been in slow retreat, originally in the face of Anglo-Norman settlers, for seven centuries. Today, Gaelic's stronghold is the far north and west, notably the Outer Hebrides and the Highlands, where there are 58,000 or so Gaelic speakers. However, increased funding for Gaelic broadcasting, especially television, since the early 1990s has resulted, ironically, in Gaelic being heard in parts of Scotland—for example, the extreme northeast—that have had virtually no Gaelic speakers for centuries.

LOWLAND SCOTS In its late medieval heyday, the Scots tongue, which evolved from a Northumbrian form of Anglo-Saxon, had roughly the same relationship to "English" that Dutch has to German. Today it is diluted and impoverished by its kinship with "Standard English," and has the further disadvantage of non-standardized spelling. However, its rich borrowings from Norse, French, German, and Dutch can still be heard, especially in the northeast, which most linguists consider to be its heartland. Even in its densest forms it roughly follows Standard English in most grammatical forms, but differs considerably in vocabulary and pronunciation.

This Gaelic sign in Fort William literally means "a hundred thousand welcomes"

Gaelic enters the vocabulary of Scots and English speakers most often in anglicized or part-anglicized place-names or topographical features such as ben, loch, strath, glen, or cairn. Sassenach, slogan, and *ceilidh* are other Gaelic words commonly encountered. As the panel at the top shows, many places on the west coast possess only a Gaelic name.

TRAPS FOR THE LISTENER The linguistic nuances of Scotland are worth listening out for. For example, there are Scots constructions using an everyday English vocabulary. "I'll see you the length of the bus-stop" is all but opaque to many non-Scots, yet does not use any exclusively "Scots" words. It means "I will escort you as far as the bus-stop." There are single words which mean something different to Scots and English. "Messages" means shopping to most Scots (and French, for that matter), with the mysterious "going the messages," that is, doing the shopping, a further complication.

Dingwall in Highland Region also uses the traditional Gaelic welcome

SCOTS: A SEPARATE LANGUAGE? Perhaps the listener will skite (slip) on a creishy (greasy) chip paper on a dreich (dull) day, accidentally breenging into (colliding with) the farm's dour (unfriendly) orraman (spare hand) daundering (walking slowly) down to the roup (auction)!

Language experts talk of "the great vowel shift," that is, the change in vowel qualities that took place in medieval times (and makes the works of English medieval writer Geoffrey Chaucer difficult for English speakers today). This shift did not occur in northern word forms. Thus "take" is "tak," "bowl" is "bool," "cow" is "coo," and "most" is "maist" (and so on) in Northeast Scotland today. Then listen for a scattering of surviving weak Anglo-Saxon plural forms: "shoes" are "sheen," "eyes" are "een." Add Scottish constructions to the northern vocabulary and characteristic pronunciation, and it takes a brave linguist to say that Scots is just a dialect of English.

But do not worry—you will be understood everywhere and might hear no Scots tongue at all. Bilingual Scots, in the sense of those who can still speak "dense" Lowland forms as well as English, modify their language into a near Standard English (with a Scots accent, naturally) for the benefit of everyday intercourse with the rest of the English-speaking world.

❑ If you are a non-Scot and your car breaks down—beware. A mechanic telling you "I doubt you'll need a new starter motor" is giving you bad news, not good. In Scotland "I doubt" often means "I regret that..." or "I am afraid that..." ❑

ENGLISH IN SCOTLAND The overheating of England's property market in the mid-1980s saw many English people take advantage of the high selling prices in the south to move into rural Scotland where property was much cheaper. It is possible to travel in many parts of the Highlands and hear no local native voices at all.

❑ The linguistic historian Billy Kay has memorably described Lowland Scots as "a language spoken by consenting adults in private." ❑

In the Scotland of old, diet and wealth were interrelated; the same is true today. But instead of trips to the supermarket to load up the car, the wealthy merchants and lairds and the powerful clan chiefs took advantage of direct trading links across the North Sea to acquire the dainty spices and French wines that went with their status.

A MEAGRE DIET It is significant that Scotland's most famous dish, haggis, is an ancient folk recipe for using up the cheapest cuts of meat. In a nation with a somewhat unpredictable climate and a history of economic uncertainties, everyday Scots cooking in the past had much to do with eking out ingredients.

Today, the poverty in the bleak housing schemes of deindustrialized Scotland is a factor in health statistics which no amount of tartan packaging can totally conceal. In low-income households a dependence on cheap and convenient high cholesterol and otherwise unbalanced foods ensure Scotland is a poor performer in the healthy-eating league table: Deaths through heart disease are the worst in Europe.

Paradoxically, Scotland today has numerous advantages when it comes to "local produce." Peterhead is Europe's largest white fish landing port. Scottish seafood is sought out by top chefs south of the border and in Europe. (In fact, locals grumble that the best is exported.) Aberdeen Angus beef, though eclipsed by overseas breeds in recent years, is making a comeback and still has considerable cachet. Scots farmers remind anyone who will listen that their beef is "grass-fed" on natural pastures. Meanwhile, Scottish farmed venison, with all its low-fat virtues, is often available on restaurant menus.

THE SCOTS AS HOME BAKERS The largest soft-fruit growing area in the EU lies within Tayside in the hinterland of Dundee. With the prevailing climate just right for raspberries and their cousins, as well as strawberries, it is no coincidence that Dundee is famous for its jams. The Scots sweet tooth not only sends

The Waterfront Wine Bar in Leith, the port of Edinburgh

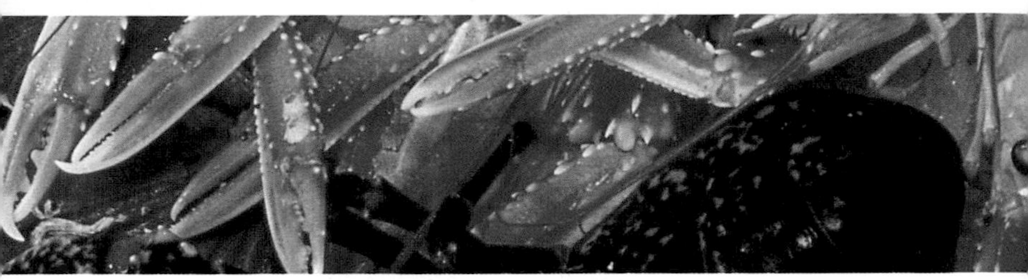

Shortbread—distinctive product and unmistakable packaging

some of its population to an early grave but also shows itself in a still sturdy tradition of home baking, including shortbread and other traditionally fattening goodies. Finally, the humble oat, until well into the 20th century still a staple of Lowland farmhands, has recently won many new converts with the discovery of its role as a good source of soluble fibre.

EATING OUT TODAY Foodies will be able to find a high standard of cuisine north of the border. Some restaurants advertise "Taste of Scotland" menus, which means they belong to an organization dedicated to high standards and the fresh and creative use of Scottish local produce. However, an establishment offering "Scottish" cuisine will not automatically be of the highest order. In a few places there still exists the ersatz Scots menu, where catering packs masquerade as tradition and even the humble cup of coffee is translated into creaking mock Scots as a "tassie o bean bree" ("tassie" is "cup," "bree" is "soup," or "brine"). There is much more to good Scottish food than "flambéeing" the steak in whisky or coating the ice cream in oatmeal, and the discriminating diner will find plenty to please, not just an updated local tradition. Other styles, from Italian to Punjabi, are also well represented, notably, but not only, in larger towns in Scotland.

❑ "The little Highland Mutton, when fat, is delicious, and certainly the greatest of luxuries. And the small Beef, when fresh, is very sweet and succulent… Amongst the poorer classes in Scotland, beef is eaten only at Martinmas, when a Mart or Ox is killed; and the only other butcher meat they eat throughout the year is an occasional Braxy."
Edward Burt's *Letters from the North of Scotland*, 1730

A "mart" is an animal, such as an ox or sheep, killed for salting for winter.
A "braxy" is a sheep that has died of braxy, an intestinal illness. ❑

To many people, especially from the more urban south, the appeal of Scotland lies in its "unspoiled" qualities: The silent hills and open skies of the northlands represent a near-mystical, changeless purity. But is the north really the untouched wilderness, a description so beloved by the writers of tourist brochures?

THE FATE OF SCOTLAND'S WOODLANDS In environmental terms, the upland landscapes that cover 75 percent of Scotland tell a sad story of destruction and forest clearance, started originally in the Southern Uplands and the Lowlands by Bronze Age man about 3,000 years ago. The needs of agriculture meant that by the Middle Ages much of the forest south of the Highlands had gone.

Harbouring wolves and brigands, the Highland forests also were destroyed. Charcoal made from Highland oaks was used in early iron smelting. Queen Elizabeth I of England (1558–1603) decreed that English trees should be reserved for shipbuilding, so her smelters turned to the Highlands, aided and abetted by Scottish Lowland businessmen. Until coke replaced charcoal around 1813, Highland forests were destroyed wholesale for smelting purposes.

By 1743 the last wolf had gone, following the brown bear, reindeer, elk, boar, and beaver into oblivion. Then the great flocks of sheep, still a feature of the Highlands today, arrived with flockmasters who fired whole hillsides, eager to extend the grazings. The modern type of sporting estate seen today, encouraging red deer on an open hillside, also evolved. High populations of nibbling sheep and deer still prevent forest regeneration. In the eastern Highlands, grouse moor management involves annual burning of open hillsides, to encourage young heather growth.

When reafforestation was at last tackled, much of it was in blocks of sitka spruce or other alien species, now seen throughout the Highlands,

The Black Wood of Rannoch—a rare surviving example of Scotland's natural pine forest

even in traditional beauty spots such as the Trossachs. Elsewhere, it is the open "hillscape," burned and overgrazed, degraded for quick profit and described by some ecologists as a wet desert, that is the wilderness enjoyed by millions each year.

FINDING THE REAL WILDERNESS Yet the picture is not all gloomy. Real wilderness, in the sense of an unchanged landscape, give or take a few ski developments, lies above 900m (2,800ft) or so. Meanwhile, on lower ground, there is a more sensitive attitude to forestry planting, at least in some places, and a wide range of habitats, many in the care of conservation bodies. Little chunks of high-grade landscape survive even in the Lowlands in the form of river gorge woodlands, Lowland raised bog, and also wetlands, notably at the Loch of Strathbeg in the northeast.

The oakwoods on the east side of Loch Lomond still ring with spring birdsong. An echo of the great wood of Caledon can be found in the Black Wood of Rannoch on the south shore of Loch Rannoch. Here the characteristic habitat survives: an open woodland of great-limbed pines, with an understorey of juniper and heather. Crossbills call in the treetops and it is still possible to see capercaillie, the big grouse of the woods. Around Rothiemurchus on Speyside, near Aviemore, and by Loch Maree in Wester Ross, on the Beinn Eighe side, wild country can be enjoyed in a comparatively "undegraded" state.

Finally, though land misuse is undeniable, the paradox is plain: Despite everything, the Highlands, with their vast stretches of open man-made moorland, remain hauntingly beautiful.

A remnant Scots pine in Glen Falloch. Overgrazing prevents its offspring regenerating

❑ The unique survival of a feudal method of landownership in Scotland—10 percent of Scotland is owned by just 13 individuals—has not always worked in favour of conservation and healthy land use. The financial worth of sporting estates is partly measured in deer numbers, so the incentive exists to keep stocks at artificially high levels, to the detriment of the Highland habitat. ❑

Why do many Scots still write "Scottish" and not "British" in passports and hotel guest-register books? In 1997, the Scottish electorate threw out the only British Parliamentary party still in favour of the Union with England in its present form. For Nationalists, mild or rampant, there are interesting times ahead.

WHO FEELS BRITISH? In 1707, during the rounds of negotiations and bribes in Westminster that ended with the Union of Parliaments and the loss of Scotland's independence, the proposals for each day of negotiation were laid before the Scots who were left to argue among themselves. The English Parliament continued its business. When the deal was concluded, nothing had changed for English parliamentary representatives. There were new Scots faces at Westminster—but nothing was fundamentally altered to make the English feel British. Neither do many Scots, even to this day.

By the 19th century, the Liberal Party and a succession of other pressure groups had pledged themselves to Home Rule for Scotland. They flourished and withered over the decades. In 1928, the forerunner of the Scottish National Party (SNP) was formed. They gained 11 MPs by 1974 while campaigning under the slogan "It's Scotland's Oil," though these were reduced to three throughout the 1980s.

By that time, Scotland had become a Labour Party stronghold, with the ruling Conservatives' policies deeply unpopular north of the Border. A wave of well-off southerners who had capitalized on the mid-1980s property boom and were snapping up highly desirable property all over Scotland further increased resentment. Before the key general election of 1992, the media—much of it London-based and supporting the Conservative government—talked up the Nationalists' chances, seeing them as the "second force" in Scottish politics. However, the SNP's breakthrough did not occur, though its share of the vote increased—as it did again in 1997. From 1992 to 1997, Scotland was governed by a party with barely enough Scottish Conservative MPs to man the Scottish Office in Edinburgh.

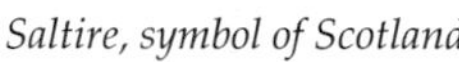

Saltire, symbol of Scotland

They, in turn, were completely wiped out in the 1997 general election, when the Scottish people delivered their verdict on the Conservatives' pro-Unionist agenda.

THE SCANDINAVIAN MODEL

Nationalists argue that Scotland is self-sufficient in food and energy, while proportionately exporting 21 percent more for every manufacturing worker than the UK as a whole. Of the 11 nations that have overtaken the UK in the world wealth league in the last 30 years, seven are small European nations. And of those, three—Finland, Iceland, and Norway—have become independent this century. Nationalists in Scotland look closely at the Scandinavian model of economic success and point to the influence of Denmark, for example, within the EU; with its similar population size, climate, resources, and economy. Far older, they point out, than the present Union with England, is the Auld Alliance—the historical tendency for Scotland to unite with France against England. Old trading alliances with the Low Countries, too, are reminders that Scotland formerly looked to Europe and may do so again.

The commitment of the Labour government, elected in 1997, to a Scottish Parliament sharpened the minds of many Scots, and also the media, to contemplate going beyond this half-way house in a way that had not been discussed in Scotland for three centuries. Now, with the Scottish Parliament in place, the SNP is the largest opposition party in the face of a Labour-Liberal Democrat Alliance. Whether or not it attains "critical mass" and leads Scotland on to full independence, precipitating the break-up of the UK, only time will tell.

The magnificent new buildings of the Scottish Parliament opened for business in 2004

❑ Linda Colley, a professor of history at Yale University, describes Scotland's situation: "the alienation of the Celtic fringe is not a recipe for a healthy democracy, nor for a happy and long-lasting union." ❑

SCOTLAND FREE OR A DESERT

Political message on a disused railway viaduct, north of Montrose

One fact is certain: Scotland as the "Workshop of the Western World" has gone for ever, the nation's smokestack industries, dependent on coal and iron, mostly reduced to dereliction and the memories of old men...

Harvesting in Fife: Agriculture now plays a lesser role in the economy

Even as late as the mid-1960s, manufacturing made up 32 percent of Scotland's GDP and employed 35 percent of its workforce. By the mid-1990s, manufacturing was down to 22 percent with only 20 percent of the workforce in this sector—below the UK average. Today, seven out of ten workers are now in the service sector and not manufacturing anything. However, Scotland is not yet quite a nation of waiters and tartan gift-shop assistants.

ELECTRONICS—THE SUNRISE INDUSTRY Silicon Glen was the apt name coined to describe the sunrise industry of electronics, which currently employs 41,000 people north of the Border. At least 28 percent of personal computers and 80 percent of workstations sold in Europe are actually built in Scotland, thanks to financial incentives for inward-bound companies, plus a skilled workforce. Scotland is now home to more than 500 companies in the electronics sector, many of them household names, including four of the world's top eight computer and office-equipment manufacturers.

EXPORTS AND EARNINGS

Scotland's most famous export, whisky, continues to be important, though the degree of Scottish control within the industry is limited, as most brands belong to multinationals based outside the country. Roughly 65,000 jobs directly or indirectly depend on it UK-wide, while exports per employee are six times the UK average and in total came to £2.3 billion in 2002. Curiously, 55 percent of production and 70 percent of the workforce are in the Lowlands, in spite of the product's Highland associations.

Another sector currently hitting the headlines is biotechnology. Perhaps the most headline-conscious of them all was Dolly the Sheep, created by PPL Therapeutics, in collaboration with the Roslin Institute at a secret site near Edinburgh. Dolly represented the first sheep cloned from an adult cell.

Elsewhere, Scotland's food industry sales were of the order of £7.3 billion by 2003, with £2.4 billion worth of exports. This in turn supports the 50,000 people engaged in processing a wide range of foodstuffs, not just whisky, but also seafood, meat, cheese, and even shortbread.

BLACK GOLD FROM THE NORTH SEA

Oil has made a substantial impact on the Scottish economy since the late 1960s, turning upside-down the local economies of places like Aberdeen, often described as Scotland's oil capital, and Peterhead, a leading fishing port on the northeast coast, whose harbour of refuge found a new role in sheltering and servicing oil supply vessels. In fact, more than 41,000 jobs in Grampian depend on oil. However, some say the boom has passed, not just because the easier finds have been exploited, but also because increasing offshore automation requires fewer workers, while onshore supply bases also require fewer staff. Meanwhile, optimists point to the imminent opening up of a second exploration front in the waters west of Shetland (the so-called "Atlantic frontier") where surveys have revealed enormous accumulations of untapped oil.

OTHER SECTORS The impact of tourism itself should not be overlooked. It contributes £4.5 billion annually to the Scottish economy and supports 197,000 jobs, including 13 percent of the Highlands and Islands workforce. The Scottish voice is perceived as a friendly one, and Scotland has become Europe's leading location for telephone- and web-based contact centres—a 21st-century industry that employs around 46,000 people here. Meanwhile, fishing, fish farming, agriculture, the financial industry, plus the rump of the surviving engineering sector (which still includes names like Weir Group, British Aerospace, Howden Group, John Brown, and Motherwell Bridge) should continue to ensure a measure of prosperity north of the Border.

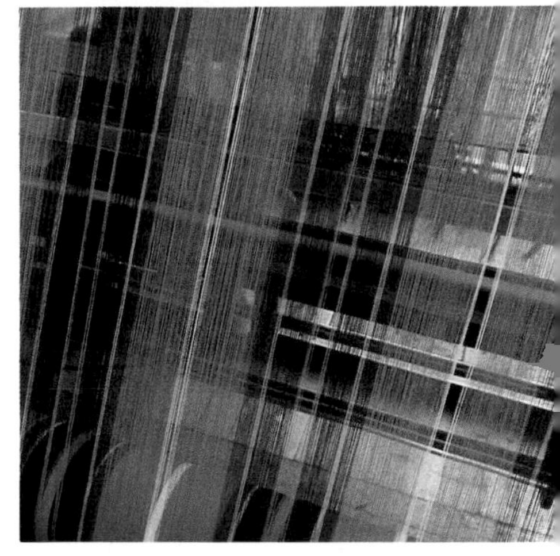

Textile manufacture—still important in the Borders' economy

❑ Oil experts estimate the recoverable reserves in the fields west of Shetland at five billion barrels—roughly equivalent to the entire North Sea production for between seven and eight years. However, rigs will have to combat Atlantic swell, strong winds, and twice the water depth of the North Sea to gain this new oily bonanza. ❑

Ravenscraig—the heavy industry of yesterday?

Scotland's position on the edge of continental Europe, surrounded by sea on three sides, helps explain her unpredictable weather. The country is a battleground between the continental climate of Europe and the weather systems coming off the Atlantic Ocean.

NOT TRULY TROPICAL The Gulf Stream is often heralded as the saving grace of Scotland's weather. Much emphasized in holiday brochures, this warming oceanic current reaches Scotland as the North Atlantic Drift. It hardly lends a "sub-tropical air" to the west coast (as is sometimes claimed in print) but it is appreciated by tender tree ferns and cabbage palms at places like Logan Botanic Garden in Galloway and Inverewe Garden in Wester Ross (at the same latitude as Moscow).

Hebridean rain on Berneray, one of the smaller Western Isles

WHERE TO FIND GOOD WEATHER Sunshine in Scotland is most likely to be encountered away from the prevailing southwesterlies: The east coast "resorts"—Dunbar, St. Andrews, and Lossiemouth—all have encouraging statistics. The west is far wetter than the east. While Dunbar gets away with 555mm (22in) annual rainfall (less than Rome), Inveraray on Loch Fyne enjoys 2,036mm (81in). For many visitors, wet weather is a risk worth taking. The popular tourist area of Lochaber is one of the wettest parts and July one of the wetter months in the west, but also one of the busiest for tourists.

When it is not raining, the sparkling colours of the hills and sea lochs of the west make some of the finest landscapes anywhere in the world. Besides, the dreaded east coast haar, a summer sea fog, also complicates the picture. Scottish weather is a highly localized gamble, with few rules—except to expect the worst and be pleasantly surprised.

❑ The summit of Ben Nevis has a mean annual rainfall that is rather generous: It is twice that of Fort William—which is only 6km (4 miles) away and gets 1,980mm (79in). But if you really want to test your waterproofs, visit the head of Glen Garry which offers 5,000mm (200in) every year. ❑

Glencoe, one of Scotland's five ski developments

Scotland Was

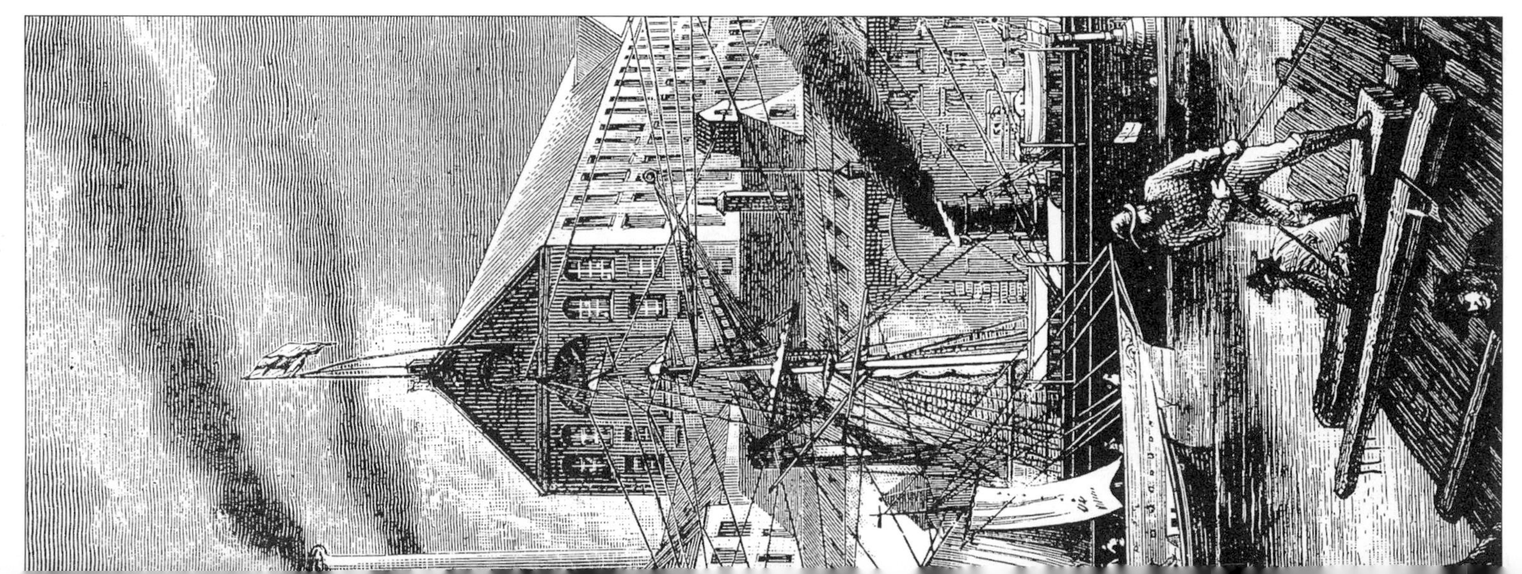

The scanty clues from "shell-middens," the rubbish dumps of early man, suggest that Scotland was first colonized about 8,000 years ago, after the last Ice Age. Over the millennia, different races blended together, leaving only their grave goods, standing stones, and cairns as mysterious evidence for today's archaeologists. Then Celtic invaders from Europe arrived about 500 BC *with superior metalworking techniques. The Romans came and failed to subdue the northlands, finally withdrawing shortly after* AD *212.*

After the Romans, "Scotland" roughly comprised a British kingdom in Strathclyde and the southwest, with a capital at Dumbarton. ("Dun-Briton" means the fort of the Britons, who had been the main Celtic tribe until pushed west by European invaders.) A Pictish confederation controlled the north. Within a couple of centuries a new wave of Celtic settlers arrived, this time from Ireland. These were the Scots who established the kingdom of Dalriada, with its centre at Dunadd near Crinan in Argyll.

THE SHAPE OF SCOTLAND The Angles arrived in the southeast in the 5th century. This Germanic tribe created a powerful Northumbrian kingdom, which took in the Lothians (around present-day Edinburgh). Thus, along with the three Celtic ethnic groups (Britons, Picts, and Scots), a fourth, non-Celtic power base became important.

The northern expansion of this Anglo-Saxon grouping was checked at the Battle of Nechtansmere in Angus in 685, when the Pictish King Brude defeated the Angles under Egfrith, one of the important events which influenced the final form of Scotland. It also shifted the power base in England south from Northumbria to around the Thames, where it has remained ever since, so the shadowy northern Picts altered the course of English history as well.

Christianity played its part in Scotland's story. A Galloway-born

The Stones of Stenness, Orkney

Dun Troddan Broch, Glenelg

❑ The Roman historian Tacitus records a tantalizing snippet on Scotland's first named battle, when red-haired warriors with painted bodies were defeated by a Roman force at Mons Graupius, a site as yet unidentified. There are traces of Roman marching camps as far north as the Moray Firth, though their greatest monument is the remains of the Antonine Wall (AD 142–143), across the waist of Scotland. ❑

Briton, St. Ninian, is the first recorded native Christian. However, the later St. Columba is better known. He came from Ireland to Iona in Dalriada in AD 563 to convert the northern Picts. As the Britons were already Christian by this time, this forged closer links between the two groupings.

Yet another factor was at work in shaping Scotland. The depredations of the Vikings troubled both the northern Picts and also the Scots on the western seaboard. Some say the repeated pillaging of the Christian settlement and seat of learning at Iona set back the course of civilization for centuries. The Picts were so weakened by Norse incursions that Kenneth MacAlpin, King of Scots, was able to extend his kingdom north and east. He was crowned King of Scots and Picts in 844.

Thereafter MacAlpin strengthened an alliance with the Britons, further extending his sway. However, only after the Battle of Carham (on the English side of the Border near Coldstream) in 1025, when the Scottish King Malcolm I defeated the Northumbrians, did they give up the southeast so that the Lothians became part of Scotland.

Finally, the marriage in 1070 of King Malcolm III to Margaret, a daughter of the English King Edward the Confessor, set a pattern of intermarriage between the royal houses of Scotland and England that would also strongly influence the fate of Scotland.

❑ Tacitus uses the word *Picti*—painted people—as well as *Caledonii* (hence Caledonian) to describe the northern tribes. Later, Alba (hence Alban and Albion) was the Gaelic word which described the combined Scot-Pictish kingdom north of the rivers Forth and Clyde. ❑

The Wars of Independence refer to a period in Scottish history when Scotland's right to exist as an independent nation was threatened by the expansionist aspirations of the English Plantagenet kings. But it was not quite as simple as that. Nothing between Scotland and England ever was simple.

THE ENGLISH OVERLORDS? In 12th-century Scotland, notably in the time of King David I (ca1080), the Norman feudal system had taken root. David had married the daughter of an English earl, gaining lands near Cambridge in England. In feudal terms, land meant an obligation to the overlord, in this case the English king. This bowing of the knee as an English landholder by David (and earlier kings) reinforced a view that the Scots were under English command. This was strengthened by the Treaty of Falaise in 1174, signed by King William the Lion, who, seeking territorial gains, joined a revolt by English barons against King Henry II of England. The barons were defeated; William was captured and forced to sign a treaty of allegiance, confirming the feudal overlordship of England. (Scotland later bought its "independence" back when King Richard the Lionheart needed money for a crusade.)

Bannockburn prelude—Robert Bruce kills Sir Henry de Bohun in single combat

A TRAGIC FALL King Alexander III of Scotland ruled a comparatively peaceful kingdom until 1286 when he died after falling from his horse. Through intermarriage, King Edward I of England was the great-uncle of the heir to the Scottish throne, Margaret of Norway. Acting as arbiter, he suggested she marry his son, thus securing close union between the two kingdoms. The Scots agreed but the Maid of Norway unfortunately died, leaving 13 other claimants with varying degrees of legitimacy.

Edward seized his chance in the power vacuum and demanded acknowledgment of his own claim as overlord of Scotland. The claimants complied and Edward chose John Balliol, who became a puppet king, ever after known in Scotland as "Toom Tabard"—empty coat. However, even he was pushed too far by Edward who demanded his services against the French. Balliol sided with France and saw his army crushed at Dunbar by Edward's forces in 1296. Scotland was occupied by the English thereafter. The Scots aristocracy, spectacularly sycophantic, secured their property by meekly swearing allegiance to Edward. He then destroyed many of Scotland's own records and carried off a variety of relics among them the Stone of Destiny, which was not to be returned to Scotland until November 1996.

This was the background to the campaign called the Scots Wars of Independence. In the midst of Edward's policy of dismantling Scotland's administration and machinery of nationhood, there arose the first of her freedom fighters, William Wallace, who achieved some successes before his betrayal in 1305.

Queen Mary Gardens beside Stirling Castle

> ❑ William Wallace's most famous victory was at the Battle of Stirling Bridge in 1297, where, within sight of the English-held Stirling Castle, Wallace's men fell upon and defeated the opposing forces while they attempted to cross the narrow bridge. ❑

THE BANNOCKBURN CAMPAIGN

Robert Bruce now saw his chance. Bruce came from an old Norman family (de Brus refers to a Normandy place-name and is often anglicized as the Bruce), and, like other Scots nobles, he played his part in the complex politics of English court life. His grandfather had been one of the original 13 claimants to the Scottish throne. He was crowned King of Scotland in 1307 and initiated a seven-year military campaign, which ended at the Battle of Bannockburn in 1314 with a (historically rare) Scots victory. Thereafter, though Scotland and England were not at peace, Scotland won almost 400 years of independence from England.

Scotland's churchmen were unreservedly nationalist throughout the struggle. With the Pope still believing in England's right to rule Scotland they met to prepare Scotland's most famous document, the Declaration of Arbroath, in 1320: "For so long as a hundred of us remain alive we shall never accept subjection to the domination of the English..."

Robert Bruce, victor at Bannockburn

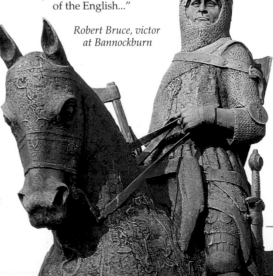

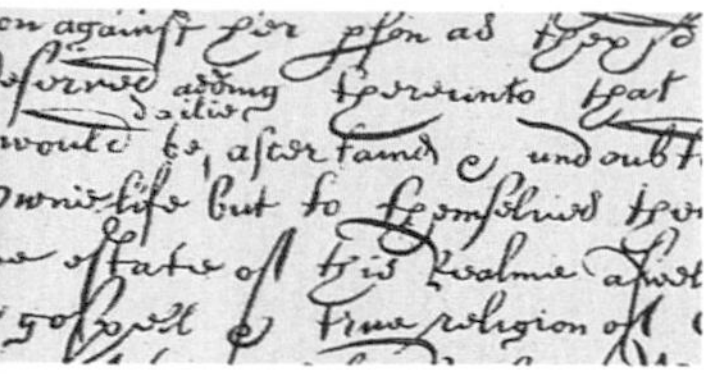

Mary was queen for only seven years but she played her part in a large-scale drama involving the royal houses of Scotland, France, and England. Since her death more than 400 years ago, she has become perhaps the best-known figure in Scotland's history.

Mary, Queen of Scots (1542–1587) was at the heart of political upheavals even as a small child. The Stuart monarchs of Scotland had the inconvenient habit of dying when their offspring were too young to rule. Mary's father, King James V, died a week after hearing of his daughter's birth. Within three years this led to English attacks on Scotland—the destructive episodes known as the "rough wooing." This was King Henry VIII of England's less than subtle attempt to marry off his own young son Edward to the infant Mary. To get rid of the English invaders, the Scots called on the French for help. The price for this was the removal of Mary to France in 1548 for marriage to the Dauphin, the young French prince, in order to secure a Catholic alliance against England.

SCOTLAND'S TRAGIC QUEEN On her return to Scotland in 1561, Mary was a young and beautiful widow. The Dauphin had died, still in his teens. With Scotland in the throes of the Reformation and a widening Protestant–Catholic split, Mary was, politically speaking, hot property. Politicians (Scottish and English) soon worked out that finding Mary a Protestant husband might offer the best chance of stability.

However, Mary fell for the dubious charms of the lanky young Lord Darnley. (Mary, being very tall, may have enjoyed the novelty of being looked down on.) Though at first she described him as the "lustiest and best proportioned lang man," the marriage proved a disaster. Darnley took to tavern life in solace, finding that Mary soon excluded him from any real authority. In short, he sulked.

The murder (by Darnley and others) of her secretary and favourite, David Riccio, witnessed by Mary while six months pregnant, indicates the ruthlessness of the conspirators ranged against her in that age of political and religious instability. The birth of a son—the future King James VI of Scotland, James I of England—and his baptism in the

Mary, Queen of Scots

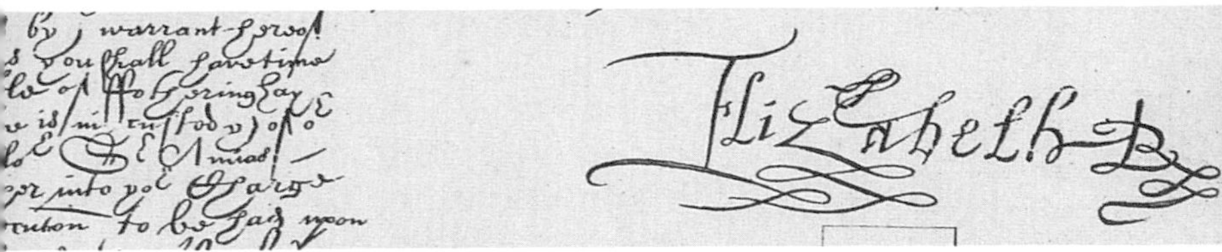

Catholic faith at Stirling Castle were a cause for alarm amongst the Protestant factions.

PLOT AND COUNTERPLOT More controversy followed. The house in which Lord Darnley was convalescing after illness blew up one night. Darnley was found strangled in the adjacent garden, his body unmarked by the explosion. Exactly what happened that night in February 1567 remains one of Scotland's great historical mysteries, but suspicion still falls on the third man in Mary's life, the earthy James Hepburn, Earl of Bothwell. Before Darnley's death it was well known both that Mary's reconciliation with him had failed, and that she was pregnant again. Rumours were rife at court about the possible father of her child. In any event, Mary married Bothwell after his acquittal of Darnley's murder.

The last Scottish scenes in the drama saw the rising of a confederacy of the Protestant Lords of the Congregation against her new liaison, which led to Mary's surrender and imprisonment in Loch Leven Castle. Her pregnancy ended with stillborn twins.

A few months later, in May of 1568, she escaped, gathered an army and suffered defeat at Langside at the hands of the Protestant faction. Subsequently she fled to England, crossing the Border only 11 days after escaping from Loch Leven. There she remained a political pawn in the hands of Queen Elizabeth I, her cousin, who signed her death warrant in 1587.

❑ David Riccio was ugly, small, and hunched (though a fine lutenist) and it is unlikely that his role extended beyond that of musician and chief secretary to the Queen. Court gossip, however, suggested otherwise. ❑

Renaissance stonework on Falkland Palace, hunting lodge of the Stuarts

The Union of Parliaments and Scotland's loss of independence is a live issue among Scots, in a way it has never been in England. Now, in the early days of a new Scottish Parliament, there is a strong sense north of the border that history has come full circle.

SCOTLAND'S FOREIGN VENTURE

After the Union of the Crowns in 1603, when James VI of Scotland became James I of England, Scotland shared a monarch with England but had its own parliament. Poorly developed Scotland assumed that this would mean sharing in trade with England's burgeoning colonies. When it became clear that England intended to keep the economic benefits to herself, the Scots decided to found their own colonies. The Darien Scheme, the establishing of a settlement on the disease-ridden isthmus of Panama in 1698, proved a financial catastrophe. Fever struck the colonists and neighbouring Spanish possessions rose against them. The Scots appealed to nearby English colonies for aid. This was refused for fear of upsetting Spain.

Everything was abandoned, ruining both the Scottish aristocracy and the ordinary folk who had put up funds. By 1701 anti-English feeling was running high. There was also a crisis of succession for Scotland and England. The Scots Parliament attempted blackmail. They stated that unless Scotland gained trading rights in English markets, they would not choose the same monarch as England. Instead of favouring the Protestant Hanoverian succession, they would

Christmas in Parliament Square, on Edinburgh's Royal Mile

❑ The Earl of Seafield, as Lord Chancellor instrumental in carrying forward the legislation, touched the written Act with the Royal Sceptre (symbolizing royal assent) and consigned Scotland to history. As he handed the Sceptre back to a clerk, he was heard to mutter "Now, there's an end of an auld sang". Three centuries later, with a new Scottish Parliament, he has been proved wrong. ❑

turn instead to the exiled Catholic Stuart dynasty. Once more for England the threat of a Scottish alliance with Catholic France presented itself.

POLITICAL HORSE-TRADING The foolish blackmail attempt caused England to retaliate with the Alien Act of 1705. This prevented Scots from holding properties in England and banned the purchase of all Scottish goods and services in England. England's parliament thus alarmed the now penniless Scots nobility, many of whom also had English properties, and also closed off Scotland's main market.

The price of peace was accepting the Hanoverian succession and the end of an independent Scottish parliament. As a trade-off, England offered access to her markets in the colonies. In addition, an English army stationed itself at Newcastle, close to the Scottish Border. Discussions began in London, with the Scottish representatives aware that if agreement to England's terms was not secured, Scotland would be invaded.

BOUGHT AND SOLD FOR ENGLISH GOLD? When the final votes were taken, the nobility were heavily in favour and the popular representatives more evenly divided. This is hardly surprising. The Scottish landowners could recoup their losses after the Darien disaster, since bribes were standard parliamentary practices for moving through legislation. The Duke of Atholl was recompensed generously for not making trouble. The Duke of Argyll became a general, his brother Archie acquired a peerage. Altogether, about £20,000 was spent in buying off the Scottish aristocracy.

Later, the Scots said the deal was crooked, though the machinations were everyday parliamentary routine and only marginally less subtle than modern practices. Robert Burns wrote the song still sung in Scotland today:
"We are bought and sold for English gold,
Such a parcel of rogues in a nation."

VOTING FOR A NEW PARLIAMENT
Shortly after taking office in May 1997, the Labour government held a referendum, in which almost three-quarters of the Scots who voted were in favour of the principle of a new parliament. The Labour Party were keen to stress the devolution aspect, and emphasized that it would strengthen rather than weaken the UK. Subsequently, the Scotland Bill of 1998 paved the way for the new body, which came into being in 2000.

James Ogilvy, 1st Earl of Seafield, as portrayed by Sir John Baptiste de Medina

In about a century, the Jacobites went from feared political and military force to a suitable sentiment for Victorian drawing-room song. Most celebrated of all is Prince Charles Edward Stuart, the Bonnie Prince Charlie of Jacobite hagiography.

WHO WERE THE JACOBITES? Decades of conflict between the monarch, the church, and the state (both in Scotland and England) came to a head with the exile of the Catholic King James VII (II of England) in 1689.

Though opinion on the matter was divided, a Convention of Estates (political representatives who formed a decision-making committee) in Scotland eventually went along with England and accepted William of Orange, husband of Mary, the daughter of the exiled King James VII. The Scottish supporters of the exiled James were furious. Thus originated the Jacobites (from the Latin Jacobus, for James). They rallied round John Graham of Claverhouse, the "Bonnie Dundee" of later Jacobite image-building.

He led them against a government army in the Battle of Killiecrankie in 1689. Fortunately for later tourism, he chose a most scenic location in Perthshire for his side's victory and his own demise, killed by a stray bullet.

The Jacobites had created their first saint, but, deprived of a figurehead, they were soon stopped in their tracks at nearby Dunkeld. There the grimly fanatical Cameronians, earlier persecuted by the Catholic faction, took their revenge.

"IT WAS A' FOR OOR RIGHTFU' KING..." (It was all for our rightful king.) It is sometimes forgotten that the exiled Stuarts were actually the rightful blood line. This belief in the justice of their cause was instilled into James Francis, the Old Pretender, King James VII's son, as he grew up on the Continent. In turn, it was also fostered in the last Stuart king's grandson, Italian-born Charles, the Young Pretender, who as Bonnie Prince Charlie became the most famous Jacobite of all.

UPRISINGS Encouraged by Catholic France and Spain, this court in exile waited for

Highlander statue on top of the Glenfinnan Monument

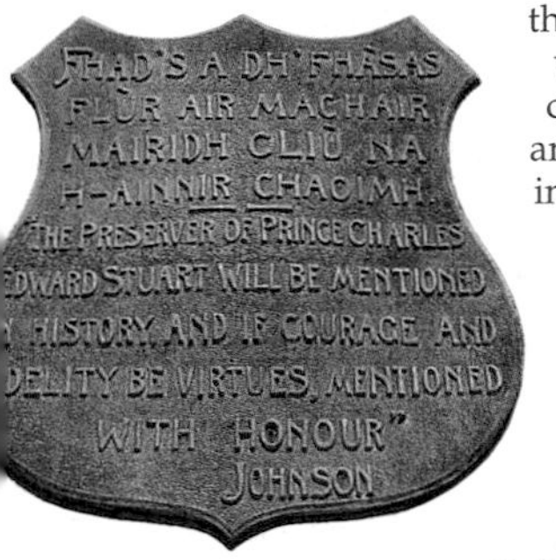

FHAD'S A DH'FHÀSAS
FLÙR AIR MACHAIR
MAIRIDH CLIÙ NA
H-AINNIR CHAOIMH.
"THE PRESERVER OF PRINCE CHARLES
DWARD STUART WILL BE MENTIONED
HISTORY AND IF COURAGE AND
DELITY BE VIRTUES, MENTIONED
WITH HONOUR"
JOHNSON

the call, which came with an uprising in 1715. Its leader, John, Earl of Mar, was known even in his own lifetime as Bobbin John, from his habit of changing sides—an indication of the political complexities of the times. Mar led an army out of the hills to an inconclusive battle above Stirling on the hillslopes of Sheriffmuir. The affair had fizzled out by the time the Old Pretender "James VIII" actually landed on Scottish soil at Peterhead, so he wisely did not stay long.

The 1719 rebellion was even more farcical. Spanish mercenaries were landed on the northwest coast near Dornie. They linked up with local Jacobites in Glen Shiel. Mortar fire from a detachment of government troops soon dealt with the matter. "Sgurr na Spainteach," Spaniards' Peak, in Glen Shiel, commemorates the incident. In between times, there were other plans and other invasion fleets which failed to materialize or were blown off course by storms.

THE LAST REBELLION Later, France and Britain went to war. Eager to encourage any destabilization of her island neighbour, France fitted out the hot-headed, handsome Bonnie Prince Charlie and sent him off to Scotland in 1745 to raise support. After some successes, the mad escapade ended with Charles's army cut to pieces on the battlefield of Culloden. Charles was in Scotland for less than a year. The Jacobites were never a threat again. Soon the bloodshed had been sanitized and transformed into romantic notions of exiled kings across the water and a great many maudlin songs.

When Charles first landed on Scottish soil on Eriskay in the Outer Hebrides, he was told by the local chief to go home. He said he had come home. Only about 6,000 of the 30,000 fighting men in the Highlands of the time rallied to his cause.

35

❑ King James VII was the last of the Catholic Stuart dynasty, a line which had originated with the grandson of Robert the Bruce. ❑

Glenfinnan, where Bonnie Prince Charlie landed on the Scottish mainland some 260 years ago on 19 August, 1745

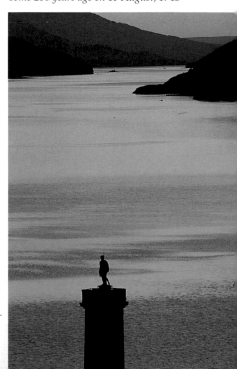

Far from being absorbed by the expanding greater Britain, Scotland retained its identity in the 18th century with an intellectual renaissance which tended towards a liberal-minded patriotism. It played an important role in the international movement known as the Age of Reason.

Some people label the entire period between the Union of the Crowns in 1707 and the death of the influential writer Sir Walter Scott in 1832 as the Scottish Enlightenment. However, if Scotland did have a true post-Union Golden Age, then most commentators place it within the second half of the 18th century.

EDINBURGH'S GREATNESS In its heyday, the movement was focused upon Edinburgh. The New Town was its architectural expression, but the Enlightenment embraced many other fields from medicine to philosophy, agriculture to economics. This was the time of Edinburgh-born David Hume, one of the more influential philosophers of the Western world; of Kirkcaldy-born Adam Smith, who wrote *Wealth of Nations* as the cornerstone of the new science of political economy; of Edinburgh's pioneering geologist James Hutton; of chemists such as Joseph Black, discoverer of carbon dioxide, and of many more who laid the foundations of a range of modern disciplines, many of them flowering out of the seedbed of Edinburgh University.

Sir Walter Scott, author of novels that still enthrall readers today

INTELLECTUAL LIFE Edinburgh was the first university in the world to introduce a chair of English Literature, and it also led the way in important pioneering medical work. No less than three generations of Monros held the Professorship in Anatomy. Glasgow-born William Cullen not only established a tradition of chemical research work, but also became Professor of Chemistry at Edinburgh in 1756 and lectured in clinical medicine at the Royal Infirmary, exploring the links between the two disciplines.

Between 1750 and 1790 Edinburgh was certainly a stimulating place to live. It was also a place where those creating the intellectual wealth were well aware of their role. They recognized the paradox that a lead in so many fields had been taken by a poor nation that had so recently lost status.

Even with New Town construction under way, the sheer proximity of many families of both high and

❑ George III's chemist, Amyat, commenting on the intellectual life of Edinburgh society in the 1750s, remarked: "Here I stand at what is called the Cross of Edinburgh, and can, in a few minutes, take 50 men of genius and learning by the hand." ❑

A map of Scotland dating from 1797

humble birth in the tall cramped tenements of Edinburgh's Old Town seemed to generate a special atmosphere, a cross-fertilizing of ideas which was widely commented upon by outsiders. They noted the debating and literary societies, the interest in written essays and stimulating conversation, as well as in the concrete forms of communication, such as building roads, bridges, and canals. Referring to this ready access to scientists, engineers, and all kinds of thinkers and writers, the English visitor Amyat (chemist to King George III) wrote that the philosophers in Scotland "tell us what they know, and deliver their sentiments without disguise or reserve."

By 1789, Thomas Jefferson, while travelling in Europe on political business, wrote that "no place in the world can pretend to be competition with Edinburgh." Yet half a century later, the light had dimmed. An urge for rapid political change, embodied in the French Revolution and the Romantic movement, had overwhelmed the moderation and harmony which were the goals of the greatest Enlightenment thinkers.

The Royal Society of Edinburgh, founded in 1783

❑ David Hume to Elliott of Minto in 1757: "Is it not strange...that, at a time when we have lost our Princes, our Parliaments, our independent Government, even the presence of our chief Nobility, are unhappy in our accent and Pronunciation... speak a very corrupt Dialect of the Tongue...is it not strange...we shou'd really be the People most distinguish'd for literature in Europe?" ❑

The great mercantile cities of the Lowlands went about their business of making money. The powerful Highland landowners were similarly motivated. To improve their estates, they cleared their tenants from ground they had worked for centuries. Today this process might be called ethnic cleansing.

The series of evictions and forced emigration known as the Highland Clearances did not happen immediately after the defeat of the Jacobite rebel forces at Culloden in 1746. Nevertheless, after Culloden, the old-style clan chiefs were stripped of their powers. The reality of hard economics asserted itself in the poor lands of the north.

An abandoned croft at Arnol, on the Isle of Lewis in the Western Isles

THE IMPROVING LANDLORDS A system of improvements was implemented by new landowners, only some of whom were still of Highland stock, as they tried to make money from their property. The second half of the 18th century saw the founding of state-sponsored fishing stations such as Tobermory and Ullapool. The potato was first grown and soon became a staple. Better nourishment allowed the Highland population to expand.

A SHORT-LIVED PROSPERITY
Britain's wars employed Highland manpower and were also a market for Highland produce such as cattle, fish, and meal. Also, kelp was gathered, dried, and burned and the ash used in the manufacture of soap and glass. This made money for landowners with coastal properties.

The landowners raised rents to increase profits and altered leases to reduce individual landholdings, in order to compel tenants to spend more time fishing or kelp-gathering. Far from evicting tenants, landowners in the first decades of the 1800s—the majority of whom were absentees—actually required manpower to make money.

The slump came at the end of the Napoleonic Wars in the early 19th century, when the market for cattle collapsed. Agricultural improvements, successful in the Lowlands, simply did not work on the thin, acid Highland soils. New chemical processes made kelp-gathering unnecessary, and even the fishing became unprofitable. The landowners turned to sheep to make money. Unfortunately, the tenants' farming activities—the growing of potatoes and the pasturing of cattle—conflicted with the needs of the new-style Cheviot or black-face breeds.

❑ "Much the same thing is done today by town councils who uproot people from their old shabby but neighbourly streets and place them in ultra-modern, clinically clean but often inhuman high-rise flats, usually against their will."
Dunrobin Castle Guidebook, printed 1991. Dunrobin was the home of the initiators of the Sutherland Clearances. ❑

VIOLENCE IN THE GLENS The people of the glens were evicted. The violence that accompanied the policy flared up in a now infamous list of Highland place-names, of which Strathnaver on the Sutherland Estates is perhaps the best known.

In 1785, the last Earl of Sutherland's daughter, Elizabeth Gordon, married one of the richest men in England, George Granville Leveson-Gower, second Marquess of Stafford. He had made a fortune in coal and wood and owned a vast estate in England. With his marriage came most of the northern Scottish county of Sutherland, including Dunrobin Castle in Golspie.

In the system of estate improvements, around 5,000 Highlanders were cleared up to 1821. They were either settled on narrow coastal strips or forced to emigrate, mostly across the Atlantic. In Strathnaver, many of the tenants were unable to salvage their belongings as their houses were burned before their eyes. The estate factor, Patrick Sellar, was even charged with arson and homicide, as some homes were fired with old people still inside them. He was acquitted.

The same pattern of evictions by landowners—titled aristocrats, entrepreneurs, and industrialists—stretched from Shetland to Perthshire. Many sincerely believed it was for the best. Today, in the Highlands, with their silent glens admired by city-dwellers, visitors creep reverently round the treasures in the castles of the descendants of these "improvers."

Dunrobin Castle, Golspie, Sutherland

The Scots have always been adventurers. Soldiers and merchants travelled in Europe from the very early days of the Scots nation. Then, when ships became large enough to undertake longer voyages, Scots left their homeland and became entrepreneurs and explorers, as well as simply colonists, all over the globe.

In 1297, Sir William Wallace, the Scottish freedom fighter, wrote to the Senators of Lübeck and Hamburg thanking them for helping Scottish merchants and offering safe conduct for any of their representatives at Scotland's ports. This is an early reference to Scots entrepreneurs abroad. It is estimated that Poland had 30,000 Scots living and operating in business there in the 17th century.

Dunbar acknowledges its famous son, John Muir

TO THE FOUR CORNERS OF THE GLOBE Scots were prominent in the Far East. William Jardine, born in Lochmaben (Dumfriesshire), was an independent China trader who joined forces with James Matheson to form the Hong Kong-based Jardine Matheson of today. Its early profits were amassed in the unsavoury opium trade. Hugh Falconer from Forres and William Jamieson of Leith were early pioneers of tea plantations in India. Fraserburgh-born Thomas Glover introduced modern technology to Japan, particularly in shipbuilding. He ordered Japan's first slip dock, which in turn led to the expansion of the now multinational company Mitsubishi.

Not only was Thomas Glover a trusted adviser and personal friend of Mitsubishi's founder, Yataro Iwasaki, he also imported the first steam locomotive and the first telegraph line. Incidents in his extraordinary life are said to have inspired Puccini's opera *Madame Butterfly*.

The Scots turned westwards as well, building Glasgow's early wealth on plantations of Virginia tobacco and Jamaican sugar. Later developments such as the Prairie Cattle Company Limited, Texas's first major joint stock venture in cattle ranching, were actually Edinburgh based. More than half the Hudson Bay Company's senior staff were Scots. Even more significantly, at least 13 US presidents claimed Scots ancestry.

These emigrant Scots or their descendants became involved in every sphere. The son of a poor country tailor in a small parish in Aberdeenshire went on to found *Forbes Magazine*, the still-successful US financial journal. Bertie Charles Forbes (1880–1954) became a millionaire in the process. James Gordon Bennet (1795–1872) left his native Keith in Moray in the north-east, and went on to found the *New York Herald*. In industry, the best-known Scot is the steel magnate Andrew Carnegie from Dunfermline; his name has become a byword for

philanthropy. The squalor of the Glasgow slums of the early 19th century produced Allan Pinkerton, the founder of the oldest and largest private investigation agency in the world. In 1867, a young Scottish emigrant, John Muir from Dunbar, began to develop the idea of environmental conservation while walking in the Sierra Nevada. It was to lead to the founding of the conservation movement in the USA.

There were, naturally, the oddities: the Scots who suddenly popped up in unexpected places, like the businessmen who formed the African Lakes Corporation in 1878, or the Scottish lace workers in Spain who founded the first Spanish football club. Less surprising, perhaps, is a certain James Chisholm, who founded the first pub in Sydney, called the Thistle Tavern—presumably around the same time as another Scot, Lachlan Macquarie, brought order as the first governor of the former penal colony of New South Wales.

Dunfermline-born industrialist Andrew Carnegie

THE HOMELAND Whatever the reason—religious persecution, lack of opportunity, forced clearance, voluntary emigration, or just a sense of adventure—Scots men and women have been the country's leading export over the centuries. Small wonder the Clan Donald has over 100,000 members worldwide. For many the call of the homeland is still strong. Libraries throughout Scotland, carrying records on microfiche formerly only available at New Register House in Edinburgh, do brisk business with genealogical enquiries.

❏ The word Scot in Polish also means a commercial traveller, and the Poles have a simile "as poor as a Scots pedlar's pack." Evidently not all Scots were successful in business. ❏

The image of Scotland as a resourceful, industrial place sits uncomfortably with the more romantic notion of misty bens and glens. Yet, in times gone by, the output of heavy industry and, in particular, shipbuilding, ensured that Scottish products went around the world and that "Clyde built" (that is, a product of the many shipbuilding yards along the River Clyde) meant the very finest of its kind.

The Scottish industrial belt was formerly a diagonal corridor across the waist of Scotland, less than 48km (30mi) wide from coast to coast. It took in the coalfields of Ayrshire and the south of Edinburgh, the Vale of Leven dyeing industries south of Loch Lomond, and Angus textile manufacturing (all now mere vestiges of their former size, if there at all). Paradoxically, it also included some of Scotland's best farmland.

THE KEY TO PROSPERITY: COAL AND IRON Among these activities, those based on locally available coal and iron had the highest profile—if only because of the effect they had on the environment and landscape. It is arguable that the real cradle of the Industrial Revolution in Scotland lay east of Glasgow, in the Falkirk area, where the Carron Company was founded in 1760, close to iron mines.

However, by the early years of the 19th century, the easily workable blackband iron ore of Lanarkshire had been discovered. What had been the fruit garden of the west of Scotland was demolished in a search for this important mineral. The air of Lanarkshire filled with grime and smoke as ironworks sprang up, using local coal to fuel the furnaces. The stage was set for Clydeside to become one of the world's greatest shipbuilding centres. Though England's River Tyne was also important, most of the developments in ship design and, in particular, marine engines and boilers, were made on Clydeside.

The Clydeside birth of a Cunarder, the Queen Mary

❑ The Carron Company's most famous product was the carronade, a short-barrelled, large-bore cannon used in Britain's imperialist wars. ❑

THE SONG OF THE CLYDE Formerly, the shipyards stretched practically unbroken all the way downstream to Greenock, but these days most are long gone. Even as recently as 1929, the Clyde built 20 percent of the world's shipping. Then the so-called Clyde symphony or the "song of the Clyde" was at its height: the noise of thousands of riveters banging home the red hot rivets that held together the locally made steel plates.

Sunset over the Clyde shipyards

THE ROMANCE OF SHIPS Glasgow, of course, had all kinds of other manufacturing operations, including the production of railway locomotives. Dundee and the Angus hinterland thrived on textiles, Edinburgh had her printing and publishing industries, as well as shale oil extraction to the west. Even modest Aberdeen could claim a surprisingly large engineering sector, while the Borders were well known for textiles.

Yet only shipbuilding and the proud and graceful products that sailed the waters of the globe acquired the romance and mystique that come with the associations of distant places. Though the local coal and iron that helped build the ships have long been worked out, the hammers are not yet silent. The Clyde still sees the launch of large vessels—as ever, diagonally into the narrow river. But on the banks of today's Clyde there are also long stretches of filled-in docks and redeveloped sites. Only at places such as the Denny Ship Model Experiment Tank at Dumbarton (see page 140) are there echoes of the great, grimy days of the Clyde, the river that made Glasgow.

❑ During World War II, the Clyde shipyards still had the capacity to build 2,000 ships, repair more than 23,000 and convert hundreds more. To put it another way, the workforce built or repaired 13 ships every day for five years. ❑

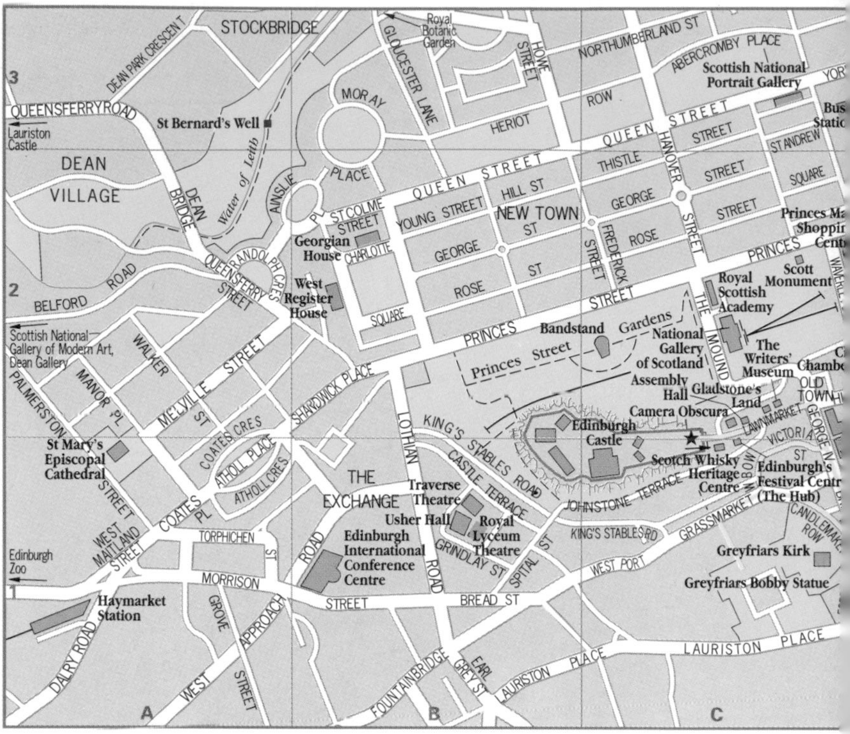
STOCKBRIDGE
Royal Botanic Garden
GLOUCESTER LANE
HOWE STREET
NORTHUMBERLAND ST
ABERCROMBY PLACE
Scottish National Portrait Gallery
YORK
DEAN PARK CRESCENT
QUEENSFERRY ROAD
Lauriston Castle
St Bernard's Well
MORAY
HERIOT
ROW
QUEEN STREET
HANOVER
STREET
Bus Station
ST ANDREW
SQUARE
DEAN VILLAGE
DEAN BRIDGE
Water of Leith
AINSLIE
PLACE
QUEEN STREET
HILL ST
THISTLE
STREET
ST COLME STREET
YOUNG STREET
NEW TOWN
GEORGE
STREET
Princes Mall Shopping Centre
Georgian House
CHARLOTTE
GEORGE
ST
FREDERICK STREET
ROSE
PRINCES
Scott Monument
WAVERLEY
QUEENSFERRY STREET
RANDOLPH CRES
ROAD
BELFORD
West Register House
ROSE
ST
STREET
Royal Scottish Academy
THE MOUND
SQUARE
PRINCES
Bandstand
Gardens
National Gallery of Scotland
The Writers' Museum
Scottish National Gallery of Modern Art, Dean Gallery
WALKER
STREET
MELVILLE
Princes Street
Assembly Hall
Gladstone's Land
OLD TOWN
MANOR PL
SHANDWICK PLACE
Camera Obscura
LAWNMARKET
GEORGE IV
PALMERSTON
ST
COATES CRES
KING'S STABLES ROAD
Edinburgh Castle
VICTORIA
St Mary's Episcopal Cathedral
ATHOLL PLACE
LOTHIAN
CASTLE TERRACE
Scotch Whisky Heritage Centre
BOW
Edinburgh's Festival Centre (The Hub)
STREET
THE EXCHANGE
Traverse Theatre
JOHNSTONE TERRACE
ATHOLL CRES
COATES PL
Usher Hall
Royal Lyceum Theatre
GRASSMARKET
CANDLEMAKER ROW
WEST MAITLAND STREET
TORPHICHEN
ST
Edinburgh International Conference Centre
KING'S STABLES RD
SPITAL ST
GRINDLAY ST
ROAD
Greyfriars Kirk
Edinburgh Zoo
MORRISON
WEST PORT
Greyfriars Bobby Statue
Haymarket Station
STREET
ROAD
BREAD ST
GROVE
APPROACH
DALRY ROAD
LAURISTON PLACE
WEST
STREET
FOUNTAINBRIDGE
GREY ST
EARL
LAURISTON
PLACE
3
2
1
A
B
C

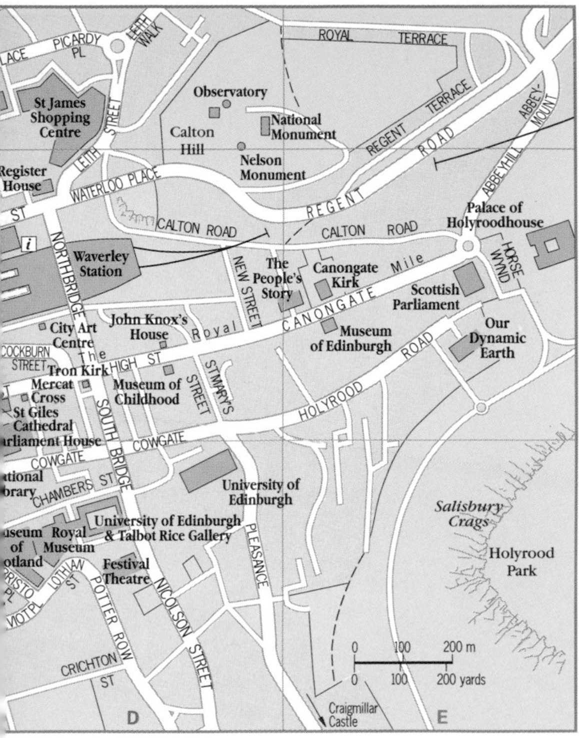

STIRRING FIRST IMPRESSION By road, only a couple of hours or less from the border with England, the A68 plunges over the edge of the Southern Uplands to reveal the Lothians, Edinburgh's countryside, spread out below: the sweep of the Pentland Hills stopping short at the edge of the city; farther round, the dark profile of Arthur's Seat dominating the other more gentle rises on which Scotland's capital is built; then the long reach of the Firth of Forth with just a hint of the Highlands beyond. This is the setting for one of the world's most distinguished cities, now once again the seat of the Scottish Parliament.

From the air, on the final approaches, the city map is plain: The castle on its high rock and the Palace of Holyroodhouse in its Royal Park act as head and tail for the backbone of the Royal Mile, which runs through the Old Town. Across the green space of Princes Street Gardens, symmetrical patterns reveal the plan of the neoclassical New Town. Moments after this port-wing view, and over the high spans of the Forth rail and road bridges, the traveller touches down.

By rail, you reach the centre at Waverley Station. On emerging, the skyline seems familiar: The profiles of castle and battlement, the gothic-spired Scott Monument and Greek-porticoed art galleries, popular postcard images, are known worldwide.

From every angle, Edinburgh strikes theatrical poses. The neoclassical collection of monuments on top of Calton Hill seems about to frame some Greek tragedy. Above the rooftops of the Royal Mile, the long red ridge of

Edinburgh Castle dominates the city skyline

▶▶▶CITY HIGHLIGHTS

Salisbury Crags skirts the rocks of Arthur's Seat—it could well be a painted backdrop for one of Sir Walter Scott's melodramas. At one o'clock each afternoon a cannon cracks out, puffing blue smoke over the castle battlements. This is not another uprising, only Edinburgh squeezing extra drama out of a time check. Edinburgh generates excitement and a sense of expectation. This is where things happen…

OLD EDINBURGH Edinburgh's **Castle Rock** dates from the last Ice Age. An eastward grinding glacier nibbled away at its hard volcanic plug, leaving three steep sides and a ramp running down eastwards. An archaeological dig in the 1990s to establish the age of settlement on the Rock found some chewed herring bones, now carbon-dated to around 800 BC.

The Castle Rock was a Dark Age stronghold, fortified by the Saxon King Edwin in the 7th century. The oldest building in Edinburgh today is the 11th-century **St. Margaret's Chapel** within the castle, named after Queen Margaret. She married King Malcolm, whose Celtic court was at Dunfermline, then the capital. As a Saxon southerner she persuaded the court to move to the Saxon-influenced Lothians. Edinburgh became the capital thereafter.

By the 12th century, the huddle of little houses protected by the castle had spilled down the ramp—the embryonic **Royal Mile**—perhaps as far as today's Tron Kirk in the High Street. Margaret's son, King David, founded **Holyrood Abbey**, another landmark in the shaping of the old city.

The castle was sacked by King Edward I of England in 1296 and many of the nation's records were destroyed. After the English withdrew, Edinburgh became a royal burgh in 1329, and thereafter faced the wars and vicissitudes of Scotland's long struggle under a weak monarchy with a powerful and ambitious neighbour on her southern border. The High Kirk of St. Giles was burned in 1385 by King Richard II of England, the Royal Mile torched in 1542 during the "rough wooing" (see page 30).

As a means of defence, Edinburgh was a walled town. Bits of wall survive today, near St. Mary's Street and above the Grassmarket. In the main, the community remained within its high walls until the mid-18th century.

Then it crossed the marshy defensive gap, now the site of Princes Street Gardens, to found the New Town.

NEW EDINBURGH In the creative heat and spirit of optimism of the Age of Enlightenment, the city laid the foundations of the townscape of today. The first **New Town** comprises the rectangle bounded by **Charlotte** and **St. Andrew squares** to west and east and **Princes** and **Queen streets** to the south and north. Other development schemes followed on around Moray Place and, less successfully, along Royal Terrace.

The great public buildings and monuments which enhance the city environment so much today were built at the same time: the **Royal Scottish Academy** and the **National Gallery of Scotland**, honey-coloured columned temples floating in garden greenery when viewed from the east; the fluted shapes of more columns of Calton Hill's unfinished National Monument, which block and change the views east along Princes Street from every angle.

Amid all this neoclassicism, the **monument to Sir Walter Scott** shoots out of the trees like a Gothic sky-rocket. Architecturally isolated, Scott's immortalization in sandstone plays its part in the theatrical quality of Edinburgh and has become an essential symbol of the city. Towering above the Palace of Holyroodhouse, the impossible profile of **Arthur's Seat** looks like a backdrop for one of Scott's own theatrical melodramas—or an entirely appropriate setting for the cultural overkill generated annually through the Edinburgh International Festival, the Fringe, and other attendant festivals.

For all its swingeing parking fines and crowds, as well as the proportion of well-meant but uninspiring productions that turn the Fringe into something of a lucky dip, Edinburgh undoubtedly remains an exciting place. Away from the city centre's cosmopolitan throng, life in the New Town goes on pretty much as it has done for more than two centuries, below the plasterwork in elegant drawing-rooms or amid the shade of the private gardens overlooked by palace-fronted façades: a curious meeting of past and present.

SCOTLAND'S BURGHS
A Scottish burgh, a term first used in the 12th century, was a town with certain rights; when these rights were granted by the monarch, a town became a royal burgh. The rights were mainly to do with mercantile matters, such as the granting of the right to hold fairs or markets, in order to raise money for the Crown, as well as for the community itself. Characteristics of a burgh usually included a mercat (market) cross, to indicate the place of the market and the town centre, as well as a tolbooth—a civic building that served as an administrative centre—and, very often, a courtroom and prison too. Burghs disappeared with a local government reorganization in 1975.

Calton Hill commands some fine views over Edinburgh—see page 49 for an example

 Calton Hill *45D3*

Robert Louis Stevenson's favourite view of Edinburgh was from this hill to the east of Princes Street. Even in Stevenson's day it carried its extraordinary neoclassical collection of buildings: the **Old Observatory** (the only surviving building by New Town planner James Craig), the **City** or **New Observatory**, the **Dugald Stewart Memorial** (loosely based on the temple of Lysicrates in ancient Athens), the unfinished **National Monument,** and the **Nelson Monument** which ignores its neoclassical neighbours and is shaped instead like an upturned telescope. If the walk up the steps to the hilltop is too much, take the car. Look for the turning by the former Royal High School. The hill is open at all times.

Visitors view the former Royal High School near Calton Hill

► Camera Obscura and World of Illusions *44C1*

549 Castlehill (tel: 0131 226 3709; www.camera-obscura.co.uk)
Open: Apr–Jun, Sep–Oct, 9.30–6; Jul–Aug, 9.30–7.30; Nov–Mar, daily 10–5. Admission: moderate

This building has a varied history: The lower storeys were built in the 17th century, and the upper castellated storeys added in 1853, when the building first became a camera obscura. As well as panoramic projections of Edinburgh, thanks to its revolutionary design and mirrors, the centre offers Edinburgh-related exhibitions.

► Canongate Kirk *45D2*

Canongate (tel: 0131 556 3515)
Open: Jun–Sep, Mon–Sat 10.30–4.30, Sun 10–12.30 all year. Admission free

This church was built in 1688 for the congregation when King James VII converted the abbey kirk at Holyrood into a chapel for the Knights of the Thistle. Of greater interest, is the **graveyard**. Graves include that of Mrs. McLehose, who was abandoned by her husband. Robert Burns conducted a passionate correspondence with her (just that and no more, since he was confined to his Edinburgh lodgings with a twisted knee). She outlived him by 45 years. Also here is the grave of Robert Fergusson, the Edinburgh poet who inspired Burns, though they never met. When Burns visited, he was shocked to find Fergusson's grave unmarked, and paid for his headstone.

EDINBURGH'S UNFINISHED PARTHENON

The prolific architect William Playfair had a hand in many Edinburgh streets and buildings. He is also less happily associated with the National Monument, the columned facade on Calton Hill. Intended to be an exact copy of the Parthenon in Athens and a tribute to the dead of the Napoleonic Wars, it was started in 1822. Money ran out in 1829 and the work has been left unfinished ever since. It has become known as "Edinburgh's Disgrace." but it has a certain appeal in its present state.

Itinerary

Three days in Edinburgh
DAY 1 Rampart views from **Edinburgh Castle** aid orientation in this fairly simply laid-out city, and a self-guided castle tour, taking most of a morning, is worthwhile. Then go downhill, diverting for **Victoria Street** shopping. (Use the steps at West Bow.) Try Jacksons on the **Royal Mile** for lunch, or head to the Kalpna by Nicholson Street, or take a chance with a pub lunch anywhere on the Mile.

Be selective if time is short. The **Museum of Childhood** is fun, or continue to the **Museum of Edinburgh**. The **Palace of Holyroodhouse** is also popular, though this option may give too much history. Alternatively, go to **Calton Hill** for city views, en route for the **National Gallery** at the foot of the Mound. You should just catch it before closing.

DAY 2 Yesterday the Old Town, today the New. Start at the **National Portrait Gallery**, then go on to the **Georgian House**. In between, try Jenners in Princes Street for shopping. For lunch, choose from the many options nearby: La Lanterna on Hanover Street if on a budget, or Martin's on Rose Street North Lane. In the afternoon, explore northwards through the New Town to reach the **Royal Botanic Garden**, then return via Stockbridge and shops. In the evening, check out Leith's eating places, or, if the weather is fine, walk in the Royal Park to enjoy great views from Arthur's Seat, followed by a beer in the Sheep's Heid at Duddingston.

DAY 3 The **Princes Mall** is useful for last-minute souvenir shopping. If you have time, revisit the Royal Mile. The **Scotch Whisky Heritage Centre**, the **Writers' Museum**, and **Gladstone's Land** are all within easy reach of the centre.

TIME-KEEPING
The firing of the one o'clock gun from the ramparts of Edinburgh Castle originated from a request by the Leith Dock Commission in 1861 to locate a time ball on top of the Nelson Monument (which was visible from the docks). Punctually every day since then (except in wartime and on Sundays) an audible signal has boomed out across the city and simultaneously the time ball has dropped down its pole on the monument, enabling mariners of old to check their chronometers and nowadays making tourists jump visibly as they stroll along Princes Street at lunchtime.

Edinburgh Castle from Calton Hill

A ROYAL MYSTERY
In 1830, workmen discovered a tiny coffin hidden in the royal apartments in Edinburgh Castle. Within was a baby with an embroidered "J" legible on the golden shroud. This added to rumours that Mary, Queen of Scots' own infant had died and been substituted. The prime suspect is the Countess of Mar, since the future King James VI was brought up with the Earl and Countess' own son, whom he resembled closely, as contemporary portraits show.

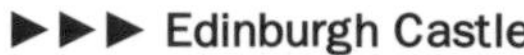

►►► Edinburgh Castle 44B1

Open: Apr–Sep, 9.30–6 daily; last entry 5.15; Oct–Mar, 9.30–5 daily; last entry 4.15. Admission: expensive (tel: 0131 225 9846; www.historic-scotland.gov.uk)

Possibly Scotland's most famous landmark, Edinburgh Castle dominates the city centre with its silhouette of ramparts and rooftops. Over a million visitors every year swarm over its buildings, from the 11th-century chapel to its latest addition, a restaurant with one of the finest views anywhere in the city.

Edinburgh Castle was an important royal court from at least the 11th century. Through the Middle Ages, its buildings were mainly around the highest point of the Castle Rock. King David II built the first strong defensive line across the eastern neck after 1356.

Little of the very early works survives. Today's **Great Hall** of King James IV dates from the early 16th century, but has been much altered. The massive **Half Moon Battery** dates in part from the latter half of the 16th century. As the castle's royal role became less important than its military one, successive waves of buildings and defences were dictated by military needs and warfare, which severely damaged the castle on many occasions.

The castle fired its last shot in anger in 1745 at Bonnie Prince Charlie's men, who failed to take the high rock. Thereafter, as well as a barracks and administrative centre, the castle also became a military prison. It still serves as a military headquarters.

Start your tour by the **Esplanade**, the mid-18th-century parade ground. Beyond the Victorian gatehouse, you find yourself below the vast walls of the **Half Moon Battery** and **Forewall Battery**. Beyond the **Portcullis Gate** the upper levels are reached.

Reminders of a constant military presence include the handsome **Governor's House**, dating from 1742, now the Officers' Mess, and the **New Barracks**, whose bold blocking has dominated the skyline since the 1790s. The former hospital, to the right (beyond tiny St. Margaret's Chapel), is now part of the **Scottish United Services Museum**, a place of monosyllabic attendants and immaculate uniforms. (The main historic collection is in the Queen Anne Barracks.)

St Margaret's Chapel is the oldest and simplest structure within the castle. Dating from the 12th century, it honours the memory of Margaret, wife of Malcolm III, and is still used for occasional weddings. Beside it stands the mighty cannon **Mons Meg** (see panel opposite). The dank vaults of the castle contain the **Prisoners of War** exhibit, showing the conditions endured by 18th-century prisoners of various nationalities.

Back above ground, on Crown Square, is the **Scottish National War Memorial**, an emotional ambush of grey light, tattered flags, and endless names. Opposite is the anticlimax of the **Great Hall**. Like the small room in the Palace in which Mary, Queen of Scots gave birth to the James who was to rule both Scotland and England, this just fails to grab the imagination. However, also here is a very illuminating display on the story of the castle, plus the **Honours of**

The Scottish United Services Museum, Edinburgh Castle

Scotland Exhibition. This is a highlight, where you can view the oldest regalia in Europe: the Scottish crown, sceptre, and sword of state. The **Stone of Destiny**, crowning seal of the Scottish monarchs, is also here. It was returned from England in 1996, having been stolen by King Edward of England in the 14th-century wars of independence.

▶ City Art Centre *44C2*

2 Market Street (tel: 0131 529 3993; www.cac.org.uk)
Open: Mon–Sat 10–5; Sun 12–5. Admission free
The city's own art gallery is housed in a six-floored former warehouse. It stages changing exhibitions and displays the city's collection of Scottish paintings. It brings world-class exhibitions to the city, from the Chinese Warriors to *Star Wars.*

▶ Craigmillar Castle *45D1*

Off the A7 (tel: 0131 661 4445; www.historic-scotland.gov.uk)
Open: Apr–Sep, daily 9.30–6.30; Oct–Mar, daily 9.30–4.30 (last entry 4pm). Admission: inexpensive
If Edinburgh Castle were less of a magnet, and if Craigmillar Castle were not situated quite so near one of Edinburgh's less salubrious housing developments, then the impressive Craigmillar would have many more visitors. In Mary, Queen of Scots' time, the imposing fortress was held by Sir Simon Preston, one of her staunchest allies. Behind the massive curtain wall, somewhere in the 16th-century range of buildings, the murder of her husband Darnley was planned (see pages 30–31).

City Art Centre

THE SCOTTISH REGALIA
On 24 June, 1953 the Regalia of Scotland were taken from the castle to St. Giles Cathedral, where they were presented to Her Majesty the Queen. The galaxy of lords and earls who guarded the Honours of the Nation were dressed in ermine and grand costumes. The Queen, however, wore a simple coat and hat. Still clutching her handbag, she touched the oldest crown in Europe. The incongruity is still remembered in Scotland to this day, though in the official portrait of the event, by Stanley Cursiter, the handbag has been carefully painted out.

MONS MEG
This siege gun or bombard was made in Mons in the 1440s and sent by its owner, the Duke of Burgundy, to his nephew by marriage, King James II, in 1457. The gun had a firing rate of, at the most, one cannonball every 30 minutes. Though cumbersome to move over the rough roads of its day, it did take part in sieges before finally bursting while firing a salute in 1680. It was later displayed in the Tower of London, before its return to Edinburgh Castle.

Edinburgh Castle from Princes Street Gardens

Looking east down the Royal Mile in the direction of the Palace of Holyroodhouse

Walk

A taste of old Edinburgh

A pleasant stroll to attractions on both sides of the Royal Mile, before dropping down to the Grassmarket and a fine view of the castle. Allow 2 hours; *see map on page 44.*

Amid the general visitor mêlée on Castlehill at the very top of the **Royal Mile**, look out for the **Witch's Well** (on the wall) which recalls the last witch burned here in 1722. Nearby is **Cannonball House**, which has a cannonball embedded in the gable with a variety of explanations as to how it got there. Farther down the hill are the **Camera Obscura** (see page 48) and the **Scotch Whisky Heritage Centre** (see page 63). Keep on down the hill to the roundabout.

In the Lawnmarket, there are numerous souvenir shops to distract you, but for a hint of old Edinburgh, turn right just after the roundabout into the short Upper Bow. Go to the end of this truncated street and look over the railings to see Victoria Street curving down below. Now imagine the shape of the town before Victoria Street was built: Upper Bow plunged steeply down to join the lowest point of Victoria Street, called West Bow, which leads into the Grassmarket. The insignificant lane you have just come down used to be the main road into old Edinburgh from the west. Return to the Lawnmarket on the Royal Mile. Opposite is **Gladstone's Land** (see page 55), one of a number of restored 17th-century properties in this area.

The Writers' Museum (see page 57) Is also on the north side of the street—cut through an alleyway to reach it, with **Deacon Brodie's Tavern** occupying the corner site. Deacon Brodie, a respectable locksmith by day and a villain by night, inspired Robert Louis Stevenson's *The Strange Case of Dr. Jekyll and Mr Hyde.*

Turn right into George IV Bridge and right again to reach Victoria Street, which has a good range of shops and cafés. West Bow leads into the **Grassmarket**. The right to hold regular markets here was granted by King James III in 1477. The area gained notoriety as the hanging place of common criminals, as well as Covenanter martyrs (see page 55). Look for the **St. Andrew's Cross**, railed and set into the cobbles, which marks the gallows site.

For an impressive view of the castle, cross over the Grassmarket, go halfway along, and follow The Vennel up in a series of steps to a well-preserved portion of the city wall. This is **Telfer's Wall,** 1628–1636, which now defines the boundaries of George Heriot's School beyond. From here, there is an excellent view north to the castle. Return to the Grassmarket, then bear right, passing **Mr. Wood's Fossil Shop** which offers souvenirs with a difference (very small trilobites are a snip). Then go up **Candlemaker Row**, where tourists risk life and limb standing in the middle of the road to photograph the statue of **Greyfriars Bobby** (see page 54) at the far end. Make your way back to the Royal Mile along George IV Bridge.

❑ Beneath Edinburgh City Chambers in the High Street lies Mary King's Close. This narrow street was abandoned after the plague of 1645, and sealed off to prevent the disease from spreading. It was later covered by the foundations of the later buildings on the High Street. The 17th-century time capsule can be visited on conducted tours (tel: 08702 430160; www.realmarykingsclose.com. *Open* daily. *Admission* expensive. ❑

❑ Right up to the 18th century, and even later, the Old Town was a rather smelly place. This fact was recorded by numerous visitors. Household wastes of every description were emptied from the tall tenements into the narrow High Street with a warning cry of "gardyloo" from on high (the phrase comes from the French *gardez l'eau*—"beware, water"). This was the cause of great embarrassment to James Boswell as he escorted the distinguished man of letters, Dr. Samuel Johnson, up the Royal Mile before they set off for their Hebridean Tour in 1773. The odour is also remembered by a famous fiddle tune, somewhat ironically entitled "The Floo'ers (flowers) o' Edinburgh." ❑

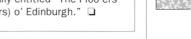

The City Chambers, built as the Royal Exchange

"THE CADIES"
In the Old Town there used to be an entirely unofficial part-courier, part-guide, part-security service known as "the cadies." They knew every nook and cranny in the warrens around the Royal Mile and no visitor could arrive in town without their knowledge. For generations, Edinburgh had fewer robberies and less housebreaking than other Scottish cities simply because of the all-seeing eyes of the cadies. The word, from the French *cadet,* survives today as caddy, the term now used for someone who helps with golf clubs.

The Georgian House, Charlotte Square

Greyfriars Bobby, Edinburgh's best-known dog

►► Our Dynamic Earth 45E2

Holyrood Road (tel: 0131 550 7800; www.dynamicearth.co.uk) Open: Apr–Oct, daily 10–5, last entry 3.50; Jul & Aug, daily 10–6, last entry 4.50; Nov–Mar, Wed–Sun 10–5, last entry 3.50. Admission: expensive

Opened in July 1999 on a prime location near the new Scottish Parliament building, Our Dynamic Earth has 11 galleries featuring impressive wrap-around, hi-tech imagery. On a journey back through time to the creation of the earth, visitors experience a variety of special effects including a flight up a glacier (not recommended for air-sickness or vertigo sufferers) as well as an erupting volcano, a mini-earthquake—the floor really moves—and a humid tropical rainforest.

Although it is very much a visitor-processing machine and hardly a relaxing experience, Our Dynamic Earth is proving a popular attraction. Try to visit outside peak times if you can.

► Fruitmarket Gallery 44C2

Market Street (tel: 0131 225 2383; www.fruitmarket.co.uk) Open: Mon–Sat 11–6, Sun 12–5. Admission free

Another of Edinburgh's high-profile arts venues, the Fruitmarket emphasizes contemporary art and design with a strong international flavour. Combine it with a visit to the City Art Centre opposite (see page 51).

►► Georgian House 44A2

7 Charlotte Square (tel: 0131 225 2160; www.nts.org.uk) Open: Apr–Jun, Sep–Oct, daily 10–5; Jul–Aug 10–7; Nov and

Mar, daily 11–3; last entry 30 mins before closing. Admission: moderate

Right in the middle of Robert Adam's magnificent palace-fronted block at No. 7 Charlotte Square, the National Trust for Scotland has re-created the look of 1796, when the elegant building was new. From the magnificent drawing-room with its candlesticks aglitter, to the well-scrubbed areas below stairs, it demonstrates the impact that the New Town made on Edinburgh life for its wealthier residents.

► Gladstone's Land *44C1*

477B Lawnmarket (tel: 0131 226 5856; www.nts.org.uk)
Open: Easter–Jun, Sep–Oct, daily 10–5; Jul–Aug, daily 10–7
Admission: moderate

When local merchant Thomas Gledstanes acquired the property that now bears his name in 1617, it was a typical 16th-century building. Gledstanes modernized it by adding a stone front and stone arcading. Like so much of the Royal Mile, this ancient tenement was scheduled to be swept aside, but instead a purchaser presented it to the fledgling National Trust for Scotland in 1935. The Trust restored it and uncovered its by then hidden arcades, now unique in Edinburgh. Some fine painted ceilings also survive from Gledstanes' time and are set off by period room settings.

The Covenanters Prison in Greyfriars Kirkyard

► Greyfriars Kirk *44C1*

Greyfriars Place (tel: 0131 226 5429; www.greyfriarskirk.com)
Open: Kirk Apr–Oct, Mon–Fri 10.30–4.30, Sat 10.30–2.30; Nov–Apr, Thu 1.30–3.30: churchyard daily. Admission free

King Charles I's attempt to introduce the English Episcopal Service Book to Scotland in 1637 was widely opposed. The following year a large crowd gathered in the churchyard of the Greyfriars to sign the National Covenant. This important manifesto professed loyalty to the king but warned him not to interfere in the affairs of the Kirk. It can be seen to this day within the church. Thus were born the Covenanters, participants in the religious wars of the 17th century. The kirkyard itself, where 1,400 Covenanters were imprisoned in 1679, is on the site of a 15th-century Franciscan friary and has many 17th-century grave monuments.

►► Museum of Edinburgh *45D2*

Canongate (tel: 0131 529 4143; www.cac.org.uk)
Open: Mon–Sat 10–5; during Festival Sun 2–5. Admission free

This 16th-century building houses the city's museum of life over the centuries. Local silver, glass, pottery, shop signs, and a host of other artefacts are all displayed in a warren of interconnecting rooms. It helps to know a little about the history of Edinburgh before you browse around so that, for example, the artefacts connected with King George IV's visit, or the original New Town plan signed by James Craig, are more significant.

REGISTER HOUSE
Record keeping in Scotland has had a troubled history. King Edward I of England vindictively destroyed the country's earliest records in the 13th century. Register House was sited in the castle by the mid-16th century, and then in the Tolbooth a century later. Only in 1774 was a foundation stone laid for a custom-built Register House, designed by Robert Adam, and partly financed by funds raised from the sale of estates forfeited by Jacobite lairds (see page 38). The building, at the east end of Princes Street, is still in use today, guarded by a famous statue of Wellington.

From its earliest days as Scotland's capital, Edinburgh has had strong literary connections. Thomas Nelson, J. Bartholomew, Oliver & Boyd, and W&R Chambers are some of the famous publishing houses with origins in Edinburgh.

SCOTLAND'S POETIC GOLDEN AGE

Medieval Edinburgh was a literary place. Gavin Douglas, ca1474–1522, Dean of St. Giles, translated the *Aeneid*, the first translation of a Latin poet ever printed in English.

William Dunbar, ca1460–ca1520, was a court poet whose work was in print by 1508, the earliest example of Scottish typography. Sir David Lyndsay of The Mount scandalized the courtiers with his *Satyre of the Thrie Estatis* in 1540. The piece returns regularly to the Edinburgh Festival.

Originally a wig-maker in the Grassmarket, the poet Allan Ramsay later set up Britain's first circulating library, and his is the first of the "modern" names associated with literary Edinburgh. Then came Robert Fergusson, who captured the spirit of the Enlightenment in Edinburgh and inspired a later generation, among them Robert Burns.

A vibrant literary community Conspicuous in the 19th century was Sir Walter Scott, writing of "mine own romantic town" from his house in Castle Street. As a teenager, he had once met Burns at a local literary gathering. Edinburgh's literary life, with its publishers, tavern life, and buzzing creativity, attracted writers from all over the world. It was the first city to recognize the achievements of Charles Dickens by making him a freeman. Charlotte Brontë was also enthralled by the place. Her brother, Branwell, wrote to the influential Edinburgh-based *Blackwood's Magazine* asking for a job when he was 15. His letter was ignored at the time but is now in the National Library.

Edinburgh in its prime Robert Louis Stevenson was a native of Edinburgh and became one of its most famous Victorian writers. Stevenson wrote of the city not just in romantic terms but in a style which still brings its taverns and low life alive. Scotland's most influential 20th-century poet, Hugh MacDiarmid, also had strong Edinburgh connections through a variety of publishing enterprises. The novelist Muriel Spark was educated at James Gillespie's High School for Girls, model for the Marcia Blane School in her novel *The Prime of Miss Jean Brodie*.

Modern writers such as Ian Rankin and Alexander McCall Smith continue the popular literary traditions, and today it is still possible to rub shoulders with poets and writers, even moderately famous ones, in one of the city's "literary" pubs such as Milne's Bar on Hanover Street.

Burns' memorabilia, The Writers' Museum

Lauriston Castle near Cramond

▶ John Knox House 45D2

43–45 High Street (tel: 0131 556 9579)
Open: Mon–Sat 10–6, Sun 12–6. Admission: inexpensive
Nobody seems to know if John Knox (see panel) really did live in this house in the High Street. However, a folk tradition was enough to save it when threatened with demolition in 1849. The late 15th-century building, with its projecting first-floor gallery, is a reminder of what the Royal Mile would once have looked like: narrow and lined by tenements with their projecting floors shutting out the light. The house was damaged by the English Earl of Hertford's men in 1544, when it was owned by Mariota Arres and James Mossman. Their initials are on the wall above the shop door. Mossman was the keeper of the Royal Mint to Mary, Queen of Scots, and was hanged for his allegiance. Today there is an exhibition on the lives of Mossman and Knox within the property.

▶ The Writers' Museum (Lady Stair's House) 44C2

Off Lawnmarket, Lady Stair's Close (tel: 0131 529 4901; www.cac.org.uk)
Open: Mon–Sat 10–5, during Aug Sun 2–5. Admission free
This building, bearing the date of 1622, was only later associated with the first Earl of Stair's widow, who died in 1759. The close on which it was built was at one time the main communication between the Old Town at the Lawnmarket and the New Town. The house was given to the city in 1907, and it is now a museum of Burns, Scott, and Stevenson memorabilia.

▶ Lauriston Castle 44A2

Off Cramond Road South (tel: 0131 336 2060; www.cac.org.uk)
Open: Apr–Oct, Sat–Thu 11–1, 2–5; Nov–Mar, Sat–Sun 2–4. Grounds open all year 9am–dusk. Admission: grounds free, castle moderate
A little away from the main tourist thoroughfares, Lauriston Castle makes a worthwhile excursion, perhaps combined with a quiet walk along the River Cramond. Built in 1593 on the site of a tower destroyed in 1544, the castle's original owner was John Napier (1550–1617). This Scottish mathematician was the inventor of logarithms. The castle was presented to the city in 1926 and its Edwardian interiors are carefully preserved.

JOHN KNOX

Born at Haddington (see page 115), John Knox (1513–1572), architect of the Reformation in Scotland, became filled with Lutheran reforming zeal in 1544 and was called to the ministry in 1547. He led an adventurous life, including a spell as a French galley slave, following capture at St. Andrew's Castle. He preached in England and on the Continent, as well as making his mark in Scotland, where his views were uncompromisingly antagonistic to those of Mary, Queen of Scots.

EDINBURGH'S OLDEST HOUSE

Moubrey House, next door to John Knox House, is probably even older than its more famous neighbour and can therefore claim the distinction of being Edinburgh's oldest dwelling, built by Andrew Moubrey ca1472.

The National Gallery of Scotland

►►► Museum of Childhood 45D2

42 High Street (tel: 0131 529 4142; www.cac.org.uk)
Open: Mon–Sat 10–5, Sun 12–5
Admission free

If you have never quite forgotten your last trainset or your doll's house, then the Museum of Childhood should awaken echoes of those lost days. There is a collection of older material such as Victorian dolls and German automata, but the eerie part is the objects half recognized from one's own childhood. There, behind glass, is that even larger set of Meccano to which you always aspired. If you have children, then you should consider visiting, though the younger members may be overcome by the massed ranks of historic teddies. Even without children, this museum should still be on the "must visit" list.

This museum, the first in the world to show the history of childhood was founded in 1955 by local councillor, Patrick Murray (see panel).

►► Scottish National Portrait Gallery 44C3

Queen Street (tel: 0131 624 6200; www.nationalgalleries.org)
Open: Fri–Wed 10–5, Thu 10–7. Admission free

The Scottish National Portrait Gallery was built with much Caledonian zeal following the impetus given by the funding provided by John Ritchie Findlay, who owned *The Scotsman* newspaper. At its opening in 1889 it was stated that "a gallery such as this is…the highest incentive to true patriotism we can possibly have." Since then, the images of the famous Scots who stare down from the walls have become part of Scotland's fabric, reproduced both in scholarly books and on shortbread tins, so that the viewer coming upon Nasmyth's Robert Burns may find it quite familiar—a veritable icon of Scotland.

Take time, however, to look at the setting of these famous Scots. The architect Robert Rowand Anderson was an Edinburgh native but amid the orderly neoclassicism on the very edge of the first phase of the New Town, he created a Gothic palace, now one of Edinburgh's few monuments to Gothic revivalism. Inside, the late Victorian fashion for mural painting found expression in a

A MUSEUM FOR ADULTS?

The founder of the Museum of Childhood, Patrick Murray, an Edinburgh town councillor, insisted it was a museum portraying a specialized field of social history. A bachelor, he did not actually like children—or at least he pretended not to. He formerly displayed in the museum entrance hall a design for a memorial window to "good" King Herod!

processional frieze of famous Scottish figures—a miniature portrait gallery in itself—with other wall-sized scenes from Scotland's story, set between the sandstone columns.

The Stuart monarchs are here, naturally, including the only portrait of Mary, Queen of Scots in the collection which was made in her lifetime—a small bronze bust of Mary, aged around 17 years. Flora Macdonald, who played her role in later Jacobite schemes, is also on view, as is King George IV entering Holyroodhouse in 1822. This visit of the monarch marked the rehabilitation of tartan, which is much in evidence in many other works.

Historical figures, such as Sir Walter Scott (by Sir Henry Raeburn) are also on display, along with with modern icons, including John Bellany's Sean Connery and David Mach's portrait of sports personality Alex Ferguson, bringing the collection up to date. There are also regular photography exhibitions.

On the same site, the Scottish National Photography Collection has over 27,000 images dating from the 1840s to the present day.

A GREAT ARCHITECT
William Henry Playfair (1789–1857) not only designed the National Gallery (which was finally completed in the same year that he died), but is also associated with many other buildings in and around the New Town, which still lend distinction to the city's profile. These include Donaldson's Hospital, St. Stephen's Church, and, on Calton Hill, the National Monument, the New Observatory, and the monument to Dugald Stewart.

Roman treasure in the Royal Museum of Scotland collections

▶▶▶ National Gallery of Scotland *44C2*

The Mound (tel: 0131 624 6200; www.nationalgalleries.org)
Open: Fri–Wed 10–5, Thu 10–7. Admission free

William Playfair's National Gallery was completed in 1857 and rates among the top two or three classical designs in Edinburgh. Its sparingly ornamented length, honey-coloured in the thin Edinburgh sunlight, has a simple dignity entirely in keeping with its role as a repository for Scotland's finest art.

Inside, its human scale makes it easily accessible. Against a rich red background, many paintings are hung very high and close together. Visit it for some of the best Old Masters in the United Kingdom outside London, for its Impressionists and, naturally, for its Scottish paintings and for important collections of drawings, prints, and watercolours. The refurbished adjacent Scottish Academy and Playfair Project Underground Link (a pedestrian walkway opened in 2004) provide further wall space for the nation's collection.

The Museum of Childhood, a top attraction on the Royal Mile

Looking over Hillend Ski Centre towards Edinburgh

Walk

From Swanston to Colinton Dell

A rural walk south of Edinburgh in the footsteps of Robert Louis Stevenson, with spectacular views back towards the city. Allow about 3 hours for the walk (one way).

Take a bus or car to the southern edge of the city. Bus travellers can alight at the Hillend Ski Centre on the A703 and cross Lothianburn Golf Course by a path to reach the attractive little hamlet of Swanston to the west. Those with a car can take it all the way to the hamlet, where parking is available.

The Hermitage of Braid, on the way from Edinburgh to Swanston

Swanston is associated with Robert Louis Stevenson—his family had a summer cottage there—and is part of the setting for his unfinished novel *St. Ives*. The former Stevenson family home (private) is still there as described in the work: "It had something of the air of a rambling infinitesimal cathedral... grotesquely decorated with crockets and gargoyles, ravished from some medieval church." (In real life, these were salvaged from the restoration of St. Giles.)

For a longer expedition (than just to Swanston itself), which needs good footwear and the best part of a morning or afternoon, follow the track into the Pentland Hills south of Swanston. The objcctive is the broad ridge, seen to the south, of Caerketton and Allermuir Hills, two of the Pentland "tops." Alternatively, Caerketton (the one with screes) can be reached by missing Swanston entirely and going up towards the ski centre at Hillend, striking upwards on a path to the left of it. Either way, you join a skyline path westwards along the heathery hilltops, enjoying superb city views. Take in Capelaw Hill before descending an easy path and track to Bonaly Country Park. (There is parking for those making a separate excursion.) Follow Bonaly Road down into the suburb of Colinton to reach Spylaw Park. Turning right (towards town) soon brings you to Colinton Parish Church above a bend in the Water of Leith, another place which Stevenson knew well; his maternal grandfather, the Reverend Dr. Lewis Balfour, was minister here. It is childhood memories of this leafy dell with its mossy banks and river that Stevenson recalls in his lines: "Here is the mill with the humming of thunder./Here is the weir with the wonder of foam." Buses run from Colinton back into the city centre.

▶ Palace of Holyroodhouse *45E2*

Open: Apr–Oct, daily 9.30–6; Nov–Mar, daily 9.30–4.30. Admission: expensive (tel: 0131 556 5100; www.royal.gov.uk)

As late as the 1890s, Robert Louis Stevenson in his *Picturesque Notes on Edinburgh* observed that "The Palace of Holyroodhouse has been left aside in the growth of Edinburgh, and stands grey and silent in a workman's quarter among breweries and gasworks." This was the low point in the story of what is still the official residence of the royal family in Scotland. The palace evolved from the guest-house of the adjacent Holyrood Abbey, now a ruin.

The first palace, started by King James IV, was damaged during the English raids of 1544, part of the "rough wooing" (see page 30), though the northwest tower (or the King James V Tower—the left-hand tower on the frontage) survived the flames to be rebuilt.

Holyrood was ablaze again in 1650, the same year as Cromwell and his troops stayed there while occupying the north. He ordered some repairs but in the main the work seen today is the result of a major remodelling between 1671 and 1680, during the reign of King Charles II.

However, it is most strongly associated with Mary, Queen of Scots (see page 30) though the site of the murder of Riccio is no longer marked with red paint but instead by a discreet plaque. After such highlights as grand levees held by the transient Bonnie Prince Charlie and later by King George IV in his 1822 visit, it fell into decline, though Victoria and Albert used it in 1850. Much restoration work this century has restored its dignity. As well as portraits of monarchs (some of them mythical) there are tapestries and fine furniture from the royal collections. It closes to visitors and transforms itself from a tourist centre to a high-security establishment whenever a member of the royal family comes to visit. The elegant, modern **Queen's Gallery**, by the palace gate, shows works of art from the Royal Collection (joint ticket with palace available).

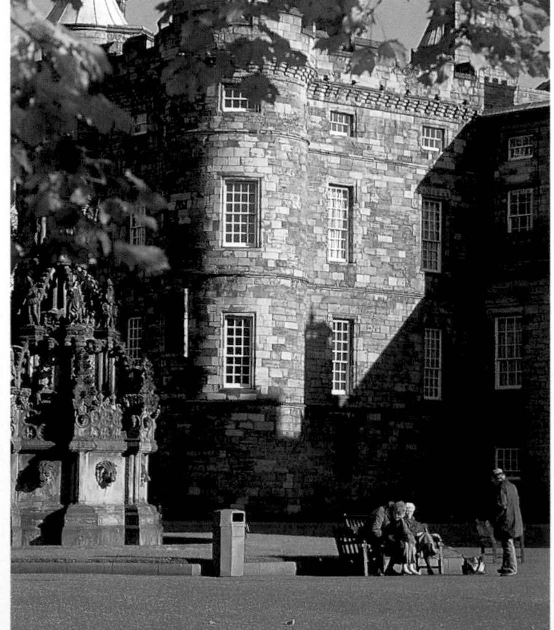

Palace of Holyroodhouse—detail of entrance gates

THE LAW COURTS
Behind St. Giles, Parliament House, the seat of Scottish government until 1707, now houses the Supreme Law Courts of Scotland. There are portraits by Raeburn among other artists, as well as a hammerbeam roof to admire.

ROYAL PORTRAITS
Jacob de Witt, a Dutchman living in Edinburgh, signed a contract with His Majesty's Cash Keeper in 1684 to deliver 110 portraits of Scottish kings within two years at £120 per year. These ran from the possibly mythical King Fergus I to the then contemporary King Charles II—so at least in one case de Witt had a likeness from which to work. The painter fulfilled his contract at more than one a week and at least 80 of the portraits can be seen today.

Palace of Holyroodhouse, officially the Scottish residence of the royal family

THE OLD PHYSIC GARDEN
Few of the passengers arriving at Waverley Station notice the plaque which records the site of the first public botanic garden in Edinburgh. The Old Physic Garden was in the hollow now occupied by the station and the post office next to it. The area saw many changes, not the least of which was the draining of the Nor' Loch which once provided Edinburgh Castle's defences to the north (in part of today's Princes Street Gardens). The partial draining of the ancient loch flooded the Old Physic Garden in 1689 and many of its precious plants were lost.

►► People's Story 45D2

163 Canongate (tel: 0131 529 4057; www.cac.org.uk)
Open: Mon–Sat 10–5; during Aug, Sun 12–5
Admission free

The People's Story is just that—a museum recording the experiences of the ordinary folk of Edinburgh from the 18th century to the present day. As such it does not portray a sanitized view of a city in which bad housing and poor working conditions co-existed with a genteel preoccupation with middle-class respectability.

►►► Royal Botanic Garden Edinburgh 44B3

20A Inverleith Row (tel: 0131 552 7171; www.rbge.org.uk)
Open: Apr–Sep, 10–7; Oct and Mar, 10–6; Nov–Feb 10–4.
Admission free; glasshouses: inexpensive

One of Edinburgh's most precious recreational assets, the garden is "strollable" from Princes Street via Stockbridge, though you may wish to take the bus back up the hill. It is especially suitable for children as it is dog-free—though the squirrels can be a bit persistent. As well as its large rhododendron collection and a magnificent rock garden (best in May), there are substantial areas under glass. The highest point of the garden has a fine view of the city.

Royal Botanic Garden—an all-weather, all-year attraction

►► Royal Museum of Scotland and Museum of Scotland 44C1

Chambers Street (tel: 0131 247 4422; www.nms.ac.uk)
Open: daily 10–5. Admission: free

This lofty Victorian building, with its soaring columns and galleries, houses the national collection of scientific, natural, historical, geological, and archaeological objects, and much more, and is currently undergoing renovation.

The adjacent Museum of Scotland houses a collection of artefacts and treasures that relate specifically to Scotland, including Pictish carvings, the famous Lewis chessmen, chairs by Charles Rennie Mackintosh, items relating to Robert Burns and steam engines of the industrial age.

A PRESBYTERIAN PROTEST
A humble cabbage-stall owner called Jenny Geddes earned her place in history on 23 July, 1637. King Charles I had declared St. Giles a cathedral and had ordered the use of the Anglican service book. No sooner had the Dean of Edinburgh started this unfamiliar service to the staunchly Presbyterian congregation than Jenny Geddes threw her prayer stool at him, screaming "Daur ye say mass in my lug! (Dare you say Mass in my ear?)." More missiles followed and a full-scale riot ensued. Her great gesture over, Jenny quietly returned to cabbage selling.

►► Royal Yacht *Britannia*

Ocean Drive, Leith (tel: 0131 555 5566; www. royalyachtbritannia.co.uk)
Open: Apr–Oct, daily 9.30–4.30; Nov–Mar daily 10–3.30.
Admission: exepnsive

For 40 years, *Britannia* served the royal family, travelling over a million miles to become the most famous ship in the world. The on-shore visitor centre sets the scene, telling the history of the ship. A well-spaced, self-guided tour using handsets makes for a pleasant wander around the yacht itself. Pre-book at peak times.

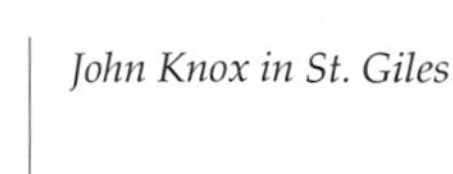

John Knox in St. Giles

► St. Giles: the High Kirk of Edinburgh *44C1*

High Street (tel: 0131 225 9442; www.stgilescathedral.org.uk)
Open: Oct–Apr, Mon–Sat 9–5, Sun 1–5; May–Sep, Mon–Fri 9–7, Sat 9–5, Sun 1–5; and for services. Admission free

Often called St. Giles' Cathedral, though purists argue it only achieved this status briefly, St. Giles was at one time the only kirk within the walls of old Edinburgh. The tower of St. Giles, whose crown was completed in 1500, is one of the few remaining examples of 15th-century work to be seen in the High Street today. Much of the kirk has been altered and reworked over the centuries. Today's dull cladding is the result of 19th-century "restoration." Only the tower and crown escaped this grey stone.

Once the church even had a long arcade of booths, the "krames," leaning against the north side. These were removed in 1817 along with the "luckenbooths," other small shops that contributed to the crowded narrowness of this part of the High Street. Just to the west of the kirk is the site of the Old Tolbooth, also removed in 1817. Causeway stones mark the spot in the shape of a heart.

► Scotch Whisky Heritage Centre *44C1*

354 Castlehill (tel: 0131 220 0441; www.whisky-heritage.co.uk)
Open: Sep–May, daily 10–5; Jun–Aug, daily 9.30–7
Admission: expensive

The problem with whisky-making is that it is not a dramatic process. The Scotch Whisky Heritage Centre injects fun into the subject with its hi-tech approach of talking tableaux and commentary, all viewed while riding along very slowly on a hollowed-out whisky barrel.

THE OLD TOLBOOTH
It was formerly considered good luck to spit on the heart shape which marks the Old Tolbooth site beside St. Giles. This was perhaps a contemptuous gesture towards the town authorities who used the Tolbooth as a prison.

JOHN KNOX
John Knox's statue can be seen inside St. Giles, but the fiery reformer's grave is no longer marked. He was buried in the old St. Giles churchyard, which is now covered by flagstones.

ST. GILES
St. Giles, the kirk, was probably founded by Benedictine followers of Giles, the saint, who brought the name from the south of France. In 1466, the Preston Aisle of the kirk was completed, in memory of William Preston who had acquired the armbone of the saint in France. This relic disappeared about 1577, but St. Giles' other arm-bone is still in St. Giles Church, Bruges.

The story of Scottish whisky is told on the Royal Mile

The Scottish patriot Fletcher of Saltoun wrote in 1698: "As the happy situation of London has been the principal cause of the glory and riches of England; so the bad situation of Edinburgh has been one great occasion of the poverty and uncleanliness in which the greater part of the people of Scotland live."

Top: an ornate ceiling inside the head office of the Royal Bank of Scotland at 36 St. Andrew Square

An 18th-century vision Many stories of the squalor of the Old Town of Edinburgh are documented. As the more peaceful 18th century began in Scotland, improvements began within the Old Town itself. But the long-term solution was for the city's inhabitants to escape entirely from the rocky ramp running down from the castle.

George Drummond, Lord Provost of Edinburgh, had a clear vision of a new Edinburgh rising on what was then only a low ridge between the castle and the sea. A competition to design a new town was organized, which was won by a young and unknown architect, James Craig. His 1767 design shows a simple grid of streets balanced by a square at either end. This is the Princes Street to Queen Street area, with Charlotte Square and St. Andrew Square at either end.

THE MOUND

In the great building spree that went on in 18th-century Edinburgh, somewhere had to be found for the material dug out for foundations. In the case of the Royal Exchange (today's City Chambers) the rubble became the Castle Esplanade. Meanwhile, Geordie Boyd, a local tailor, started dumping earth into the quagmire of the old Nor Loch. So did everyone else, and "Geordie Boyd's mud brig" grew and grew. Two million cartloads later, in 1830, it became The Mound, the elegant roadway linking the Old and New Towns.

Princes Street If you stroll along Queen Street today, you can see how it echoes Princes Street: it is built up on one side only and has gardens (still private) opposite. Down amid the hubbub and "High Street" shopfronts on Princes Street, it is hard to believe that in Craig's original scheme the area was meant to be entirely residential. He designated today's Thistle and Rose streets, lesser byways between the grand thoroughfares, as the abode and business place of tradesmen and shopkeepers. The use of the lanes behind Thistle and Rose streets to service the back doors of the wealthier residents was a clever element in his deceptively simple scheme.

Princes Street did not remain residential for long. The main tide of commercial developments began to flow from east to west by the mid-19th century. Before that, the residents, whose grand drawing-rooms looked out to the castle over the trees in the gardens, had fought another battle. A speculator wanted to build along the south side of Princes Street and the indignant citizens,

Period atmosphere in elegant Charlotte Square

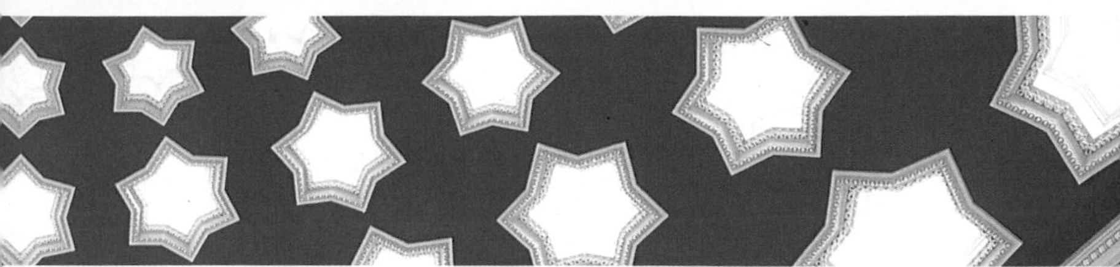

determined to preserve their views, had to take their case to the House of Lords before the project was stopped. (The city fathers of the day were quite happy to allow the speculator to build.) Today's low-profiled Princes Mall is a reminder of those far-off legal battles.

String-pulling Stand on what used to be the bare ridge and is now George Street, about halfway along, and look up and down the street. In Craig's plan the two squares, Charlotte and St. Andrew, at either end of the view, also had churches. While the green copper dome of the former St. George's (now West Register House) is plain on the western skyline, to the east in St. Andrew Square there is a fine town house instead of a church.

A place of worship was never built there because of civic string-pulling by Sir Laurence Dundas. Rich, power-

PRINCES STREET
Princes Street was to be called St. Giles Street, but King George III objected as it reminded him of the St. Giles district of London, which was notorious for its lowlife at the time. So the most famous street in Scotland became Prince's Street after the Prince Regent, before assuming its plural form in 1848.

The grand facades of Edinburgh's New Town

ful, and one-time Commissary General of the army in Flanders, Dundas acquired the site and altered the plan to suit himself. He employed Sir William Chambers to design the magnificent façade which is seen today, and this fine town house is now the headquarters of the Royal Bank of Scotland. It has ornate ceilings in its main hall and is well worth going inside to see it. The city fathers got their kirk eventually, built on a less satisfactory site, round the corner in George Street. This is St. Andrew's, still in use today and open to visitors.

By the end of the 19th century, the first New Town was complete, paving the way for further phases to the north, east, and west, and creating Edinburgh's unique neoclassical ambience.

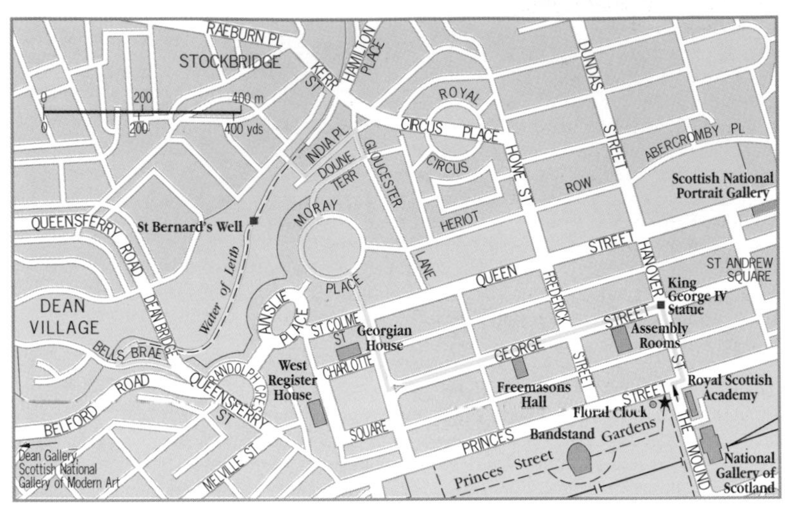

Walk

The New Town

Discover the surprisingly intact second phase of the New Town in the streets that lie north of Charlotte Square. Allow 3 hours.

Starting from the **Floral Clock** on Princes Street, opposite the Royal Scottish Academy, walk north to George Street, turning left at the **statue of King George IV**. Go past the **Assembly Rooms**, now a major Festival Fringe venue, where Sir Walter Scott publicly admitted to writing the "Waverley" novels during a grand dinner in 1827.

Continue down George Street to **Charlotte Square** at the west end, which balances **St. Andrew Square** at the east. The Robert Adam-designed north façade of Charlotte Square is impressively harmonious, while intrusive dormers and other additions detract from the other three sides.

Continue downhill to **Moray Place**, typical of the New Town with its private gardens, cobbled roads, and grand façades. Leave by **Doune Terrace**. Cross the **Water of Leith** to shop in Stockbridge, otherwise turn left along undistinguished India Place. Keep going to enter the wooded valley of the Water of Leith and go down steps by the bridge. **St. Bernard's Well**, half-hidden in the greenery, is a former mineral spring in the shape of a Grecian temple with a statue of Hygeia, designed by Alexander Nasmyth in 1789.

The footpath continues to **Dean Village**. Overhead is Thomas Telford's road bridge, built in 1832. A 1643 Baxters (Bakers) "coat-of-arms" survives on the abutment of the original bridge below. Climb back to the busy streets by cobbled Bell's Brae, the former main road.

St. Bernard's Well

▶ Scottish National Gallery of Modern Art *off 44A2*

Belford Road (tel: 0131 624 6200; www.nationalgalleries.org)
Open: daily 10–5. Admission free

Housed in former school premises to the west of the town, an excursion here could be made via a stretch of the Water of Leith footpath, joining it perhaps at Dean Village. Scotland's own collection of modern art includes works by Derain, Matisse, Picasso, Giacometti, Hockney, Hirst, and Hepworth among many others. Scotland's own artists are not neglected, with the Scottish colourists—Peploe, Cadell, Fergusson and Hunter—well represented. The gallery also has a popular café. Opposite is the Dean Gallery, with its outstanding collection of Dada and surrealist art.

▶ (Edinburgh) Zoo *44A1*

134 Corstorphine Road (tel: 0131 334 9171; www.edinburghzoo.org.uk)
Open: Apr–Sep, daily 9–6; Mar, Oct, daily 9–5; Nov–Feb daily 9–4.30. Admission: expensive

Edinburgh Zoo is a good example of how a visitor attraction—like an endangered species—must adapt to survive. Some years ago it suffered all the problems of financing a long-established traditional wide-ranging animal collection at a time when visitors suddenly found an ever-increasing choice of attractions to divert them.

Penguins at Edinburgh's Zoo

These days the emphasis is on education, and the displays modified to make life more interesting for the creatures within them. With or without children in tow, the zoo is worth a visit just to see how an establishment once described as "the dinosaur of the leisure industry" has got its act together, modernized, considered visitors' needs and now offers a very worthwhile "infotainment" experience. The new generation of animal exhibits really are quite exciting—the aerial walkway across the rolling hillocks occupied by the painted hunting dogs, for example, while the African plains and several other artfully designed enclosures give a sense of spaciousness.

The zoo is particularly associated with penguins, and the underwater views of swimming penguins are also excellent. The sloping site has been addressed with a road train that runs around the park. Overall a visit to the zoo, both for the animals and for the great city views, should still be part of the Edinburgh experience.

PENGUINS ON PARADE
Edinburgh Zoo's "Penguin Parade" is an old-established institution. The penguins are shepherded out of their modern, spacious enclosure daily in the summer months and trundle round a grassy area nearby. Formerly, they were walked right out of the zoo, but their appearance on the pavements by Corstorphine Road caused traffic accidents as drivers were distracted. Their perambulations these days are less extensive.

RESERVING ACCOMMODATION
Tel 0845 225 5121;
www.visitscotland.com

Accommodation

Sit on the top deck of a bus coming in on the main road from Cameron Toll through the district of Newington and you can get some idea of the range of accommodation that is available. The hotels and guest-houses are lined up as far as the eye can see—and that is just one street, though it changes its name as it heads towards The Bridges and central Edinburgh.

However, do not be misled into thinking that finding the right place to stay will be easy, since Edinburgh is a hugely popular destination. If you are visiting specifically to "do" Edinburgh at Festival time, then book well ahead. Otherwise, late August and early September are best avoided altogether.

Finding somewhere at a reasonable rate will be much easier outside that period, and easier still out of season (November to Easter). If you do find yourself in the city during the Festival and need somewhere to stay, it's worth persevering with the Edinburgh and Scotland Information Centre at 3 Princes Street (tel: 0845 225 5121), who will certainly assist. It would be misleading to suggest that accommodation is impossible, more that things are *very* busy.

HOTELS Many international chains are represented in Edinburgh, for example the Edinburgh Sheraton, with its views of the castle. Then there are the city's former railway hotels: the grand Caledonian Hilton with its sumptuous Pompadour Restaurant and, dominating the skyline at the other end of Princes Street, the equally luxurious Balmoral. (This used to be called the North British, taking its name from the other pre-1923 railway company which ran services into Edinburgh.)

Also in the expensive bracket are: The Howard in Great King Street; the classically elegant Scotsman on North Bridge; newly refurbished Prestonfield House, set in rolling parkland only five minutes from The Royal Mile. Medium and budget hotels can also be found in the heart of the city.

Quality can be enjoyed without paying the earth. Notable for its service and country-club atmosphere in the

Echoes of the great railway age—the Caledonian Hotel

A Princes Street landmark—the clocktower of the Balmoral Hotel

city is Channings on South Learmonth Gardens. The Malmaison, with a strong French influence, is in a quiet location close to the waterfront in Leith, yet only 10 minutes from the middle of the city.

GUEST-HOUSES There is a wide choice of guest-houses. Many can be found south of the city centre. As a general rule, the smaller establishments tend to be some distance from the city centre—though this should not be a problem as Edinburgh bus services are adequate. Remember if coming by car to enquire about parking at the establishment of your choice, since Edinburgh traffic wardens strike without mercy after 8AM.

Rates during the off-season period between November and Easter are always cheaper and there are often special break prices or other kinds of deals from the larger hotels.

HOSTELS There are four Edinburgh youth hostels at: 7 Bruntsfield Crescent (tel: 0870 004 1114), 18 Eglinton Crescent (tel: 0870 004 1116), Edinburgh Metro at 11/2 Robertson's Close, Cowgate (tel: 0870 004 1115, summer only), and Edinburgh International, Kincaid's Court, Guthrie Street (tel: 0870 004 1117, summer only). These are supplemented in summer by additional hostel accommodation using university student residences. For advance bookings, contact Central Reservations (tel: 0870 155 3255; www.syha.org.uk—you can book online). All are within easy reach of the main visitor attractions.

OUT OF TOWN Choosing accommodation outside the city is another option. The Norton House Hotel and the Edinburgh Marriott are on the west side of the city within easy reach of Edinburgh Airport. To the south, the Roslin Glen Hotel in the conservation village of Roslin is close to Rosslyn Chapel, with its medieval stonecarving.

HISTORIC FEATURES
You might notice the extra-wide front doors in some of the city's New Town properties that are now hotels. Together with generous hallways between inner and outer doors, these were originally built to park sedan chairs when not in use! Similarly, the New Town's George Street was not built so broadly with central parking in mind but to let a coach-and-six do an easy U-turn!

Food and drink

Edinburgh's colourful pub signs

Edinburgh sees itself as a cosmopolitan city so you will find cuisines from around the world on offer in its restaurants. However, many establishments come and go, and chefs move around, so it is always best to take up-to-the-minute local advice if you want a meal to remember.

RESTAURANTS In addition to a wide choice of independent restaurants, the main hotels all have good restaurants, with Number One at the Balmoral Hotel and Rhubarb restaurant at the Prestonfield being particularly notable ones. On the other hand, the area surrounding the university, especially around Nicolson Street, has a number of eating places offering particularly good value. Leith, Edinburgh's seaport, is the venue for a number of enterprising restaurant developments and should not be overlooked. This is a place to head for in the evening to eat and drink, and to see and be seen in one of the trendy wine bars.

For consistent quality, Martins in Rose Street North Lane and The Vintner's Rooms down in Leith are examples of top-flight imaginative cuisine, but it is almost unfair to single them out as the city has so many good restaurants to choose from: Atrium, Haldanes, Stac Polly, Blue, Restaurant Martin Wishart, The Witchery by the Castle.

If you want quality on a budget, try Kalpna in Nicolson Street, with its reasonably priced, inspiring Gujarati vegetarian cooking; to join a complete cross-section of the

IN THE HAGGIS SEASON...
Haggis may be Scotland's national dish, but it can be dull, or dry, or greasy, or gritty—though it can also be spicy and delicious. If you want to try it, you will sometimes find it on Scottish-themed restaurant menus as a starter.

Bags of atmosphere at the Café Royal Oyster Bar

Scotland's sweet tooth—Casey's sweet shop

locals enjoying a good evening out, try The Waterfront in Leith, or Conran's Zinc Bar and Grill in Ocean Terminal, one of the city's newest shopping and entertainment complexes.

The only thing that is really hard to track down in Edinburgh is an easily identifiable local cuisine, though the East Lothian countryside is market-garden country, supplying plenty of local produce. The other name for Edinburgh's eastern hinterland is "Scotland's Granary," which has in turn helped to develop a tradition of fine baking, though probably no more so here than in other parts of Scotland. Local food-lovers are more likely to whisper reverently about the near-legendary Valvona and Crolla delicatessen and café at 19 Elm Row (tel: 0131 556 6066; www.valvonacrolla.co.uk), with its authentic Italian ambience. They also have a wine bar/café in the new central shopping hotspot near Harvey Nichols.

WHOLEFOODS Edinburgh's fairly enlightened attitude (for Scotland) to food can be deduced from the success of Henderson's in Hanover Street. This vegetarian wholefood self-service restaurant is not a new place capitalizing on the current trend for healthy eating. Instead it has survived and prospered on the same site for decades—since long before the notion of healthy food reached the rest of high-cholesterol Scotland.

The heavyweight traditional Scottish breakfast is still available in most guest-houses and B&Bs, but you can skip it and linger instead over a croissant and coffee in one of the city's numerous café bars. Home-baked cakes for afternoon tea are easily found—try Clarinda's in the Canongate—and the Balmoral Hotel's famous afternoon tea, or its Thursday night chocolate buffet.

EDINBURGH ROCK The quintessential Edinburgh souvenir is sold at any number of tourist shops, and could be just the gift for someone with a (very) sweet tooth. If you prefer a different kind of food souvenir, look for authentic Scottish cheese at Ian Mellis's shop on West Row.

ROLL PLAY

An Edinburgh baker's is a good place to note the regional differences in the names for various bread goods and fancies. Muffins describe at least two types of bun. Pancakes are even more of a problem. Are they the same as crumpets, or even pikelets? Aberdeen rolls in most Edinburgh bakers are butteries, sometimes rowies. And what exactly are Jap cakes and German biscuits? If you think this is complicated, try ordering a pound of potted hough from the butcher next door.

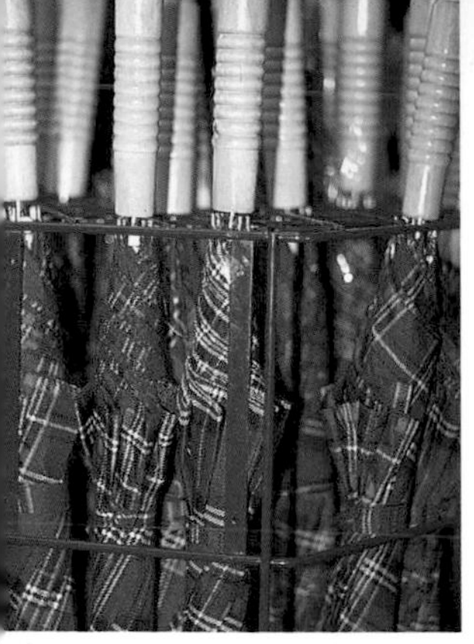

Tartan brollies—practical souvenirs of Edinburgh

Shopping

MAIN SHOPPING AREAS Do not make the mistake of assuming that Edinburgh's shopping ends with Princes Street. This is far from the case. With the exception of the famous Jenners department store, and a very few other places, Princes Street has little more to offer than can be found in a dozen other British towns. This is not to say that the shops are necessarily bad—just that there is not a huge choice of unique or characterful Scottish wares along its length.

Within a few moments' walk of Princes Street are the St. James Centre and the Princes Mall, both covered. Nearby George Street offers exclusive boutique-style shopping.

SCOTTISH GOODS Shopping in Edinburgh is worthwhile, as the city offers a good range of Scottish products. But the best shops are not all in one place. Shops selling imported souvenirs abound along the Royal Mile, but there are several high-quality outlets as well.

The Tartan Weaving Mill and Exhibition, at 555 Castlehill, offers a good cross-section of Scottish wares made on the premises, including bagpipes and kilts. Palenque, at 56 High Street, has a fine selection of contemporary silver and gold jewellery. Anta, at 93 West Bow, has a range of stylish ceramics and tartan textiles designed and made in Scotland.

OPEN FOR BUSINESS
Especially in the height of the season, many shops catering for visitors are open every day. Off-peak, the city has late night opening on Thursdays (7.30–8PM), and superstores stay open late right through the week, all year round.

SPECIALIST SHOPS Small individual businesses still survive in Victoria Street. A little farther on in the Grassmarket, among the odd mixture of down-and-outs and exclusive designer shops, is Mr. Wood's Fossils, which, as you would expect, sells all kinds of fossils. Also within easy reach of Princes Street is the William

The elegant interior of Jenners

Street/Stafford Street area, where there are a number of smaller specialist fashion and gift shops, of which Studio One in Stafford Street is a long-established example.

SHOPPING OUT OF THE CENTRE Farther afield, the districts of Bruntsfield and Morningside are worth a stroll along the main streets, down the high canyons of the Edinburgh tenement blocks. Stockbridge, towards the Water of Leith, is also worth a look, and only minutes from the city centre. Edinburgh Crystal at Penicuik, about half an hour from the city centre by car, runs factory tours showing the glass-blowing process and has hand-cut products. (You can also buy this range in the city.)

A Royal Mile souvenir shop—tartan all the way

BOOKSHOPS Edinburgh's literary leanings are confirmed by the large number of bookshops scattered around, many of which are second-hand shops. Among new book retailers are Borders Books and Waterstones. These, and many more, some with late opening hours, make the city a browser's paradise.

ART AND ANTIQUES Antique shops seem to come and go, but try Bruntsfield Place or Causewayside where they gather in clusters. It is best to ask around for up-to-the-minute information. Some antique shops have a good selection of Scottish paintings, but Edinburgh is exceptionally well-endowed with specialized galleries, with selections of both contemporary and antique material.

The Firth Gallery in William Street specializes in living Scottish artists. Gallery 41 in Dundas Street tends towards contemporary work as well as wood sculpture and pottery, while Stills on Cockburn Street exhibits work by both Scottish and international photographers. For those who hunt around, bargains and high-quality work can be found in the city. If tracking them down takes you off Princes Street then that is all the better—the real Edinburgh can be found en route.

JENNERS
Jenners has been an Edinburgh institution since 1838. It offers a good range of wares, from Edinburgh Crystal to exclusive fashions and a large toy department. This traditional department store is housed in a handsome building of 1895, with lots of baroque detail outside and a mock Jacobean galleried interior.

Nightlife

It may not be Paris or Las Vegas, but Edinburgh belies its sober and respectable image with a vibrant nightlife.

The annual rash of Fringe posters

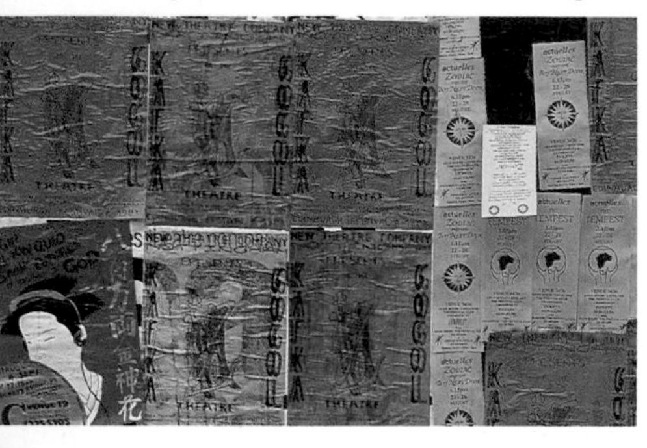

THEATRE AND CONCERT HALLS The Traverse Theatre on Cambridge Street (tel: 0131 228 1404) puts on the most stimulatingly experimental material, while the Royal Lyceum Theatre on Grindley Street (tel: 0131 248 4848) stages more "middle-of-the-road" plays. The Kings Theatre on Leven Street (tel: 0131 529 6000) has varied lightweight events including variety and pantomime. The Usher Hall on Lothian Road (tel: 0131 228 1155) is the city's old-established concert venue, while the Festival Theatre on Nicolson Street (tel: 0131 529 6000) is equally prestigious. The Queen's Hall on Clerk Street (tel: 0131 668 2019) is a more intimate concert setting, while The Playhouse, Greenside Place (tel: 0870 606 3424) sees a lot of big showbiz names.

FESTIVAL NIGHTS
Remember that Edinburgh's nightlife, like the city itself, moves up a gear during the Festival (see page 13). Everywhere is crowded and full of visitors. This is the season when Edinburgh appears truly cosmopolitan.

FILM The independent Dominion on Newbattle Terrace in Morningside (tel: 0131 447 4771) is particularly good, while the Filmhouse on Lothian Road (tel: 0131 228 2688) is the place to see off-beat, less commercial, or foreign-language films.

OTHER KINDS OF NIGHTLIFE The city's casinos include the Stanley Berkeley in Rutland Place (tel: 0131 228 4446) and Stanley Martell on Newington Road (tel: 0131 667 7763). Both will offer free membership with 24 hours' notice.

Alternatively treat yourself to a Scottish evening, with lots of songs and dancing at the Thistle Edinburgh Hotel, Leith Street (tel: 0131 556 0111).

There are at least half a dozen club venues that offer something for fans of techno, rave, chart sound, mainstream, and/or the gay scene. Try the Bongo Club (tel: 0131 558 7604), Po Na Na (tel: 0131 226 2224) or Blue Moon (tel: 0131 557 0911).

LISTINGS
For up-to-the-minute events information in Edinburgh, try *The List* (www.list.co.uk) available from all city-centre newsagents, or *The Scotsman* (www.scotsman. com) on Saturdays, whose weekend section is very strong on entertainment events throughout Scotland, but emphasizing Edinburgh. The latter is a useful place to find information on folk music in the capital.

Fringe actors—an encounter at every street corner

Practicalities

AIRPORT TRANSFERS Edinburgh Airport, Edinburgh EH12 9DN (tel: 0870 040 007) is 9.6km (6mi) from the city centre. Airport buses run at peak times every 10 minutes (every hour off-peak) between the terminal building and Waverley Bridge. They take 30 minutes and cost roughly a quarter of the taxi fare.

ARRIVING BY TRAIN OR BUS Waverley Station could hardly be closer to the city centre and there is a taxi rank right within the station. The main bus station has been refurbished and is at St. Andrew Square, moments away from Princes Street along which run the principal city bus services (see below).

TOURIST INFORMATION For the main Edinburgh Tourist Information Centre see page 272. For information about Edinburgh at the airport, check with the Tourist Information Desk in the terminal building.

GETTING AROUND BY BUS Edinburgh has an extensive bus network, with two main bus companies covering most of the routes. On Lothian Buses plc (LRT) maroon and white buses, you pay the driver on entry with the exact fare. They offer a variety of unlimited travel tickets to visitors. Further information from the office at Annandale Street, Edinburgh (tel: 0131 554 4494).

On First Edinburgh purple and cream buses, you pay the driver on boarding, and change is given. Some services are small coaches known as Citysprinters. Obtain more information from Traveline Scotland—public transport information (tel: 0870 608 2608).

TAXIS Black taxis are widely available within the city. There are a number of taxi ranks, and taxis showing an illuminated "For Hire" sign can be hailed in the street. Black taxis cannot be picked up at Edinburgh Airport, but a fleet of other licensed cabs (usually saloon car types) is available there.

TRAVEL TO THE AIRPORT
Both main railway lines converging on Edinburgh, from Glasgow and from the north, pass the airport practically next to its perimeter. So far, nobody has thought to build a station. Airport to city-centre connections are by road, through the suburb of Corstorphine, which can get very busy at peak times, to Princes Street. Allow a good hour before check-in time if you are catching a plane.

If time is short—take a bus tour

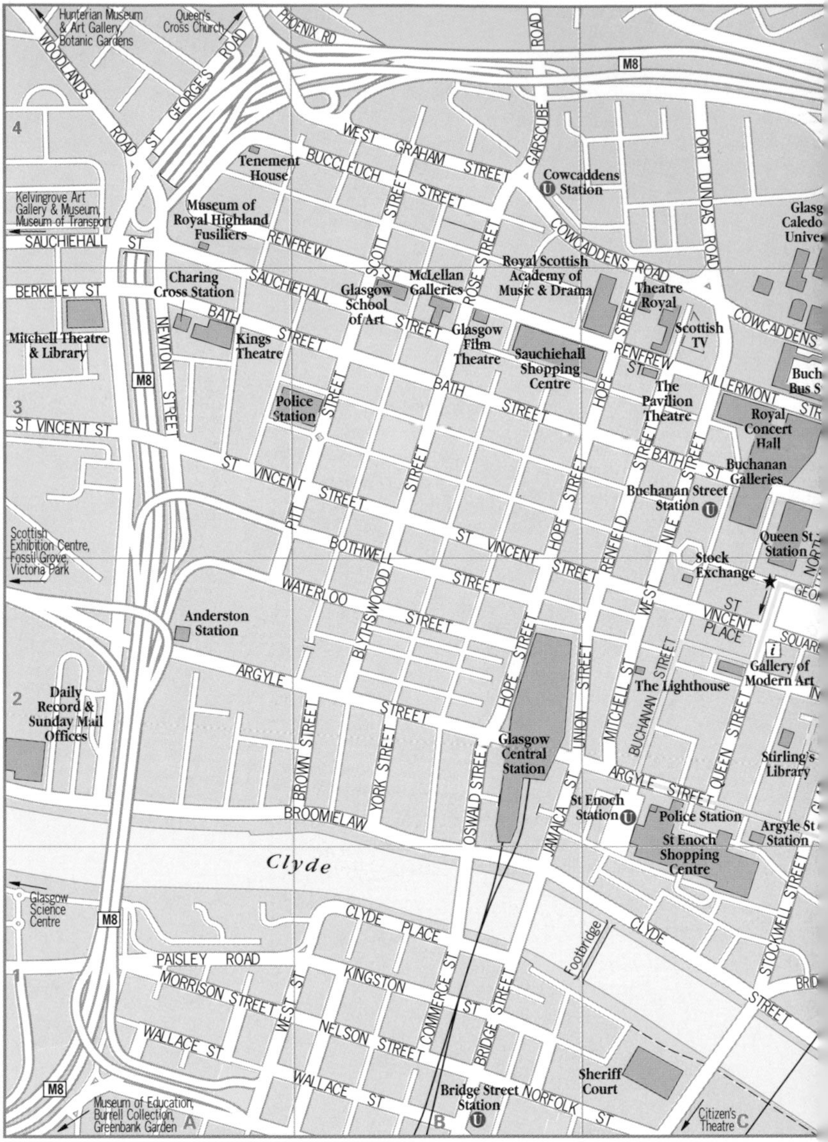

Hunterian Museum & Art Gallery, Botanic Gardens
Queen's Cross Church
WOODLANDS ROAD
ST GEORGE'S ROAD
PHOENIX RD
M8
GARSCUBE ROAD
PORT DUNDAS ROAD
4
WEST GRAHAM STREET
BUCCLEUCH STREET
Tenement House
Cowcaddens Station
Kelvingrove Art Gallery & Museum, Museum of Transport
Museum of Royal Highland Fusiliers
SAUCHIEHALL ST
RENFREW
SCOTT ST
ROSE STREET
COWCADDENS ROAD
Royal Scottish Academy of Music & Drama
Theatre Royal
BERKELEY ST
Charing Cross Station
SAUCHIEHALL STREET
Glasgow School of Art
McLellan Galleries
Glasgow Film Theatre
Sauchiehall Shopping Centre
Scottish TV
Mitchell Theatre & Library
BATH STREET
Kings Theatre
NEWTON STREET
M8
HOPE STREET
RENFREW ST
The Pavilion Theatre
KILLERMONT ST
Royal Concert Hall
3
ST VINCENT ST
Police Station
PITT STREET
BATH STREET
BATH ST
Buchanan Galleries
ST VINCENT STREET
Buchanan Street Station
Scottish Exhibition Centre, Fossil Grove, Victoria Park
BOTHWELL
ST VINCENT STREET
RENFIELD
NILE STREET
Queen St Station
Stock Exchange
WATERLOO
BLYTHSWOOD
STREET
WEST
ST VINCENT PLACE
Anderston Station
STREET
Gallery of Modern Art
ARGYLE
MITCHELL ST
BUCHANAN STREET
The Lighthouse
2
Daily Record & Sunday Mail Offices
STREET
HOPE STREET
UNION STREET
Glasgow Central Station
BROWN STREET
YORK STREET
OSWALD STREET
QUEEN STREET
Stirling's Library
ARGYLE STREET
BROOMIELAW
JAMAICA ST
St Enoch Station
Police Station
Argyle St Station
St Enoch Shopping Centre
Clyde
Glasgow Science Centre
M8
CLYDE PLACE
Footbridge
CLYDE STREET
STOCKWELL STREET
PAISLEY ROAD
1
MORRISON STREET
WEST ST
KINGSTON ST
COMMERCE ST
BRIDGE STREET
WALLACE ST
NELSON STREET
Sheriff Court
M8
WALLACE ST
Bridge Street Station
NORFOLK ST
Museum of Education, Burrell Collection, Greenbank Garden
A
B
Citizen's Theatre
C

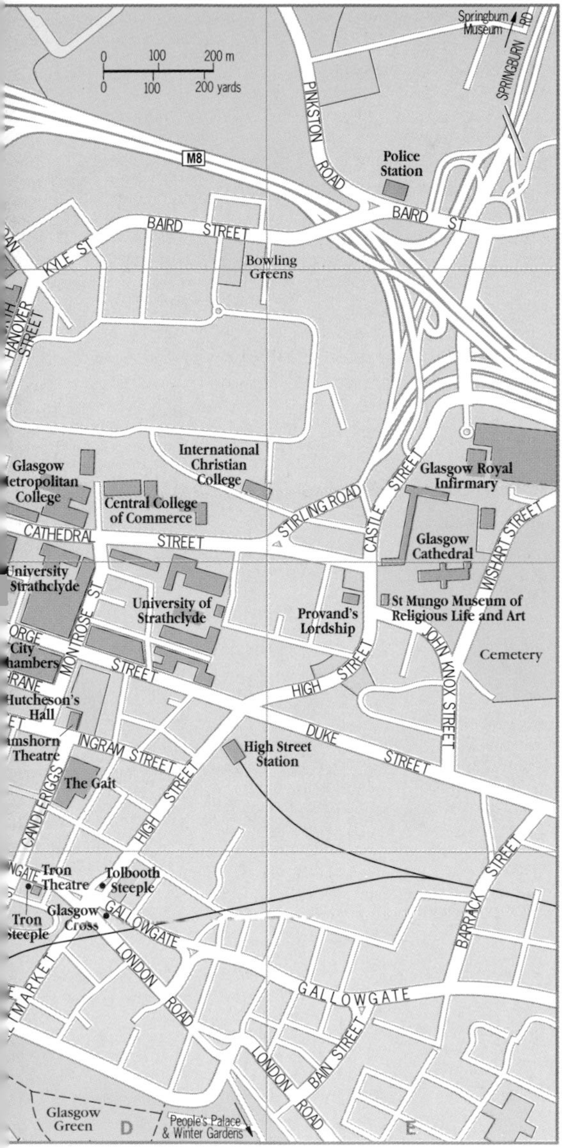

CHANGING IMAGE It was not so long ago that the idea of down-to-earth Glasgow becoming a serious challenger to Edinburgh's supremacy in the cultural and entertainment stakes would have been dismissed as impossible (especially by the complacent capital). But throughout the 1980s Glasgow ran a broadly based campaign to change its image. The native Glaswegians' friendliness, adaptability, and innate loyalty to their native city was harnessed to turn Glasgow into one of the most exciting places in Britain. Today, a thousand cameos of downtown Glasgow with its fine civic buildings rival the grand panorama of Edinburgh. The buoyant enthusiasm of the folk of the west make Edinburgh's stand-offishness seem

Look up for the best details on Glasgow's buildings

all the more absurd. Glasgow's choice of cultural, entertainment, eating, and shopping attractions matches anything the capital can offer, except perhaps at Edinburgh Festival time. In short, Glasgow has arrived.

The story of the city is essentially one of trade, though long ago it was a religious centre of some importance. St. Kentigern, or Mungo (ca518–603), is said to have built its first church on the site of the present cathedral, thereby founding the settlement which later became a royal burgh, though not until 1611. This status gave certain trading rights, though the prosperity of the city's traders and burgesses grew slowly at first, their activities hindered by the shallow silty river. Only after the Reformation, which ended Glasgow's role as a religious seat, did commerce really get under way. By 1688, the first pier had been built on the Broomielaw, on the riverside.

After the Union of 1707, the pace accelerated as it became easier to trade with the English colonies in America. Set on the western seaboard, Glasgow was well placed for this trade, and it soon began to rival Bristol in importance. In came rum, cotton, and tobacco; out went manufactured goods such as hats, shoes, and linen. One group of merchants in particular came to rival the aristocracy because of their wealth and power: Glasgow's Tobacco Lords.

"WORKSHOP OF THE WESTERN WORLD" The Glasgow talent for adaptability and resourcefulness showed itself in the way that new markets were founded following the collapse of the tobacco trade after America became independent in 1775. Using the nearby resources of coal and ironstone, Glasgow was soon a city with a heavy

▶▶▶ CITY HIGHLIGHTS

Typical Glasgow street scene—St. George's Tron Church closes off the view west down George Street

manufacturing base in the throes of the Industrial Revolution. At its height it became the "Second City of the British Empire" and was the "Workshop of the Western World" throughout the 19th century. This confidence expressed itself in fine civic buildings, both in the Merchant City—that part of Glasgow lying west of the old High Street—and farther west in the streets that were built on a relentless grid. It is in this inner city that the finest architecture can be seen today.

However, the ores and the coal which formed the backbone of the heavy industry, in particular around Lanarkshire immediately to the south, gradually became worked out. Even by the early years of the 20th century, Glasgow was losing touch with the shifting patterns of the world economy. By mid-century, many of the shipyards were uncompetitive and its locomotive works were finding it difficult to compete for orders.

Glasgow today is a postindustrial city, now emerging from a phase of urban renewal, with something of the spirit of the enterprising Victorians playing a part in the city's rebirth. Indeed, Glasgow was the 1999 UK City of Architecture and Design.

The city still has some problem peripheral housing schemes (but then so indeed has Edinburgh). There are still holes in the Merchant City, a few sites with grand plans still unfulfilled. But anyone strolling through the fashionable Italian Centre (an 18th-century warehouse conversion) or the sophisticated Princes Square (everything that a modern shopping mall ought to be but more often than not isn't) can see that the new Glasgow has something rather special.

The Glasgow Science Centre—a modern icon

THE RIVER CLYDE
Mention the River Clyde to the locals and soon the phrase "doon the watter" (down the water/river) will be heard. This refers to the now all-but-vanished summer holiday tradition of the toiling masses in the Clydeside conurbation who escaped from the shipyards, foundries, engineering works, mills, and offices, on a trip by steamer down the Clyde to the playground of the lower estuary—to Rothesay, Dunoon, Helensburgh, or any one of the other Clyde resorts (see Bute, page 231).

A CLEAN RIVER
Salmon returned to the River Clyde in 1983. Because of pollution, they had not been found there for the previous 120 years.

Medieval stained glass at the Burrell Collection (see page 81)

AN EXPLODING MYTH
One enduring Glasgow myth is that the Kelvingrove Art Gallery and Museum was built back to front, and that the architect committed suicide by jumping from the tower. It isn't and he didn't!

►► Art Gallery and Museum (Kelvingrove) *76A3*

Kelvingrove Park (tel: 0141 287 2699; www.glasgowmuseums.com)
Open: Mon–Thu, Sat 10–5, Fri, Sun 11–5

This arresting early 20th-century building in red sandstone is in Kelvingrove Park. It reopened after major refurbishment in 2006, and resumed its role in the leisure time of Glaswegians, both with its historical artefacts and with one of the finest civic art collections in Europe. The collection ranges from the Old Masters (with 17th-century Dutch work prominent) to the "Glasgow Boys" a later 19th-century flowering of Scottish artists (though not necessarily Scottish subject matter).

The new displays are contained in 18 major galleries where objects are shown in ways to help visitors understand them and in stories that help to interpret them. Each gallery is targeted towards a key audience (such as families or children), and there is a dedicated area for under-fives. Visitors can handle objects from the collections and experience multi-sensory learning activities.

► Botanic Gardens *76A4*

730 Great Western Road (tel: 0141 334 2422; www.glasgow.gov.uk)
Open: grounds daily 7–dusk. The glasshouses are open daily 10–4.45. Admission free

The original botanic collection was in a physic garden of the university, which moved to its present site on Great Western Road in 1842. The centrepiece of the garden today is the magnificent Kibble Palace of 1863 (restored in 2006), a sort of glass "big top" originally built for a merchant called John Kibble. He decided to give it to the city, provided he could use it for 20 years, and it was reassembled in the garden in 1871. Exterior features include a herb garden, sequential border, and arboretum. The garden has renowned orchid collection and the national collection of begonias.

The 18th-century elegance of Pollok House, in whose grounds the Burrell Collection now stands

▶▶▶ Burrell Collection 76A1

Pollok Country Park, 7km (4mi) southwest of Glasgow (tel: 0141 287 2550; www.glasgowmuseums.com). Open: Mon–Thu, Sat 10–5, Fri, Sun 11–5 Admission free

Sir William Burrell was a wealthy Glasgow shipowner with a wide-ranging taste for *objets d'art*. He started collecting as a boy and was still acquiring pieces at the time of his death in 1958, aged 96. Even by 1901, when the city staged the Glasgow International Exhibition, Burrell was the largest single lender for the displays, which included medieval tapestries, ivories, wood and alabaster sculpture, stained glass and bronzes, Roman glass, 16th- and 18th-century Dutch, German, and Venetian table glass, plus silver, furniture, Persian rugs, and many paintings including works by Manet, Whistler, and Monticelli. He acquired his first Degas just a little later, an indication that his eclectic tastes were already fully formed. In 1944 he gave the whole collection of 8,000 or so items to the city, along with almost half a million pounds to build a suitable home for them. As one of the conditions attached was a rural and pollution-free setting, matters languished for some years but a site was found by 1967 and, after a competition and a 12-year building phase, the magnificent Burrell Collection opened in Glasgow's Pollok Park in 1983.

▶▶▶ Gallery of Modern Art 76C2

Royal Exchange Square (tel: 0141 229 1996; www.glasgowmuseums.com) Open: Mon–Wed 10–5, Thu 10–8, Fri 11–5, Sat 10–5, Sun 11–5. Admission free

Opened in 1996, the gallery started life as a tobacco baron's mansion in 1780, then became a bank, an exchange or meeting and entertainment place for businessmen, then a library. The gallery is one of Scotland's major contemporary art venues, on four floors, each identified by one of the elements: fire, earth, water, or air, with appropriate signage. It displays Glasgow Museums' collection of art, craft, and design from 1950 to the present. Artists who have become internationally known since the 1980s are emphasized, and the gallery acquired works from beyond Scotland, including Papua New Guinea and Ethiopia. The gallery has wide-ranging temporary exhibitions and events and makes a substantial impact on the contemporary arts in Scotland.

At the Art Gallery and Museum, Kelvingrove

POLLOK HOUSE
Pollok Park, the setting of the Burrell, comprised the former policies (grounds) of Pollok House, donated to the city in 1967. Five minutes from the Burrell Collection, Pollok House, built ca1750 with later additions, now houses a further European painting collection as well as furniture, ceramics, glass, and silver.

The Kibble Palace, Glasgow Botanic Gardens

BUYING WORKS OF ART
Sir William Burrell used 28 school exercise books between 1911 and 1957 to record the purchase of each item. He bought cautiously, and though he used trusted dealers in London and Paris, he often sought a second opinion and liked to haggle over prices. Though wealthy, he was up against the even greater wealth of a number of American art magnates such as John Paul Getty.

EARLY 18TH-CENTURY GLASGOW
The writer Daniel Defoe was most impressed by Glasgow and wrote in his *Tour Through the Whole Island of Great Britain*: "It is a large, stately, and well-built city, standing on a plain...and the five principal streets are the fairest for breadth, and the finest built that I have ever seen in one city together." This was before rapid industrialization brought its special problems of poor housing and degradation.

►► Glasgow Cathedral 77E2

Cathedral Street (tel: 0141 552 6891; www.historic-scotland.gov.uk). Open: Apr–Sep, Mon–Sat 9.30–6, Sun 1–5; Oct–Mar, Mon–Sat 9.30–4, Sun 1–4 Admission free

Now a little isolated from the main thrust and vigour of the modern city centre, Glasgow Cathedral is one of the oldest and most historic sites in the city. The short trip eastwards is well worth making and is an easy walk from the Merchant City. The site has been occupied since the early days of Christianity here and is associated with Glasgow's patron saint, St. Kentigern or Mungo. He founded a church here, possibly in the early 7th century. The earliest identifiable work is 13th century.

There are five elements to the cathedral, which has an unusual shape: the nave, the choir, the upper and lower chapter houses, the lower church, and the Blacader Aisle. The late-medieval roof, 32m (99ft) above the nave, incorporates 14th-century timber. The choir and nave are separated by a 15th-century screen or pulpitum, a rare survivor from pre-Reformation times. The unique lower church, below the choir, was a 13th-century extension on the sloping site, and contains St. Mungo's tomb. The Blacader Aisle, where spotlights pick out the fascinating ceiling bosses, is the "youngest" part of the fabric, built by Archbishop Blacader (1483–1508). The Necropolis behind the cathedral is likewise worth a stroll.

Glasgow Cathedral

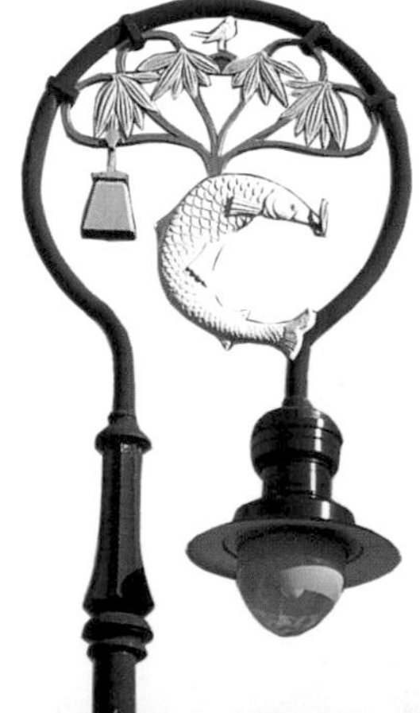

► (Glasgow) City Chambers 77D2

George Square (tel: 0141 287 4018; www.glasgow.gov.uk) Open: Mon–Fri, tours at 10.30 and 2.30 Admission free

The turreted, colonnaded facade of the City Chambers, topped by a tower and festooned with carving, is exotic enough, but inside it verges on the outrageous. The mosaic basilica of an entrance hall, marbled staircases, and galleries epitomize the "over the top" exuberance of high Victoriana. The building was intended to restore confidence after the City of Glasgow Bank collapse.

Glasgow's transformation from religious seat to commercial centre resulted in the original community expanding westwards from its High Street, cathedral, mercat cross, and other trappings of a market town. It was this "new town," at the heart of Glasgow today, that became the Merchant City.

The growth of trade Glasgow's expansion could only be funded by trade, but the shallow, silty nature of the river at first hindered the aspirations of the traders and burgesses. The first pier was built on the nearby Broomielaw by 1688 and over the years the river was deepened. Gradual commercial expansion meant that the rural grazings west of the High Street were required for commerce. Various manufacturing concerns, as well as vast warehouses and the grand mansions of the successful traders sprang up in successive waves. Expansion gathered pace in the 18th century as a planned development of gridded streets.

Glasgow became one of Europe's most important tobacco ports, with its nerve centre within the Merchant City. The ships that came in with the golden leaf from Virginia sailed again with cargoes ordered by the planters on the far side of the Atlantic. Thus the Merchant City prospered, even surviving the economic hiccup of the American colonies gaining independence.

Architectural style The city developed urban characteristics unique in Scotland. Most notable of these is the compact Glasgow square, usually enclosing a church: One example is at Nelson Mandela Place, west of Queen Street Station. Another feature is the deliberate placing of prominent buildings to close off vistas.

The Victorians, with their emphasis on civic pride, brought other styles to the Merchant City. However, decline set in during the 20th century, when the 18th-century warehousing became redundant, and the old tobacco exchanges out- moded. The area became a little run-down until the design-led late 20th-century renaissance. Now the Merchant City is again the focus of innovation, thoughthis time it is the small, specialist (and exclusive) retailers of fine clothes, furniture, and other chic supplies who have brought new life to this fascinating, historic area.

Top: chimney pots are numbered for each tenement flat

COTTON
After American Independence the business community of the Merchant City diversified by investing in cotton spinning. Glasgow became second in importance only to Manchester, England, in this industry.

The Duke of Wellington *by Marochetti*

Glasgow offers the best shopping choice in Scotland

Walk

Glasgow city centre

A walk that takes in the architectural riches, past glory, and modern regeneration of the Merchant City area. Allow 2.5 hours; *see map on pages 76–77.*

Near Queen Street Station, admire the early French Gothic style of the **Glasgow Stock Exchange** (built in 1875). Go down Queen Street, with its views across statue-spiked George Square, to the **Gallery of Modern Art** in the former Royal Exchange. Originally a mansion, it had a colonnaded classical facade stuck on later to enhance the view from Ingram Street.

Go through **Royal Exchange Square** (where there is a good tearoom) for the shopping delights of pedestrian only **Buchanan Street**. The modern charms of the discreet **Princes Square** development, airy yet compact, contrast with the **Argyll Arcade** beyond, built in 1827 as Scotland's first shopping arcade. The arcade opens into Argyle Street. The shops move generally down-market the farther east you go, so, unless you intend a weekend visit to the flea market at the **Barras** farther yet to the east (see panel, page 86), turn up Candleriggs to reach the heart of the old **Merchant City**. Some of the 18th-century warehouses still survive. The Italianate City Hall (dating from 1817) is still a concert hall, though only the façades of the markets remain. The Merchant City is still in the throes of regeneration: note the **Café Gandolfi** in Albion Street round the corner, an example of the new Merchant City enterprise.

Thread through Wilson Street, past more interesting new shops on **Ingram Square** and the massive, classical old **Sheriff Court**. Continue west to Virginia Street, named after the New World trade. **Virginia Court**, half-way along, has cart ruts in its cobbles from times past. Nearby is the former **Tobacco Exchange**, now bookshops and antique stalls. Then make your way through to **George Square**, with Robert Adam's **Trades House** (his only surviving work in Glasgow) in the near vicinity, and, to the north, **Hutchesons' Hall** on Ingram Street.

▶ Greenbank Garden 76A1

Flenders Road (tel: 0141 616 5126; www.nts.org.uk)
Open: daily 9.30–sunset. Reception/tearoom Easter–Oct 11–5; House Easter–Oct, Sun 2–4. Admission: moderate

Greenbank is 10km (6mi) south of town in fairly plush Clarkston. Set around a fine Georgian house, originally built for a Glasgow merchant, the 5ha (12-acre) policies (grounds) include a big walled garden. Greenbank is run as a demonstration garden, with a variety of small-scale features. It is owned by the National Trust for Scotland.

▶▶ Hunterian Museum and Art Gallery 76A4

Gilbert Scott Building, University Avenue (tel: 0141 330 4221; www.hunterian.gla.ac.uk)
Open: Mon–Sat 9.30–5 (Mackintosh House closed 12.30–1.30). Admission free

William Hunter (1718–1783) trained at Glasgow University and became a famous physician in London. He bequeathed substantial scientific collections to his parent university and the Hunterian opened in 1807 as Scotland's first public museum. The emphasis is now on geology, archaeology, coins, and art. Exhibits include the fossil of the Bearsden shark (named after a suburb of Glasgow) as well as the city's own meteorite!

The Hunterian Art Gallery has existed as a separate entity since 1980. It includes European works from Rembrandt to Reynolds as well as Scottish 19th- and 20th-century work. The Print Gallery exhibits works from the largest print collection in Scotland. Furniture and fittings from the architect's home are in the Mackintosh House—a reconstruction of the principal rooms of his own home.

▶ The Lighthouse, Scotland's Centre for Architecture, Design and the City 76C2

Mitchell Lane (tel: 0141 221 6362; www.thelighthouse.co.uk)
Open: Mon, Wed–Sat 10.30–5, Tue 11–5, Sun 12–5
Admission: inexpensive

Based in a converted building designed by Charles Rennie Mackintosh, the centre includes two main exhibition areas—a permanent facility on the work of Mackintosh and a rooftop viewing platform.

CHARLES RENNIE MACKINTOSH (1868–1928)

Mackintosh gutted th end-of-terrace house at 78 Southpark Avenue, Hillhead, Glasgow and refitted it in his own unique style. It came into the hands of the university in 1945 and was demolished in 1963. Prior to demolition a detailed survey was carried out and much was salvaged, ultimately to be lovingly rebuilt almost 20 years later in the Mackintosh section of the Hunterian Art Gallery.

Mackintosh's distinctive style in the Hunterian

St. Mungo, who now has a museum named after him

BARRAS FLEA MARKET

At the weekend a visit to the People's Palace can be combined with a browse around the Barras, Glasgow's flea market. It lies within easy walking distance north of Glasgow Green.

GLASGOW GREEN

In the days when Glasgow was a hotbed of communism and the struggle for workers' power, Glasgow Green was used as the Clydeside orators speaking platform. The authorities retaliated in the 1930s by planting flower-beds in strategic positions to discourage crowds from gathering.

► St. Mungo Museum of Religious Life and Art *77E2*

Cathedral Square (tel: 0141 553 2557; www.glasgowmuseums.com)
Open: Mon–Thu 10–5, Fri 11–5, Sat 10–5, Sun 11–5
Admission free

With picture windows that reveal the skyline of the soaring cathedral and the knobbly monuments of the Necropolis, this museum of religious life and art also takes a broad overview of life, death, the hereafter and how they are treated across the world. Salvador Dalí's *Christ of St. John of the Cross* is here—hung so high that it is best viewed from the gallery on the other side of the room—round the corner from a many-limbed Shiva as Nataraja, the Lord of the Dance. From Japanese shrines to Aboriginal paintings, the religious art and artefacts of many cultures are brought together. Another gallery covers birth, marriage, and so on, more anthropological, perhaps, than religious in the usual sense.

► Scotland Street School Museum *76A1*

225 Scotland Street (tel: 0141 287 0500); www.glasgowmuseums.com)
Open: Mon–Thu 10–5, Fri 11–5, Sat 10–5, Sun 11–5
Admission free

Housed in a Mackintosh building of 1904, the former Scotland Street School now pays homage to education in Scotland and gives a sense of how it felt for pupils, right down to the squeak of pencils on slate. Inside are period classrooms from various eras, and changing exhibitions.

►►► Museum of Transport *76A3*

Kelvin Hall, 1 Bunhouse Road (tel: 0141 287 2720; www.glasgowmuseums.com)
Open: Mon–Thu 10–5, Fri 11–5, Sat 10–5, Sun 11–5
Admission free

This spacious site round the back of the Kelvin Hall holds all kinds of historic transport exhibits. It is great fun, and not just for children, with huge steam locomotives, brooding and awesome, tramcars and buses, Hillman Imps (Scotland's fairly awful last home-produced motor car), and other gleaming vehicles from past eras. The fire engines and ship models are hugely popular and there is also an

At the Museum of Transport

evocative 1938 Glasgow street scene. The museum is just across the road from the Art Gallery and Museum at Kelvingrove with the Hunterian within easy reach.

A shopfront from a Glasgow street in the excellent Museum of Transport, where it always remains 1938

►►► People's Palace and Winter Gardens *77E1*

Glasgow Green (tel: 0141 271 2962; www.glasgowmuseums.com)
Open: Mon–Thu 10–5, Fri 11–5, Sat 10–5, Sun 11–5
Admission free

In the heart of the ancient park known as Glasgow Green, the People's Palace, as the name implies, is for and about the people of Glasgow. This late Victorian sandstone edifice has a museum at the front and a huge glass conservatory, the Winter Gardens, at the back. The latter is heated so that palms and other tender plants can flourish. There is also a café, which makes it a popular place for idling and for posing for wedding and other photographs. To go from the clear light and bustle of the Winter Gardens through the swing-doors to the museum is an odd experience, a little like discovering someone's attic.

The story of the Tobacco Lords is told in the museum, together with those of the radical weavers, the temperance and Co-operative movements, and women's suffrage, alongside the ephemera of everyday lives, from tram tickets to ration books, as well as reconstructions of typical Glasgow working-class tenements.

Just down the road, off the Green, is the former **Templeton's Carpet Factory**, yet another of Glasgow's exuberant pieces of Victoriana, sometimes called the Doge's Palace. Multi-coloured brick and tile have been used to create an extraordinary Venetian-style facade (the building can only be viewed from the outside). The **Doulton Fountain**, a 14m (43ft) high terracotta extravaganza, formerly an important exhibit at the 1888 International Exhibition at Kelvingrove, was restored to its place in front of the People's Palace in 2005 after major refurbishment.

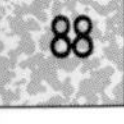

Provand's Lordship, one of only two remaining medieval buildings in Glasgow

Charles Rennie Mackintosh: architect, designer, water-colourist, and leading exponent of art nouveau in Scotland

▶ Provand's Lordship *77E2*

3 Castle Street (tel: 0141 552 8819; www.glasgowmuseums.com)
Open: Mon–Thu and Sat 10–5, Fri and Sun 11–5. Admission free

Close to the cathedral, this is Glasgow's only other central medieval building. A "Provand" is a clergyman who is paid from cathedral revenue and officiates there. The Provand of Balornock once inhabited the house.

It was built in 1471 as a manse (minister's house) for the long-vanished hospital next door. With its characteristic steeply pitched roof with crow-stepped gables and armorial panels, it was, in its day, a suitably dignified residence for churchmen. Now a lone survivor, Provand's Lordship has become a city museum housing period furniture.

▶ The Mackintosh Church at Queen's Cross *76B4*

870 Garscube Road (tel: 0141 946 6600; www.crmsociety.com)
Open: Mon–Fri, 10–5; Mar–Oct, Sun 2–5. Admission inexpensive

This is the only church designed by Charles Rennie Mackintosh. Built between 1897 and 1899 it is now the headquarters of the Charles Rennie Mackintosh Society, with a small exhibition area, library, and shop.

▶ (Glasgow) School of Art *76B3*

167 Renfrew Street (tel: 0141 353 4526; www.gsa.ac.uk)
Open: tours Oct–Mar, Mon–Sat 11 and 2; Apr–Sep, daily 10.30, 11, 11.30, 1.30, 2, 2.30 (booking advisable. Please telephone during June for hours). Admission: moderate

This is Mackintosh's masterpiece, a work of world stature, though crowded by later developments, and is still a breathtaking design. The School of Art is sometimes described as the first and finest architectural work of the modern European movement. Here all of the Mackintosh characteristics are seen to good effect: the sinuous swirls of the forms of nature, the bold and uncluttered lines, the detailing and supreme awareness of the effect of light and shadow.

▶▶▶ Glasgow Science Centre

50 Pacific Quay (tel: 0141 420 5000; www.glasgowsciencecentre.org)
Open: Nov–Mar, Tue–Sun 10–6, Apr–Oct, daily 10–6. Admission: expensive

Glasgow Science Centre makes a refreshing change from Scotland's heritage overdose, with four floors of thought-provoking and entertaining hands-on demonstrations, experiments and things to do. Although intended for children of all ages, adults may find themselves elbowing the younger ones aside! The sheer size of the venue is impressive. Allow plenty of time, especially if you want to take in the on-site Planetarium, as well as enjoying an educational show on Scotland's only IMAX screen presentation.

▶▶ The Tall Ship at Glasgow Harbour

100 Stobcross Road (tel: 0141 222 2513; www.thetallship.com)
Open: Mar–Oct, daily 10–5; Nov–Feb 10–4. Admission: moderate

The century-old tall ship *Glenlee* is by the new Pumphouse Visitor Centre. The only Clyde-built sailing ship afloat in the UK, it houses an exhibition called "The Glenlee Story"; showing conditions a hundred years ago. The Pumphouse has exhibitions on Clyde and nautical themes.

▶▶ The Tenement House 76B4

145 Buccleuch Street (tel: 0141 333 0183; www.nts.org.uk)
Open: Mar–Oct, daily 1–5, last admission 4.30
Admission: moderate

A young girl moved into the tenement building with her mother in 1911. They were pleased to have such well-appointed accommodation. The young girl was a certain Miss Toward. She never married and after her mother's death lived there alone until 1965. A relative who bought the flat realized that it was a "time capsule" of Glasgow life, because Miss Toward had never thrown anything away and had never changed the layout of her home. Here, preserved in its entirety, was a slice of tenement life from the early years of the 20th-century.

The flat consists of a hall and four rooms: the bedroom (reserved usually for the lodger in Miss Toward's case); the parlour or best room, used for special occasions, for example when the kirk elder or a minister called; the bathroom—a sure sign that this was a very well-appointed tenement for its date (it was built in 1892); and the kitchen, complete with a large black cooking range with coal bunker.

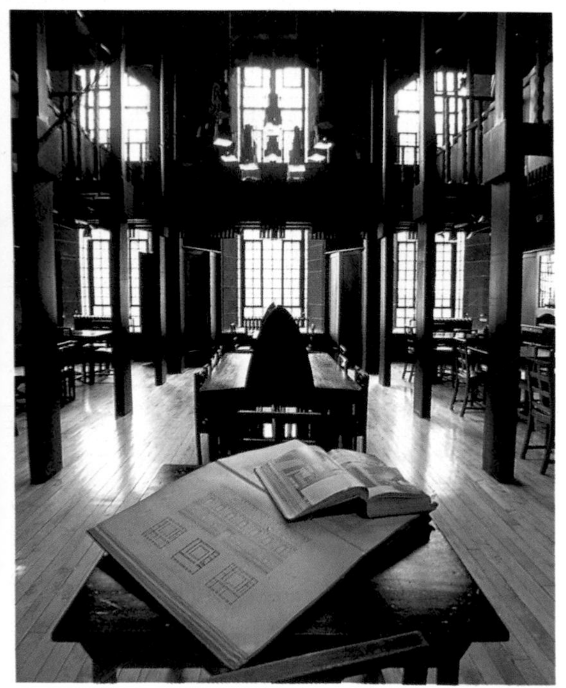

Glasgow School of Art, a remarkable example of Mackintosh design

FOSSIL GROVE
Among Glasgow's many green spaces, Victoria Park is notable for its Fossil Grove. This is a roofed area in which excavations have exposed the fossilized stumps and roots of trees which grew here 330 million years ago.

THE COAL BUNKER
Miss Toward of the Tenement House had a kitchen coal bunker which held half a ton at a time and would have been typical of that era. Pity the poor coalmen on the Glasgow tenement stairs!

Accommodation

As befits Scotland's largest city and one where tourism is a main industry, Glasgow has a very reasonable choice of accommodation at all price levels. An increasing number of quality hotels have opened up quite close to the heart of the city, mainly to serve the business and conference market but partly because of the Scottish Exhibition Centre down by the Clyde. Another trend has been the welcome arrival of a few smaller, intimate, town-house establishments amid the city's Georgian terraces. Accommodation in the university halls of residence should not be overlooked at the budget end of the market. Check out last-minute offers and book on-line at www.visitscotland.com.

OUT OF TOWN It is easy to get into the countryside from Glasgow—-Loch Lomond is only half an hour away—so it is also worth considering out-of-town accommodation if exploring the city. Organizations such as Scottish Farmhouse Holidays (Renton Terrace, Eyemouth TD14 5DF, tel: 01890 751830; www.Scotfarmhols.co.uk) offer farmhouse accommodation in the silence of the moors and upland grazings of the Campsie Hills, for example, both of which are well within an hour's journey of the city centre.

Though Glasgow does not have quite the same accommodation bottlenecks as Edinburgh, it nevertheless gets quite busy. Don't forget that there are Tourist Information Centres, which can find accommodation, both in Paisley and also at Glasgow Airport, as well as the main city-centre office.

TOP HOTELS Starting at the top end, the Glasgow Hilton has all the style and high levels of service (and, of course, prices) you would expect from this international chain. (Driving there is tricky, though the tall building is

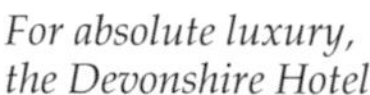

For absolute luxury, the Devonshire Hotel

Many original features survive in the elegant Victorian town houses of Devonshire Place, including stained glass at the Devonshire Hotel

visible enough. The hotel even goes to the length of providing a little map to help you find your way to the parking area.)

The Glasgow Marriott (right in the city-centre) and the Radisson SAS Glasgow (likewise in the thick of things) are both worth considering if you are looking for the no-nonsense professionalism of the larger establishment. There are also plenty of moderately priced hotels and guest houses within walking distance of many visitor attractions. They can be large enough to have a good range of facilities, yet still small enough to be friendly. (The locals' "genius for instant friendship" is most noticeable in the service industries—receptionists sometimes genuinely remember guests.)

The Devonshire Hotel at 5 Devonshire Gardens is a town house of deluxe standard just by Great Western Road. (Do not confuse this with One Devonshire Gardens a couple of doors down, which is equally luxurious and slightly more expensive.)

Also at the top end and out of town is the Devere Cameron House Hotel, on the banks of Loch Lomond, with a superb range of leisure facilities

Other possibilities, if you want a country base with easy access to the city centre, are the areas around Balloch (at the south end of Loch Lomond), Helensburgh (a Clyde resort), and Drymen, east of the loch

HALLS OF RESIDENCE For visitors on a budget there is a good selection of all kinds of bed and breakfasts and guest-houses available, as well as university halls of residence (see panel).

Locations include Sauchiehall Street, ideal for the shops; Clyde Street, a good base for the Merchant City; and Cathedral Street; all offer reasonable value for money.

Glasgow also has a large youth hostel which is in a good location at 8 Park Terrace (tel: 0870 004 1119).

CAMPUS ACCOMMODATION

For details of Glasgow's on-campus accommodation—there are at least six halls of residence for Glasgow University alone—contact Glasgow University's Conference and Visitor Services, No. 3, The Square, Glasgow G12 8QQ (tel. 0141 330 5385), or Strathclyde University Residence and Catering Services at 50 Richmond Street, Glasgow G1 1XR, tel: 0141 553 4148).

PACKAGE DEALS

Glasgow is now a popular destination for English-based coach firms and other operators who offer a complete package of travel and accommodation. For more details telephone 0845 225 5121 or visit www.visitscotland.com and ask for the latest list of package holidays.

Food and drink

As in other cities, fashionable places to eat and drink in Glasgow come and go, as do chefs. You need to strike up a conversation with a local or follow the recommendations of local restaurant critics (see panel page 96) for up-to-date news. There is also a core of well-loved favourites which are easy to track down. Glasgow has ambience in plenty when it comes to eating and drinking: It's all part of its downtown vibrancy and new-found confidence and it's probably the most exciting place to be in Scotland for an evening out.

Glasgow specializes in the kind of place which offers competent cuisine along with bags of atmosphere, so that any minor shortcomings are easily forgiven. Another characteristic is the many pubs and restaurants that now occupy buildings originally designed for other commercial uses—you can catch yourself staring upwards from your glass of beer at the fine old woodwork of a former bank, or the decorated tiles of a Victorian insurance office. There are also themed places, which are very popular with locals. Yet another category is the restaurant with a pub or café attached.

Scotland's patriot, William Wallace, has given his name to several pubs

ASK A CABBIE
One way of getting a really up-to-date tip on the best places to eat is to ask a taxi driver. Certainly, Glasgow is noted for its friendliness (though the same can be said about plenty of other places in Scotland). However, Glasgow's talkative cabbies definitely made an impression on the American Society of Travel Agents when it held its annual conference there in 1997. Their helpful-ness was officially recognized by Visit Scotland, which awarded a commemorative plaque to the local taxi drivers' association in acknowledgment of their role as "outstanding ambassadors of tourism."

RECOMMENDED RESTAURANTS The Ubiquitous Chip, a well-loved establishment off Byres Road, is situated in a covered and cobbled courtyard where you can eat on the ground floor surrounded by plants or upstairs in the more conventional dining room. It offers an original menu and is probably as near as you can get to a local cuisine, with a pronounced Scottish flavour. Much the same can be said about the Buttery in Argyle Street, with its Victorian decor. Another popular haunt, with a loyal clientele, is the long-established Rogano in Exchange Place, which first opened its art deco doors in 1935. It is well-known for its seafood.

A Glasgow institution for Italian cuisine is La Parmigiana on Great Western Road, which has a local following for its tuna with borlotti beans, rabbit *alla cacciatore*, and other slightly out-of-the-ordinary dishes. Also hugely popular, especially with the business crowd, is Gamba on West George Street, where the Mediterranean interior provides a striking setting for superb seafood, making strong use of Scottish ingredients. Stravaigin, on Gibson Street, looks world-wide for its inspiration; it has a refreshingly laid-back attitude, but the quality of its cooking, in the harissa-marinaded venison, or the seared west coast scallops with crab ravioli, is top-notch. If you want to splash out, try the restaurant at One Devonshire Gardens for painstakingly prepared modern cuisine.

PUBS Glasgow's pubs are quite varied, but city-centre ones can be very spruce. Typical of this kind is the Drum and Monkey, formerly banking premises in St. Vincent Street. It is popular with business people who have lunch in its small and intimate back room with its dark wooden pews, and it has a more boisterous main hall. Babbity Bowster, on Blackfriars Street, has folk music on Saturday nights, and a licensed beer garden. Close to Central Station is one of Glasgow's most famous pubs, The Horse Shoe bar in Drury Street, which claims to have the longest continuous bar in the UK.

TEAROOMS Glasgow's tearooms have always been something of an institution. The Willow Tearoom is a surviving, though restored, typical Mackintosh design in Sauchiehall Street and Buchanan Street.

These days, tea and coffee are also served throughout the day in any of a number of bistros. Miss Cranston's, on Gordon Street, is another traditional tearoom, set above a bakery and patisserie. Heart Buchanan, on Byres Road in the West End, is a café/deli selling great Scottish produce available to buy or eat-in.

The Rogano, an old-established part of Glasgow's restaurant scene

A STREET NAME
Sauchiehall Street is really sauchie-haugh street: "sauchies" are willows and a "haugh" is a watery field. The willow reference is echoed in the Willow Tea Room on the street.

FOR SHOPPERS
Princes Square has a good standard of refreshments. Try the October Café right on the top floor, with its noticeably bright atmosphere—perhaps an effect of being so near to the glass roof.

Byres Road pub

the old
, St.
s now a
r-cover shop-
touch better
1990s malls
its interesting
cture, with
sed girders and
es. However, it is not
elegant and intimate
as Princes Square.

Shopping

There are more shops in Glasgow than anywhere else in Scotland. All the usual well-known names can be found but, thanks partly to the Merchant City enterprise, there is also a very good selection of smaller specialist outlets. Glasgow is style- and fashion-conscious, so clothes shops proliferate, though not all of them prosper.

MAIN AREAS The main shopping streets are found from Argyle Street northwards as far as Sauchiehall Street, taking in streets on both sides of pleasingly pedestrianized Buchanan Street, northwest of which is a grid of streets well worth exploring. The Merchant City lies to the east of it and should be explored. There are further shopping possibilities around Byres Road to the west which should not be overlooked. Except for Byres Road, most of Glasgow's shops are within easy walking distance of Buchanan Street. The best of the malls is Princes Square, at the bottom of Buchanan Street, with its elegant shops selling designer clothes. Shops in the Buchanan Galleries, at the top of Buchanan Street, are mostly chain stores.

OUTLETS FOR SCOTTISH GOODS If you are looking for high-quality Scottish wares, then Geoffrey (Tailor) Kiltmakers and Weavers—quite far along Sauchiehall Street (but worth the walk)—is just the place for Scottish knitwear or tweed souvenirs, or for an entire Highland outfit. Hector Russell, Kiltmaker, in Renfield Street will also oblige in much the same market niche.

Borders Books at 98 Buchanan Street has a wide-ranging selection of material on Scotland and Glasgow. Postcards home could be written with something exclusive picked up at the Pen Shop in Princes Square, which is a stylish shopping mall for gifts as well as fashions, including knitwear at Jumper.

The Barras (or Barrowland) is an essential part of the Glasgow shopping experience—but don't make it the only one!

DESIGNER SHOPS If you ask about designer shops in the Merchant City, locals may suggest Mademoiselle Anne in Stockwell Street, which has women's collections. Cruise in Ingram Street is the destination for designer clothes for men and women. For shoes, Soletrader specialize in trainers to labels: Paul Smith, Diesel, Hugo Boss. The atmospheric Argyll Arcade (dating from 1827) offers a choice of 25 jewellers' shops selling modern and antique designs. Catherine Shaw, in Gordon Street and the Argyll Arcade, has giftware in Charles Rennie Mackintosh's style. Victorian Village in West Regent Street is a collection of small antique outlets offering silver, jewellery, porcelain and clothes. Tim Wright Antiques at Richmond Chambers in Bath Street has a tremendous range of items.

Typifying the new Glasgow style is the Italian Centre, just off Ingram Street, of which the city is inordinately proud, particularly because this gathering of shops includes labels seen nowhere else in the UK outside London.

FLEA MARKET If you tire of the chic shops of the Merchant City, then a trip to the Barras flea market will prove a refreshing antidote—though remember that the market is open at weekends only. The Barras is a reminder that Glasgow has not yet become too precious in its new image. The name may have been translated into "Barrowland" in an attempt to prettify it, but it still remains a boisterous flea market in a mixture of sheds and warehouses. There at least, the prospect of a real bargain flits just ahead at the next stall, and even if it remains out of reach, the market nevertheless provides great entertainment.

PADDY'S MARKET
Do not confuse the Barras with Paddy's Market, near the river. Paddy's Market gets its name from the penniless Irish immigrants of a century ago who would literally sell the shirts off their backs, so desperate was their poverty. Something of the same air of desperation still hangs around today. This little lane of stalls belies Glasgow's upbeat new image.

Princes Square—modern shopping at its most sophisticated

Nightlife

Glasgow has a huge selection of pubs and bistros, plus a range of venues offering musical entertainment from proper ceilidhs (not fake affairs for tourists) to new wave.

THEATRE AND CONCERT HALLS The city's cultural flagship is the Royal Concert Hall in Sauchiehall Street (tel: 0141 353 8000), a first home for the Royal Scottish Orchestra, which, along with Scottish Ballet and Scottish Opera, has its headquarters in the city. The Royal Scottish Academy of Music and Drama in Stevenson Hall on Renfrew Street (tel: 0141 332 4101) offers a variety of international performances. The Tramway on Albert Drive (tel: 0845 330 3501) is an exciting venue for opera, drama, and dance. The Tron Theatre in Trongate (tel: 0141 552 4267) offers the best of contemporary Scottish and international theatre. The Pavilion Theatre on Renfield Street (tel: 0141 332 1846) puts on variety shows, and rock and pop concerts, while the Kings Theatre on Bath Street (tel: 0141 240 1111) has drama and popular productions. With the Citizens' Theatre on Gorbals Street (tel: 0141 429 0022), the City Hall, and the Henry Wood Hall, these are just some of the performing spaces on offer.

…ww.list.co.uk), …rom all …re newsagents, …nformation on …ts in Glasgow and …nburgh. *The Herald* …ewspaper on Saturdays lists entertainment activities with a Glasgow emphasis.

FILM An alternative to the regular cinema chains, the Glasgow Film Theatre, Rose Street (tel: 0141 332 8128) is an independent concern, offering new releases, classic revivals, and popular re-runs.

OTHER NIGHTLIFE These are some examples from the broad spectrum: Glasgow's "Grand Ole Opry" at 2 Govan Road (tel: 0141 429 5396) is where the local cowboys hang out for the country and western music. Archaos on Queen Street (tel: 0141 204 3189) is the biggest club in Glasgow and offers an eclectic musical mix on its three dance floors. The Arches on Midland Street (tel: 0141 565 1023) has house, techno, and big music names at one of the city's largest venues. Victoria's on Sauchiehall Street (tel: 0141 332 1444) is a popular nightclub with supper bar: the hunting ground of professional footballers and models, with several floors to suit all musical tastes. The Riverside Club in Clyde Street (tel: 0141 248 3144) is *the* ceilidh place in town, like an upstairs barn with a tiny stage. The Ferry on Anderston Quay (tel: 0141 248 5376) looks like a floating conservatory but is actually the former Renfrew ferry: another great ceilidh place with other kinds of music as well (best to check the local press for details). The Scotia Bar on Stockwell Street (tel: 0141 552 8681) is an old-fashioned little pub with lots of impromptu performances, mostly of folk music.

The ground-breaking Citizens' Theatre, at the heart of Glasgow's art scene

Practicalities

AIRPORT TRANSFERS Glasgow Airport (tel: 0870 040 0008) is 13km (8mi) from the heart of the city with a reasonably priced express bus service that takes 30 minutes. These buses connect with the hourly service to central Edinburgh. There is also a railway station at Paisley Gilmour Street, about 3km (2mi) away. Metered taxis are available, with fares upwards of £12 to the centre.

For accommodation contact www.visitscotland.com or telephone 0845 225 5121.

The Drum and Monkey, St. Vincent Street

ARRIVING BY TRAIN OR BUS Glasgow Central is the city-centre train terminus for services from the south (London Euston is about five hours away). Glasgow Queen Street is the terminus for services from Edinburgh (around 45 minutes by rail) and the north and west (Aberdeen and Fort William for instance). Glasgow's main bus station is Buchanan Bus Station, Killermont Street (tel: 0141 333 3708).

PUBLIC TRANSPORTATION WITHIN GLASGOW Glasgow is the only Scottish city with an underground network, a modernized and useful service open 6.30–11.30 daily with trains every six to eight minutes all day. Flat-rate tickets are on sale at all stations on the underground, which takes the form of a large circle. For information call Traveline Scotland (tel: 0870 608 2608). They are an important source of travel information for Glasgow's excellent fully integrated transportation network and they can also supply details of Glasgow's extensive suburban rail network.

There are many bus companies operating within the city. Several different types of multi-journey or flexible tickets are available, some combining rail, bus, and underground. The Family Day Tripper Ticket, allowing travel as far afield as Loch Lomond, is good value.

TAXIS Black cabs are widely available throughout the city, and main taxi ranks are located at the stations. A fleet of airport taxis operates the service from the airport.

TRANSPORT TIP
First ScotRail operates a service every 15 minutes between Edinburgh and Glasgow Queen Street Station—very handy if you are combining both these exciting cities as part of your holiday.

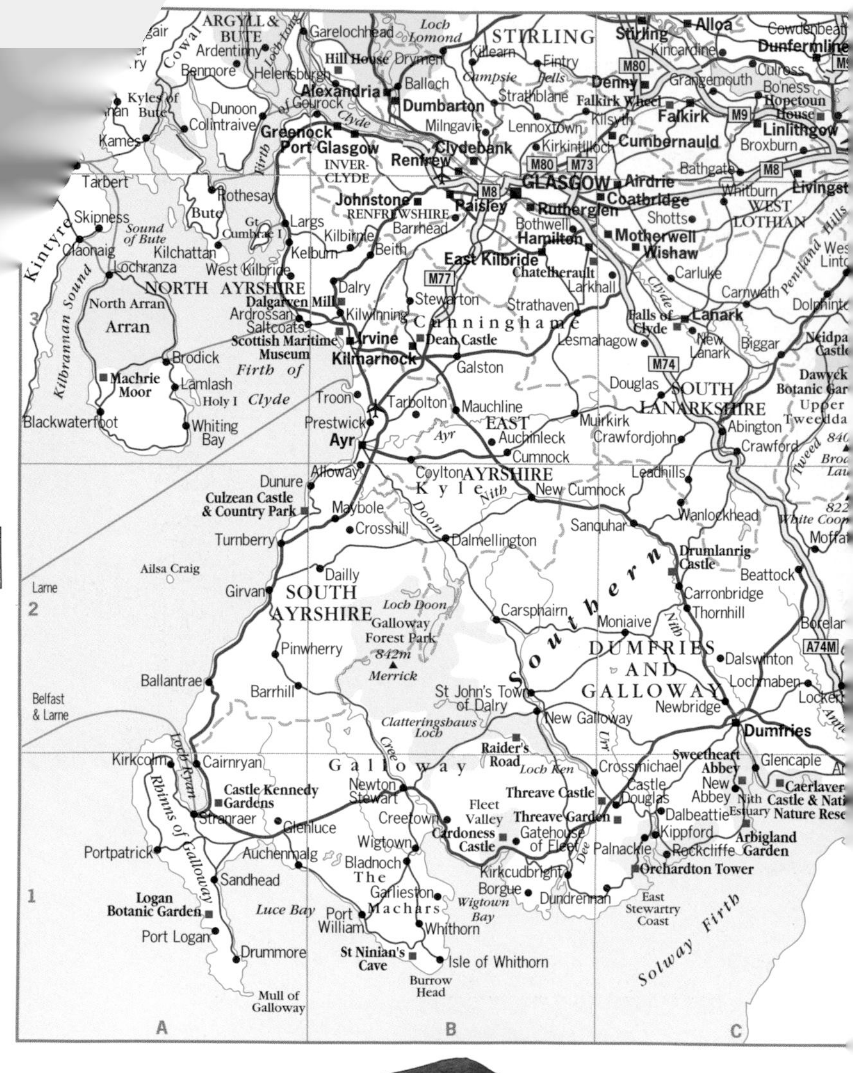
ARGYLL & BUTE
Cowal
Loch Long
Garelochhead
Loch Lomond
STIRLING
Stirling
Alloa
Kincardine
Dunfermline
Ardentinny
Benmore
Helensburgh
Hill House
Drymen
Killearn
Fintry
Campsie Fells
M80
Culross
Grangemouth
Bo'ness
Denny
Kyles of Bute
Dunoon
Gourock
Alexandria
Balloch
Dumbarton
Strathblane
Falkirk Wheel
Hopetoun House
Falkirk
M9
Linlithgow
Colintraive
Greenock
Clyde
Milngavie
Lennoxtown
Kilsyth
Kames
Port Glasgow
Clydebank
Kirkintilloch
Cumbernauld
Broxburn
Firth of Clyde
INVERCLYDE
Renfrew
M80
M73
Bathgate
M8
Livingston
Tarbert
Rothesay
Johnstone
M8
GLASGOW
Airdrie
Coatbridge
Whitburn
Bute
RENFREWSHIRE
Paisley
Rutherglen
WEST LOTHIAN
Skipness
Sound of Bute
Gt Cumbrae I
Largs
Barrhead
Bothwell
Shotts
Kintyre
Claonaig
Kilchattan
Kilbirnie
Hamilton
Motherwell
Kelburn
Beith
Wishaw
Lochranza
West Kilbride
East Kilbride
Chatelherault
Pentland Hills
Carluke
NORTH AYRSHIRE
M77
Larkhall
Dalry
Clyde
Carnwath
North Arran
Dalgarven Mill
Stewarton
Strathaven
Ardrossan
Kilwinning
Arran
Saltcoats
Cunninghame
Falls of Clyde
Lanark
Kilbrannan Sound
Scottish Maritime Museum
Irvine
Dean Castle
Lesmahagow
New Lanark
Biggar
Brodick
Kilmarnock
Galston
M74
Machrie Moor
Lamlash
Firth of Clyde
Douglas
Holy I
Troon
Tarbolton
Mauchline
SOUTH LANARKSHIRE
Blackwaterfoot
Whiting Bay
Prestwick
EAST
Muirkirk
Abington
Ayr
Auchinleck
Crawfordjohn
Ayr
Cumnock
Crawford
Tweed
Alloway
Coylton
AYRSHIRE
Leadhills
Dunure
Kyle
Nith
New Cumnock
Culzean Castle & Country Park
Doon
Maybole
Wanlockhead
Crosshill
Sanquhar
Turnberry
Dalmellington
Ailsa Craig
Drumlanrig Castle
Beattock
Larne
Dailly
Girvan
SOUTH AYRSHIRE
Loch Doon
Carronbridge
Galloway Forest Park
Carsphairn
Thornhill
Southern
Moniaive
Nith
Pinwherry
842m
DUMFRIES AND GALLOWAY
Dalswinton
Merrick
Ballantrae
Barrhill
St John's Town of Dalry
Lochmaben
Belfast & Larne
Newbridge
Clatteringshaws Loch
New Galloway
Dumfries
Cree
Raider's Road
Urr
Kirkcolm
Cairnryan
Galloway
Loch Ken
Crossmichael
Sweetheart Abbey
Glencaple
Loch Ryan
Castle Kennedy Gardens
Newton Stewart
Threave Castle
Castle Douglas
New Abbey
Caerlaverock Castle & Nature Reserve
Rhinns of Galloway
Fleet Valley
Threave Garden
Nith Estuary
Stranraer
Glenluce
Creetown
Dalbeattie
Cardoness Castle
Gatehouse of Fleet
Kippford
Portpatrick
Auchenmalg
Wigtown
Palnackie
Rockcliffe
Arbigland Garden
Bladnoch
Dee
Kirkcudbright
Orchardton Tower
Sandhead
The Machars
Garlieston
Borgue
Dundrennan
Logan Botanic Garden
Luce Bay
Port William
Wigtown Bay
East Stewartry Coast
Solway Firth
Port Logan
Whithorn
Drummore
St Ninian's Cave
Isle of Whithorn
Mull of Galloway
Burrow Head
A
B
C
1
2
3

SCOTLAND

The South

Kirkcaldy
FIFE
Burntisland
Firth of Forth
Dirleton Castle
North Berwick
Bass Rock
Tantallon Castle
Queensferry
Gullane
Scottish Seabird Centre
Dalmeny House
Dunbar
EDINBURGH
East Linton
Musselburgh
Haddington
Cockburnspath
EAST LOTHIAN
St Abb's Head
Dalkeith
Gifford
Coldingham
St Abbs
533m
Eyemouth
Rosslyn Chapel
Grantshouse
Newtongrange
Lammermuir Hills
Burnmouth
LOTHIAN
Crichton Castle
Preston
Chirnside
Duns
Manderston House
Moorfoot Hills
Thirlestane Castle
Berwick-upon-Tweed
Greenlaw
Swinton
Lauder
Stow
Gordon
The Hirsel
Peebles
659m
Eildon & Leaderfoot
Mellerstain House
Coldstream
Walkerburn
Galashiels
Uplands
Innerleithen
Melrose
Floors Castle
Tweed
Traquair House
Abbotsford House
Kelso
St Boswells
Dryburgh Abbey
Bowhill House
Selkirk
Town Yetholm
Ancrum
SCOTTISH BORDERS
Jedburgh
Teviotdale
Denholm
Ettrick
Hawick
The Cheviot Hills
620m
Windy Gyle Hill
Grey Mare's Tail
Carter Bar
Teviothead
Border Forest Park
Eskdalemuir
Hermitage Castle
Liddel
Esk
Newcastleton
Langholm
Ecclefechan
ENGLAND
Gretna
Gretna Green
Esk
Carlisle
0 10 20 30 40 50 km
0 10 20 30 miles
D
E

ACROSS THE BORDER Unless indulging in the tartan frolics of Gretna or Gretna Green—"Joke Anvil Weddings Performed Here" says one advertisement—crossing the border is a low-key affair. (It was different when eloping couples from England came to Gretna Green, where Scots law allowed them to marry simply by declaration before witnesses; this became illegal in 1940.) Sometimes a piper plays at Carter Bar where the A68 enters Scotland, but otherwise at first sight things look much the same.

However, Scotland is distinct from England, even in its southern sector—from banknotes to buying beer in pubs, a subtly altered culture is all around. Geographers call the area the Southern Uplands—blue waves of hills, resonant with tales of ancient skirmishes in these fought-over lands—a dramatic sight from Carter Bar. Farther west, in the Galloway Forest Park north of Newton Stewart, the end of the park road is within walking distance of The Merrick,

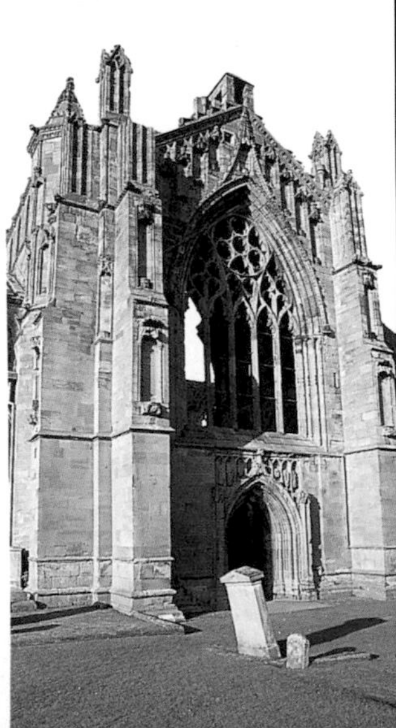

the highest mountain (842m/2,763ft) in southern Scotland, with a vista of dark lochs, birchwoods, and purple slopes, resembling the Trossachs farther north (see pages 160–161).

AYRSHIRE Continuing north from Galloway, the sheep-cropped moors and conifer blocks blend into Ayrshire, another area with a highly characteristic landscape. There is a lushness in the river valleys, woods, and hedgerows reminiscent of South Wales—a parallel sustained by the signs, in places, of now-vanished heavy industry, coal, and ironworks, backed by green hills. Farther north, the typical Ayrshire view is across hawthorn hedge and pasture to a long horizon dominated by the smudgy profile of Arran and Kintyre, a setting more Highland than Lowland.

Beyond the geological edge of the Southern Uplands, and into the southern part of the central corridor across Scotland, the scenery changes again. The summer-yellow grainfields of East Lothian have red-pantile roofed villages with hills as a backdrop, or even the sheer unexpectedness of the vista from the prehistoric site on the top of Cairnpapple Hill behind Linlithgow, with the Forth Valley spread out like a geography lesson.

Border at Coldstream

As well as its fine landscapes, southern Scotland has highly individual townscapes and communities of character. The typical pastel-washed frontages and wide streets of the Galloway towns are surprising for anyone with preconceptions of dour grey Scottish communities. No one who accidentally stumbles upon a Common Riding in one of the Border

Borders landscape near Galashiels

Typical river scenery near W[illegible] west of Galashie[illegible]

towns can fail to notice the groundswell of loyalty to place and culture. These are mainly modern revivals of the historic customs of marking out the bounds of the community, as well as great celebrations of horsemanship—another Border tradition. (A Scottish Border MP once requested that the date of a general election be changed so that it did not clash with the Selkirk Common Riding, which he enjoyed attending.)

LAND OF BURNS Similarly in Ayrshire, where you cannot turn a corner without finding a signpost pointing to some aspect of the life of Robert Burns, there is a genuine and unique regard for Scotland's poet. This is not something that tourism promoters have foisted upon reluctant communities, but instead an affection for the ploughman poet and pride in his achievements.

From bards to model villages by the tumbling cataracts of New Lanark, from stern Border towers to the softness of East Lothian, from the faded Victorian resorts of the golf-mad Clyde coast to the breathtaking bird cliffs of St. Abbs, the south of Scotland offers a slice of real Scotland without too much tartan ribbon (even if you can find a pipe band in a Border town just as easily as farther north). In fact, the area's variety and complex character may ultimately satisfy much more than that of the weather-dominated north. It is not an area to hurry through.

THE RIVAL COUNTY TOWNS

After Berwick became English, Greenlaw saw its chance to become the county town of the Scottish county of Berwickshire. However, nearby Duns also wanted this status and managed to achieve it several times. Each time it did so, little Greenlaw built another fine civic building. A 17th-century courtroom and prison, an 18th-century hotel to accommodate visiting lawyers and court officials, and a 19th-century town hall all add to the fine townscape of today's Greenlaw. It was superseded by Duns for the last time in 1903.

AYRSHIRE ELECTRIC ILLUSIONS

The A719 at a point within sight of Culzean Castle, 14km (9mi) south of Ayr, is called Croy Brae, or more familiarly, Electric Brae. Because of a particularly effective optical illusion, the road gives the impression of going downhill when it is actually going up. The site got its name as it was formerly thought that electricity had some part to play in the phenomenon, though this is now known not to be the case. Take care when travelling on this road as you are likely to encounter puzzled motorists freewheeling "uphill" to satisfy their curiosity.

.GH LIGHT

Scott was a ...an at heart, landowner's ... an ordered soci- ...here everyone ...v their place. He and ...ne friends founded the ...dinburgh Light Horse, a ...ind of "Home Guard," in response to a threatened Napoleonic invasion in 1797. They galloped around enthusiastically but saw little real action. However, in the troubled times when workers began to protest about working conditions, Scotland's champion did manage to threaten to sabre some mill workers at Moredun Mill and took a few pot shots at dissenting miners at Cross Causeway, both in Edinburgh.

▶▶▶ Abbotsford House 99D3

Off B6360 (tel: 01896 752043; www.scottsabbotsford.co.uk)
Open: mid-Mar–Oct, Mon–Sat 9.30–5, Sun 2–5
Admission: moderate

Sir Walter Scott's creation of his own version of Scotland and its heroic past is embodied in the house that was his life. Here is the door from the Old Tolbooth in Edinburgh, there is the desk made with wood from a Spanish Armada ship. Look at Rob Roy's gun, Bonnie Prince Charlie's quaich (cup), James IV's hunting bottle (did he club game with it?), the keys of Lochleven Castle, and other treasures.

▶ Ayr 98B3

A preference for a fortnight in the Mediterranean sun instead of a traditional seaside holiday, plus the demise of traditional industries such as coal mining, have left Ayr and its hinterland facing a challenging future. Nevertheless, Ayr is a bustling place (but take care with the parking system which needs vouchers from local shops and garages). It makes a good base for keen golfers.

Non-golfers can pursue the life of Burns. There seem to be so many places in the vicinity in which Burnsiana is displayed that after a day or two you will recognize his handwriting from several paces off. Take your pick from the **Auld Kirk**, where many of Burns's contemporaries are buried, the **Twa Brigs o' Ayr**, the older of which is 15th-century or earlier, plus the odd statue or two...then follow signs to Alloway.

Scottish memorabilia from Abbotsford

Alloway▶▶, a pleasantly leafy suburb of Ayr, is disturbed only by incessant coach loads from all nations on their way to the shrine of Scotland's national bard. **Burns Cottage,** with a museum next door (*Open* Apr–Oct daily 9.30–5.30; Nov–Mar daily 10–5. *Admission: inexpensive*. Tel: 01292 443 700; www.burnsheritagepark.com), is an excellent starting point. Down the road the **Tam o'Shanter Experience** brings to life the poem *Tam o'Shanter* in a three-screen audio-visual event (*Open* Apr–Oct, daily 9.30–5.30; Nov–Mar, daily 10–5. *Admission: inexpensive*. Tel: 01292 443700). Nearby, the Burns Monument's neoclassical columns rise from a clipped garden. Also moments away are the **Auld Brig o' Doon** and **Alloway Kirk**, both immortalized in *Tam o'Shanter*, a tale of drunkenness and orgy in a setting now taken over by suburban respectability. All of the previous Burns locations in Alloway are part of the Burns National Heritage Park.

Dalgarven Mill

On the Burns trail Incurable romantics will pursue the poet east to **Mauchline,** a village sitting dourly on a grassy ridge in the hinterland of hawthorn-hedged fields. There they will find the **Burns House Museum** (tel: 01290 550045. *Admission: free)* and a breathtaking view from the **Burns Memorial Tower** just up the road. Burns signposts are everywhere. You can follow them to the grimly workaday town of **Kilmarnock**, where in a country park stands **Dean Castle.** A rare volume, the first or Kilmarnock Edition of Burns poetry is on display, but just as interesting are the early musical instruments and European armour collections (*Open* castle Apr–Oct, Wed–Sun 11–5; Nov–Mar, Wed–Sun 11–4. Grounds daily dawn–dusk. *Admission free*. Tel: 01563 522702; www.deancastle.com).

Elsewhere in Ayr's hinterland, **Dalgarven Mill**—the Ayrshire Museum of Country Life and Costume—north of Kilwinning, is in a restored water-powered flour mill (*Open* Nov–Mar, Tue–Fri 10–4, Sat 10–5, Sun 11–5; Apr–Oct Tue–Sat 10–5, Sun 11–5. *Admission: inexpensive* Tel: 01294 552448; www.dalgarvenmill.org.uk). Also within easy reach of Ayr are the **Magnum Leisure Centre** (*Admission: moderate*. Tel: 01294 278381; www.themagnum.co.uk), much trumpeted for its modern approach to leisure now that the traditional Clyde Coast seaside holiday is out of favour, the **Scottish Maritime Museum** (see page 117), and **Culzean Castle** (see page 110).

THE SOUTHERN UPLANDS FAULT

The Southern Uplands Fault, where the midland plain gives way to the high ground of southern Scotland, is most conspicuous in the east. Running into East Lothian and prominent from the main A68 south of Dalkeith (Midlothian), the ancient tough rocks of the Lammermuir Hills form an escarpment above the soft sandstones to the north. A convenient layby on the A68 at Soutra Hill offers superb views back to the Pentlands, Edinburgh, the Firth of Forth, and beyond.

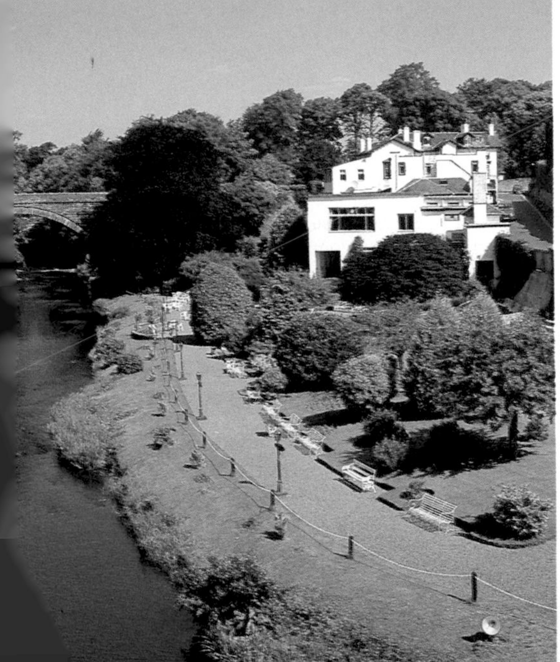

The gardens beside the Brig o' Doon in Ayr

Robert Burns (1759–1796) is the best-known figure in Scottish literature, though whether for his poems or for his pursuit of the lasses is perhaps another matter. Large tracts of Ayrshire and the area around Dumfries have plenty of sign-posted places of interest associated with his life.

SATIRICAL OBSERVATIONS

As an observer of others' follies, Burns wrote plenty of scathing and satirical observations of both people and state. A poem to the "Scotch Representatives in the House of Commons" contains the line, often quoted by the distilling industry: "Freedom and Whisky gang thegither" (go together). It also contains this observation on the Scots army regiments:

"But bring a Scotchman frae his hill
Clap in his cheek a Highland gill
Say, such is royal George's will
And there's the foe,
He has nae thought but how to kill Twa at a blow."

[A gill is a measure of whisky; royal George means King George.]

Robert Burns

Ayrshire beginnings With his farming background and his daily toil, Burns might have lived and died anonymously as just another Ayrshire farmer, struggling with poor soil and the primitive agricultural practices of the day. Instead, his immortality was assured through poetry filled with shrewd observations on human nature, with lyricism and optimism, and above all, belief in the brotherhood of man.

His father was a farmer who moved to Ayrshire from Kincardineshire, on the east coast, and built a cottage on some land he had acquired. This "auld clay biggin" still stands, a shrine to the thousands who have flocked there since the beginning of the 19th century. Burns's father was a hard worker determined to educate his family. Robert and his brother Gilbert acquired a reasonable, if sporadic, education. Robert read avidly when he was not helping on the farm. He had committed "the sin of rhyme" by the time he was 15 years old, while on the farm of Mount Oliphant.

Poems and passion After his father's death in 1784, he and his brother rented the farm of Mossgiel near Mauchline. Robert soon gained a local reputation as a maker of rhymes (among his other vices). In a period when passion and poverty went together with fierce creativity, Burns wrote some of his best-known works. This culminated in the publication of the famed Kilmarnock Edition of *Poems, Chiefly in the Scottish Dialect* in 1786. Around the same time there were writs from Jean Armour's father, livid at his daughter's association (pregnancy, to be precise) with Burns, the poor farmer; penance in the local kirk (for fornication); thoughts of emigration—only "the feelings of a father" kept him in Scotland; and also an affair with Highland Mary which ended in mysterious circumstances. Highland Mary (Mary Campbell) is a figure about whom very little is known. She died in October 1786, possibly after bearing him a child. Certainly, Burns felt terribly guilty about her in later years. It is said she consented to be his wife, but he was already committed to Jean Armour, whom he later married.

Through the success of the Kilmarnock Edition, Burns gained sudden fame. He was soon lionised by the literary classes of Edinburgh and welcomed as a ploughman poet into genteel drawing-rooms. He went along happily with the image

The songwriter Burns was also a maker of songs. In 1787 he started his completely unpaid contribution to James Johnson's *Scots Musical Museum*, reworking and improving many songs and fragments, a huge body of work still popular to this day. By 1788 he was back once again with Jean Armour. He married her and gave up the hopeless struggle of farming at Mossgiel, deciding instead to move to Ellisland Farm not far from Dumfries. He took up employment with the Excise, although he was still determined to succeed as a farmer. The farm at Ellisland failed in 1791.

In between his commitments to the Excise and the needs of the farm, he worked on with further volumes of *The Scots Musical Museum* as well as his own poetic outpourings. Illness and low spirits dogged him as the 1790s progressed. Rheumatic fever took its toll in 1795 as he struggled to maintain the output for *A Select Collection of Original Scottish Airs for the Voice.* By July 1796, at the age of 37, he was dead.

Burns Cottage in Alloway, near Ayr

Memories of Burns The Burns "industry" followed on thereafter. The first of many biographies was published by 1797, the year after his death, and the Irvine Burns Club, started in 1826, claims to be the oldest continuously operating club of its kind. Today, his birthday (25 January) is celebrated throughout Scotland—and far beyond, wherever Scots gather—with Burns Suppers, a unique format of haggis, whisky, poetry, and song. No other British poet has achieved anywhere near the same kind of popular appeal. On Burns Night even buttoned-up Scots have a good time, with their stern Calvinistic streak temporarily obscured by the outlook that, at least for one evening

"...man to man, the warld o'er
Shall brithers be for a' that."

Burns would certainly have approved.

THE BROW WELL

Though places associated with Burns are scattered throughout Ayrshire and Galloway, perhaps the saddest lies next to the B725 southeast of Dumfries. The Brow Well is a rock-cut well close to the sea. It was once famed for its mineral properties, and the poet, desperately ill with rheumatic fever and possibly bacterial endocarditis, visited it while sea-bathing nearby, in a last attempt to recover his health. He died three days after he returned from Brow.

AE FOND KISS

The curious affair by post (see page 48) which Burns had with Mrs Agnes McLehose in Edinburgh resulted in a great deal of correspondence, some frigid literary exercises in neoclassical idiom and one great, truly great, love poem and song of parting, "Ae fond kiss and then we sever," with its haunting fourth verse:

Had we never lov'd sae kindly,
Had we never lov'd sae blindly!
Never met—or never parted,
We had ne'er been broken hearted.

This was written in 1791, as "Clarinda," as Burns addressed her, was preparing to rejoin her husband in the West Indies. Burns never saw her again.

▶ Biggar *98C3*

The town of Biggar, equidistant from Glasgow and Edinburgh, has retained its own character and a sense of heritage. The original settlement is associated with 12th-century Flemish immigrants who arrived under the patronage of the Scottish kings. The incomers built "mottes," earthen mounds once topped with wooden castles. A motte survives behind today's High Street.

Biggar is essentially a centre for a rural hinterland, and the **Corn Exchange**, with its clock tower, still dominates the wide main street, scene of former markets. **St. Mary's Kirk** dates from 1545—the last kirk to be built before the Reformation—and is open to view. It is a collegiate church, founded by Lord Fleming, Mary, Queen of Scots's uncle, to support teaching priests. All this can be taken in on a few minutes' walk from the main street. The town also has a puppet theatre—not a common feature of Scottish towns—as well as several museums.

Biggar Gasworks (no longer operating) is Scotland's oldest surviving rural gasworks (1839)

Gladstone Court Museum, a tribute to the energy of the local museum trust, is an indoor "street" of shops with a good range of nostalgia-inducing artefacts (*Open* Easter–mid-Oct, Mon–Sat 11–4.30, Sun 2–4.30. *Admission: inexpensive*. Tel: 01899 221050). The **Greenhill Covenanter's House,** downhill towards the Biggar Burn behind St. Mary's, is a 17th-century farm relocated stone by stone. It sheds some light on the Covenanting movement (see page 55) and the complexities of the Scottish religious wars by way of artefacts and displays (*Open* Apr–mid-Oct, Sat and Sun 2–4.30. *Admission inexpensive*). For a total contrast, visit **Biggar Gasworks Museum▶** (*Open* Jun–Sep, daily 2–5. *Admission: inexpensive*. Tel: 01899 221050). Thanks to North Sea Gas, traditional gasworks have vanished from most places, but not from Biggar. Sometimes they fire it up, creating an

An old-fashioned chemist's shop at Gladstone Court Museum, Biggar

olfactory trip down memory lane for some. **Moat Park Heritage Centre** tells of Biggar's early history, and also focuses on embroidery, with samplers and patchwork coverlets, and on geology (*Open* Easter–mid-Oct, Mon–Sat 11–4.30, Sun 2–4.30. *Admission: inexpensive.* Tel: 01899 221050).

▶▶▶ Caerlaverock Castle and National Nature Reserve *98C1*

Open: Apr–Sep, daily 9.30–6.30; Oct–Mar, daily 9.30–4.30. Admission: moderate (tel: 01387 770244; www.historic-scotland.gov.uk)

Caerlaverock Castle is unique in Britain. No other castle builder employed this odd triangular moated design. The castle sits in its moat, massive and menacing in red sandstone, and offers another puzzle. Nobody knows who built Caerlaverock, which is of late 13th-century origin. It was taken by King Edward I of England around 1300 and regained by the Scots by 1312, only to suffer further in later Anglo-Scots conflicts. Unexpectedly, for this frontier fortress, there is an ornate 17th-century range within: Nithsdale's Building, built by the Lords Maxwell. This building is all but ruinous—a troubled history in stone.

Caerlaverock National Nature Reserve▶▶▶ Combine a castle visit with deluxe birdwatching on the marshes: particularly good away from high summer, best of all on a calm winter's day. Among the birds here are 13,000 barnacle geese from Spitzbergen, with superb views possible of the flocks from the visitor centre or from the conveniently placed hides. This is one of Scotland's major wildlife spectacles if you time it right. The reserve is open all year.

▶▶ Castle Kennedy Gardens *98A1*

Open: Apr–Sep, daily 10–5. Admission: inexpensive (tel: 01581 400225; www.castlekennedygardens.co.uk)

The Earl of Stair built these pleasure grounds. As a Field Marshal, instead of toiling with a wheelbarrow and shovel, he used his troops to build the main landscape features. (They were supposed to be chasing Covenanters.) The result is gardening on a grand scale, with vistas down the avenue of monkey puzzle trees, lakes and swathes of rhododendrons in spring. May is probably the best month to visit. The gardens are well worth the excursion, and could easily be combined with a visit to Logan Botanic Garden (see page 120).

CASTLE REMAINS
Within Castle Kennedy Gardens is the shell of Castle Kennedy, burned down in 1716, but now lending an antique air to the parklands. The Victorian Lochinch Castle in the grounds is strictly private.

THE DEBATABLE LAND
The Debatable Land was the name given to disputed territory between England and Scotland, between the rivers Sark and Esk, not far from Carlisle, England. Grazing was its only use as buildings were forbidden. In 1552 it was split in two and a settlement agreed.

Two sides of Caerlaverock Castle's triangular moat

The magnificent Adam interior of Chatelherault Lodge, near Hamilton

The past uniform of the famous Coldstream Guards

► Castle Douglas *98C1*

This is a cheerful sort of place, with its busy main street at the centre of a simple grid. The town's designer, Sir William Douglas, was a rich local merchant who rebuilt the old village in 1792. Now bypassed by the A75, Castle Douglas has plenty of shops to make strolling worthwhile.

Nearby Carlingwark Loch was once a source of marl, the limey clay used as fertilizer, which originally made the town prosperous. To the northeast is the Motte of Urr, the largest man-made castle mound in Scotland. The former 12th-century administrative headquarters of the de Berkeleys is now an impressive green hump by the river.

A few minutes from Castle Douglas, **Threave Garden►►** is the training ground for the National Trust for Scotland's gardeners. There are always fresh plantings and new ideas within its 26ha (64 acres). Early spring (April) has spectacular drifts of daffodils with over 200 cultivars. Later, the peat garden is a high point (*Open* daily 9.30– sunset; walled garden and greenhouses daily 9:30–5; visitor centre Nov–Dec, Feb–Mar, daily 10–4; Apr–Oct, daily 9.30–5.30. *Admission: expensive*. Tel: 01556 502575; www.nts.org.uk). The Scottish baronial mansion has been restored to its 1930s glory, and may be seen in guided tours (*Open* Apr–Oct, Wed–Fri, Sun 11–3.30).

Threave Castle►► This gaunt 14th-century tower rising out of the watery scenery on an island in the River Dee was once owned by Archibald the Grim. It is an appropriate setting for the name. The Lord of Galloway built his fortress to intimidate. Formerly the main power-base of the Black Douglases, the strongest of the Scottish nobles until they overreached themselves in a conflict with King James II, Threave was successfully besieged in 1455 by the king's forces. Excavations have revealed a lot about medieval defensive buildings as well as the most complete medieval riverside harbour in Scotland. There is a pleasant walk, though wet in places, from the parking area in the farmyard to the riverside. Ring a bell for the boatman. Even when the castle is closed, the walk is still worthwhile, with close-up views from the bank (*Open* Apr–Sep, daily 9.30–6.30. *Admission: inexpensive*. Tel: 07711 223101; www.historic-scotland.gov.uk). Threave Wildfowl Refuge is nearby.

►► Chatelherault *98B3*

The wealthy Duke of Hamilton asked William Adam to design a hunting lodge and kennels within the grounds surrounding Hamilton Palace. Chatelherault was part of one of the most ambitious landscaping works in 18th-century Britain. Nothing remains now of the 5km (3mi) avenue, the lake, or the canalized River Clyde. Hamilton Palace was demolished in 1927 after most of the land was sold for mining. Today there is only a country park, plus a £7 million restoration of Adam's one-room-deep façade, part of which is a visitor centre telling the extraordinary story. It is well worth the diversion from the M74 (*Open* daily Mon–Sat 10–5, Sun 12–5. *Admission free*. Tel: 01698 426213).

► Coldstream *99E3*

A pleasant village just north of the border, Coldstream, like Gretna Green, once did a brisk trade in marrying elopers. This is recalled on a plaque by the little tollhouse on the Scottish side of John Smeaton's elegant 1760s bridge. Coldstream is also associated with the Guards regiment of the same name. Items from their past can be seen in the Coldstream Museum (*Open* Easter–Sep Mon–Sat 10–4, Sun 2–4; Oct, Mon–Sat 1–4. *Admission free*. Tel: 01890 882630).

North of the village is **The Hirsel ►**, once the home of Sir Alec Douglas-Home, Lord Home of The Hirsel, who was Prime Minister from 1963 to 1964. Walks through very varied habitats of woodland (with rhododendrons in spring), farm, and loch, are enjoyed by birdwatchers in particular. A craft complex and visitor centre in a converted farm building sheds light on the life of a Borders country estate (*Open* grounds daily, sunrise–sunset; museum and crafts centre Mon–Fri 10–5, Sat–Sun 12–5. *Admission free; parking charge*. Tel: 01890 882 834; www.hirselcountrypark.co.uk).

Threave Castle, near Castle Douglas

THE COLDSTREAM GUARDS

The primacy of the Grenadier Guards as the senior regiment in the Guards Division of the British Army is disputed by the Coldstream Guards. Both regiments share 1660 as their official founding date. When on parade the Coldstreamers will not stand next to the Grenadiers, instead taking the left of the line. Their motto is *Nulli secundus*—second to none.

FOUND IN THE LOCH

Not only valuable marl came out of Carlingwark Loch by Castle Douglas. Among other historical artefacts, a forge was once recovered from the waters. It is thought to have been used by King Edward I's forces as they passed this way during one of their forays in around 1300.

FLAT
floor of ... f Culzean ... t at the dis- ... eral Dwight ... wer as a token ... ottish people's ... e for his role as ... ne Commander of ... llied Forces in ... ope in World War II. It ... as become known as ... he National Guest Flat and its story is told in the Eisenhower Room in the castle today.

AN ITALIAN INFLUENCE?
The unique studded facade of Crichton Castle dates from the 1580s. The Palazzo Steripinto in Sciacca, Sicily (1501) is a possible source of inspiration, as the 5th Earl of Bothwell was in exile in southern Italy.

►► Crichton Castle 99D3

Open: Apr–Sep, daily 9.30–6.30. Admission: inexpensive (tel: 01875 320017; www.historic-scotland.gov.uk)

This forbidding, brooding castle is easily missed if you hurry along the A68, intent on Edinburgh. It is worth stopping, not least because of the fine Lothians countryside in which the castle is set. Built between the late 14th and late 16th centuries, it is associated with the Earls of Bothwell. Mary, Queen of Scots was here in January 1562, attending the wedding of her half-brother to Lady Janet Hepburn. The son of that marriage, the 5th Earl of Bothwell, often in exile, commissioned the castle's unique feature: the diamond-faceted façade of the north range. A pathway leads to Borthwick Castle (a private hotel).

►►► Culzean Castle and Country Park 98A2

Open: house Easter–Oct, daily 10.30–5 (last entry 4); country park daily 9–5.30. Admission: expensive (tel: 01655 884455; www.nts.org.uk or www.culzeancastle.net)

Culzean, pronounced "Kul-*ain*," is the National Trust for Scotland's most popular attraction. Set on its clifftop perch, it has been associated with the Kennedy family since the 14th century. The present building was commissioned by the 10th Earl of Cassillis, and is one of Robert Adam's most famous designs, taking 20 years to reach completion in 1792. The structure itself, with its ornate plasterwork, oval staircase, and round drawing-room, plus 230ha (570 acres) of "policies" (grounds), came into the hands of the National Trust in 1945, to be held for all time. Now the once-private grounds swallow up more than half a million visitors every year, though fewer visit the castle itself. Stabilizing the wind- and salt-eroded sandstone of the structure and the outbuildings was only one problem for the Trust to solve. Simply running the estate is a huge operation. This is conservation and countryside education on a large scale. Within the extensive policies are woodland walks, a walled garden, a swan pond, deer park, and vinery, as well as a helpful Ranger Service, based in a reception and interpretation centre.

Culzean Castle has fine Adam architecture, extensive gardens, and superb views to Arran and Ailsa Craig (a steep, rocky island once the plug of a volcano)

► Dalbeattie 98C1

Dalbeattie presents an uncharacteristic Galloway townscape of silver granite, like a little detached chunk of Aberdeen, but its granite has brought prosperity—even the Grand Harbour of Valletta in Malta used it. The town is a good base for exploring the coastline, especially around Rockcliffe and Kippford. Kippford is popular with sailing enthusiasts, while Rockcliffe has the air of a retirement haven. Farther up the Water of Urr is Palnackie, where a flounder tramping festival is held annually in the muddy creek. Also nearby is Orchardton Tower, a 15th-century tower house unique in Scotland because it is circular.

The beach at Yellowcraigs, Dirleton, with Fidra offshore

THE JUBILEE
Rockcliffe is Kippford by the Path, through tr by the sea edge views to the blue shallows of the Wat Urr estuary. It makes very pleasant stroll, w a drink to follow at the local hotel in Kippford. Note that though only 1.6km (1mi) apart by the Jubilee Path, the two places are 8km (5mi) apart by road.

►► Dawyck Botanic Gardens 98C3

Open: Apr–Sep 10–6; Mar, Oct, 10–5; Feb, Nov, 10–4
Admission: inexpensive (tel: 01721 760254; www.rbge.org.uk)
On the B712 southwest of Peebles, this specialist garden of the Royal Botanic Garden in Edinburgh lies a little off the main tourist routes and as such is often overlooked. It is worth seeking out, especially in late spring and early summer when the garden is ablaze with rhododendrons. The plantings here are on a large scale, with grand conifers and shrubs and woodland walks.

►► Dirleton Castle 99D4

Open: Apr–Sep, daily 9.30–6.30; Oct–Mar, daily 9.30–4.30.
Admission: moderate (tel: 01620 850330; www.historic-scotland.gov.uk)
Overlooking the village green of Dirleton, parts of this fortress date to the early 13th century, when its great circular towers, now overlaid with later work, were built by the Anglo-Norman de Vaux family. The strategically important castle, commanding east–west routes round the Lammermuirs, was captured by King Edward I of England in 1298. It has a pit-prison, cut from the solid rock. Ruined by Cromwell's troops in 1650, the castle became part of the Archerfield estate. The site lies within a much later wall enclosing a 17th-century bowling green, ancient yews, and a fine garden.

The Victorian garden, which is at its best in high season, includes the world's longest herbaceous border. Combine a visit with a coastal walk at Yellowcraigs. An access road is signed just east of the castle.

LITERARY CONNECTIONS
Conspicuous offshore at Yellowcraigs (by Dirleton) are the island of Fidra and its lighthouse. This is one of the places said to be the inspiration for the topography of Robert Louis Stevenson's *Treasure Island*. Certainly, Stevenson knew this part of the coastline well, using other nearby coastal features in *Catriona*.

...NG AT ...AR

...ssing his chances ...uring the throne of ...land, Robert the ...uce (see page 29) had ... deal with other powerful families with Scottish interests at the English court. For this purpose the encounter was typical of the murky politics of the day. He met with John Comyn (the Red Comyn) at Greyfriars Kirk in Dumfries. Most historians believe that they had been jointly plotting against King Edward of England and that Comyn had let the English know about this. Bruce had been warned and left England in great haste. At his meeting with Comyn he accused him of treachery, and the fatal stabbing followed. The game was up. To return to King Edward was impossible. Bruce had to declare his intention: To win Scotland's Crown.

Decorative tiles in a Dunbar shop

▶ Dumfries 98C2

With its old bridges, museum and Camera Obscura, a reasonable range of shops, and plenty of Burns strands to follow, Dumfries is a pleasant rather than breathtaking town. Known as the Queen of the South, it is the largest centre for some distance around, with a good mix of light industry and commerce, tourism and historic sites. Now that it is bypassed by the terrifyingly busy A75, the town

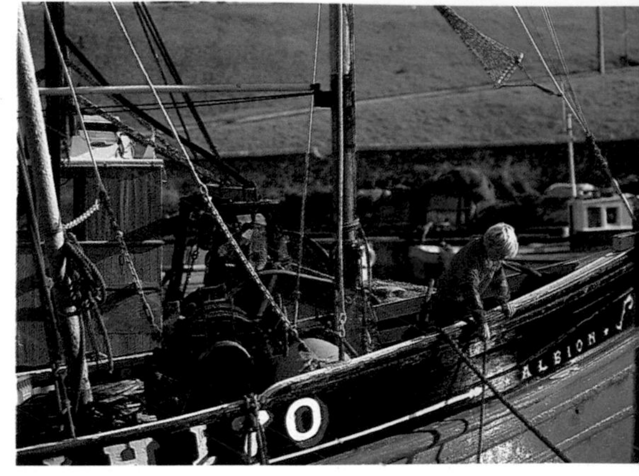

environment has greatly improved. The prevailing street colour is the distinctive pink of the local sandstone. Dumfries grew up around the ford on the River Nith, becoming a royal burgh in the 12th century.

The now-vanished Greyfriars was the scene of the stabbing of the Red Comyn by Robert the Bruce, an incident that led to the Scottish Wars of Independence (see panel). Much later, and flying in the face of Jacobite romantic myth, Dumfries wanted no truck with Bonnie Prince Charlie, who helped himself to town funds as well as the lead off the church roof.

Like Ayr, Dumfries has capitalized on its Robert Burns connections (see pages 104–105). He moved here in 1791 to take up his post as an Excise officer and now lies buried in a grand mausoleum in St. Michael's churchyard. The house he died in is also a museum (*Open* Apr–Sep, Mon–Sat 10–5, Sun 2–5; Oct–Mar, Tue–Sat 10–1, 2–5. *Admission free*. Tel: 01387 255297; www.dumgal.gov.uk/museums). The Globe Inn, known to Burns, is still a pub, complete with the chair he used and the window on which he scratched some radical verses.

Robert Burns Centre▶ Modern input to the Burns cult takes the form of this handsome former mill building by the River Nith. The centre offers an exhibition on the Dumfries Burns connection (*Open* Apr–Sep, Mon–Sat 10–8, Sun 2–5; Oct–Mar, Tue–Sat 10–1, 2–5. *Admission free; small charge for audio-visual*. Tel: 01387 264808).

▶▶ Dunbar 99D4

Boasting high sunshine records—when the coastal "haar" (sea fog) stays away—and low rainfall, Dunbar is a mix of traditional resort, decayed port, and elegant Georgian sea town. By the harbour are fragments of one of medieval Scotland's most important fortresses, controlling a coastal

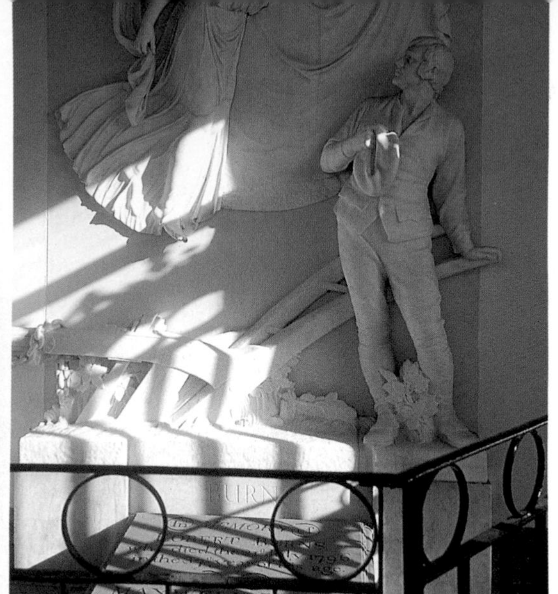

FIRST STEAM
Dalswinton Loc
10km (6mi) nort
Dumfries. The firs
powered boat ever
was tested on its wa
in 1788. The designer
William Symington, an
engineer who was born
far off at Leadhills. His engine developed 0.45 horsepower (0.34KW), barely enough to turn the cranks.

Burns's Mausoleum, one of many stops in and around Dumfries on the Burns trail

route used by the English invaders. The Scots were defeated here in 1296. In 1650, the Covenanting army met the same fate at the hands of Oliver Cromwell.

Today, the townscape owes its origins partly to funds generated by intense trading activities in the 18th century, which included, briefly, whaling. The handsome 17th-century town house pre-dates these times, though Dunbar or Lauderdale House, blocking the eastward High Street view, was built by one of the powerful trading families in the town. There are other fine buildings to be admired, but a stroll will inevitably lead seawards, past the Cromwellian Old Harbour to the New or Victoria harbour, dating from 1842. In spring, kittiwakes nest on the old castle and other harbourfront buildings.

Dunbar lies next to the **John Muir Country Park▶▶**, 70ha (175 acres) of excellent coastal habitat, varying from salt marsh to sea buckthorn, around the Tyne estuary. It offers plenty of walks at all seasons and has the further attraction of completely altering its character at high tide.

AN UNFORTUNATE NAME
The former county town of Duns is recalled in the uncomplimentary word "dunce." This is ironic, as it refers to John Duns Scotus (1266–1308), a philosopher and leading divine said to have been born in the town. The modern usage came about through later criticism of his teachings.

▶ Eyemouth Museum *99E3*

Open: Easter–Sep Mon–Sat 10–5, Sun 11–2; Oct Mon–Sat 1–4. Admission: inexpensive (tel: 01890 750678)

A converted Georgian church in the fishing port of Eyemouth is the setting for this successful community venture. Eyemouth Museum was set up in 1981 to record the centenary of the Great East Coast Fishing Disaster of October 1881, when 189 fishermen lost their lives in a sudden hurricane. The tale of the disaster is commemorated in a magnificent tapestry, and the museum also touches on other aspects of folk life in the area, including agricultural developments. A visit here could be combined with birdwatching around St. Abbs' Head.

► Galashiels *99D3*

A sturdy, workaday mill town, rather than a picturesque place, "Gala" has lots of shops to browse in for knitwear bargains. In fact, the textile theme is inescapable, notably at **Lochcarron Cashmere Woollen Mill**►► (*Open* Mon–Sat 9–5, also Sun 12–5 Jun–Sep. Tours Mon–Fri only. *Admission: inexpensive.* Tel: 01896 751100; www.lochcarron.com). The museum there, with its traditional spinning and weaving artefacts, tells the story of the town's development as an important textile manufacturing centre. There is also a factory tour and a mill shop.

Lochcarron Cashmere Woollen Mill, Galashiels

►► Galloway Forest Park *98B2*

Between the rivers Cree and Ken, the open moors below the grey hills of Galloway lost their original tree cover long ago. From 1922 onwards the Forestry Commission reclothed many of the slopes using alien species, designating the area a Forest Park in 1943. Like all Forestry Commission properties, it offers unlimited public access unless areas are closed for tree felling. There are marked trails and opportunities to fish or camp, and the park is also bisected by the Southern Upland Way (a long-distance footpath). Points of interest are the 16km (10mi) forest drive near Clatteringshaws Loch, the Raider's Road, linking the A712 and the A762, views from the road end at Glen Trool, and the Bruce's Stone, commemorating the first victory in the Independence Wars.

THE QUEEN'S WAY
The A712 between Newton Stewart and New Galloway as it passes through the Galloway Forest Park is known as the Queen's Way. The original Queen's Way was the old pilgrim road used by Mary, Queen of Scots, among many other monarchs, that led down to Whithorn (see page 120).

►► Gatehouse of Fleet *98B1*

This peaceful mill community on the edge of the hills was founded in the 1760s. Just to the southwest is 15th-century **Cardoness Castle**, a typically austere tower house (*Open* Apr–Sep, daily 9.30–6.30; Oct–Mar, daily 9.30–4.30. *Admission: inexpensive.* Tel: 01557 814427; www.historic-scotland.gov.uk). The B796 north out of Gatehouse gives a taste of the empty hinterland and high hills of Galloway, and a long view to the viaduct over the Big Water of Fleet. If you are visiting the **Gem Rock Museum** at Creetown (*Open* Easter–Sep, daily 9.30–5.30; Oct–Nov, Mar–Easter, daily 10–4; Dec and Feb, Sat–Sun 10–4. *Admission: inexpensive* Tel: 01671 820357; www.gemrock.net), this road is much more attractive than the A75.

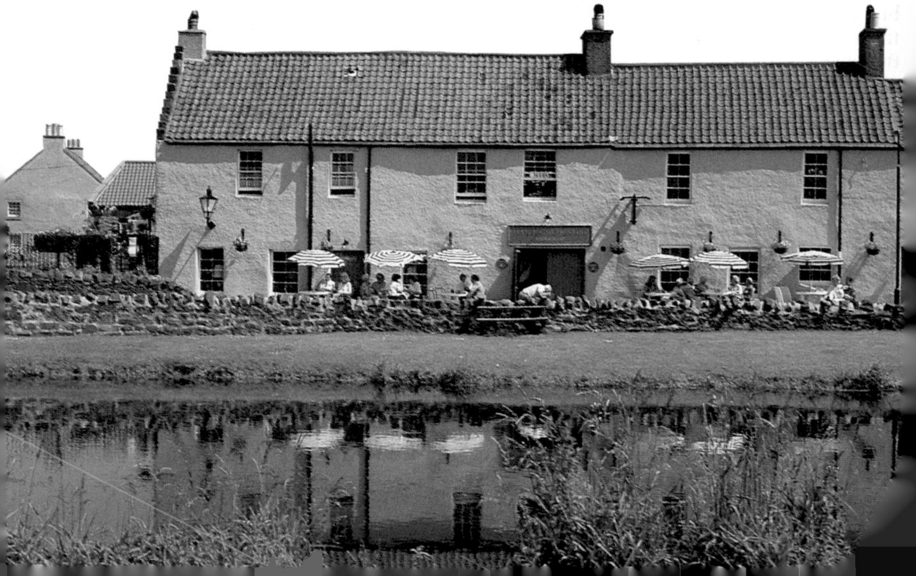

Outdoor refreshments by the Tyne, Haddington

Mill on the Fleet►►► (*Open* Easter–Oct daily 10.30–5. *Admission: free*. Tel: 01557 814099; www.gatehouse-of-fleet.co.uk), a visitor centre in a former bobbin mill, tells the tale of Gatehouse's cotton spinning, offering a hi-tech interpretation. Visitors are provided with hard hats at the entrance, inside which are tiny loudspeakers that are activated at various points in the displays to provide commentary.

A gentle corner of the Galloway landscape in Scotland's southwestern corner

►►► Haddington 99D4

One of the most pleasing towns of the Lothians, the counties surrounding Edinburgh, Haddington was the administrative headquarters of the old county and for centuries played an important part in Lothian affairs. A 12th-century royal burgh, it lay at the centre of one of the best agricultural regions of Scotland, and had continental trade through the now silted up port of Aberlady to the north.

Today it retains its triangular medieval street plan, and the fine, mainly Georgian, buildings of the town centre have been preserved and carefully painted to create a co-ordinated and harmonious façade along a High Street rivalled by few other Scottish towns. The air of a prosperous old community is enhanced by other trappings of a Scottish burgh: the impressive town house originally built by William Adam, the market cross, courthouse, and 14th- to 15th-century St. Mary's Church, with its warm, red stones reflected in the river. This is a town to study at a slow pace, admiring the detailing of wrought-iron balconies, ornamental urns, cornice-decoration, and so on. Note also the closes running off the main thoroughfares. Tucked round a corner in Sidegate, a plaque records the exact heights of the River Tyne floods: The last big one was in 1948.

SCOTTISH TWEED

The traditional explanation for the name "tweed" is that a merchant in London received a consignment of Scottish cloth and misread the word "tweel" (twill). Because of the River Tweed the name stuck. This is probably a myth, though at least two Scottish tweed mills claim they sent the consignment. There is a written reference from Aberdeen in 1541 to "small twedlyne"—tweedling. According to philologists, the words tweel and tweeling, tweed and tweedling have been around a long time and have nothing to do with rivers. Besides, the traditional version does not explain Harris tweed, given that Harris in the Outer Hebrides is so far away.

LONG RIDE
Mary, Queen of Scots rode from Jedburgh to Hermitage Castle and back in a day, just over 80km (50mi), to visit the wounded Earl of Bothwell, trusted lieutenant on Border matters. Though this is sometimes romantically described as a foolhardy venture undertaken on her own, it was not in fact unusual to cover such a distance in a day and, besides, the Queen was in company with many members of her court and a squad of soldiers.

▶ Hawick 99D2

Hawick is the largest of the Border towns. Its long and bustling main street is worth a browse for woollen shops with keenly priced cashmeres. At one end is **Drumlanrig's Tower** (*Open* Mon–Sat 10–5 (Apr–Sep, Mon–Sat 10–5, Sun 12–3). *Admission: inexpensive*. Tel: 01450 377615). This visitor centre portrays the local history of the area. **Wilton Lodge Park** is also attractive, with Victorian walled gardens and its own museum and art gallery (*Open* Apr–Sep, daily 7.30–4.15; Oct–Mar, 8–3.30. *Admission free*. Tel: 01450 378023).

▶ Hermitage Castle 99D2

Open: Apr–Sep, daily 9.30–6.30. Admission: inexpensive (tel: 01387 376222; www.historic-scotland.gov.uk)

Off the B6399 in bleak Border country, the grimness of Hermitage Castle echoes the emptiness around. Hermitage is particularly impressive if the clouds are low on the hills. One of the tales about this 14th-century keep concerns Lord Soulis, who was so cruel that the locals eventually revolted, wrapped him in lead, and boiled him to death in a cauldron.

▶ Innerleithen 99D3

A compact mill town by the confluence of the Leithen Water and the Tweed, Innerleithen is home to famous knitwear names, notably Ballantynes. Sir Walter Scott used it as the setting for his novel *St. Ronan's Well*, published in 1821.

A Borders' time capsule

Robert Smail's Printing Works▶▶▶, run by the National Trust for Scotland, is perhaps the main attraction within the town (*Open* Easter, Jun–Sep Thu–Mon 12–5, Sun 1–5. *Admission: moderate*. Tel: 01896 830206; www.nts.org.uk). The local printers, which served the community for well over a hundred years, remained in the original family's hands until purchased by the Trust in 1986. The Victorian office, paper store, composing room, and machine room all survived as a unique time capsule. Most importantly, so did 50 "guard books"—a record of every item ever printed at the works, as well as ephemera from the past. There are now print demonstrations.

Just minutes away to the south is one of the most interesting grand homes in the Borders. **Traquair House▶▶▶** (*Open* Apr–May and Sep daily 12–5; Oct daily 11–4; Jun–Aug, daily 10.30–5. *Admission: moderate*. Tel: 01896 830323; www.traquair.co.uk) boasts that it is the oldest continuously inhabited house in Scotland and that it has been associated with the Stuarts or Maxwell-Stuarts, the Lairds of Traquair, since 1491. Before that it was a hunting lodge used by the Scottish monarchs. Over the centuries it has been transformed from a grim Borders keep to a stately mansion, and has remained practically unchanged since the end of the 17th century.

ST. RONAN'S WELL
The sulphurous waters of St. Ronan's Well were said to be particularly effective for "ladies desirous of becoming in an interesting condition." According to local legend, the sulphur content is the result of the local holy man, St. Ronan, catching the Deil (Devil) with his shepherd's crook and immersing him in the waters.

A total of 27 Scottish and English monarchs have been guests at Traquair, and Bonnie Prince Charlie is said to have visited. Family lore and the paraphernalia and treasures of generations, including notable Mary, Queen of Scots' relics, are further attractions of the house, which is also pleasantly unintimidating in scale. If there is only time for one Borders house, then make it Traquair.

▶ Irvine 98B3

Scattered around the riverside area of the New Town of Irvine, the **Scottish Maritime Museum▶** has a collection of craft moored at pontoons, including the puffer Spartan. (Puffers were small flat-bottomed cargo vessels used to supply west-coast communities; you can always board at least one vessel.) Farther along the harbour is the Tug Quay and main Museum Wharf. Visitors can board the Garnock, the last Irvine tug. Indoors, there is a special maritime exhibition, with changing themes. The Shipyard Workers Tenement Flat is a restored room and kitchen of the early 20th century, showing typical accommodation.

Several craft offer trips at events, some weekends and holidays, including the S.Y. *Carola*, the oldest seagoing steam yacht in Great Britain, built 1898 as a private family yacht. (*Open* daily 10–5. *Admission: inexpensive*. Tel: 01294 78283; www.scottishmaritimemuseum.org).

THE CLOSED GATE
Traquair House has parallel drives, one of them ending at permanently closed gate. When Bonnie Prince Charlie rode out after a visit to Traquair in the autumn of 1745, the 5th Earl wished him success and closed the gates behind him, vowing they would never be opened again until a Stuart was on the throne.

Traquair Castle, left, a fine fortified Borders castle, and below, the Traquair coat of arms

117

A HISTORIC HECKLER
In the old part of Irvine is the Glasgow Vennel, formerly the main road out of town. Robert Burns came here to learn to dress flax, a process known as heckling. (Hecklers tended to be politically argumentative types, hence the modern usage.) The venture came to an end when Burns' partner's wife dropped a candle during a drunken Hogmanay Party. The dried flax caught fire and the business was burned down. The thatched Heckling Shop has been restored, along with Burns' lodgings nearby.

Above: Jedburgh's mercat cross, symbol that the town enjoyed certain trading rights. Right: Kelso Abbey, at the heart of the town Sir Walter Scott described as the most beautiful in Scotland

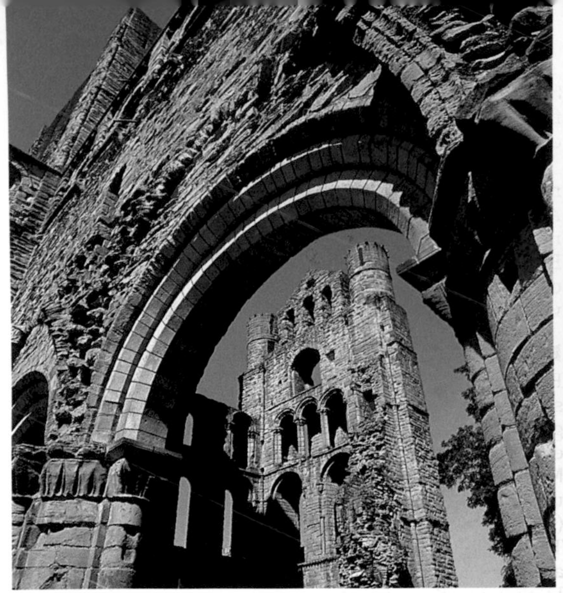

▶▶ **Jedburgh** *99D3*

Jedburgh, on the A68, is a typical Borders town, with a history of tweed making. The local weavers were the first to combine two colours in their weave, thus inventing tweed. Even the Tourist Information Centre and parking area are on the site of a former mill. The original woollen developments were focused on the activities of the monks in the Border abbeys, of which Jedburgh's is the best preserved.

The shell of the once great **Jedburgh Abbey**▶▶▶ still dominates the town skyline though it was destroyed by English forces during the "rough wooing" (see page 30). The Abbey visitor centre makes an excellent introduction to the vanished monastic life of the Borders (*Open* Apr–Sep, daily 9.30–6.30; Oct–Mar, daily 9.30–4.30. *Admission: moderate.* Tel: 01835 863925; www.historic-scotland.gov.uk). Also of note is **Mary, Queen of Scots' House**, a near-contemporary fortified or "bastel" (like the French bastille) house, now a museum (*Open* Mar–Nov, Mon–Sat 10–4.30, Sun 11–4.30. *Admission: inexpensive.* Tel: 01835 863331). The former prison on the site of the castle (Castle Jail), once a Georgian model prison, is now a **museum**. The town also has associations with Sir Walter Scott and Bonnie Prince Charlie.

▶▶ **Kelso** *99E3*

When the writer H. V. Morton passed here in the 1920s, he was struck by the appearance of the main square in Kelso. "Surely I was in France! An enormous *grande place* paved with whinstone forms the heart of the town. Round it rise those tall, demure, many-storied houses...which seem to know almost as many stories as a concierge." Little has changed except the traffic. Stroll from the square past the poignant fragment of **Kelso Abbey**, severely damaged by the Earl of Hertford's forces in 1545. All 112 inhabitants were slaughtered. The Tourist Information Centre is almost opposite. Rennie's handsome bridge of 1803 spans the Tweed moments farther on. From the parapet there is a fine view to **Floors Castle**▶ (*Open* Easter–Oct, daily 10–5. *Admission: moderate.* Tel: 01573 223333; www.floorscastle.com), the largest inhabited house in

A FLATTERING DESCRIPTION
With its long waterfront, Lord Cockburn described Kirkcudbright as "the Venice of Scotland." Clearly, he never saw it with the tide out.

THE UNION CANAL
Linlithgow is a good place to discover the Union Canal, ideal for strolls along the towpath. There is an impressive aqueduct about 3km (2mi) to the west. Linlithgow has a canal museum and cruising opportunities. Enquire at weekends in summer.

Scotland. It offers glittering excesses of fine French furniture, porcelain, paintings, and tapestries, as well as extensive parkland and walks.

Mellerstain House▶▶ is a highly attractive Adam mansion to the northwest of Kelso. It has typically ornate Adam plasterwork and decoration and also beautiful terraced gardens, from which there are fine views (*Open* Easter, May–Sep Sun–Mon, Wed–Thu 12.30–5; gardens open 11.30–5.30. *Admission: moderate.* Tel: 01573 410225; www.mellerstain.com).

▶▶▶ Kirkcudbright *98B1*

Pronounced "kir-*coo*-bree," Kirkcudbright has a typically spacious Galloway layout and its Georgian streetscapes give it a dignified and harmonious air. The 16th-century exception to the prevailing 18th-century work, **Maclellan's Castle** is a ruined turreted mansion conspicuous on the skyline and set in the middle of the town (*Open* Apr–Sep, daily 9.30–6.30. *Admission: inexpensive.* Tel: 01557 331856; www.historic-scotland.gov.uk). There are a few antique shops to browse around, as well as the Harbour Gallery, though the main artistic connection is **Broughton House**, with its collection of the works of Edward Hornel (1864–1933) of the famed "Glasgow Boys" (*Open* Easter–Jun, Sep–Oct, daily 12–5; Jul–Aug 10–5. *Admission: expensive.* Tel: 01557 330437; www.nts.org.uk). The picturesque Tolbooth and mercat cross complete the harmonious groupings in this Solway town. The **Stewartry Museum**▶▶ is a traditional museum (*Open* Mar–May, Oct, Mon–Sat 11–4; Jun–Sep, daily 11–4; Nov–Feb, Sat 11–4. *Admission inexpensive.* Tel: 01557 331643; www.dumfriesmuseum.demon.co.uk). Visitors can discover the Dorothy L. Sayers connection and find out why the founder of the American navy was once locked in the local tollbooth.

FIVE RED HERRINGS

The renowned detective novelist Dorothy L. Sayers had two aunts and an uncle in Kirkcudbright. She used the local area as a setting for one of her Lord Peter Wimsey novels, *Five Red Herrings*, published in 1931. Another and more famous work set in Galloway—at least in part—is John Buchan's *The Thirty-Nine Steps* (published in 1915).

The Scottish Parliament met in 15th-century Linlithgow Palace on several occasions, most "recently" in 1646

▶ Linlithgow Palace *98C4*

Open: Apr–Sep, daily 9.30–6.30; Oct–Mar, daily 9.30–4.30
Admission: moderate (tel: 01506 842896; www.historic-scotland.gov.uk)

Birthplace of Mary, Queen of Scots, this once magnificent royal palace is now a cold shell. It was burned, probably accidentally, during the last Jacobite rebellion in 1745. It is, however, worth a diversion from the M90.

...gan
..., it is
...e the
...ure of a sea-
...Built originally
...as a source of
...sh for nearby
... House, it contains
... cod which can be
... by hand. Curiously,
...he pond was damaged by
a wartime mine.

A RECORD CLAIM
The Whithorn excavation team reconstructed a Viking Age house on the site of their dig for the benefit of visitors. It was built of poles and brushwood and sadly it burned down. Seeking compensation through their insurers, the team made the first ever Viking Age insurance claim.

►► Logan Botanic Garden 98A1

Open: Apr–Sep, daily 10–6; Mar and Oct, daily 10–5. Admission: inexpensive (tel: 01776 860231; www.rgbe.org.uk)
Galloway trumpets its prevailing mildness to persuade visitors to stay. Nowhere is the benign influence of the North Atlantic Drift more apparent than in Logan Botanic Garden. This specialist garden of the Royal Botanic Garden in Edinburgh specializes in tender plants that would not survive in other parts of Scotland. It has much success with exotic Australasian tree ferns, cabbage palms, and a whole range of southern hemisphere species.

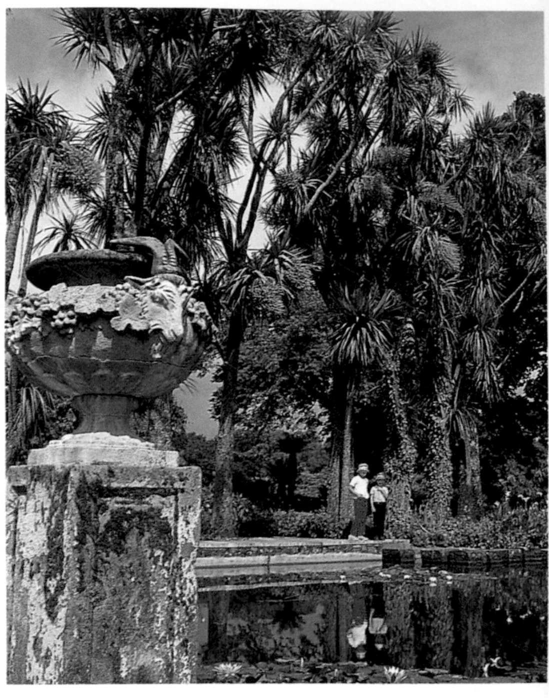

Logan Botanic Garden, where many species from the southern hemisphere enjoy some of Scotland's mildest air

►► The Machars 98B1

Lush green is the first impression of the Machars, to which is added the yellow splash of gorse on the little rough hillocks. This is gentle, rolling countryside, with the big hills of Galloway receding to the north. A triangle lying between Wigtown Bay and Luce Bay, the Machars are sometimes overlooked by visitors but have a curious serenity. Perhaps this echoes their early religious links. Here, at Whithorn, not on the island of Iona, is the cradle of Christianity in Britain.

Whithorn Story and Whithorn Priory Museum►► This archaeological attraction (*Open* Apr–Oct, daily 10.30–5. *Admission: inexpensive*. Tel: 01988 500508; www.historic-scotland.gov.uk) is on the site of the first Christian community in Scotland and displays material from AD 400 dug up on the site. Whithorn is associated with St. Ninian. His chapel on a grassy headland at Isle of Whithorn (not actually an island) is an anticlimax, though his cave makes a worthwhile walk down a lane and along the pebbly shore.

Wigtown is also attractive, with a wide main street. It is associated with the drowning of two Covenanter martyrs, tied to a stake before the incoming tide in 1685. You can visit the site, down by the endless mud flats of the shore. More cheerfully, Wigtown is heavily promoted as Scotland's book town. The arrival of several book businesses in recent years is turning this sleepy Machars' town into a browsers' paradise.

A grim reminder of the Covenanters at Wigtown

▶▶▶ Melrose *99D3*

Melrose is a tweedy town that is almost too neat to be true. It has a romantically ruined red sandstone abbey, visible from the road. Next door, the National Trust for Scotland sells various gifts and dried flowers grown in Priorwood Garden (*Open* Easter–Dec, Mon–Sat 10–5, Sun 1–5. *Admission: inexpensive*. Tel: 01896 822493; www.nts.org.uk). There are plenty of gift and clothes shops. Melrose is overshadowed by the beautiful Eildon Hills where a stiff walk (starting across the golf course) offers outstanding views.

The **Three Hills Roman Heritage Centre** ▶▶ This is a fascinating account of one of the Romans' main forts in Scotland, Newstead, which is just a few fields away (*Open* Apr–Oct, daily 10.30–4.30. Site walk: Jul and Aug, Tue 1.30–5.15; all year Thu 1.30–5.15. *Admission: inexpensive*. Tel: 01896 822651; www.trimontium.freeserve.co.uk). Alternatively there are a number of excursions from Melrose, including Dryburgh Abbey and Scott's View (see page 126).

The River Bladnoch as it reaches the sea near Wigtown; it rises high on the Galloway moors

▶ Moffat *98C2*

The ram statue on the Colvin Fountain in the middle of the town square is a reminder of Moffat's origins in the wool trade, though it also had a reputation in the 18th century as a spa town. The woollen bargains at Moffat Weavers at the southern end of town are popular with tourists. Moffat is on the A701, a scenic route to Edinburgh known as "the Beeftub road." As well as the **Devil's Beeftub**, a hollow carved out by a glacier at the head of the valley, there are more glacial features to be seen up the Moffat Water by the A708. This passes the Grey Mare's Tail, a geologically classic waterfall pouring over the lip of a hanging valley. Hardy walkers can penetrate beyond the waterfall, either to circle round Loch Skeen or to reach the broad rounded summit of **White Coomb**, which at 822m (2,696ft) is one of the highest hills in the Southern Uplands.

A CANNY LOCATION

Why did the Romans build their main fort at Trimontium? According to the Trimontium Exhibition in Melrose, when the legions came over the Cheviot Hills, they made for the most conspicuous landmark, the triple-peaked Eildon Hills, instantly recognizable from any angle, and right in the centre of southern Scotland.

…CAN …ION

…d Garden can be …ned with a visit to …theart Abbey. The …en is attractively …ltered by mature …ees, and has a …leasantly tinkling burn, a Japanese Garden, poolside primulas, and sea views. However, its claim to fame is its connection with John Paul Jones, the founder of the American navy. He was born in a cottage on the estate and worked in the gardens as a boy. A museum tells the story (*Open* May–Sep, Tue–Sun 2–6).

▶▶ New Abbey 98C1

This little village on the A710 is dominated by the red ruins of **Sweetheart Abbey**, a religious seat founded in 1273 by Devorgilla, wife of John Balliol. On his death she had his heart embalmed in an ivory and silver casket, an act recalled in the abbey's name. The abbey suffered from its proximity to the Border in the Wars of Independence. At the Reformation its riches were disposed of, and the building gradually deteriorated. Today, visitors can stroll through the pointed Gothic ruins. The 18th-century **New Abbey Corn Mill**▶ is close to the abbey (*Open* abbey and mill Apr–Sep, daily 9.30–6.30; Oct–Mar, Sat–Wed, 9.30–4.30. *Admission: inexpensive.* Tel: 01387 850260; www.historic-scotland.gov.uk). The great grinding stones, powered by water via an impressive set of gearing, produce oatmeal of various grades. Walk a bit further to reach the **Shambellie House Museum of Costume**, an outstation of the Royal Museum of Scotland. It shows material from the National Costume Collection (*Open* Apr–Oct, daily 10–5. *Admission: inexpensive.* Tel: 01387 850375; www.nms.ac.uk).

Shambellie House Museum of Costume

▶▶▶ New Lanark and the Falls of Clyde 98C3

The River Clyde seems a world away from its downstream industry here amid the farms and orchards of Lanarkshire on the edge of the hills. It roars through a wooded gorge over spectacular waterfalls ("linns") in a setting unique in Scotland. The river was harnessed to power cotton mills in an unusual experiment in workers' welfare. The model village of New Lanark has survived intact and there is a visitor centre within the mill complex (*Open* daily 11–5. *Admission: moderate.* Tel: 01555 661345; www.newlanark.org).

The corn mill at New Abbey, which, along with a picturesque abbey and a museum of costume, makes the village worth seeing

A remarkable industrial and social experiment, embodying the principles of welfare and worker care, took place in the upper reaches of the River Clyde in the late 18th and early 19th centuries. Two hundred years later, there is still a lot to see.

In 1783 a successful Glasgow businessman, David Dale, bought this wooded bowl with its roaring river as a potential site for a spinning mill. Before the end of the century New Lanark had become the single largest industrial enterprise in Scotland. Some of the river's force was diverted, a little way downstream, to turn giant water-wheels which, with belts and drives, powered noisy cotton looms housed in vast mill buildings. In 1793, over 1,100 employees tended these machines, of whom 800 were young boys and girls.

Social benefits Dale the master was no despotic employer. Hours were long, but substantial housing was provided as well as educational facilities. Many of his child-workers were orphans who were, by the standards of the day, well fed and cared for. Another source of workers was Highland emigration: New Lanark employed people who would otherwise have headed for the New World because of repression and depressed economic conditions in their native lands to the north.

Robert Owen This Welshman was born in 1771 (32 years after Dale) and also made his way in the spinning industry. He had strong ideas about equality and social welfare. In 1799 he married David Dale's daughter. Along with two partners he then bought New Lanark and assumed management in 1800. Already embodying principles of welfare and worker care, the model village became the setting for Owen's own social experiments and even more benevolent management style.

After some business vicissitudes in the early years of the 19th century, Owen was able to put his principles into practice with new Quaker backers. To the four great mills and blocks of workers' houses were added the New Institute for the Formation of Character (1816) and Robert Owen's School (1817), as the first steps in the creation of his vision of a society without crime, poverty, or misery—the fundamentals of "Owenism."

THE FALLS OF CLYDE
The "linns" that comprise the Falls of Clyde are in a delightful wooded river gorge and are well worth the walk upstream. (Go through the gap in the wall at the far end of the village.) Some of the water is diverted through tunnels to run a hydroelectric power station. When this is not operating, for example during station maintenance work, the falls are at their best.

Bell tower on Spinning Mills New Buildings, New Lanark

Robert Owen, an entrepreneur of vision who transformed the banks of the Clyde at New Lanark with his model working village

NO CARE FOR TREES
Neidpath Castle eventually came into the hands of the Douglas Earls of March. The 3rd Earl inherited it but cared little for this country property, instead leading a spendthrift life in London. He even sold for timber a fine stand of ornamental trees planted by his father and grandfather. This vandalism was subsequently condemned by William Wordsworth's *Sonnet Composed at Neidpath Castle*:
"Degenerate Douglas! oh the unworthy Lord!"

► Newton Stewart *98B1*

A kind of gateway between the Machars and the Galloway Forest Park, Newton Stewart has a good range of shops (including antiques). Nearby, the Wood of Cree is a Royal Society for the Protection of Birds nature reserve, the largest oak wood in the southwest. Species include several summer warblers, plus dippers and grey wagtails. The scenically outstanding Glen Trool road (see page 114) is easily reached from the town.

►► North Berwick *99D4*

Within easy commuting range of Edinburgh, North Berwick has developed from a small fishing port into a holiday resort. Its little harbour is jammed with pleasure craft, its harbourfront granary is converted to flats, and its fine quality Victorian and Edwardian architecture likewise suggest prosperity. Behind the town is the cone of the **North Berwick Law**, a 187m (613ft) high volcanic plug. Views from the top are excellent.

The Scottish Seabird Centre► at the harbour uses the latest technology to capture pictures of seabirds nesting on the nearby cliffs and islands, as well as interactive and multimedia displays for families (*Open* Apr–Oct, daily 10–6; Nov–Jan, Mon–Fri 10–4, Sat, Sun 10–5.30; Feb–Mar, Mon–Fri 10–5, Sat, Sun 10–5.30. *Admission: moderate*. Tel: 01620 890202; www.seabird.org).

East of the town, on the way to Tantallon, is another fine beach at Seacliff. Other nearby attractions include the historic aircraft collection at the **Museum of Flight** at East Fortune, complete with a Concorde (*Open* Apr, Jun, Sep–Oct, daily 10–5; Jul–Aug 10–6; Nov–Mar, Sat, Sun 10–4. *Admission: moderate*. Tel: 01620 897240; www.nms.ac.uk/flight).

Tantallon Castle►►► This 14th-century stronghold straddles a headland, a grim fortified wall of eroded red sandstone (*Open* Apr–Sep, daily 9.30–6.30; Oct–Dec, Sat–Wed 9.30–4.30. *Admission: moderate*. Tel: 01620 892727; www.historic-scotland.gov.uk).

Traditional ironmongers, Peebles

▶▶ Peebles 99D3

Peebles is well within day-trip range of Edinburgh and is accordingly busy throughout the year. There is a good choice of shops for antiques and fashions. The town was the birthplace of William and Robert Chambers, of Chambers Dictionaries fame. After making their fortune in Edinburgh, they endowed their home town with the impressive municipal buildings on the main street, now housing a library and museum.

Neidpath Castle▶▶ (*Open* Easter, Jul–early Sep, Mon–Sat 11–6, Sun 1–5. Open bank holiday Mondays. *Admission: inexpensive.* Tel: 01721 720333). A few minutes west of the town, this stronghold can be reached on foot along the River Tweed as a pleasant alternative to going by car. An L-plan tower house, originally built by the Hayes family, Neidpath has survived remarkably intact. It was "modernized" for comfort in the 17th century, though retaining its medieval outward appearance, but fell into decay by the 19th century. The present owners, the Earls of Wemyss, restored it.

▶▶ Rosslyn Chapel *99D3*

Open: Apr–Sep, Mon–Sat 9.30–6; Oct–Mar, Mon–Sat 9.30–5; Sun 12–4.45 all year. Admission: moderate (tel: 0131 440 2159; www.rosslynchapel.org.uk)

The finest example of medieval stone carving in Scotland (if not Britain) can be found a few minutes' stroll beyond the village of Roslin. Perched above Roslin Glen, Rosslyn Chapel was founded in 1446 by William Sinclair, 3rd Earl of Orkney. Still used as a place of worship, it is really only the choir of a larger design which was never completed.

▶ Scottish Railway Preservation Society (Bo'ness and Kinneil Railway) *98C4*

Open: Apr–Jun, Sep–Oct, weekends plus major holidays; Jul–Aug daily. Special events in Dec
Admission: moderate (tel: 01506 822298; www.srps.org.uk)

At Bo'ness on the Forth, a typical Scottish branch line has been re-created, offering a 6km (4mi) trip uphill to Birkhill (with extensions likely) where a former clay mine can be visited. It captures the feel of a vanished age and could be tied in with a trip to Linlithgow.

"Maude" (former Class J36) at Bo'ness

LITERARY VISITORS
Rosslyn Inn (now a private house), adjacent to the Chapel, was the main lodging for many famous folk who came to see the wonders of the place. The Wordsworths stayed there, leaving very early to visit Sir Walter Scott at his first marital home at nearby Lasswade (the Scotts were still in bed when they arrived). Before that, Robert Burns stayed, and Dr. Samuel Johnson and James Boswell took lunch and tea there, on their way back from their Hebridean tour.

A branch line—re-created

BASS ROCK BIRDS
The gannet's Latin name, *Sula bassana*, recalls its long association with the Bass Rock. Gannets occupy about 14,000 nest sites on the Bass. There are smaller numbers of kittiwakes, guillemots, razorbills, and puffins. Boat trips go from North Berwick.

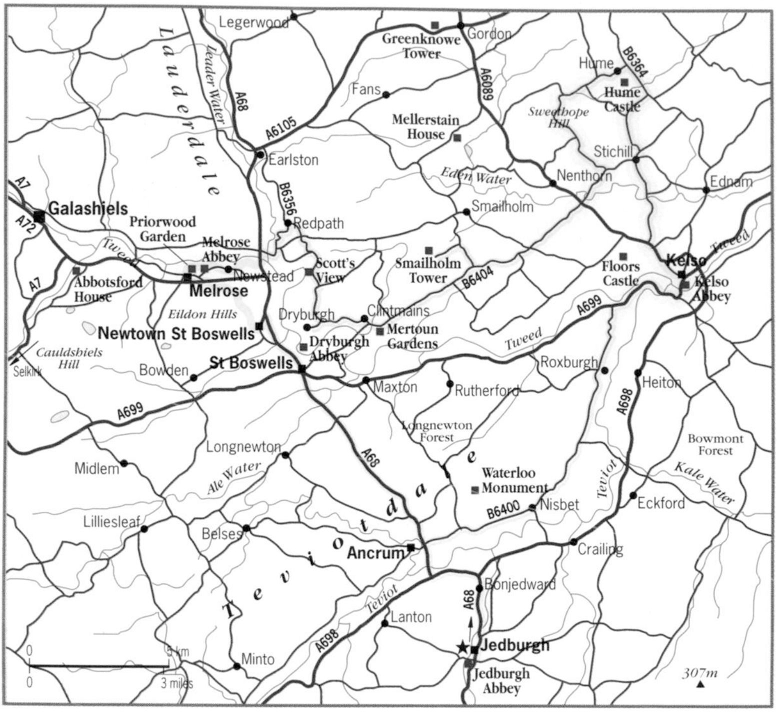

126

Drive

Border views and abbeys

Smailholm Tower for Border views

The river valleys and rounded hills of the Borders make rewarding country for touring. This route is 64km (40mi), and is easily driven in a day if no diversions are taken along the way.

Take the A68 north from Jedburgh, then the B6400 east. The unmistakable high tower of the **Waterloo Monument** on an ancient earthwork was raised in 1815 on the instructions of William Kerr, 6th Marquis of Lothian.

Continue past Roxburgh, to reach **Kelso** with its ruined abbey.

Take the B6364 northwards and soon you will see a dark square of battlements rising ahead. Take a minor road to Hume. Built by Lord Hume in the 1790s on the site of the original **Hume Castle**, the site offers one of Scotland's best views.

Travel west to cross the A6089 at a staggered crossroads for the view from **Smailholm Tower**, a 16th-century fortified border keep associated with Sir Walter Scott. Then drop gently down westwards to find signs for the peaceful riverside **Dryburgh Abbey**.

Scott's View, Scott's favourite viewpoint for the Eildon Hills, is signposted. The minor road leads to the A68 and Melrose, with its abbey. Detour to Selkirk, or return to Jedburgh on the A68.

► Scottish Mining Museum 99D3

Newtongrange (tel: 0131 663 7519; www.scottishminingmuseum.org). Mar–Oct, daily 10–5; Nov–Feb, daily 10–4. Admission: moderate

Newtongrange was once the largest planned mining village in Scotland. Built to service the Lady Victoria Colliery, it now has a major visitor centre instead of a coalmine. Hi-tech displays tell the story of coal, and there are interactive displays with a "virtual" coalface, and "magic helmets" to provide a commentary. There is an informative film, and a tour includes an impressive steam winding engine.

A vanished way of life at Newtongrange

►► Selkirk 99D3

Sir Walter Scott presided as sheriff in Selkirk, and his **Courtroom** (*Open* Apr–Sep, Mon–Fri 10–4, Sat 10–2; May–Aug also open Sun 10–2; Oct, Mon–Sat 1–4. *Admission free*. Tel: 01750 20096) tells of his life, writings, and time as a judge. **Halliwell's House►►** is an interesting museum. Ask to see the excellent videos about the Common Ridings (*Open* Apr–Sep, Mon–Sat 10–5, Sun 10–12; Jul and Aug Mon–Sat 10–5.30, Sun 10–1; Oct Mon–Sat 10–4. *Admission free*. Tel: 01750 20096). **Abbotsford House** is nearby (see page 102).

► South Queensferry 98C4

South Queensferry makes a pleasant evening excursion from Edinburgh to view the great bridges both upriver and down. Or tie it in with a day visit to **Hopetoun House►** to the west, where architects William and John Adam created a spectacular mansion, now filled with valuables (*Open* mid-Apr to Sep, daily 11–5.30, last entry 4.30. *Admission: expensive*. Tel: 0131 331 2451; www.hopetounhouse.com). Also nearby is **Dalmeny House**. Some of the Rothschild Mentmore porcelain collection forms part of the impressive items on display (*Open* Jul–Aug, Sun–Tue 2–5.30. *Admission: moderate*. Tel: 0131 331 1888; www.dalmeny.co.uk).

The Yellow Drawing Room at Hopetoun House

QUEEN MARGA

The queen in th South (or North) Queensferry refers Queen (and Saint) Margaret, the Saxon of the uncouth King Malcolm. She is associated with the ancient ferry-crossing here, which connected the old capital at Dunfermline with the Lothians.

AN EARLY FORTH BRIDGE DESIGN

Commenting on the flimsiness of an 1818 design for a chain bridge across the mighty Forth near South Queensferry, a later Victorian engineer noted "it would hardly have been visible on a dull day and after a heavy gale it would no longer be seen on a clear day either."

The Forth estuary was the last great challenge of the Victorian railway age. In 1873, the railway companies of the east coast trunk route oversaw the laying of a foundation stone for a Forth Bridge designed by Sir Thomas Bouch. But then the Tay Bridge—which he had designed—fell, and his plans for the Forth were abandoned.

MAINTENANCE COSTS
The phrase "painting the Forth bridge" has passed into common usage to describe a never-ending job. The painting area has been estimated as 59ha (146 acres) and 38,000 litres (8,400 gallons) of Forth Bridge oxide of iron brushing paint are needed to coat it from end to end. Originally, many of the bridge painters were ex-sailing ship crew, accustomed to shinning up and down holding only a rope. Today, hydraulic lifts and cradles are used.

A new Forth design was supplied by Benjamin Baker of the engineering company Fowler and Baker. This was based on the cantilever principle, invented in the Far East, and used steel instead of the treacherous cast iron of the first Tay Bridge. The contract for the work was signed in 1882, with William Arrol as the main contractor.

Building progress The next four years were taken up with building the coffer dams, sinking the caissons (watertight chambers used for laying foundations underwater) and building the piers on which the huge weight of steel would rest. The superstructure was built in the next four years. While the first Tay Bridge has sometimes been described as an optimist's bridge, the Forth is a pessimist's bridge. The engineers were all too aware of the effects of lateral wind pressure, which had been the downfall of the Tay design. Exhaustive scale-model tests were carried out and all the various calculations were based on a "worst-case scenario"—the freak hurricane that blew its way up one side of the Forth and down the other.

Facts and figures The bridge cost 57 lives during construction before it was opened in March 1890—and still proves an endless source of astonishing statistics, not the least curious of which is the fact that the bridge is almost a metre (3ft) longer on a hot summer day than in midwinter. It consumed 55,000 tons of steel, 148,300 cubic metres (194,300 cubic yards) of granite (on the approach viaducts), 21,330 tons of cement and almost seven million rivets. The last one was banged into place by the Prince of Wales at a spot marked by a plaque. It was the monument of the age.

The Forth Bridge, impressive from every angle

▶▶▶ St. Abbs 99E4

The great seabird colonies of northern Scotland, particularly Shetland, are justly famous. But there is one place in southern Scotland where, for very little effort, in May and June in particular, a spectacular "bird city" can be seen that rivals anything the north can offer. The cliffs and stacks of St. Abbs Head are favoured by 10,000 guillemots alone. This portly, penguin-like auk is just one of the many species that make the experience a cacophony of noise, and, not least, smell (a distinctly fishy one). Razorbills, fulmars, and kittiwakes add to the din. The cliffs can be viewed with relative ease, as some of them are offshore stacks. A signposted walk takes you from the visitor centre to the cliffs, from where the route goes west to reach the lighthouse and the easily viewed seabird colonies. (Elderly visitors can take the car all the way from the visitor centre to the lighthouse.) There are magnificent sea views all the way, with the biggest seabird colonies bursting into view by the lighthouse itself. Birdwatchers haunt the spot at autumn migration time as well. There are lots of rare birds—ask the warden for details.

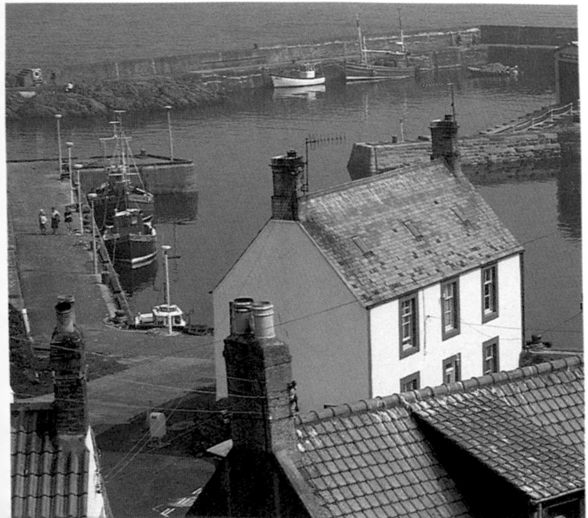

St. Abbs, where clear waters and a diverse underwater flora create a Mecca for divers

▶ Wanlockhead 98C2

Wanlockhead is Scotland's highest village, though it is a considerable distance from the Highlands. It stands among the bald, bleak domes of the Lowther Hills, a strange, almost claustrophobic, gathering of steep-sided glaciated bumps buffering Strathclyde and Galloway. The Lowthers are cut by impressive road passes, notably the Dalveen and the Mennock, the latter leading to Wanlockhead and nearby Leadhills.

Britain's most important non-ferrous metal mining area used to be there, in the endless winds and open moors. Gold was found in the reign of King James IV, but lead made fortunes for local landowners. The mine closed in the 1930s, a story told in the **Museum of Lead Mining** (*Open* Apr–Oct, daily 11–4.30; Jul–Aug 10–5, last tour 4. *Admission: moderate.* Tel: 01659 74387; www.leadminingmuseum.co.uk). There are several other historical threads to follow, ranging from the vanished branch line, once Britain's highest railway, to the Covenanters, whose strongholds were here.

BIRD SPE

St. Abbs H
in autumn m
include sooty
shearwaters an
and great skuas.
Summertime sees
of gannets going to
from the Bass Rock
breeding grounds near
North Berwick.

EARLY CHARITY

In the early 19th century, the Wanlockhead proprietor, the Duke of Buccleuch and Queensberry (owner of Drumlanrig Castle), passed through and gave £5 to the miners to drink his health. Instead they "considered they should testify their respect and gratitude by making the £5 the commencement of a charitable fund for the relief of miners when sick, or rendered unfit for work by age, as also for the benefit of their widows." Whether or not this gave the duke food for thought is not recorded.

Gulls on offshore rocks, St. Abbs

d

LIGHTS

Nicoll Moncrief's gratitude seems to be as much to King James (VI of Scotland, I of England) as to God. This carving is in the village of Falkland

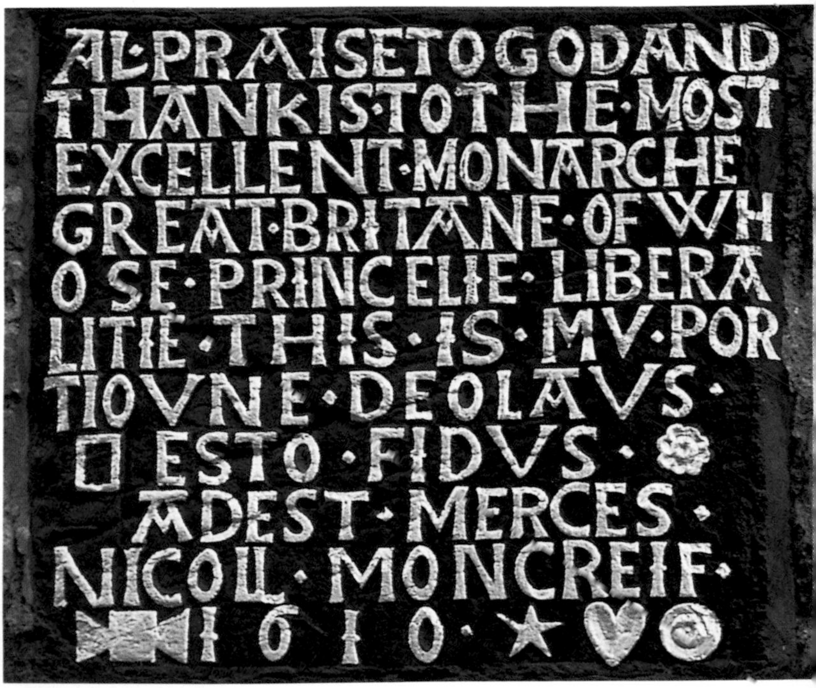

AL·PRAISE TO GOD AND
THANKIS TO THE·MOST
EXCELLENT·MONARCHE
GREAT·BRITANE·OF WH
O SE·PRINCELIE·LIBERA
LITIE·THIS·IS·MV·POR
TIOVNE·DEO LAVS·
ESTO·FIDVS·
ADEST·MERCES·
NICOLL·MONCREIF·
1610·

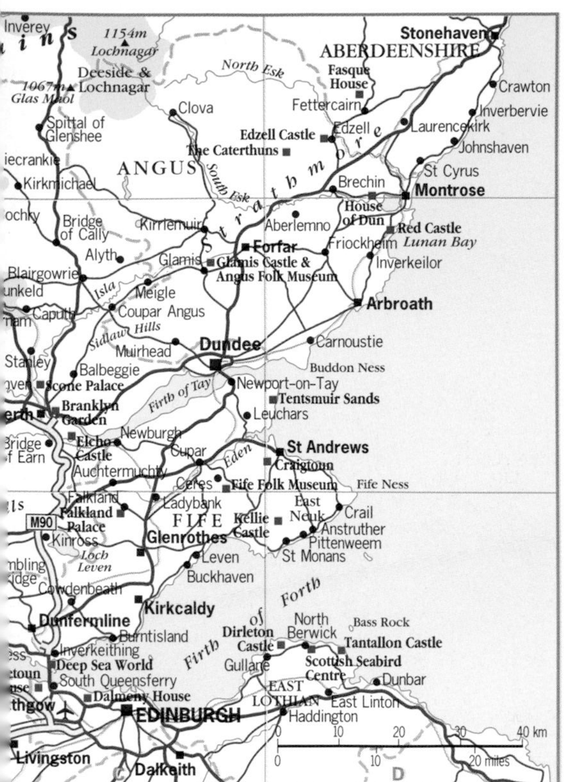

A MEETING OF TWO CULTURES This region has two distinct characters because it bridges the Highland Line, or, more accurately, the Highland Boundary Fault. This is not just a geological distinction but a real divide between two cultures, Highland and Lowland, separated by a mountain barrier and, formerly, also by language and traditions.

It was in the Highland part of Central Scotland that the cult of the picturesque first took root. From the cities of the central belt, the first tourists admired the beauties of the Trossachs and Loch Lomond—not just because they were attractive, but also because they were the first bit of wild Scotland that was accessible from the Lowlands. This led to the growth of resort towns which still cater for visitors today: places such as Callander, Crieff, Dunkeld, and Pitlochry, all of which have long-established reputations as holiday spots in or near the Highlands.

The feeling of entering or leaving different cultures is an important element in the Central Scottish "experience." Ben Ledi looms at the end of Callander's main street as a reminder that there is real grandeur beyond the cut-price woollen mill sales. At Dunkeld, there is a strong sense of passing between the Highland portals. Alternatively, drive up any of the Angus Glens—or follow back roads beyond Alyth—for a full taste of the openness in the silent, rounded hills of the Grampian edge. From the unexpected drama of the Reekie Linn waterfall near Kirriemuir, Scotland's mini-Niagara

ROMANTIC PROSPECTS
Though Sir Walter Scott is often said to have put the Trossachs on the tourist map, he was certainly not the first to discover them. As early as 1794 the Statistical Account of Scotland noted under the heading "Romantic Prospects" that "The Trossachs are often visited by persons of taste, who are desirous of seeing nature in her rudest and most unpolished state."

THE HEART OF SCOTLAND
Breadalbane is an ancient name for the heart of Scotland in central Perthshire. Crianlarich, Killin, and, farther east, Aberfeldy, with all the high hills around, are considered to be within it. The name is derived from two Gaelic words: *braghaid*, the upper part, and *Alban*, Scotland, hence Breadalbane means "the uplands of Alban," an appropriate enough name for this wild country.

VIEWING THE FAULT LINE
Perhaps the best vantage point for viewing the Highland Boundary Fault is from the top of Conic Hill behind Balmaha on the shores of Loch Lomond. The climb can be made along part of the West Highland Way. From the hilltop, the fault line runs out and through the main Loch Lomond islands to the west, while it disappears eastwards towards Callander. The pink and pebbly conglomerate rock is characteristic of the geology of the edge of the Highlands.

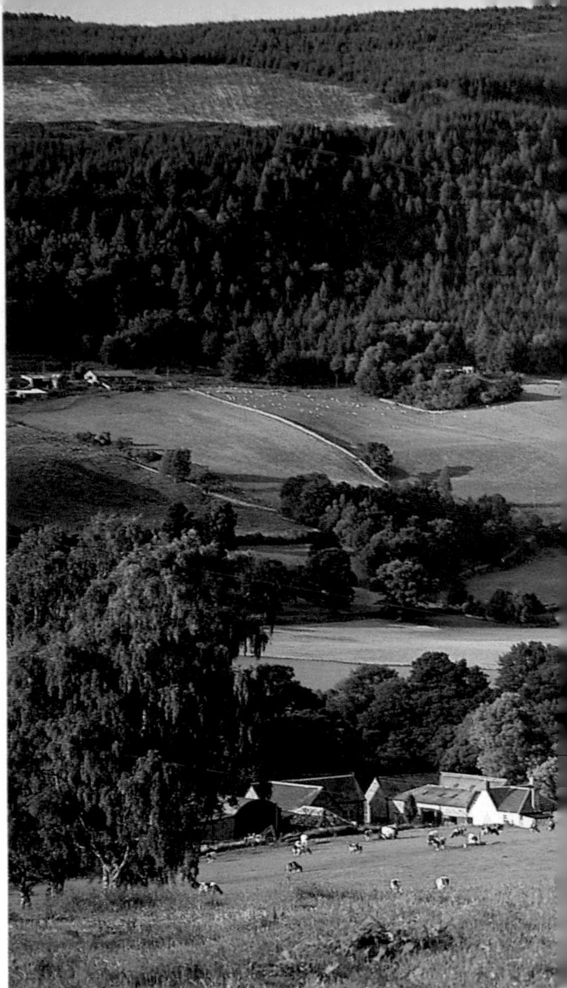

smoking its way over a high ledge, to the heights of Ben Lawers, Central Scotland's much trampled-upon highest mountain, scenic drama can be found in plenty.

Yet Central Scotland is not without a very attractive Lowland character. Northeast Fife, with its long beaches backed by finely trimmed golf courses, seems a long way both from the Highlands and the legacy of the Industrial Revolution. This portion of Fife missed out on the effects of industry, so plain in other parts of the Lowlands. Instead, it kept its essentially rural character. Its European heritage from its early trading links with the Low Countries is seen today in architecture, especially on the coast. Thus St. Andrews and the East Neuk of Fife have very distinct personalities, being Scottish without being either tartan or grimy. Angus is almost wholly rural, though here the Grampian Hills are always a backdrop, forming one side of Strathmore, the long rural corridor which leads northeastwards from Perth up to the Mearns on the edge of the old county of Kincardineshire.

Central Scotland's industrial background includes linoleum at Kirkcaldy, Dunfermline's specialized damask ware, and also industries based on the city of Dundee, still

The Tay Valley in Perthshire. The river begins life in Loch Tay and reaches the sea at Dundee

noted for its jam and journalism. Brewing is still associated with Alloa in the old county of Clackmannan below the Ochil Hills. Perhaps the most interesting chunk of industrial heritage can be found at Culross overlooking the Forth, where a small Scottish burgh seemed to be passed over by progress for more than two centuries until restoration.

Just as the shipyard workers of the industrial Glasgow of old would escape at weekends to the mountainous beauty of the Trossachs and the millworkers of Dundee would go northwest to the long Angus glens, so it is still the hills and mountains which inevitably call to visitors today. To take in the essence of Central Scotland, find a high point near the Highland edge: Callander Crags behind Callander, the highest section of the Duke's Road in the Trossachs, Dumyat (pronounced "De-*my*-att") behind Stirling, the delectable Duncryne Hill on the southern edge of Loch Lomond, or the Caterthun hillforts on a Grampian shoulder in Angus. Northwards, waves of hills roll on to the end of Scotland. Southwards is all the grit and liveliness of the Lowland towns. That is the essence of Central Scotland.

THE SIGNAL TOWER
The Bell Rock lighthouse by Robert Stevenson was built on the Inchcape Rock, a reef submerged at high tide, about 18km (11mi) southeast of Arbroath. It was first lit in 1811 and was a magnificent achievement for its day. To facilitate rock to shore communication when the lighthouse was under construction, a signal tower was built, which was also the shore base for the light. This is today's Signal Tower Museum where the story is told in full.

►► Aberfeldy 130B2

Aberfeldy is a pleasantly peaceful place. It makes a good centre for exploring the local walks and trails, notably along the Moness Burn to view the "**Birks of Aberfeldy**" in the wooded den. These birchwoods were made famous by Robert Burns who penned the lyrics of the Scottish song of the same name. Aberfeldy itself has a watermill and a distillery to visit, which is the setting for **Dewar's World of Whisky** (*Open* Apr–Oct, Mon–Sat 10-6, Sun 12–4; Nov–Mar, Mon–Sat 10–4, last tour one hour before closing. *Admission: moderate*. Tel: 01887 822010; www.dewarswow.com). **Castle Menzies** is nearby to the northwest on the B846 (*Open* Apr–mid-Oct, Mon–Sat 10.30–5, Sun 2–5, last entry 4.30. *Admission: inexpensive*. Tel: 01887 820982). This 16th-century, fortified Z-plan tower is in the care of the Clan Menzies. To reach it by road means crossing the River Tay by the finest of General Wade's bridges (see panel).

► Arbroath 131D2

A salty, seagull-strafed, seacoast town, Arbroath in Angus gave its name to the Arbroath smokie, a smoked, split

Blair Castle

haddock. Smokies can be bought from several merchants in the narrow streets of the "fishing quarter." Arbroath mixes fishing with the air of a 1950s traditional Scottish holiday resort. There is very fine coastline to explore north of the town, as well as the hinterland of Angus within easy reach. In the centre of the town stand the red sandstone walls of the 12th-century **Arbroath Abbey►** and its new visitor centre (*Open* Apr–Sep, daily 9.30–6.30; Oct–Mar, daily 9.30–4.30. *Admission: moderate*. Tel: 01241 878756; www.historic-scotland.gov.uk), scene of important events in Scotland's history (see panel). Other aspects of the town's history are portrayed in the curious **Signal Tower Museum►**, close to the harbour. The museum has a display on one of Arbroath's specialist industries: the manufacture of lawnmowers (*Open* Mon–Sat 10–5; also Sun 2–5 Jul and Aug. *Admission free*. Tel: 01241 875598).

Contributing to the town's holiday air is **Kerr's Miniature Railway►►**. This ride-on track, running parallel to the high embankment of the Edinburgh–Aberdeen railway, has delighted generations (*Open* Apr–Jun, Sat–Sun 1–4; Jul to mid-Aug, daily 2–5; mid-Aug–Sep, Sat–Sun 2–5. *Admission: inexpensive*. Tel: 01241 879249).

WADE'S BRIDGES
General Wade, the military road builder, built many fine bridges in Scotland, but none were so grand as his work at Aberfeldy. It was not to everyone's taste. Dorothy Wordsworth toured with her brother William in 1803 and, among many carping comments on things Scottish in her journal, she described how the party "crossed the Tay by a bridge of ambitious and ugly architecture. Many of the bridges in Scotland are so..."

► Balquhidder 130B2

The Braes (slopes) of Balquhidder and Balquhidder Glen, in which lie the long reaches of Loch Voil, are often missed by those rushing north on the A84 from Callander. Once a place in which desperate men from broken clans chose to settle—though it was also the stronghold of the MacLarens and the Macgregors—the area around Balquhidder has glorious scenery which is worth exploring. Many people visit the **grave of Rob Roy** (see pages 137 and 161) in Balquhidder kirkyard, something of an anticlimax, while others make their way to the end of the public road, in order to climb the choice of **Munros** (a mountain over 914m/3,000ft high) within easy reach. Another worthwhile walk is to hike up through the trees to the windy heights of Kirkton Glen (start by the church) where the little jewel of **Lochan nan Eireannaich** (Loch of the Irish) sits below the crags of an old hill pass to Glen Dochart. Listen for the ring ouzel (the mountain blackbird), which sings here in summer.

► Blair Atholl and Blair Castle 130B3

Blair Atholl is famed chiefly for **Blair Castle►►**, whose white turrets can be seen from the A9. The settlement that grew up near the castle also has a mill and a folk museum. Blair Castle itself (*Open* Apr–Oct, daily 9.30–5.30, last entry 4.30. *Admission: moderate*. Tel: 01796 481207; www.blair-castle.co.uk), the seat of the earls and later the dukes of Atholl, is the archetypal Scottish castle, dating from at least 1269.

There are many stories associated with it (and its role in the Jacobite rebellion of 1745), and many rooms full of furniture and artefacts accumulated over the centuries. There is plenty to keep you busy but you may well tire of hearing that the Duke of Atholl was the only person in Britain allowed to maintain a private army.

THE DECLARATION OF ARBROATH

In the Scots Wars of Independence, the country's leading churchmen were firmly nationalist. In 1320 they met in Arbroath Abbey to write a famous document in Scotland's story, the Declaration of Arbroath. Its most widely quoted passage is: "For so long as a hundred of us shall remain alive we shall never accept subjection to the domination of the English. For we fight not for glory, or riches or honour, but for freedom alone which no good man will consent to lose but with his life."

THE FALLS OF BRUAR

North of Blair Castle, accessible from the old A9, these falls are within the extensive landholding of the Blair Charitable Trust. Robert Burns visited on his Highland tour and suggested to the Duke of Atholl that he might plant more trees to create even more beauty around the falls. The suggestion was taken up and the falls today are noted for their mature larch trees.

Near Aberfeldy: fishing the River Tay, and Castle Menzies (detail)

THE BRACKLINN FALLS
For a wager, Sir Walter Scott once rode a pony across the rickety old bridge that spanned the gorge below the Bracklinn Falls. Today's bridge is more substantial, but take care with children on the slippery rocks and tree roots near the edge of the gorge, beyond the bridge.

► Blairgowrie *131C2*

A busy place with a good range of shops, Blairgowrie first prospered from the River Ericht as it powered its way out of the Highlands. Flax mills were built on its bank and by the early 19th century the town was booming. A second wave of prosperity followed after raspberry growing on a commercial scale was introduced. Today, the crop is still important, with the long rows of raspberry canes in the surrounding fields looking a little like vineyards.

En route to the town, the A93 is bordered for 520m (1,700ft) just beyond the River Isla by the 30m (100ft) high **Meikleour Beech Hedge**. This extraordinary living wall, of branches stretches for over 500m (1,640ft) and is sometimes described as the highest hedge in the world. The trees were planted in 1745.

►► Callander *130B1*

Right on the Highland edge, with Ben Ledi looming at the end of the main street, Callander seems busy throughout the year. The town's bustle is a reminder of its role as a gateway not just to the Highlands but specifically to the Trossachs. The old village of Callander was rebuilt and extended after 1763, when the authorities took over the land of the Drummonds, who forfeited them after the 1745 Jacobite rebellion. It is an example of early town planning, and soon Callander took on its role of servicing visitors, which it has had ever since. Escape from the tartan wares of the shopping street to discover picturesque **Bracklinn Falls►►**, signposted from the east side of the town (see the walk opposite). North-westwards, where the hills close in, is the Pass of Leny. A path from the main road goes down to another cataract, the Falls of Leny. Though the shortest approach is from the north or main road side, the Falls can be reached on foot from Callander via a former railway trackbed on the south side of the river.

Bracklinn Falls: natural beauty within easy reach of Callander

SOFT FRUITS
Around Blairgowrie and up into Strathmore is the largest soft fruit growing area in the EU. Raspberries, tayberries, loganberries, and strawberries thrive in the balance of sunshine and moisture.

Walk

The Bracklinn Falls

Only minutes from Callander's busy main street lies an escape on the very edge of the Highlands. Allow 1 hour to the Falls, or 3 hours for the Callander Crags circuit.

The Bracklinn Falls are signed north (right if coming from Stirling) up a street near the Roman Camp Hotel sign. If travelling by car, drive up this road, soon entering attractive mixed woodland for a short way until you come to the parking area on the right.

Take the level path running east from here. Soon the pines flanking the path end to reveal to a pleasing green prospect back across the Lowlands. Continue through a double kissing gate, with the falls sounding close at hand. Descend steps to a bridge over the white water. The path peters out on the far side, among the oak trees.

Retrace your steps. The energetic can walk uphill along the road from the parking area into open country with views north of an attractive glen. It is possible to circle back to Callander via the Callander Crags on the skyline, but you will need a stout pair of walking shoes.

Slightly more demanding (for pedestrians) are the **Callander Crags**▶▶, overlooking a dense bowl of woodland immediately behind the town and threaded by sheltered paths. Waterfall and woodland can be combined in a single excursion by penetrating farther up the signposted road into an attractive Highland glen.

Rob Roy and the Trossachs Visitor Centre▶▶ This tourist centre interprets the life of Rob Roy Macgregor, Scotland's Robin Hood, by means of audio-visuals and fairly hi-tech displays (including a talking cow). It also sets the folk hero firmly in the Trossachs landscapes (see page 161) (*Open* Jan and Feb, daily 11–4; Mar–May, Oct, daily 10–5; Jun–Sep, daily 10–6; Nov–Dec, daily 11–4. Last admission 45 mins before closing. *Admission: inexpensive.* Tel: 01877 330342).

▶▶ The Caterthuns *131D3*

These 2,000-year-old ramparts are Scotland's prehistory at its best. To stand in the centre of a great ring of broken stone with only a curlew call for company is certainly atmospheric. It is well worth the effort of seeking out this breezy high place on the shoulders of the Grampians near Edzell in Angus, with superb views to the Lowlands. The builders of the White and Brown Catherthun hillforts must have been capable of organizing manpower in plenty to quarry and build such defences.

Callander's Rob Roy and the Trossachs Visitor Centre makes good use of a redundant church

▶▶ Crieff 130B2

A town at the edge of the Highlands, Crieff seems all hills. Until 1770 it was an important cattle market and the Crieff Visitor Centre expands on this theme. This attraction is down by the River Earn on the A822 and is also an on-site pottery. Opposite is **Stuart Crystal▶** with Stuart, Waterford, and Wedgwood wares (*Open* Jun–Sep, daily 10–6; Oct–May, Mon–Sat 10–5, Sun 11–5. *Admission free*. Tel: 01764 645004). Just down the road is the sunken Italian garden of **Drummond Castle▶**, with formal terracing ideal for strolls (*Open* gardens only Easter, May–Oct, 1–6, last entry 5. *Admission: moderate*. Tel: 01764 681433; www.drummondcastle gardens.com). North of the town the **Glenturret Distillery▶▶**, is home to the Famous Grouse Experience, offering enertainment aside from the process of distilling. (*Open* daily 9.30–4.30. *Admission: moderate*. Tel: 01764 656565; www.famousgrouse.com).

▶▶▶ Culross 130B1

Because of its very early involvement in coal mining and salt pans, Culross ought to have been just another nondescript industrial community on the banks of the Forth. Instead, after the town's early economic prosperity, the Industrial Revolution bypassed the town for a variety of economic reasons, and it was all but forgotten. Thus Culross enters the 21st century with many 17th- and 18th-century domestic buildings intact. The streetscapes have been preserved and the attractive dwellings, with their red pantiled roofs, restored. Cobbled streets and the old mercat cross give the place the air of a film set (which it is on occasion), but this is a lived-in community.

There are some interiors to see, notably the **Culross Palace** (really the town house) of Sir George Bruce, Culross's 16th-century entrepreneur (*Open* Palace, Town House and Study Easter–Sep, daily 12–5. *Admission: expensive*. Tel: 01383 880359; www.nts.org.uk).

EARLY INDUSTRY
Throughout the 17th century, Culross was the sole maker of baking girdles (griddles). It is said the local smiths invented them after King Robert the Bruce ordered them to provide iron plates so that his soldiers could cook their oatcakes.

The Palace, Culross

▶ Cupar 131C2

Cupar is a handsome enough, typical Lowland Scottish town in the centre of a rural and agricultural area, the Howe (hollow) of Fife. It once made money with its linen manufacture and still maintains its role as the administrative headquarters of the old county of Fife. A network of rural roads includes a fine ridge route to Falkland (see page 145). It is also worth visiting **Hill of Tarvit Mansionhouse▶▶**, an Edwardian mansion (*Open* house Easter–Sep, daily 1–5; gardens daily dawn–dusk. *Admission: expensive.* Tel: 01334 653127; www.nts.org.uk).

▶▶ Deep Sea World 131C1

Open: Mon–Fri 10–5, Sat–Sun 10–6; last entry 1 hour before closing. Admission: moderate (tel: 01383 411800; www.deepseaworld.com)

In this visitor centre in North Queensferry, a moving walkway carries you unnervingly along an underwater transparent viewing tunnel where sharks swim by. This is probably as close as you will ever get to knowing how a fish feels in an aquarium. There are also coral reef displays, rock pools to fumble in, and a variety of other marine exhibits.

The medieval castle of Doune dominates the local landscape

▶▶ Doune 130B1

Doune was once the Scottish centre for manufacturing pistols. Today this little place with winding streets is chiefly visited by those going to **Doune Castle▶▶▶**, the finest surviving medieval castle in Scotland (*Open* Apr–Sep, daily 9.30–6.30; Oct–Mar, daily 9.30–4. *Admission: inexpensive.* Tel: 01786 841742; www.historic-scotland.gov.uk). The 14th-century fortress is built to a simple plan: a formidable range of buildings surrounding an inner courtyard. Note the security features, such as a separate stairway for each main hallway and the duke's bedroom's emergency exit. As well as allowing the main quarters to be sealed off if intruders gained the courtyard, the design allows for some comfort: The guest bedrooms are built above the kitchen, with its 5.5m (18ft) wide fireplace.

DROVE ROADS
The Crieff tryst or cattle market was an important affair in the days when the Highland black cattle were walked from their pastures in various parts of Scotland to an annual autumn fair. Throughout the north there was a network of "drove roads" used by the cattle drovers. These old ways through the glens flowed together like tributaries and converged on major markets such as Crieff. The trade ended when railways arrived and could move stock more quickly.

HILL OF TARVIT HOUSE
This magnificent mansion was rebuilt in 1906 by Sir Robert Lorimer, the famous Scottish architect for the Dundee industrialist Mr. F. B. Sharp. The house was designed to provide a setting for his collections of fine furniture, paintings, porcelain, and bronzes. The gardens were also designed by Lorimer.

▶ Dumbarton *130A1*

There are two main reasons for visiting this shipbuilding town. The first of these, **Dumbarton Castle▶** (*Open* Apr–Sep, daily 9.30–6.30; Oct–Mar, daily 9.30–4.30. *Admission: inexpensive.* Tel: 01389 732167; www.historic-scotland.gov.uk), is built on Dumbarton Rock, a volcanic plug. Little remains from its early pre-Viking defensive days, but the fortress is associated with Mary, Queen of Scots. She was held there in safety before her departure for France at the age of five. The **Denny Ship Model Experiment Tank▶▶** was the world's first commercial experimental tank for shipbuilders' scale-models, built in 1882 by William Denny (*Open* Mon–Sat 10–4. *Admission: inexpensive.* Tel: 01389 763444; www.scottishmaritimemuseum.org/dumbart.htm).

AN ANCIENT WALK
The Darn Road is an ancient route (used by the Romans) which links Dunblane with Bridge of Allan for foot traffic. It makes a pleasant afternoon's walk. On the way, the path passes a cave overlooking the Allan Water, which is associated with Robert Louis Stevenson. He used to holiday nearby as a boy.

▶ Dunblane 130B1

The little city of Dunblane has winding streets and, thanks to a bypass, is a peaceful place, especially around the **Cathedral▶▶**. The seat of the Bishop of the Diocese of Dunblane since the 13th century, this is the usual Scottish mix of early architecture and more recent restoration work. It demands a slow walk to examine the 15th-century misericords, early effigies, and other points of interest (*Open* Apr–Sep, Mon–Sat 9.30–6.30; Oct–Mar, Mon–Sat 9.30–4.30, Sun 2–4.30 and for services. *Admission free.* Tel: 01786 823388; www.historic-scotland.gov.uk). **Doune Castle** (see page 139) is close by.

▶ Dundee *131C2*

Dundee sits on slopes facing south over the River Tay estuary. Scotland's fourth city promotes itself as the "City of Discovery" (a reference to RRS (Royal Research Ship) ***Discovery*▶▶**, berthed at the Discovery Point floating exhibition). The vessel was used by Captain Scott (of Antarctic fame) and built in Dundee in 1901 (*Open* Apr–Oct, Mon–Sat 10–6, Sun 11–6; Nov–Mar, Mon–Sat 10–5, Sun 11–5. *Admission: moderate.* Tel: 01382 201245; www.rrsdiscovery.com). The nearby frigate ***Unicorn*** is the oldest British warship afloat—built in England in 1824

Though now surrounded by the urban development of Dundee, Claypotts Castle is one of the most complete examples of a 16th-century Z-plan tower house

Scott of the Antarctic's ship Discovery

(*Open* Apr–Oct, daily 10–5; Nov–Mar, Wed–Fri 12–4, Sat, Sun 10–4. *Admission: inexpensive.* Tel: 01382 200900; www.frigateunicorn.org). The **McManus Galleries▶** is the city's main museum and art gallery (Closed for major refurbishment; check ahead. Tel: 01382 432084; www.mcmanus.co.uk). The **Verdant Works▶▶**, the European Industrial Museum of the Year, 1999, tells the story of jute in a former jute mill (*Open* Apr–Oct, Mon–Sat 10–6, Sun 11–6; Nov–Mar, Wed–Sat 10.30–4.30, Sun 11–4.30. *Admission: moderate*; joint ticket with Discovery Point. Tel: 01382 225282; www.verdantworks.com).

Dundee Contemporary Arts▶▶ is helping to change the city's old grimy, post-industrial image to something much more vibrant. The gallery includes a cinema, print studio, visual research centre, café, and shop (*Open* Tue–Sat 10.30–5.30, late opening Thu until 8.30pm, Sun 12–5.30. Café open daily 10.30–midnight. Tel: 01382 909900; www.dca.org.uk).

On the outskirts of the city, to the east, is **Broughty Castle Museum▶** (*Open* Apr–Sep, Mon–Sat 10–4, Sun 12.30–4; Oct–Mar, Tue–Sat 10–4, Sun 12.30–4). *Admission free*. Tel: 01382 436916; www.dundeecity.gov.uk) with tales about whales and local historical matters. Then there is the **Mills Observatory** (*Open* Oct–Mar, Mon–Fri 4pm–10pm, Sat–Sun 12–4; Apr–Sep, Tue–Fri 11–5, Sat–Sun 12.30–4. *Admission free*. Tel: 01382 435967; www.dundeecity.gov.uk), opened in 1935, a sweet factory in the style of the 1940s, also open to visitors, and country parks in the Angus hinterlands, while it is not far to the Angus glens.

THE DOGGEREL POET
William McGonagall, the Scottish doggerel poet (1830–1902), is strongly associated with Dundee. His uniformly bad verse soon met with acclaim, notably from the student and legal fraternity. His eulogies to the Tay Bridge and the stranding of the great Tay whale are just two occasions when his special talents (a complete disregard for metre in particular) were brought to bear.

Dunblane Cathedral, stained glass

Andrew Carnegie in Pittencrieff Park

INDUSTRIAL ESPIONAGE

Dunfermline was already engaged in spinning when, in the early 18th century, Huguenot master weavers set up in Edinburgh using a secret process to make patterns on plain linen cloth. The new damask was a huge success. Dunfermline weaver James Blake got himself a job cleaning the Huguenot looms, memorized the process, then built his own loom. Thus began Dunfermline's damask linen industry.

▶ Dunfermline *131C1*

"What Benares is to the Hindu, Mecca to the Mohammedan, Jerusalem to the Christian, all that Dunfermline is to me." Thus eulogized Dunfermline's most famous son, Andrew Carnegie. The Dunfermline of today is still full of Carnegie associations—it even has a Carnegie Hall—but this "auld grey toun" above the Forth goes much further back. It was the capital of Scotland in the time of the 11th-century King Malcolm Canmore (the Gaelic *ceann mohr* means great head or chief). This Celtic warlord married Margaret of the English royal house after she was shipwrecked nearby while fleeing the Norman Conquest in 1070. Margaret was later canonized and under her good influence, Dunfermline became the religious centre of Scotland.

Dunfermline Abbey▶ with its adjoining monastery and the royal palace still survive, though they have been rebuilt over the centuries. Today there is a strong sense of layers of history around the historic heart of the town, though sorting them out takes quite a long time. There are plenty of explanatory panels and models within the palace complex which help to clarify matters (*Open* Apr–Sep, daily 9.30–6.30; Oct–Mar, daily 9.30–4.30. *Admission: inexpensive.* Tel: 01383 739026; www.historic-scotland.gov.uk). The 12th-century work in the abbey church may be the finest surviving Scottish-Norman architecture in Scotland. Robert the Bruce is buried here: His name is written on great stone blocks on the church tower.

Andrew Carnegie Birthplace Museum▶▶ Dunfermline soon turned to commercial matters: brewing and weaving. Andrew Carnegie (1835–1919) was the son of a weaver who emigrated to the USA. In due course Carnegie's business acumen in the steel industry made him rich enough to give away $350 million. Exactly how is told in this museum. The adjacent Memorial Hall is filled with an extraordinary assemblage of Carnegie memorabilia, including numerous "freedom caskets"—the ornate boxes in which grateful communities gave him the metaphorical keys to their towns and cities (*Open* Apr–Oct, Mon–Sat 11–5, Sun 2–5. *Admission: inexpensive.*Tel: 01383 724302; www.carnegiebirthplace.com).

Dunkeld "Little Houses" (private)

Dunfermline's Carnegie Library was the first of nearly 3,000 worldwide. This and other amenities, including the local museum, the Music Institute, the Carnegie Centre (complete with ornate Turkish baths), and the substantial Pittencrieff Park all indicate the generosity of this extraordinary "local boy made good" who transformed his home town from a grey workaday place into a well-resourced community. Dunfermline may not be the most picturesque of Scotland's towns, but it has an interesting story to tell.

▶ Dunkeld *131C2*

A classic Highland-edge community, Dunkeld has benefited environmentally (if not commercially) from the A9 bypass. As well as some shopping and the picturesque 18th-century "Little Houses," it also has Thomas Telford's handsome bridge, opened in 1809. This was a toll bridge, and the imposition of the toll caused riots in 1868. Downstream by a footpath is the Birnam oak, last relic of Birnam Wood ("Macbeth shall never vanquished be

until/Great Birnam wood to high Dunsinane hill/Shall come against him," prophesy the witches in Shakespeare's *Macbeth*). Dunkeld also has a cathedral, founded in the 12th century and wrecked at the Reformation. Its choir has been restored as the parish church. Walk up the wooded valley of the River Braan (on the opposite side of the A9 to Dunkeld) to **the Hermitage▶▶**, the pleasure grounds of the Dukes of Atholl. On the way, what might be the tallest tree in Scotland can be seen, a 60m (200ft) or so high Douglas fir. It grows in a hollow by the river at the foot of a slope. The Hermitage is open at all times.

Loch of the Lowes▶▶ Accessible off a minor road on the A923 above Dunkeld, this Scottish Wildlife Trust reserve is a gem of Highland-edge scenery and has ospreys in summer. The visitor centre is open in summer only, but the observation hide is open all year.

Carnegie's initials on Pittencrieff Park gates, Dunfermline

LITERARY INSPIRATION
It was while holidaying in the Dunkeld area in 1893 and studying fungi that Beatrix Potter wrote an illustrated letter about a naughty and adventurous bunny to a young friend. The bunny became the famous Peter Rabbit, and an expert local amateur naturalist, Charles Mackintosh, the retired postman, is suspected of being the prototype for Mr. McGregor the gardener.

Dunkeld Cathedral and "Little Houses'"

THE HERMITAGE FOLLY
Also known as Ossian's Hall, this was built in 1758 by the 2nd Duke of Atholl's nephew. The curious belvedere overlooks the roaring waters of the River Braan. By 1783 it had acquired a set of mirrors within: A pulley slid back a partition (a painting of Ossian) to reveal them and give the illusion of water pouring in from all directions. This aristocratic toy was not to everyone's taste. It was vandalized in 1821 and again in 1869. The restored shell survives to this day.

▶▶▶ East Neuk of Fife 131D1

The chief attraction of the East Neuk of Fife, a land of well-manicured golf courses, lush hedgerows, and rich barley fields and woods all set by a glittering sea, is its little string of coastal communities. The area can easily be reached from Edinburgh, and it makes a very worthwhile day's excursion from St. Andrews (see page 154).

The eastern tip of Fife, Fife Ness, is not one of Scotland's most dramatic headlands, though birdwatchers enjoy it at migration time. However, nearby **Crail▶▶**, easternmost of the villages, is a pretty place with one of the most frequently photographed harbours in Scotland (wait for high tide). Old trading links with the Low Countries are echoed in the architecture, with crow-stepped gables and a Dutch town house whose bell, cast in 1520, has a Dutch inscription. There is a good local museum.

Maintaining the fishing fleet, Pittenweem

Moving west, next comes **Anstruther▶**, with its seafront shops selling colourful fishing nets and beach-balls as a reminder of the traditional holiday trade. The **Scottish Fisheries Museum▶▶▶** overlooks the harbour, with a comprehensive presentation on the development of fishing in Scotland, from open boats right through to the most awesome modern catching machines. There are plenty of ship models, as well as the real thing (historic vessels float in the harbour). Children will enjoy exploring the nooks and crannies of this labyrinthine complex of buildings. This museum gives a very strong sense of the endless struggle, frequent tragedy, and foundations of prosperity of many east-coast communities (*Open* Apr–Sep, Mon–Sat 10–5.30, Sun 11–5; Oct–Mar, Mon–Sat 10–4.30, Sun 12–4.30. *Admission: inexpensive*. Tel: 01333 310628; www.scotfishmuseum.org).

The East Neuk's heritage is firmly bound up with the sea

Pittenweem▶▶ offers plenty of challenge to the photographer torn between bright-hulled fishing boats and red-pantiled houses. Continuing west, St. Monan is another community tied to the sea—its kirk could not stand any closer to the waves.

Kellie Castle▶▶ (*Open* Easter, May–Sep, daily 1–5. Garden daily all year, 9.30–5.30 *Admission: expensive*. Tel: 01333 720271; www.nts.org.uk). A short way inland, this National Trust for Scotland property dates mainly from the 16th and 17th centuries and was restored in Victorian times. Its walled garden is a peaceful scented haven.

▶ Edzell 131D3

Edzell slumbers behind its ornate arch commemorating Queen Victoria's visit, and is one of those out-of-the-way places where little stirs along the wide main street. However, there are a number of points of interest nearby. **Fasque**

House▶, home of the family of the 19th-century prime minister W. E. Gladstone, is within easy reach, as are the **Caterthuns** (see page 137). **Edzell Castle▶▶** is also worth exploring. The early 16th-century red-stoned tower features an unusual pleasance or walled garden with unique heraldic and symbolic sculptures (*Open* Apr–Sep, daily 9.30–6.30; Oct–Mar, Sat–Wed 9.30–4.30. *Admission: moderate.* Tel: 01356 648631; www.historic-scotland-gov.uk).

▶▶ The Falkirk Wheel *130B1*

Open: Apr–Oct, daily 9–6; Nov–Mar, daily 10–5. Admission: free; boat ride expensive (tel: 08700 500208)

An engineering wonder, or a masterpiece of modern art? Decide for yourself as you watch the gigantic boat lift rotate silently, moving craft from one canal to another.

SCOTS NAMES

Howe in "Howe of Fife" means hollow. Neuk, as in East *Neuk*, is the Scots for corner (hence nook).

AN EDUCATIONAL VISIT

Visit the Scottish Fisheries Museum and learn the difference between fifies, zulus, and scaffies (they are all different kinds of early fishing craft).

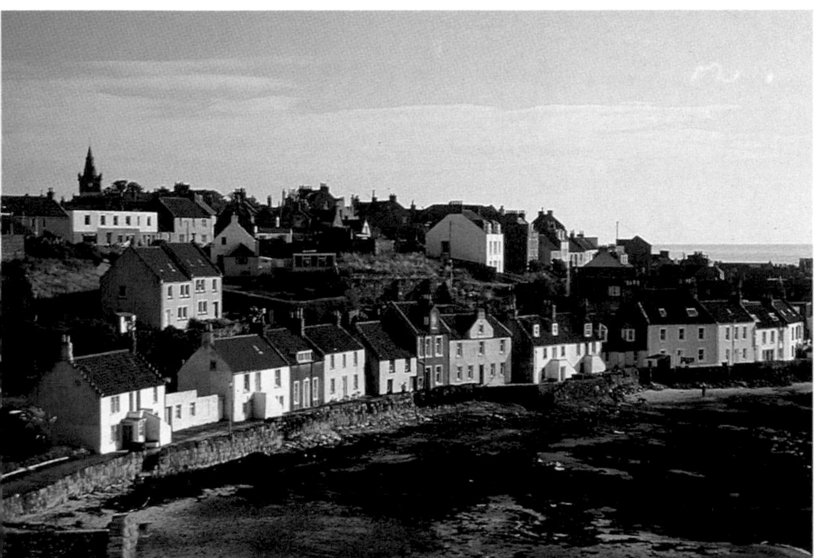

Pittenweem, one of the most picturesque of Fife's many coastal villages

▶▶ Falkland Palace *131C1*

Open: Mar–Oct, Mon –Sat 10–6, Sun 1–5.30. Admission: expensive (tel: 01337 857397; www.nts.org.uk)

The facade of this Renaissance-style former hunting lodge (1501–1541) dominates the village of Falkland, tucked below the Lomond Hills. Behind the castle are attractive gardens and a Real (royal) Tennis court dating from 1539.

▶▶ Fife Folk Museum *131C2*

Open: Easter and May–Sep, daily 11.30–4.30. Admission: inexpensive (tel: 01334 828180)

Set in Ceres, the very essence of a rural northeast Fife village, this collection of artefacts showing Fife's rural past is housed in a 17th-century weigh-house and adjoining former weavers' cottages. In the village look out for "The Provost," a curious "toby-jug" carving, set in a niche in a gable wall by the crossroads.

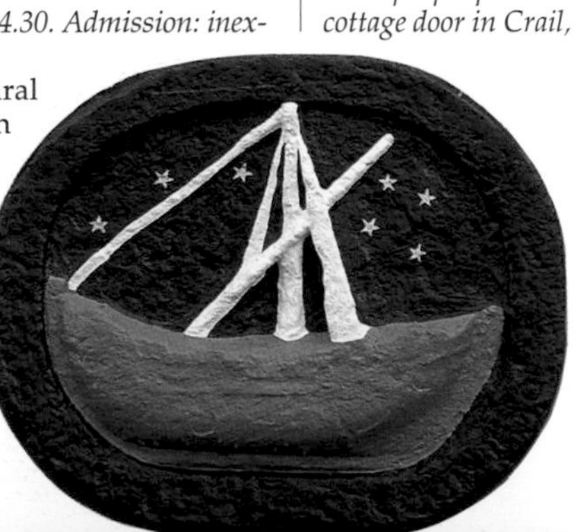

A simple plaque over a cottage door in Crail, Fife

CHILLING TALES
Glamis Castle has quite a collection of ghosts. Earl Beardie is supposed to have played cards with the devil and lost; the sad Grey Lady was seen in the vicinity of St. Michael's Chapel; a mysterious tall figure reputedly endlessly enters a locked door on the winding stair; and then there are also a black boy, a vampire legend, a mysterious grotesque monster hidden out of sight, and lots more...

THE FIRST STEAMSHIP
Henry Bell was Provost of Helensburgh in 1812. Owning a hotel there he decided to drum up trade and hit on the revolutionary idea of taking a boiler and engine and installing it in a wooden sea-going vessel in order to take potential customers from Glasgow to Helensburgh. He called his vessel the *Comet* and thus became the first to operate commercial steam navigation in Europe, 13 years before the opening of the first public steam railway.

The devil on this Helensburgh dormer stares directly at a church opposite

▶ Glamis Castle and Angus Folk Museum *131C2*

The present appearance of Glamis (pronounced "Glahms") dates from the 17th century, but the main tower is in part much older. It has fine collections of china, tapestry, painting, and furniture (*Open* mid-Mar–Dec, daily 10–6, last tour 4.30. *Admission: moderate*. Tel: 01307 840393; www.glamis-castle.co.uk). The other end of the social scale is represented at the **Angus Folk Museum▶**, a National Trust for Scotland property (*Open* Easter–Jun and Sep, Fri–Tue 12–5, Sun 1–5; Jul–Aug daily 11–5, Sun 1–5. *Admission: moderate*. Tel: 01307 840288; www.nts.org.uk). A row of 19th-century cottages have been knocked through to form a continuous passage with rooms, tableaux, and display cases covering everyday life in the rural Angus of old.

▶ Helensburgh *130A1*

Sir James Colquhoun, 8th Baronet of Colquhoun and Luss, had plans for the little *clachan* (the Gaelic for "village") near his castle, since it was the fashion of the Georgian age to improve. He bought the land and advertised for weavers but failed to attract any. Then he changed tactics, promoting the new town of Helensburgh (named after his wife) as a residential place. This plan worked, thanks in part to the later improved communications by rail and sea. Ever since, Helensburgh has retained its properous character, its wide streets and grand properties (built by well-to-do Glasgow commuters) earning it a reputation as a "museum of villas."

Hill House▶▶ Finest of all the villas is Charles Rennie Mackintosh's masterpiece, now in the care of the National Trust for Scotland. His design was so comprehensive that he even included details for light fittings, carpet patterns, and window snibs (Scots for "catches"). It was built in 1904 as the family home of the wealthy Glasgow publisher Walter Blackie (*Open* Easter–Oct, daily 1.30–5.30. *Admission: expensive*. Tel: 01436 673900; www.nts.org.uk).

▶ Hillfoots Towns *130B1*

The Hillfoots towns of Menstrie, Alva, Tillicoultry, and Dollar are strung out below the steep scarp face of the Ochil Hills east of Stirling. They formed the second largest textile manufacturing area in Scotland, using the burns running off the Ochils to power the mills, and the high green open pastures on the heights to raise the sheep whose wool was processed. Most (but not all) of the manufacturing has gone now, leaving impressive mill architecture at places such as Alva. The hill country above the towns is quite unspoilt and offers a good selection of walks into the Ochils, notably from the **Ochil Hills Woodland Park** between Alva and Tillicoultry.

Dollar▶▶ is the most attractive of the towns to the east, while Blairlogie, to the west, is a pleasant village. (The others are rather dour, their attraction lying in the countryside of the Ochils above them.) Behind Dollar, on a high shoulder above a darkly wooded

Castle Campbell above Dollar

BEN CLEUCH
The highest point in the Ochil Hills is Ben Cleuch (720m/2,363ft). If the clouds are high it offers superb views from the summit of the hills of the Central Highlands. But do not underestimate these exposed broad slopes, especially in winter: Use proper footwear and walking equipment. The Ben Cleuch path starts from Tillicoultry or Alva.

ADAM SMITH
The Adam Smith Centre, Kirkcaldy's civic centre and theatre (built in 1889 and refurbished in 1973), is named after Adam Smith, who was born in the town in 1723. A plaque near Kirk Wynd marks the site of the house where the economist wrote his influential treatise *An Inquiry into the Nature and Causes of the Wealth of Nations*.

glen, is **Castle Campbell▶▶▶** (*Open* Apr–Sep, daily 9.30–6.30; Oct–Mar, daily 9.30–4.30. *Admission: moderate*. Tel: 01259 742408; www.historic-scotland.gov.uk). This impressive stronghold is accessible by car or by a very picturesque walk, at one stage through a narrow gorge. The fortress was owned by the 1st Earl of Argyll, Chancellor of Scotland to King James IV, and comprises a basic 15th-century tower house with later additions, including a notable loggia—an arcade with arches. Rearing above the trees at the head of the valley, its setting is impressive and well worth a visit. It could be tied in with a trip to nearby Culross.

▶ Kirkcaldy *131C1*

Kirkcaldy may not be the most scenic of Scottish towns but it has good amenities, including a fine park and theatre. Visit its **Art Gallery and Museum** both for a fine collection of Scottish artists (notably Peploe) and its displays of local Wemyss ware pottery (*Open* Mon–Sat 10.30–5, Sun 2–5. *Admission free*. Tel: 01592 412860).

Ravenscraig Castle (*Open* all [reasonable] times. *Admission free*) is an austere, ruined fortress overlooking the Firth, founded by King James II in 1460 and later owned by the Sinclair Earls of Orkney. Also close at hand is picturesque **Dysart**, with attractively restored properties around a tiny harbour.

Characteristic Wemyss ware cats

One of Scotland's most famous stretches of inland water is the result of a glacier dumping its gouged-out gravels, thus creating a dam at the southern end of the deep trench it had dug. This took place 10,000 years ago, leaving Loch Lomond 8m (26ft) above sea level, in contrast to the long, narrow sea loch of Loch Long immediately to the west.

THE BANKS OF LOCH LOMOND

By yon bonnie banks and
by yon bonnie braes
Where the sun shines
bright on Loch Lomond
Where me and my true
love were ever wont to
gae
On the bonnie bonnie
banks o Loch Lomond.

Chorus

Ye'll tak the high road
and I'll tak the low road
And I'll be in Scotland
afore ye
But me and my true love
will never meet again
On the bonnie, bonnie
banks o Loch Lomond

MUSICAL CONNECTIONS

The song *The Banks of Loch Lomond* is thought to have been written by a condemned Jacobite prisoner while in jail in Carlisle, in England, after the 1745 rebellion. His lines about "yon bonnie banks" have gone round the world.

Accessibility Loch Lomond is Scotland's largest loch in surface area. Famed in song, it has exerted its pull on visitors since the late 18th century. The "bonnie banks" are indisputably bonnie—but probably no more so than those of many a Highland loch lying farther north. Loch Lomond's attraction really lies in its accessibility, a characteristic it shares with the Trossachs.

Its Lowland southern end is only about half an hour by road from Glasgow. This makes it commuter and also weekend-cottage country, as a stroll around neat little Drymen, with its exclusive shops, will confirm. The nearest point of the loch to Glasgow is at Balloch, at the head of the surprisingly industrialized Vale of Leven. Though Balloch is hardly picturesque, it is now the setting for the **Lomond Shores** complex. A great swathe of countryside hereabouts is now in the Loch Lomond and the Trossachs National Park. The new Lomond Shores is intended as an interpretative and leisure gateway. Funds were poured in to create a crescent-shaped waterside shopping experience, with the love-it-or-hate-it Drumkinnon Tower as a visitor facility. This was redesigned in 2005 as a sealife centre and aquarium (tel: 01389 721500).

Also on site, the Gateway Centre has information on the ecology and wildlife of this loved-to-near-destruction area. You can cruise the loch from here.

The eastern side Take the B837 no-through road up the eastern bank of the loch. **Balmaha**, with humpy Conic Hill behind it marking the geological line where the Highlands

begin, is the stepping-off point for boat excursions round Loch Lomond's islands. These come in various shapes and sizes, though **Inchcailloch** (Scottish Natural Heritage), with its ruined 13th-century chapel and fine woodlands, is particularly outstanding. Cruises land there from Balmaha.

Rowardennan is the end of the road for car explorers, though it is pleasant to continue eastwards on foot up the track which forms part of the **West Highland Way**. This officially signposted 157km (98mi) long-distance footpath from Milngavie, by Glasgow, to Fort William drops to the lochside at Balmaha for its journey northwards. The parking area at Rowardennan is a popular starting point for the climb up Ben Lomond, Scotland's most southerly (and probably most popular) "Munro" (see panel).

Car tourers can also sneak up on the loch via Aberfoyle to reach Inversnaid, where the road drops steeply out of the "hanging valley" of **Glen Arklet** and down to the water. This scantily populated place with its ferny banks and waterfalls is recalled in a poem by Gerard Manley Hopkins. The northern tip of Loch Lomond tails away in the marshy fields at the end of Glen Falloch.

The western side The main A82 road takes the west side of the loch, slicing away at the bonnie banks with road improvements in order to carry the tourists north at ever higher speeds. Thus many visitors miss tiny Inveruglas, from where a private road (walkers only) leads to **Loch Sloy**, the old homelands of the Clan MacFarlane, tucked behind the high hills known as the Arrochar Alps. Farther south is **Tarbet**, its name indicating a place of portage: The Vikings once carried their longships from the head of Loch Long and pillaged Loch Lomond's settlements. Also on the A82 is **Luss**, its pretty cottages part of the planned estate village originally built by the Colquhouns.

MUNROS

A Munro is a mountain in Scotland over 914m (3,000ft) high. Munro-bagging is a popular sport north of the border. The name recalls the first compiler of Scotland's heights, Sir Hugh Munro, who published a list of 277 peaks in 1891. The actual number of Munros in Scotland changes sometimes as surveys add or eliminate certain peaks. In addition, there can be problems of definition of what qualifies as a discrete mountain. For example, when does a subsidiary top of a Munro become a separate Munro? The current agreed figure is 284.

LUSS

The village name Luss is explained by a charming legend concerning the death of a local girl married to a high-ranking French officer during the 14th-century Anglo-French wars. She died in France but was buried by Loch Lomond. Fleurs-de-Lis (a species of iris and a heraldic device of the Bourbons) were scattered on her grave and, it is said, grew there ever afterwards. Though the story is romantic, it is equally likely that Luss is from the Gaelic word *lios*, meaning "garden."

THE STONE OF SCONE

The Stone of Scone, or Stone of Destiny, was the traditional coronation throne of the Scottish monarchs until it was stolen by King Edward I of England in 1297. Controversy still surrounds this stone. Some Scots believe it is a fake, and that the real Stone of Destiny was hidden before Edward's arrival and briefly found again in the early 19th century though it subsequently vanished. Whatever the truth, the Stone of Scone remains a powerful nationalist symbol in Scotland. It was returned to Scotland in November 1996, and can now be seen in Edinburgh Castle.

► Montrose *131D3*

A typical east-coast Lowland town, Montrose looks both to land and sea, with a maritime past, an involvement in North Sea oil, and one of Angus's main livestock markets. It is also something of a resort, with long beaches and a choice of old-established golf courses. Birdwatchers flock to the basin of the River Esk, which hems in the town to the west, as this Scottish Wildlife Trust reserve is an important and decidedly muddy habitat for waders and wildfowl.

Coastal scenery is impressive, with further natural history interest at **St. Cyrus** (Scottish Natural Heritage) to the north. A visitor centre here interprets the formerly important local activity of salmon netting, as well as the nearby bird and plant life. Close by to the south are the long sands of **Lunan Bay**, guarded by the ruined Red Castle above the dunes—an idyllic spot for beach strollers.

The House of Dun►►► (*Open* Easter–Jun, Sep, Wed–Sun 12.30–5.30; Jul–Aug, daily 11.30–5.30. *Admission: expensive*. Tel: 01674 810264; www.nts.org.uk). Close to the town, this National Trust for Scotland property was originally built in 1730 to a William Adam design, and has seen extensive restoration work, especially to its spectacular plasterwork. In courtyard buildings Angus Weavers produce real linen napery on traditional handlooms—a rare survivor of an industry once widespread in the area.

►► Perth *131C2*

Though built on a site still prone to flooding, Perth's strategic position as a major Lowland town with easy access to the Highlands has always given it an important role. It was the cradle of the Reformation in Scotland, after John Knox's preaching sparked off a riot in the town—and it also had bleaching and dyeing industries because of the softness and power of the River Tay's waters.

Rebuilding and renewal mean that very little is left of the ancient town. Instead, there is a grid of handsome

Scone Palace, one of the very grandest of Scotland's stately piles, is largely an early 19th-century design

Branklyn Garden, Perth

ROADS FROM PERTH
Perth offers the choice of the fast (possibly too fast) A9 heading for Speyside and Inverness, the slow A92 taking the high route over Glenshee for Royal Deeside, and the fast dual carriageway, the A90(M) via Dundee for Aberdeen. Beware if driving on the A92 in the skiing season. It leads to the ski developments at Glenshee, and the bends south of the Spittal of Glenshee are too often treated as a slalom course by car-borne skiing enthusiasts.

streets completed by the early 19th century. They obliterated much of the earlier medieval plan, but include neoclassical buildings such as Perth Academy (1807), the County Buildings (1815–1819; Perth is the county town), and the unique waterworks (1832), now a picture gallery. Meanwhile, amid these stately civic surroundings, Perth gets on with its role as a centre for a mainly rural, well-off hinterland. It has a wide range of specialist shops for antiques, crafts, jewellery, outdoor and sports equipment, a museum, an art gallery on George Street (*Open* Mon–Sat 10–5. *Admission free*. Tel: 01738 632488), and a thriving repertory theatre. The **Regimental Museum of the Black Watch** at Balhousie Castle on the North Inch tells the story of the regiment, founded in 1740 (*Open* May–Sep, Mon–Sat 10–4.30; Oct–Apr, Mon–Fri 10 3.30. *Admission free.* Tel: 0131 310 8530; www.armymuseums.org.uk).

On the edge of town, **Branklyn Garden▶▶▶** has outstanding late spring beauty from azaleas, blue poppies, and other horticultural treasures (*Open* Easter–Oct, daily 10–5. *Admission: moderate.* Tel: 01738 625535; www.nts.org.uk).

Off the Blairgowrie Road, **Scone Palace▶▶** is one of Scotland's grandest stately homes and still privately owned (*Open* Easter–Oct, daily 9.30–5.30, last entry 5. *Admission: moderate.* Tel: 01738 552300; www.scone-palace.co.uk). Scone (pronounced "skoon") was the traditional crowning place of Scottish monarchs. The site was actually the Moot Hill, within the palace grounds. Scone Palace as seen today dates mainly from the early years of the 19th century. It houses magnificent ivories, porcelain, furniture, 18th-century clocks and 16th-century needlework. There are also fine gardens.

Shopping for antiques, Perth

Clan skirmish re-enactment by Loch Achray, Trossachs

THE SOLDIER'S LEAP
The Battle of Killiecrankie in 1689 was the first attempt by the Jacobites to restore the exiled King James VII. They won after the government forces were unable to resist the wild charge of the Highland clans. However, in his victory, the Jacobite leader, John Graham of Claverhouse, Viscount Dundee, was killed by a stray bullet. Without "Bonnie Dundee's" charismatic leadership, the rebellion fizzled out. Also in this battle, a certain Donald MacBean, a government soldier, leapt 6m (20ft) across the River Garry to avoid being impaled on a Highland claymore. The spot is known as the Soldier's Leap.

►► Pitlochry *130B3*

Pitlochry claims to be the geographical middle point of Scotland. Its situation amongst the Perthshire hills was noted by Queen Victoria's personal physician when she stayed along the road at Blair Castle. His recommendations on the wholesome air led to many of the well-to-do building large mansions in this previously quiet weaving village. The Perth to Inverness railway's arrival in 1863 accelerated the growth of the fledgling resort. Hotels were built, including the Pitlochry Hydropathic, and Pitlochry developed a popularity it has retained ever since. Statistics suggest that the population of 2,500 offers 6,700 beds and plays host to nearly a million visitors a year.

Not as dull as it sounds, the **Scotish Hydro Electric Visitor Centre** (*Open* Apr–Oct, Mon–Fri 10–5.30; also Sat–Sun, Jul–Aug. *Admission: inexpensive*. Tel: 01796 473152) overlooking Loch Faskally, only moments from the main street, has a fish ladder—a stepped series of pools enabling fish to get upriver—and an explanation of the complex Tummel Valley hydroelectric scheme. You can see the fish jumping or swimming past the viewing chamber—if you are lucky. Another feature of the town is the Pitlochry Festival Theatre which shows easily digestible productions right through the main season.

Killiecrankie►►► is a dramatic battle site set amid a very scenic river gorge with woodlands and steep rocks. The National Trust for Scotland visitor centre tells the story of both the battle and the gorge itself, where there are superb walks among the tall pines and larches planted by the Dukes of Atholl. Combine a trip here with the Queen's View of Loch Tummel (*Open* site all year; visitor centre Easter–Oct, daily 10–5.30. *Admission free*. Tel: 01796 473233; www.nts.org.uk).

►► Queen Elizabeth Forest Park *130A1*

The poorly-drained, infertile uplands of Scotland have defeated many a landowner. After World War I, many of these unprofitable areas, for example around the Trossachs and Loch Lomond, were bought by the state for forestry. In 1953, approximately 170sq-km (65sq-mi) owned by the Forestry Commission in some of the most attractive landscapes of the Central Highlands became the Queen Elizabeth Forest Park. At least 100km (60mi) of forest roads are open to foot traffic. The starting point is The David Marshall Lodge Visitor Centre (*Open* Mar–Oct, daily 10–6; winter hours vary; check ahead. *Admission free; parking charge inexpensive.* Tel: 01877 382258; www.forestry.gov.uk) above Aberfoyle, with its magnificent views back to the Lowlands. As well as waymarked trails for walkers, right across the area, there is a forest drive by Loch Achray for those who cannot bear to leave their cars, as well as dedicated cycling routes. The amenity value of the forests around Loch Lomond and the Trossachs is heavily emphasized, and even though this is Scotland's best-known tourist area, it is perfectly possible to escape from people.

►►► Rumbling Bridge *131C1*

The area known as Rumbling Bridge is a geological curiosity. The phenomenon which brought generations of tourists was the sinister rumbling of boulders grinding in a deep pot called "the Devil's Mill," in a gorge which the River Devon has cut into the soft rock of the Lowland edge. The place even had its own train station, though the railway has long vanished, and excursionists would picnic by the steep and ferny banks and wander the narrow footpaths and viewing points. They also admired the quaint little bridge of 1713 which spans the gorge and is spanned in turn by a later, higher bridge of 1816, which carries today's A823. Today, there are fewer visitors as the Rumbling Bridge gorge lies in a kind of tourist no-man's land, bypassed by those rushing up the M90 or M9.

Loch Faskally, near Pitlochry, is part of the complex of lochs used for the generation of hydroelectric power

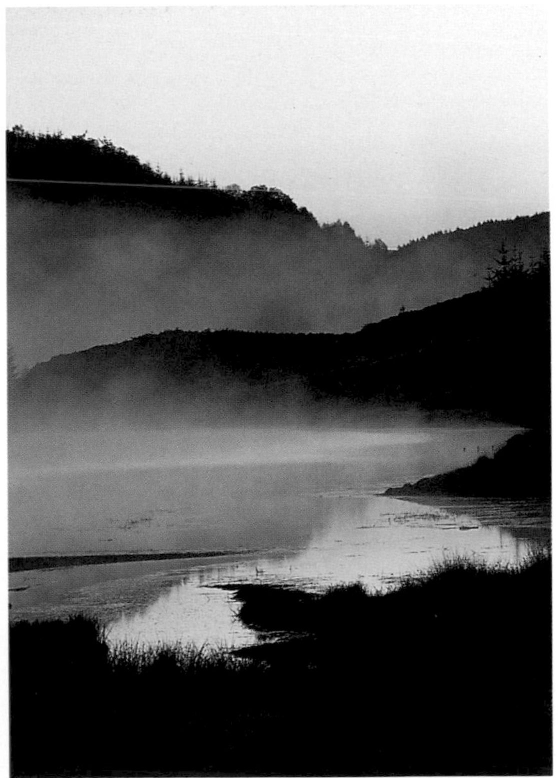

Loch Venachar is the most easterly of the Trossachs lochs, and supplies "compensation water" to the River Forth, replacing the water taken from Loch Katrine to quench Glasgow's thirst

TREE TYPES
The dominant tree species in the Queen Elizabeth Forest Park, in common with most other commercial forests in Scotland, are the alien sitka and Norway spruce, with some Scots and lodgepole pines in the drier areas. There are also some oak and beech plantings, supplementing the semi-natural oakwoods (whose bark was once harvested for tannin) as well as birch scrub—a reminder of the natural regeneration which would take place if there were fewer sheep and deer.

Not only is St. Andrews famed as the home of golf and of Scotland's oldest university, but it is also a decidedly handsome east-coast town. This is the view from the top of St. Rule's Tower, near the ruined cathedral

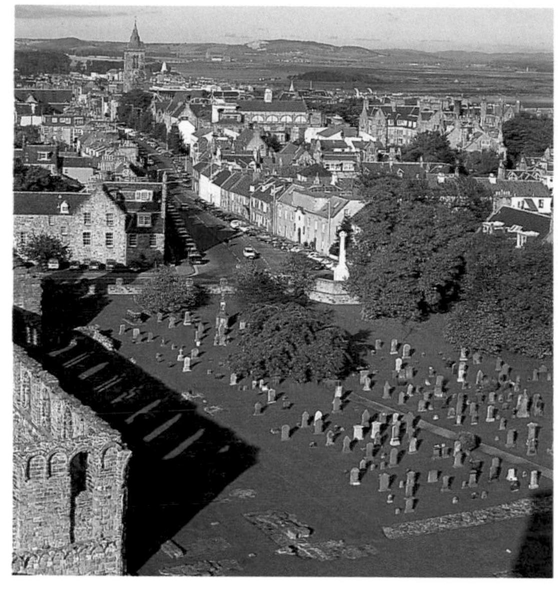

SCOTLAND'S LARGEST CHURCH
Some say that the design of St. Andrews Cathedral was in advance of the building technology of its age. It was by far the largest church in Scotland and one of the longest ever built anywhere in the UK, with a length of about 110m (350ft).

A BEACH WALK
For a change from the town, take a stroll along the beach at Tentsmuir, north of Leuchars near St. Andrews, where the pinewood-backed sandy beach goes on forever. En route, admire the fine Norman architecture of the parish church at Leuchars. Craigtoun Country Park, also near the town, is great for children.

▶▶▶ St. Andrews *131D2*

St. Andrews is unique: an ancient ecclesiastical capital, the oldest Scottish university town, and a world golfing Mecca. According to legend, a Greek monk, Regulus (or Rule), carrying relics of St. Andrew, one of Christ's disciples, was shipwrecked here and founded a church. Thereafter the cult of St. Andrew was focused on this part of Fife. The monk's name survives as St. Rule's Church (or tower) still standing near the ruined cathedral and probably from the early 12th century. Its topmost point makes a good place to view the town's medieval street plan.

Founded in 1160, **St. Andrews Cathedral▶** is now a mere ruined fragment of what must once have been awesome architecture (*Open* Apr–Sep, daily 9.30–6.30; Oct–Mar, daily 9.30–4.30. *Admission: inexpensive*. Tel: 01334 472563; www.historic-scotland.gov.uk—joint ticket for castle and cathedral available). It was damaged by natural disasters and then laid low by the Reformers, its stonework ultimately pillaged for use elsewhere in the town. The cathedral ruins are open any time, the on-site museum daily.

Teetering on the sea's brink, **St. Andrews Castle▶▶** tells a tale of drama and religious conflict, and has an impressive bottle dungeon. A claustrophobic underground experience can be had following the route of sappers as they countermined during an attempt to tunnel under the castle during a 16th-century siege. The tunnel is electrically lit now (*Open* Apr–Sep, daily 9.30–6.30; Oct–Mar, daily 9.30–4.30. *Admission: moderate*. Tel: 01334 477196; www.historic-scotland.gov.uk).

You can visit other local museums and the **St. Andrews Aquarium** (*Open* May–Nov, daily 10–6; Dec–Apr, 10–5. *Admission: moderate*. Tel: 01334 474 786; www.standrewsaquarium.co.uk), a golfing museum, excellent long beaches, and stroll round the college precincts of Scotland's oldest university.

Scotland is often called "the home of golf" and, brushing aside any suggestion that the game probably originated in the Low Countries, claims it for her own. Certainly, Scotland has a number of very old-established courses, often lying close to town centres, where, had it not been for the early rights of golfers, the land would have been swallowed up by developments long ago. Nowhere is this better seen than in St. Andrews.

Seaside pastime It is quite possible that golf came over when the medieval trading links with the Low Countries were strong. By the time of the early Stuart monarchs, a game with sticks and balls was taking up the time of both king and commoner alike. In 1457, King James II decreed that soldiers should not play golf. In 1503, King James IV treated himself to a new set of clubs.

St. Andrews, the Old Course

Some say the sport originated with a piece of driftwood, a sea-washed pebble and a rabbit-burrow—all three are found on the Fife coast among the turf, links, and dunes. In the days before mowing machines were invented, golf had to be played where grass was naturally short. Usually only on seaside links did the exposure, poor soil, and nibbling rabbits all combine to keep the turf close-cropped. Bunkers developed from natural hollows into which a golf ball would frequently roll. Wind erosion on the thin grassy skin already damaged by players' efforts to hit out would soon create a sandy hazard.

The Old Course All this substantiates St. Andrews Old Course's claims to 15th-century origins. The Old Course is still the ultimate dream of many, which may explain why, for instance, Japanese visitors have acquired a reputation for slow play over it—they want to savour every moment. It represents traditional design at its very best. However, remember that there are other courses, both adjacent to the Old Course and right along the Fife coast.

A GOLFING HAZARD

One of the former hazards of the Old Course was the goods shed of the nearby railway yard on the Fife coastline from Leuchars. This demanded a high approach shot on the 17th to clear the roof. Though the railway has gone in one of the more short-sighted closures of the 1960s, the outline of the old shed has been preserved as the golf school of the nearby luxury hotel which now occupies the site of the former sidings. Meanwhile, a campaign continues to re-open the line.

A JACOBITE BATTLE
The Battle of Sheriffmuir, on the open slopes of the Ochil Hills above Stirling, was fought in 1715 between the rebellious Jacobite forces under the Earl of Mar and the government army under the Duke of Argyll. Unusually, it ended in a draw, with each of the opposing wings pushing back the other, but neither side gaining overwhelming advantage. Argyll took his forces off to Dunblane, while Mar's men withdrew to Perth. As it was November, many of the Highland rebels wanted to go back home for the winter, and the rebellion fizzled out.

►►► Stirling 130B1

Whoever controlled Stirling controlled the Scotland of old. It was the lowest bridging point of the River Forth running east, with marshes to the west, the Campsie Hills to the south, and the Ochil Hills (and the Highlands) northwards. Stirling Castle preserves its impregnable air, rising out of the former marshlands. Downhill from the castle, the Old Town has the air of an old-established Scottish burgh, with its mercat cross, tollbooth, and Church of the Holy Rude (ca1456) as the ancient symbols of commerce, the law, and the church. Farther down, Victorian developments begin with handsome shopping streets and a railway station, and spread into the suburbs.

Stirling Castle►►► (*Open* Apr–Sep, daily 9.30–6; Oct–Mar, daily 9.30–5. *Admission: expensive*. Tel: 01786 450000; www.historic-scotland.gov.uk). Most visitors to Stirling get at least as far as the Esplanade with its breathtaking panorama, but it is well worth penetrating the castle complex itself. This former royal court with its fine Renaissance work was sadly misused after Scotland's James VI deserted it to become King of England as well. Much has been restored, including the Renaissance palace of James V and the Chapel Royal of 1594.

The National Trust for Scotland tells the story of one of Scotland's very few victories against the English at the **Bannockburn Visitor Centre►**, 4km (2.5mi) southeast of

Walk

Old Stirling

See map opposite.

Fragments of an old Scottish townscape survive in this walk through the heart of Stirling below the castle. Allow 2 hours.

Follow the rough-hewn old town wall opposite the tourist information centre up past the old school, now a hotel, to the historic buildings of St. John Street. These include the Erskine Marykirk, a grand classical church, now fronting a modern youth hostel; and the old **Detention Barracks** (1847), now the Old Town Jail museum.

The **Church of the Holy Rude** lies beyond, with Cowane's Hospital (the Guildhall, a summer ceilidh venue) nearby. A gate leads to the cemetery, with a fine view of the castle from the Ladies Rock. Steps and a gate lead to the Esplanade, next to the castle. The views here include the Arrochar Alps to the west, Ben Chonzie northwards, and the Pentland Hills behind Edinburgh.

After visiting the castle, go downhill past **Argyll's Lodging**, Scotland's finest surviving Renaissance mansion (*Open* Apr–Sep, daily 9.30–6; Oct–Mar 9.30–5. *Admission: moderate*; joint ticket with Stirling Castle available. Tel: 01786 431319; www.historic-scotland.gov.uk), and pass the facade of **Mar's Wark**, all that remains of a Renaissance palace damaged during the '45 rebellion. Broad Street, complete with cannon and tall tenements, gives way to Victorian developments and shops.

King Robert I on Stirling Castle Esplanade

Stirling (*Open* Apr–Oct, daily 10–5.30; Feb, Mar, Nov, Dec, daily 10.30–4. *Admission: moderate*. Tel: 01786 812664; www.nts.org.uk).

The National Wallace Monument▶▶ recalls Scotland's first freedom fighter (William Wallace), and has an audio-visual presentation as well as Wallace's broadsword and views from the top of the tower (*Open* Jun daily 10–6; Jul–Aug, 9.30–6; Sep 9.30–5; Mar–May, Oct 10–5; Nov–Feb 10.30–4. *Admission: moderate*. Tel: 01786 472140).

In the summer, costume dramas are set in the castle and atmospheric streets. Visitors can also see exhibitions at the Smith Art Gallery and shows at the MacRobert Arts Centre.

The view from the ramparts of Stirling Castle towards the Church of the Holy Rude

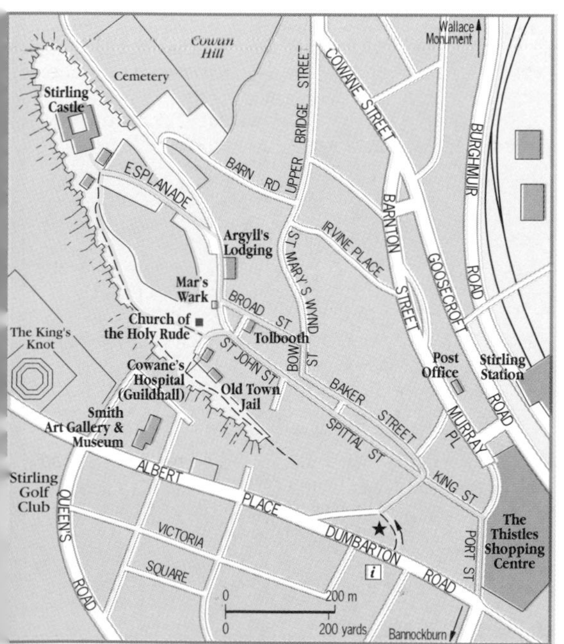

THE REASONS FOR BANNOCKBURN

The Battle of Bannockburn was not what King Robert I (the Bruce) wanted. He was forced into this pitched battle with the might of the English knights after his brother, Edward, besieging Stirling Castle, accepted an offer from its English governor that "if by midsummer a year thence he was not rescued by battle, he would yield the castle freely." This committed King Edward II of England to rescue his governor and fight the Scottish forces in a pitched battle.

Drive

Perthshire's glens

A drive round some typical Highland glens with ribbon-lochs and characteristic glaciated U-shaped profiles. This is a good autumn drive, when the roads are quiet and the colours spectacular. The trip totals 184km (114mi) via Glen Lyon but not including the Loch Tummel extension. Allow one long day, or alternatively stop overnight in the Kenmore area.

Take the A85 west from Perth, noting 15th-century Huntingtower on the outskirts of the town. On this section, south of the Highland Boundary Fault, the green landscape of well-worked farmland and woods rolls out across the shallow bowl of Strathearn, the

The Queen's View, Loch Tummel

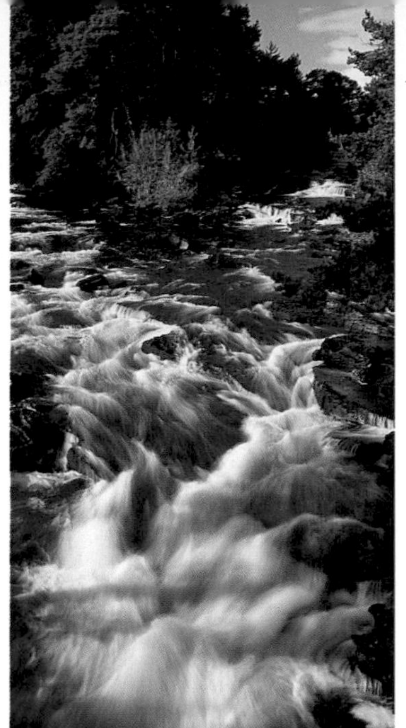

Falls of Dochart, Killin

valley of the River Earn, reaching as far south as the Ochil Hills.

Continue through **Crieff**, keeping on the A85. The town has plenty of shops and a cluster of visitor attractions on the edge of town (see page 138).

Because of its position on the Highland Boundary Fault, the village of **Comrie**, farther along the A85, is known as the earthquake centre of Scotland. **Earthquake House**, built as a recording station in 1874, lies just west of the town (*Open* Apr–Oct, view from outside only). The hills close in towards St. Fillans, on the eastern end of **Loch Earn**, a popular loch for water sports. There is a major water sports centre at Lochearnhead. Note, en route, the fine views south to the bulk of Ben Vorlich.

At Lochearnhead, turn north up **Glen Ogle**. This grand glen, according to Queen Victoria's diaries, reminded her of a print of the Khyber Pass. The old railway (closed 1965) with its decaying viaduct is now a walkway, though not totally peaceful because of the roar of peak-season traffic. Try the layby at the head of the pass for views of the **Meall nan Tarmachan** and **Ben Lawers** ranges.

After turning right at Lix Toll, on reaching Killin, watch out for pedestrians peering into cameras on the narrow bridge over the **Falls of Dochart**. There are friendly little shops in this attractive community, which has an alpine flavour when there is snow on the slopes above.

Continue eastwards, then take the unclassified road north towards Glen Lyon, unless it has recently snowed on the tops—this road traverses high ground. The National Trust for Scotland's visitor centre blights the bright green flanks of **Ben Lawers**. The Trust is a conservation body, but ironically Ben Lawers' mountain flora is threatened by too many visitors, so pass on into Glen Lyon.

Turn east down this typical Highland glen, with a "big hoose" behind its wall, warning notices to keep off the hills during stalking, forestry on the slopes, farming on the river flats, and a hydroelectric scheme at the head of the glen. Note the **Fortingall Yew** where Glen Lyon opens out. This is reputed to be more than 3,000 years old, possibly the oldest tree in Europe. The Fortingall Yew is said to be the birthplace of Pontius Pilate, whose father is supposed to have been a legionnaire stationed in Scotland. Victorian guidebook writers were notoriously imaginative.

Low-lying cloud shrouding Schiehallion and Loch Rannoch

Continue by going north to **Loch Tummel** and then circling back by way of Pitlochry, or for a more direct route rejoin the A9 east of Aberfeldy to return to Perth.

H. V. Morton in In Search of Scotland *sums up the Trossachs. He complains how a traveller can wander for months looking for essential Scotland "enduring heat, cold, fatigue, high teas, Sabbaths, kirks, and at the end comes suddenly on the whole thing in concentrated form, boiled down to the very essence..." Even more exasperating, as he points out, the place is conveniently near Edinburgh and Glasgow.*

WORDSWORTH IN THE TROSSACHS
Among the many poems inspired by his Trossachs visits, Wordsworth composed *Stepping Westward* after exploring Loch Katrine. *The Solitary Reaper* with its lines "Breaking the silence of the seas/Among the farthest Hebrides" owes its origins not to some west coast lass, but to a fieldworker the poet heard singing as she worked near Balquhidder.

Definitions The Trossachs phenomenon is a curious one. For a start, nobody can quite agree on where it is. Its heart is certainly the narrow pass that leads from Loch Achray through to the huge parking area at the east end of **Loch Katrine**. Usually it goes over the hills and knolls southward to take in **Aberfoyle** and **Loch Ard. Ben Ledi** is a part of it to the east. Sometimes it is taken to mean all of this area as far as the **Braes of Balquhidder** and the banks of **Loch Lomond** at Inversnaid.

Then nobody can agree on what the word Trossachs means. Generations of writers have accepted an early explanation that it means "the bristly country" in Gaelic—yet no Gaelic word in current use supports this. The standard work for Victorian travellers, *Murray's Handbook* of 1894, dismisses it as the rugged country. Possibly it derives from an obsolete Gaelic word *trasdaichean* meaning a transverse glen joining two others.

Popularity in the Romantic age Wherever it is and whatever it means, it was firmly on the tourist trail before the end of the 18th century, thanks to the

SS Sir Walter Scott, *steam power on popular and beautiful Loch Katrine (pronounced "Kattren")*

Romantic movement with its cult of the picturesque. A Callander minister, writing in the *Old Statistical Account* for 1794, states that "The Trossachs are often visited by persons of taste, who are desirous of seeing nature in her rudest and unpolished state." Before then, shaggy landscapes were considered uncouth and vulgar, without order or harmony—as well as being downright dangerous and probably filled with savages as well.

The Romantic poets came to admire the wooded peaks mirrored in shimmering lochs. William and Dorothy Wordsworth, accompanied by Samuel Taylor Coleridge, passed through in 1803. Though the scenery hardly needed the extra attention, Sir Walter Scott took the landscapes around Ben Ledi and Loch Katrine (as well as Stirling Castle) in *The Lady of the Lake* (1810) and peopled them with heroes, knights, hermits, and fair ladies. This dramatic verse narrative was an overnight sensation and helped propel the Trossachs towards becoming the very byword for Scottish scenery. New inns were built and roads opened up. At the eastern gateway, Callander's shopkeepers prospered.

Modern visitors The Trossachs are just as popular today, and are part of the Loch Lomond and the Trossachs National Park. The **Rob Roy and the Trossachs Visitor Centre** in Callander (see page 137) tells the Trossachs story through the eyes of the local hero and popular rogue Rob Roy Macgregor, who knew these landscapes well. (His clan found them convenient for hiding cattle stolen from Lowland farms.)

At Aberfoyle, the **Scottish Wool Centre** offers a worthwhile variation on the Scottish combination of large gift shop with attractions attached. The Story of Scottish Wool from prehistoric times to the present is told by way of a presentation in a 150-seat arena and in summer there are live demonstrations of shearing and working sheepdogs, as well as a chance to meet baby goats and lambs (*Open* Oct–Feb daily 10–4.30 Mar–Jul, daily 9.30–5; Aug, daily 9.30–5.30. *Admission: free, show inexpensive*, last show 3PM. Tel: 01877 382850). These modern developments add a wet-weather dimension to the attractions of the area. However, the best way to understand the place is to walk—up **Ben A'an** overlooking Loch Achray; round the head of Loch Katrine in Glen Gyle to discover the old Macgregor graveyard; up Ben Ledi in the heart of the Trossachs.

HILLTOP RITUALS

Ben Ledi, tallest of the Trossachs hills, is associated with Beltane rites, ancient fire ceremonies on hilltops formerly practised by the Celts. The coming of their summer was 1 May. A folk memory of this lingers on but has attached itself to Midsummer Eve instead, when the uphill path to this 879m (2,883ft) high hill can be quite busy as people gather to watch the sunset at its most northerly point.

The ferryman who takes visitors to the atmospheric Inchmahome Priory, on an island in the Lake of Menteith, near Callander

Far right: Macduff harbour
Right: whisky is exported from Scotland across the world—this bottle ended up in Australia

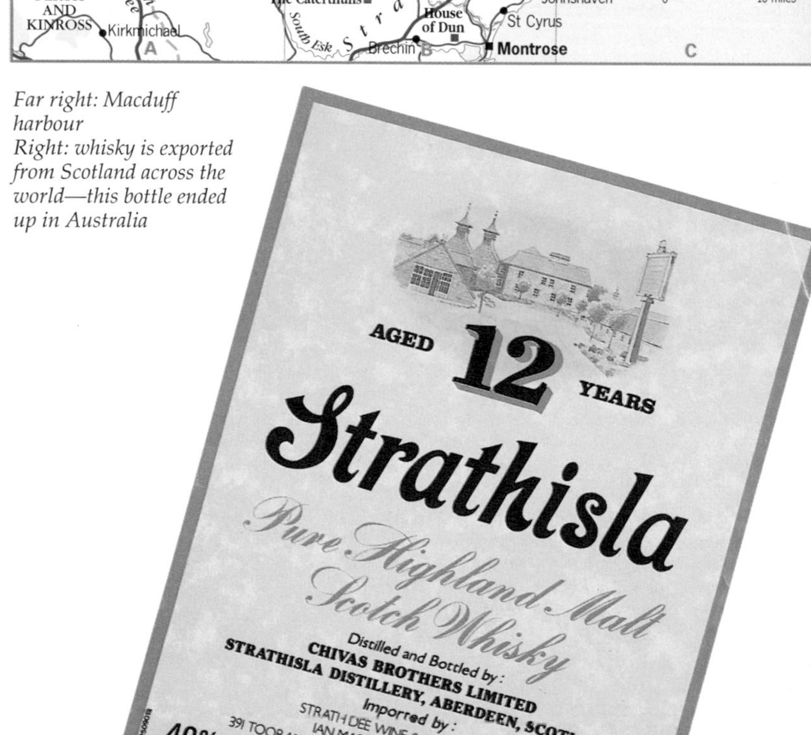

The Northeast

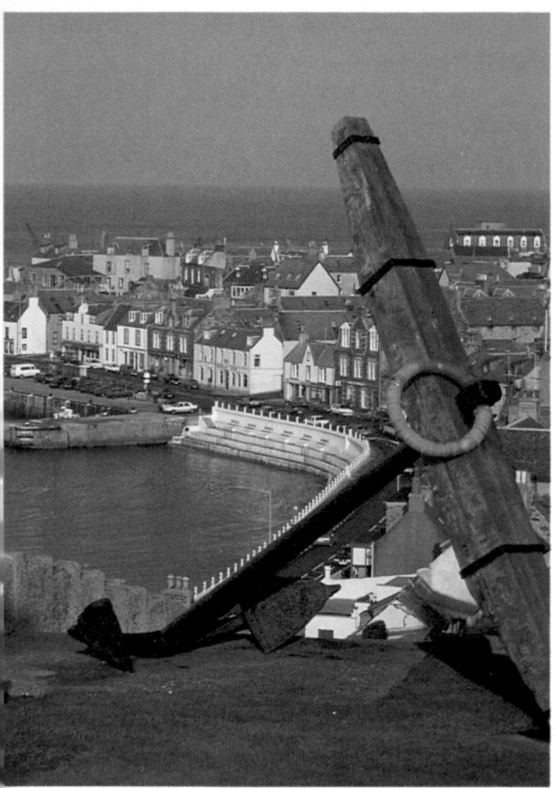

BEYOND THE GRAMPIAN HILLS The northeast region, strictly speaking, lies north of the Highland Line, the geological fault which runs from Helensburgh in the west to Stonehaven in the east. Yet the northeast has good Lowland farmlands and the densest forms of the Lowland Scots tongue. It used to be described as "the Grampian cocoon"—the land beyond the Grampian Hills, isolated from developments in Central Scotland. This may explain the survival in some vigour of its old tongue, as well as a kind of independent spirit and attitude among many of the locals. But modern communications, as well as new settlers and the impact of North Sea oil, have made their mark in this essentially rural area.

The northeast is different: not like the empty, wet, and rugged deserts of the Highlands with their original inhabitants in exile; nor even like the brisk and busy central corridor of Scotland, which spawned the industrial revolution. It is a community tied together by the twin bonds of its sea-going and its farming heritage. Its main centre, Aberdeen, the third largest city in Scotland, sometimes seems to operate like a very large market town, in spite of all the peripheral industrial estates which grew up in the wake of the oil finds in the shallow seas to the east and north.

Geographically, the northeast can be interpreted as a series of shelves, running down from the frost-shattered granite heights of the Cairngorms to the gently rolling, well-farmed Lowlands. These descending steps end

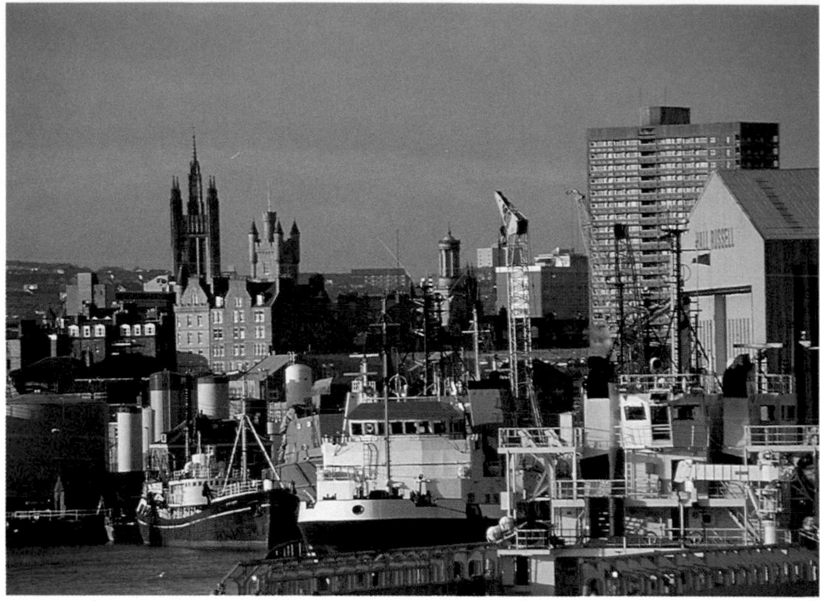

Oil supply vessels in Aberdeen harbour

spectacularly in a coastline whose beauty is hardly matched in the United Kingdom—preserved partly by remoteness, partly by the unglamorous workaday fields behind it, and also because it is usually very chilly.

CASTLES The "cocoon" effect means that many great castles have survived, away from the destructive mainstream of Scotland warfare and safely tucked out of sight behind their stone walls and woodland "policies" (grounds). Some still control farms and grand estates, others are now in the care of bodies such as the National Trust for Scotland and are open to the public. If you travel in the northeast, there seem to be signposts with castle logos at every turning.

DISTINCT AREAS The northeast splits into a number of areas. There is the city of Aberdeen itself, with its wide commuter belt, taking in places from Ellon in the north, Inverurie, Alford, Banchory, and other little country towns that expanded in the oil boom. North from this area to Kinnaird Head, the northeast tip, is Buchan, built on fishing and farming, with granite towns and villages tucked into the folds of open farmland. The old county of Banff, at least in its lowland stretches, is transitional, softening the bleak edges of Buchan and merging in turn with the softer airs of Moray, in the rain shadow of the high hills in the inner Moray Firth.

Running west of Aberdeen is the valley of the River Dee, given royal approval by Queen Victoria and still, at least in part, a playground for the wealthy, not just aristocrats on hillground and forested estates, but also the occasional foreign millionaire. Deeside eventually runs into the great whalebacks of the Cairngorms, whose northwestern slopes face Speyside and the upper reaches of Moray. North and northeast of the Cairngorm plateau are the

▶▶▶ REGION HIGHLIGHTS

Aberdeen *pages 166–168*

Ballater *page 170*

Braemar *page 170*

Crathes Castle *page 174*

Dunnottar Castle *page 183*

Fyvie Castle *page 177*

Glen Shee *page 178*

Glenfiddich Distillery Visitor Centre (Dufftown) *page 174*

Haddo House *pages 178–179*

Leith Hall *page 182*

Macduff Marine Aquarium *page 182*

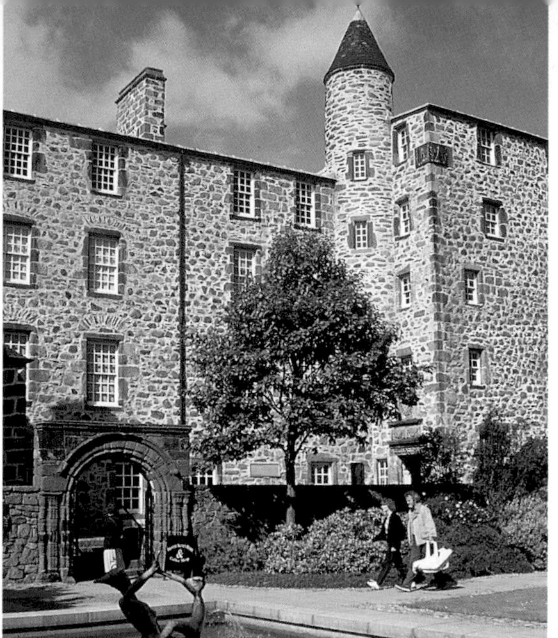

lonely glens of former upper Banffshire, once hazy with the smoke from illicit stills.

WHISKY Today the whisky industry, which is focused on the River Spey, is big business. Grand malt whisky names such as Macallan, the Glenlivet, Glenfiddich, and Glenfarclas stretch all the way to the sea, sounding every bit as distinguished as the famous wines noted as place names in France's Rhône valley.

THE TURRA COO

One tale of northeast thrawnness (stubbornness) is that of the (locally) famous Turra Coo. Turra is Turriff, a small market town, and a coo is a cow. In 1912 a local farmer refused to cooperate with the new National Insurance Act. He was fined but refused to pay. The Sheriff Officer poinded (seized) a cow. After a failed attempt to auction it in Turriff—before a crowd of 1,500 intent on merriment—it was sold in Aberdeen, but bought by sympathizers. The coo was taken back home to its first owner, watched by another large crowd and the local brass band. This spawned a minor industry in Turra Coo commemorative post-cards, pottery, glassware, etc. A memorial was erected in 1971.

Provost Skene's House, Aberdeen

King's College, Old Aberdeen

THE NORTHERN LIGHTS
The Northern Lights of Old Aberdeen is a Scottish anthem sung worldwide by Aberdonians. However, the Northern Lights are certainly not confined to the city. The *aurora borealis*—their proper name—is a not uncommon phenomenon in the north of Scotland, illuminating the sky with (usually) greenish waving curtains and beams of light at any time of year when there is sufficient darkness to view it.

►►► Aberdeen *162C2*

With a population of over 200,000, the glittering granite and spacious streets of the United Kingdom's second most northerly city (since Inverness gained city status in 2000) make an impact on first-time visitors. Built between the river mouths of the Dee and the Don, this old-established place—a royal burgh since 1124—once had strong trading links with Europe, while servicing its agricultural hinterland and developing other industries such as textiles.

Before the end of the 18th century, Aberdeen was exporting its silver-grey granite to London and other places and also building the distinctive townscape seen today around Union Street (the main shopping thoroughfare). Unlike the soft sandstones of Edinburgh and Glasgow, tough granite did not suit ornate carving. Instead it was used boldly in blocks, parapets, and spires. In sunshine, the mica chips become a million mirrors; in rain, they reflect the grey sky.

Granite detail from the entrance to St. Nicholas's churchyard

Many of Aberdeen's places of interest are within walking distance of each other. The east end of Union Street is the former centre of the early settlement, indicated by the mercat cross. Aberdeen's is one of the most splendid in Scotland, dating from 1686, and arcaded with heraldic panels and portraits.

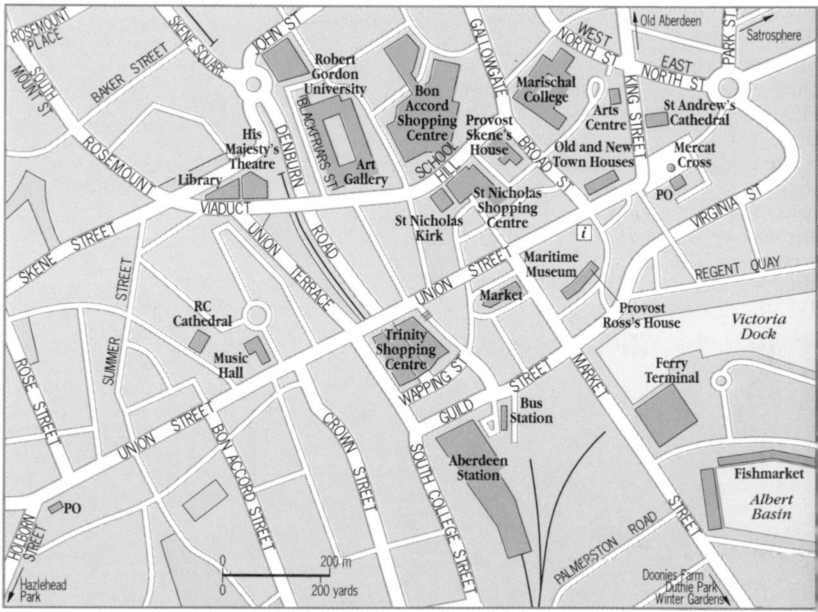

Union Street, Aberdeen

Aberdeen Maritime Museum▶ The 16th-century **Provost Ross's House** is a unique survivor on the old Shiprow, and can be found between the market-place and quayside, overlooking the harbour. The museum portrays Aberdeen's facinating sea-going past, from fishing boats and tea clippers of the early times right up to the oil boom of the late 20th century with multimedia displays and exhibitions (*Open* Mon–Sat 10–5, Sun 12–3. *Admission free*. Tel: 01224 337700; www.aagm.co.uk).

Marischal College▶▶ was founded in 1593 by the Earl Marischal as a Protestant alternative to the Catholic King's College in Old Aberdeen (see page 168). The two combined to form Aberdeen University in 1860. Marischal's arresting "Tudor Gothic" facade (with the Marischal Museum within) was built from 1891 onwards, breaking all the rules about granite and its severity. The ornate work is set off by the gilded flags, and this giant granite wedding cake is still the second largest granite building in the world(*Open museum:* Mon–Fri 10–5, Sun 2–5. *Admission free*. Tel: 01224 274301). Only El Escorial, near Madrid, in Spain, is larger.

Provost Skene's House▶ Past Marischal College and almost underneath the ugly modern block of St. Nicholas House, this steeply gabled, rubble-built structure is the remnant of a once closely packed area of town houses, and is one of the few surviving examples of early burgh architecture. It dates in part from 1545 and has now been restored as a museum of civic life with a series of rooms attractively decorated in the style of the period, and a painted chapel. There is also a café which is good for afternoon tea (*Open* Mon–Sat 10–5, Sun 1–4. *Admission free*. Tel: 01224 641086; www.aagm.co.uk).

"EDUCATION, SALVATION, AND DAMNATION"
One of the finest groupings of granite architecture in Aberdeen overlooks Union Terrace Gardens. St. Mark's Church of 1892, with its handsome dome and colonnaded portico, is flanked by the central library, inspired by Renaissance styles, and on the other side by the exuberant Edwardian flourishes of His Majesty's Theatre. Together they form a trio which was dubbed "Education, Salvation, and Damnation."

AN ABERDEEN SAYING
There is an old saying still current among Aberdonians: "Tak awa Aiberdeen and twal mile roon aboot—an far are ye?" ("Take away Aberdeen and 12 miles round about and where are you?"), meaning that without Aberdeen the area would be lost and worthless.

ROYAL CASTLE INSPIRATION
By late Victorian times the east end of Union Street, called the Castlegate, was downright seedy. Even today, respectable, upright native Aberdonians are a bit uncomfortable about it. The 19th-century city planners had the answer. Right in the middle they built a Salvation Army Citadel between 1893 and 1896. It survives as such today, with a handsome baronial tower. This castle-like design was inspired by another symbol of strength and righteousness: Balmoral Castle. The resemblance is purely external.

A TRAVELLER'S TALE
Thomas Pennant, the Welsh traveller, visited Aberdeen in 1769 and took in St. Machar's. He describes how the Reformers took the lead off the roof of St. Machar's and stole the bells. Then they "shipped their sacrilegious booty with an intention of exposing it to sale in Holland; but the vessel had scarcely gone out of port, but it perished in a storm with all its ill-gained lading." Others tell the same story of Elgin Cathedral.

Right: one of the colourful exhibits from the Aberdeen Maritime Museum

Aberdeen Art Gallery▶▶ has excellent collections of 18th- to 20th-century work (*Open* Mon–Sat 10–5, Sun 2–5. *Admission free.* Tel: 01224 523700; www.aagm.co.uk). Close by is **St. Nicholas Kirk▶**, the first place of worship in Aberdeen, founded in the 12th century (undergoing archaeological work in 2006. *Open* selected times—check ahead. *Admission free*. Tel: 01224 643494).

Old Aberdeen▶▶ was once a separate community near the River Don, and lies north of the main city near **King's College▶**. The university was founded in 1494 and its cobbled streets and artisans' cottages make it an atmospheric campus. **King's College Chapel▶▶** with its crown spire is a fine example of an early collegiate chapel (ca1500). The tall oak screen and the ribbed wooden ceiling and stalls have ornate medieval woodcarving.

Beyond the Georgian **Old Aberdeen Town House▶▶** is the Chanonry, leading to St. Machar's Cathedral and Seaton Park. The River Don curves round the park and flows under the 14th-century Brig o'Balgownie.

St. Machar's Cathedral▶ St. Columba sent St. Machar to build this church near the sea, where a river flowed in the shape of a shepherd's crook. The nave was possibly rebuilt in red sandstone by 1370, then finished in granite by the mid-15th century. The building was restored in the 19th century (*Open* summer, daily 9–5; winter, 10–4; Sun services 11–12, 6–7. *Admission free.* Tel: 01224 485988). **Cruickshank Botanic Gardens**, nearby, has over 2,500 species (*Open* daily Mon–Fri 9–4.30; also May–Sep, Sat, Sun 2–5. *Admission free*. Tel: 01224 272704).

Old Aberdeen

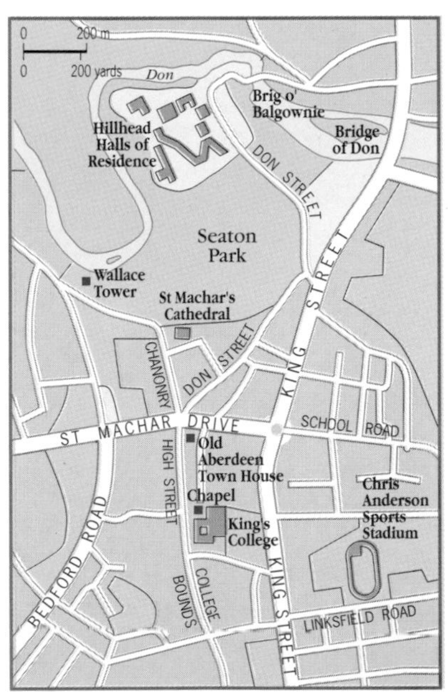

Aberdeen has sandy beaches, a funfair, leisure centres, swimming pools, and spacious parks—in short, many of the trappings of a holiday town. It also has a large number of indoor venues geared to children. If all else fails, you can always lose them for a while in the large maze in the city's Hazlehead Park.

The Satrosphere, in Constitution Street, is undoubtedly Aberdeen's top children's attraction (*Open* daily 10–5. *Admission: moderate*. Tel: 01224 640340; www.satrosphere.net). Do not be put off by the "interactive science and technology exhibition centre" description: it is a hands-on, absorbing experience for any child with imagination.

There are endless experiments and demonstrations. Children can play with mirrors and light, play tunes on 2m (6ft) pan pipes, be a TV newsreader, balance balls in streams of hot air, build a waterwheel, and be involved in lots of other activities.

Other Aberdeen attractions: Older children will enjoy the interactive computers at the **Maritime Museum** (see page 167) and some of the exhibits (probably the shrunken heads!) at the **Marischal College Museum** (*Open* Mon–Fri 10–5, Sun 2–5. *Admission free*. Tel: 01224 274301).

The David Welch Winter Gardens at **Duthie Park** are popular with families (*Open* daily from 9.30. *Admission free*. Tel: 01224 585310; www.aberdeencity.gov.uk). **Hazlehead Park** (pictured at the top of this page) has a Pets Corner that includes cute miniature donkeys (tel: 01224 208609), as has **Doonies Rare Breeds Farm** (*Open* Apr–Oct, daily 10–6; Nov–Mar, daily 10–3.45. *Admission: inexpensive*. Tel: 01224 875879), which is also worth exploring.

Scotland's largest permanent funfair (**Cordona's**) is at the beach, with much of the fairground complex and covered amusement area open all year, weather notwithstanding.

Out of town, **Storybook Glen** near Maryculter is a sheltered valley where fibreglass models of cartoon and fairy-tale characters loom disconcertingly out of the undergrowth (*Open* Mar–Oct, daily 10–6; Nov–Feb 10–4. *Admission: moderate*. Tel: 01224 732941; www.storybookglenaberdeen.co.uk).

FLORAL FACTS

Seaton Park is only one of the city's open spaces. Aberdeen lays special emphasis on flowers and is a frequent winner of the "Britain in Bloom" award. Aberdeen's flower displays were initiated using 60 tons of daffodil bulbs and 600,000 crocuses in one phase alone. Rose bushes outnumber the locals by nine to one.

A ghoulish exhibit from the Marischal College Museum

►► Ballater 162A1

Ballater has profited greatly from the needs of the royals at Balmoral. There are more "By Royal Appointment" signs here than anywhere else in Scotland.

Local excursions include the not-to-be-missed **Glen Muick** (pronounced Mick) with red deer sightings all but guaranteed. Also worth exploring are the birchwoods around Dinnet, notably **Loch Kinord** and the **Burn o Vat**, and a network of trails around **Glen Tanar**, near Aboyne. Hardy walkers can explore the **Mounth passes**—a series of high-level trails. Northwards is 16th-century **Corgarff Castle**, with its star-shaped defences added in 1748 (*Open* Apr–Sep, daily 9.30–6.30; Oct–Mar Sat–Sun 9.30–4.30. *Admission: moderate.* Tel: 01975 651460; www.historic-scotland.gov.uk).

Braemar has recorded Britain's lowest temperature: -27.2°C (-17°F)

BALMORAL
Balmoral Castle is the private holiday home of the royal family and only opens its grounds and ballroom to the public for a short time each year (*Open* daily Apr–Jul, 10–5, last admission 4.30. *Admission: moderate.* Tel: 013397 42534; www.balmoralcatle.com). Usually the ballroom houses a painting exhibition from the royal family's private collection. In August, when the royals are in residence, the castle serves as a high-security royal playground.

► Banff 162B3

Pressure from a local conservation group saved some of Banff's Georgian domestic architecture from redevelopment into the retail anonymity that blighted so many other Scottish towns, and it is worth a stroll in its own right. Its main attraction is **Duff House►**, a restored Adam mansion, now the principal outstation of the National Galleries of Scotland, with displays of Scottish portraiture of the 18th and 19th centuries and fine period furniture (*Open* Apr–Oct daily 11–5; Nov–Mar, Thu–Sun 11–4. *Admission: moderate.* Tel: 01261 818181; www.duffhouse.com).

Lonely Corgarff Castle

►► Braemar 162A1

The A93, coming west up Deeside, climbs out of the Dee valley and turns southwards, seeking a pass over the Grampians. Braemar sits on the turn. It can feel a little transitory, yet it is an old-established resort, benefiting like Ballater from the royal presence at Balmoral. The **Highland Heritage Centre** (*Open* Mon–Sat 9–5, Sun 10–5. *Admission free.* Tel: 013397 41944) takes up the theme of the royal connection and the Braemar Highland Gathering. There is an excellent selection of local excursions, including the **Linn of Dee**, a picturesque rocky cleft, west of Inverey. Nearby is the **Devil's Punchbowl**, a water-worn rock feature at the Linn of Quoich. The **Colonel's Bed** is yet more rock and water: a narrow gorge with slippery shelves in Glen Ey. For the ambitious walker, **Glen Derry** gives access to the eastern end of the Cairngorms, as well as the pass of the Larig Ghru leading through to the Spey.

The northern Picts lived in and around the Grampians between the 4th and 9th centuries AD. The Mounth, the hill ground between Deeside and Angus, was an important barrier. Moray was their final stronghold before defeat and gradual absorption by the ascendant Scots whose union with them formed the first kingdom of Scotland known as Alba (see page 27).

Burghead The most important Pictish centre was Burghead, on the coast near Elgin. A great promontory fort survived until a "new" town of Burghead was built on a grid plan between 1805 and 1809, destroying much of the Pictish ramparts and timber-laced walling that had stood there for more than a millennium. Six Pictish bull carvings survive from that time, outlined boldly in stone.

The bull is just one of the symbols which tantalize modern archaeologists and historians. The Picts left earthworks such as coastal headland forts in the northeast and inland sites like Bennachie, a hill near Inverurie, but it is their symbol stones which are the most vivid evidence of this long-gone culture. A few stones are still in their original locations, some have been re-erected or placed in museums, others have been built into walls or lost entirely.

Standing stones The **Picardy Stone** near Insch is typical, a whinstone pillar with, among other subjects, a clearly executed double-disc and Z-rod (a recurring symbol in Pictish art), serpent, and mirror. The **Maiden Stone** near Pitcaple is an impressive, red granite monolith of considerable presence, especially when slanting light highlights the curious so-called "Pictish elephant," one of the most mysterious of the designs. This is a late (9th-century) work.

Most magnificent of all is **Sueno's Stone** on the outskirts of Forres, with its many figures galloping on the face of a 2.5m (8ft) monolith. Theories abound on the meaning of this stone and all the others. Some suggest that Sueno's Stone is war reporting on a grand scale—recording, ironically, the Scots victory over the Picts. Some see the other stones as monuments, others as proclamations. Nobody knows, but the designs have both power and inspiration. Tracking them down can make for interesting excursions in this northern corner.

THE MEANING OF THE STONES

The Picts were divided into two realms, the northern and southern. Many of the finest symbol stones belong to the northern grouping. Their language was ousted by the arrival of the Scots from Ireland and they left no written records. It is known that inheritance was through the female line—though Pictish kings reigned, their sons did not succeed them. Do the symbols carved on the stones indicate lineages, alliances, and power within the leading Pictish families?

Left and below: the Maiden Stone, near Pitcaple

Whisky is one of Scotland's top exports, worth £2.3 billion in 2001, and is important in the economy of many communities. There are more than 40 distilleries in Moray alone, the greatest concentration anywhere in Scotland. More than just a distinctive plume of steam in the attractive wooded river valley, these distilleries sustain engineers, coppersmiths, painters, plumbers, maltsters, and many more trades.

DALLAS DHU
Amid all the live distilleries, you can also visit one from the past. In the care of Historic Scotland, Dallas Dhu near Forres is a time capsule from 1898 and allows a more intimate inspection than working distilleries (*Open* Apr–Sep, daily 9.30–6.30; Oct–Mar, daily 9.30–4.30. *Admission: moderate.* Tel: 01309 676548; www.historic-scotland.gov.uk).

For centuries *uisge beatha* (the Gaelic for "water of life") has been produced in Scotland from the simple ingredients of barley, water, yeast, and, usually, peat smoke. There are two main distinctions: malt whisky and grain whisky. Most drinkers would say that malt has a more complex taste and bouquet. Certainly, modern marketing techniques have given it more cachet and a higher price! Malt whisky uses only malted barley. Grain whisky may use malted barley but also other cereals, notably maize. A single malt is the product of a single distillery, while a blend is a mix of malt and grain whiskies—the higher the proportion of malt whisky, the better (or more expensive) the blend.

Experts broadly classify malt whiskies into Highland, Lowland, Islay, and Campbeltown types. This can be generalized into eastern, notably from Speyside, and western, from the islands, mainly Islay. Of the two, the western malts are noticeably "peaty." The malt that is the basis of malt whisky has usually been bought from local maltings. Malt is germinated barley that has been killed off and then dried (sometimes with peat smoke).

Copper stills at the Glen Garioch Distillery, Oldmeldrum

The whisky-making process

Grind a large quantity of malted barley and add hot water to it in a large circular vat called a mash tun. Eventually, the result will be wort, a sweet-smelling liquid. Hold this in a worts receiver or underback below the mash tun. Use the solids in the mash tun, called draff, for winter cattle food.

Take the wort and add it with yeast to another enormous vessel, known as a wash-back, where it will ferment. Then pump this liquid, called the wash, via a wash charger into a wash still, which is a large copper container. Heat it, using gas if available. Condense the vapours in a worm—a coiled

copper water-cooled tube. Repeat this process at least twice. Then run the distillate into a spirit safe. This is the part that needs most expertise. Both the beginning and end of the distilling process produce impurities. The whisky is, so to speak, in the middle.

Next, procure casks. Old sherry casks are particularly recommended. Add water to the whisky and place in the casks. Leave for several years before bottling as a single malt. Then sell worldwide as a prestige product!

Casks—and their contents—maturing at the Glenfiddich Distillery, Dufftown

Distillery tours If you attempt any form of distilling in your kitchen, Customs and Excise will be very interested. The process is strictly commercially licensed and takes place only in Scotland's distilleries (and it's most definitely "whisky," without an "e").

A typical visit includes some kind of audiovisual presentation, with the malt whisky company describing its brand as the "true taste of Scotland" and laying great store on historical roots. (Awkward facts, such as the owning company being an overseas-based multinational, are skipped over.) Then there is a tour, of varying degrees of liveliness and afterwards a return to the hospitality area where a dram is usually offered. There will often be some kind of historic exhibition and nearly always a shop. No tour of Speyside is complete without taking in at least one distillery.

Whisky festival The Spirit of Speyside Whisky Festival at the end of April is the highlight of the season, with food, fun, music and, of course, whisky tasting (tel: 01343 542666; www.spiritofspeyside.com).

THE ANGELS' SHARE
This is the name given to the whisky that was definitely there when the distillery staff put it into the cask but has gone, five or more years later, when the casks are broached for bottling or blending. Nothing untoward has taken place. There is a natural evaporation through the wood of the casks.

ay Firth contains ,est inshore of bottle-nosed ıins in Britain. (The cies otherwise prefers shore waters.) Leaping olphins can be seen anywhere at any time in the Firth. The entrances to the inner firths can be rewarding for dolphin watchers, as can the mouths of the rivers Findhorn and Spey (Spey Bay is particularly good for seals as well). The bottle-nosed dolphin can be recognized by its uniform grey with a paler underbelly and a tall dorsal fin.

▶ Craigellachie *162A2*

A typical Speyside community dependent on the whisky industry and visiting anglers, Craigellachie is noted for its cooperage, now the **Speyside Cooperage Visitor Centre▶▶**, where the skills of barrel-making are demonstrated (*Open* Mon–Fri 9.30–4. *Admission: inexpensive.* Tel: 01340 871108; www.speysidecooperage.co.uk). Also nearby is **Craigellachie Bridge▶**, designed by Thomas Telford, which crosses the Spey with an iron span cast in Wales.

▶▶ Crathes Castle *162B1*

Open: castle daily Easter–Sep, 10.30–5.30; Oct, 10–4.30. Estate and garden open all year. Admission: expensive (tel: 01330 844525; www.nts.org.uk)

This 16th-century L-plan tower house has many rare, original features, notably four rooms with painted ceilings, as well as a ghost of a green lady and some fine old furniture, locally made. Crathes is also noted for its interesting gardens, made into lots of different compartments separated by close-clipped yew hedges and containing many unusual species.

▶ Dufftown *162A2*

A planned town founded in 1817, Dufftown has wide streets that converge on a square and landmark **clock tower** (which houses the local museum). The little town is bound up with distilleries, including famous malt whisky names such as Glenfiddich, which is overlooked by the ruins of the 13th-century Balvenie Castle (itself a malt whisky name). The **Glenfiddich Distillery Visitor Centre▶▶▶** offers one of the very best audio-visuals and tours, showing all the stages of malt whisky-making from malting to bottling (*Open* mid-Jan–mid-Dec, Mon–Fri 9.30–4.30; also Easter–mid-Oct, Sat 9.30–4.30, Sun 12–4.30. *Admission free.* Tel: 01340 820373; www.glenfiddich.com). Though a planned town, Dufftown's story as a settlement goes as far back as AD 566, when Mortlach Church was founded, making it one of the earliest religious sites in Scotland. There are Pictish stones and a "leper's squint," a hole through which lepers could observe the proceedings going on inside the church.

Painted ceiling in Crathes Castle; the original castle was built in 1323 on land granted to the Burnett family by Robert the Bruce

▶ Elgin

162A3

Elgin has rebuilt its townscape over the centuries, yet retained fragments of early times. A medieval street plan can still be made out, with narrow alleyways leading off the main street. Some arcaded facades from 18th-century shops also survive. Take in the view from the top of the Lady Hill at its west end, the site of the castle occupied by King Edward I of England in the Wars of Independence.

"Acorn to Cask," the story of whisky barrels at Craigellachie

Elgin Cathedral▶ ("The Lantern of the North") was founded in 1224 and burned in 1390 by the notorious Wolf of Badenoch, the black sheep of the royal Stuart family. It was rebuilt and in use until the Reformation, when it suffered the usual fate of great religious seats in Scotland. Much of its stonework was pillaged, though the historic structure was taken into the care of the nation in 1825. The octagonal chapterhouse is a remarkable survivor (*Open* Apr–Sep, daily 9.30–6.30; Oct–Mar, Sat–Wed 9.30–4.30. *Admission: moderate.* Tel: 01343 547171; www.historic.scotland.gov.uk).

Elgin Cathedral adds distinction to the skyline of the "capital" of Moray. Much of the surviving work dates from the 13th century

Elgin Museum▶ is said to be one of the finest museums in the north. It features the oldest dinosaurs found in Britain—though, like the museum itself, they are quite small (*Open* Apr–Oct, Mon–Fri 10–5, Sat 11–4, Sun 2–5. *Admission: inexpensive.* Tel: 01343 543675; www.elginmuseum.org.uk).

Other attractions include **Johnstons Cashmere Visitor Centre**, a woollen mill specializing in cashmere (*Open* Apr–Dec, Mon–Sat 9–5.30, Sun 11–5. *Admission free.* Tel: 01343 554099; www.johnstonscashmere.com). There is also a motor museum and a preserved meal mill. On the levels of the Laich of Moray is **Duffus Castle▶**, the remains of a motte-and-bailey castle. (*Open* at all times).

Spynie Palace▶, the ruin of a former bishop's mansion with good views from the tower, is to the east. Elgin's former port, **Lossiemouth▶**, is now a resort and fishing town, with a busy air base nearby. **Pluscarden Abbey▶▶**, originally a 13th-century foundation (*Open* daily 9–5. *Admission free;* www.pluscardenabbey.org), is also nearby.

THE BATTLE OF MONS GRAUPIUS

The Roman historian Tacitus tells how Agricola's forces, ranging north in the summer of AD 83, finally brought to battle and defeated the Caledonian warriors by a hill within sight of the sea in the north of Scotland. This was the Battle of Mons Graupius, which also gave the name Grampian, possibly due to a 1470s printing error when "m" was substituted for "u." Many historians prefer a Grampian location for the battle, possibly Bennachie near Inverurie. The real battle site has never been found.

THE MOUNTH
The Mounth, from the Gaelic *monadh*—("moorland" or "mountain"), is the name given to the hill-mass south of Deeside. The Mounth passes were once important through-routes to the north. Today, they survive as hill tracks marked on maps: the Capel Mounth, the Firmouth, the Fungle; and many more, now mainly the haunt of leisure-time walkers and mountain bikers. Drivable passes include the A93 over Glen Shee and the B974 Cairn o Mount.

▶ Fettercairn *162B1*

Car travellers who tire of the fast A90 should try an interesting route to the northeast via Fettercairn, a little place on the southern edge of the Grampian Hills. Fettercairn has an 1861 Gothic arch recalling the visit of Queen Victoria and a malt whisky visitor centre (*Open* Mon–Sat May–Sep). The Fettercairn diversion leads on to the start of a scenic hill road, the B974 to Banchory, which reaches its highest point at the **Cairn o' Mount**. This hilltop cairn gives excellent views southwards over Angus and is typical of skyline cairns that have been altered by generations of travellers. Originally it dates from the 2nd millennium BC.

If travelling north to the whisky country of Moray, you could treat Fettercairn Distillery as an introduction to the typical distillery visit. The works here originally opened in 1824. Today they offer free tours of the distillery and warehouse, an audiovisual presentation and a dram of their Old Fettercairn malt (*Open* Easter–Sep, Mon–Sat 10–4. *Admission inexpensive*. Tel: 01561 340205).

▶ Fochabers *162A3*

This handsome little planned town, built by the Duke of Gordon in 1776, is worth visiting for its choice of antique shops. The Duke thought the old village was too near his castle, so knocked it down. However, he did not think of building a bypass for the A96 which makes the main street very noisy today. Fochabers is the home of Baxters, whose tinned food factory dominates the western approaches. There is an excellent view of the River Spey from a viewpoint south of the town, signposted **The Earth Pillars**, where eroded columns of red conglomerate rock form the foreground to a striking river panorama, seen through the pinewood.

Fochabers Heritage Centre and Folk Museum▶▶ is housed in a converted church and is filled with artefacts of a bygone rural life from horsedrawn carts to a turnip-chopping machine (*Open* Easter–Oct, Tue–Fri 11–4, Sat–Sun 2–4. *Admission free.* Tel: 01343 821204).

One of Fyvie Castle's main attractions is its outstanding art collection: portraits by Batoni, Raeburn, Ramsay, Gainsborough, and others

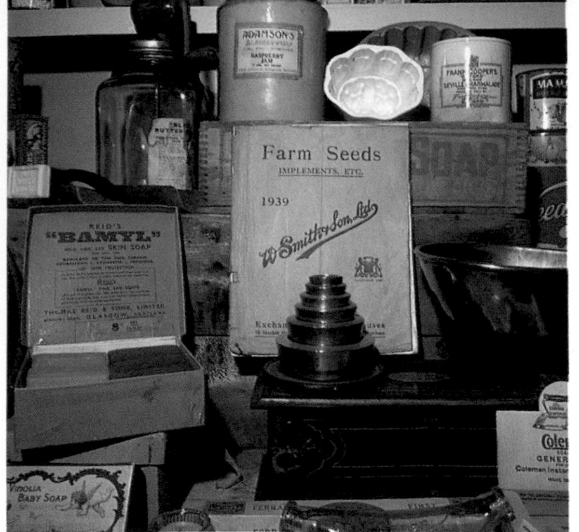

Forres's Falconer Museum has a very strong local collectior.

AN EARLY NAME
Some think that the 'Varris' on the map of Ptolemy, the 1st-century AD geographer, refers to today's Forres.

RANDOLPH'S LEAP
Randolph's Leap, a beauty spot on the River Findhorn, where the river narrows among rocks and woodlands, is unfairly named. The Randolph was Thomas Randolph, Earl of Moray. He was in hot pursuit of one Alastair Cumming who had just raided his Darnaway Castle. It was Cumming who escaped by leaping the river at this point. Judge for yourself the relative ease of choosing between a downward leap of around 3m (10ft) or being skewered on a 14th-century broadsword.

▶ Forres *162A3*

Like Elgin, farther east, Forres also maintains its medieval street plan in part. The main street bulges out at the former market-place in the town centre, though the buildings are mainly Victorian. The **Falconer Museum** (*Open* Apr–Oct, Mon–Sat 10–5; Nov–Mar, Mon–Thu 11–12.30 and 1–3.30. *Admission free*. Tel: 01309 673701) explores local history.

Brodie Castle▶▶ is a National Trust for Scotland property, to the east of Forres. Based on a 16th-century Z-plan tower house with later additions, it houses fine French furniture, porcelain, and a painting collection (*Open* Apr, Jul, Aug daily 12–4; May, Jun, Sep, Sun–Thu 12–4. *Admission: expensive*. Tel: 01309 641371; www.nts.org.uk). Well worth visiting at any season is the **Califer Braes** viewpoint, with a broad view of the Moray Firth.

▶ Fraserburgh *162C3*

Fraserburgh is a fishing port that has little merit in its townscape. However, it has a superb beach and a most interesting visitor attraction. The **Museum of Scottish Lighthouses▶▶▶** portrays the story of lighthouse service, now ending with automation. There are displays as well as a tour of Kinnaird Head lighthouse itself (*Open* Apr–Jun, Sep–Oct, Mon–Sat 10–5, Sun 12–5; Jul–Aug, Mon–Sat 10–6, Sun 11–6; Nov–Mar, Mon–Sat 10–4, Sun 12–4. *Admission: moderate*. Tel: 01346 511022; www.lighthousemuseum.co.uk).

▶▶ Fyvie Castle *162B2*

Open: Easter–Jun, Sep, Sat–Wed 12–5; Jul–Aug daily 11–5. Admission: expensive (tel: 01651 891266; www.nts.org.uk)

Five-towered Fyvie Castle epitomizes northeast castles: a rambling pile, imposing yet hidden away. The original 13th-century quadrangular fortress evolved over the centuries into a magnificent stately home. A number of famous families in the northeast held it in turn, each adding to the building. Then it was bought by Alexander Forbes Leith, a local boy made good in America. He refurbished it in parts, adding Edwardian opulence to the mix. The castle has grand interiors and fine furniture, and displays a magnificent painting collection, including a dozen Raeburns.

Falconer Museum, Forres

USUAL VEHICLE
of the exhibits in Grampian Museum ransport is the aigievar Express. This a steam-powered ricycle, and was one of Scotland's pioneering road vehicles. It was built in 1895 by the local postman to help him on his rounds. The one-cylindered, coal-fired, vertical boiler contraption took part in the 1971 London to Brighton Car Rally—and completed the course.

►► Glen Shee 162A1

Climbing to over 620m (2,000ft) at the Cairnwell, the A93 between Bridge of Cally and Braemar is the highest main road in the United Kingdom. Surrounded on both sides by Munros, it has been prey to ski developers and is very popular when snow conditions are right. The solitude of the high tops in the immediate vicinity has been invaded by parking, snow fencing, chairlifts, tows, and catering facilities. With the highest hills only about 900m (3,000ft), the downhill runs are not very long. The chairlift operates outside the winter season. On the steep south side of the pass is the Devil's Elbow, a once fearsome hairpin bend now bypassed, but still visible.

► Grampian Transport Museum 162B2

Open: Apr–Sep, daily 10–5; Oct 10–4. Admission: moderate (tel: 019755 62292; www.gtm.org.uk)

Alford offers plenty for children, in particular the Grampian Transport Museum with its extensive collection of historic vehicles and the adjoining narrow-gauge railway—built on the original site of the long-vanished "proper" railway—that runs to Haughton Country Park. Take the road north to **Suie Hill** for a peerless view over rural Aberdeenshire. If it is a summer weekend, continue over to the community hall of the enterprising village of Clatt, where the locals serve a real afternoon tea.

►► Haddo House 162C2

Open: Easter, May–Jun, Sep, Sat–Sun 11–4.30; Jul–Aug, daily 11–4.30. Admission: expensive (tel: 01651 851440; www.nts.org.uk)

There is quite a concentration of National Trust for Scotland properties in the northeast. Haddo House, with its country

Pastoral landscape near Inverurie

PITMEDDEN GARDEN
About 6km (4mi) from Haddo House, Pitmedden Garden, another National Trust for Scotland property, is at its best in high summer, thanks to 40,000 annual plants and 8km (5mi) of box hedging. This is the re-creation of a formal garden originally laid out in 1675 (*Open* May–Sep, daily 10–5.30, last entry 5. *Admission: moderate*).

Grampian Transport Museum, Alford

park, is on the **Castle Trail**, the signposted route which takes in the best of them, though this William Adam design of 1732 has an elegance far removed from the bold and battered fortresses typical of the Trail. Haddo's interiors are mostly "Adam revival" from about 1880 and the overall impression is light and cheerful, inside and out, with curving wings on either side of a harmonious façade. Combine this excursion with a visit to Pitmedden Garden (see panel).

▶ Huntly *162B2*

Huntly was the power base of the Gordons who built their castle here on a defensive site between the rivers Bogie and Deveron. Today, **Huntly Castle** stands as an imposing ruin, with heraldic adornments on its walls (*Open* Apr–Sep, daily 9.30–6.30; Oct–Mar, Sat–Wed, 9.30–4.30. *Admission: inexpensive.* Tel: 01466 793191; www.historic-scotland.gov.uk). Huntley also has an all-weather cross-country ski track down by the river.

▶ Inverurie *162B2*

Now bypassed by the busy A96, Inverurie is a locally important administrative centre in the prosperous farming area known as the Garioch (pronounced "geerie"). It is overlooked by one of the northeast's landmark hills, **Bennachie**, with its hilltop vitrified Pictish fort. There are other prehistoric sites in the vicinity (see page 171), including the **Loanhead Stone Circle**, near Daviot, 8km (5mi) to the northwest. At Oyne, 13km (8mi) northwest of Inverurie, the displays at **Archaeolink**▶▶ will tell you much about the prehistoric peoples who built these monuments (*Open* Apr–Oct, daily 11–5. *Admission: inexpensive.* Tel: 01464 851500; www.archaeolink.co.uk).

▶ Keith *162B3*

Another planned town on the main Aberdeen–Inverness road, Keith is also the gateway to the **Malt Whisky Trail** (www.maltwhiskytrail.com). This is a signposted drive—presumably for non-tipplers—around seven malt whisky distilleries, one of which, Strathisla, is in Keith, though the others lie in more picturesque settings in the attractive hinterland of the River Spey and around Ben Rinnes.

GORDON BENNETT

Few places can claim to be the home town of an expletive, but Keith was the birthplace of "Gordon Bennett." This mild oath refers to James Gordon Bennett, born in the town in 1795. He was the founder and editor of the *New York Herald*, and is sometimes described as the father of chequebook journalism, because of his innovative sensationalist style of journalism.

Drive

The northeast coast

The section of coast between the mouths of the rivers Don and Spey remains comparatively unexplored. Aberdeen to Sandend is 139km (86mi), the return along the main road 80km (50mi). Allow a full day.

Starting from Aberdeen, the A92 is set back from the coast until the Ythan estuary at Newburgh on the A975. The northern bank of the estuary is a wild habitat of dune and coastal heath, which is explained at the **Forvie Nature Reserve Visitor Centre** (run by Scottish Natural Heritage, tel: 01358 751330).

Continue north, diverting to tiny Whinnyfold, which has a view of the Bay of Cruden and the village of Cruden Bay. Bram Stoker used to holiday here, and the nearby ruin of Slains Castle reputedly inspired his *Dracula*.

At the gloomy **Bullers of Buchan**, the sea has burst through the cliff in a deep, tide-filled, kittiwake-haunted hollow. Beyond, **Peterhead**, the largest white-fish landing port in Europe, and also a North Sea oil servicing centre, has a maritime museum.

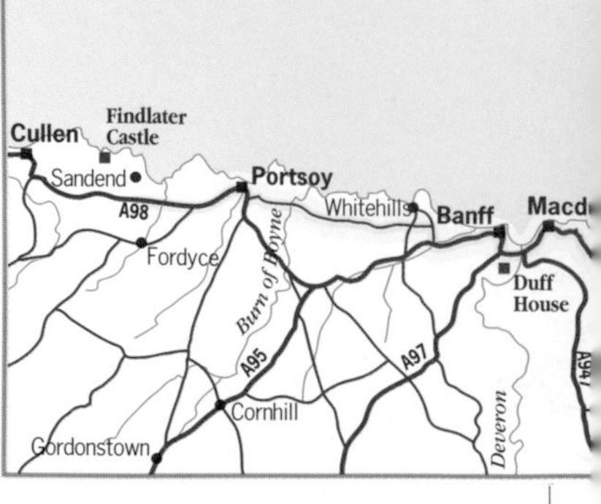

After St. Fergus comes the lonely coastline around **Rattray Head**. The **Loch of Strathbeg**, Scotland's largest land-locked coastal lagoon, is an important wintering ground for wildfowl.

Off the B9033 the fishing villages of St. Combs and Cairnbulg huddle with gable ends to the sea. **Fraserburgh**, dour in grey granite, has the **Museum of Scottish Lighthouses** on Kinnaird Head and a fine beach.

Turning west, the sands are left behind for grey rocks, which rear up beyond Rosehearty and reach impressive heights around Pennan. Seabird colonies are spectacular around the fearsomely precipitous **Troup Head** (not suitable for young children). **Gardenstown** has an attractive little harbour, as well as a fine walk to the west, to the ruin of the 11th-century Kirk of St. John the Evangelist.

Peterhead's harbour—busy with fishing boats

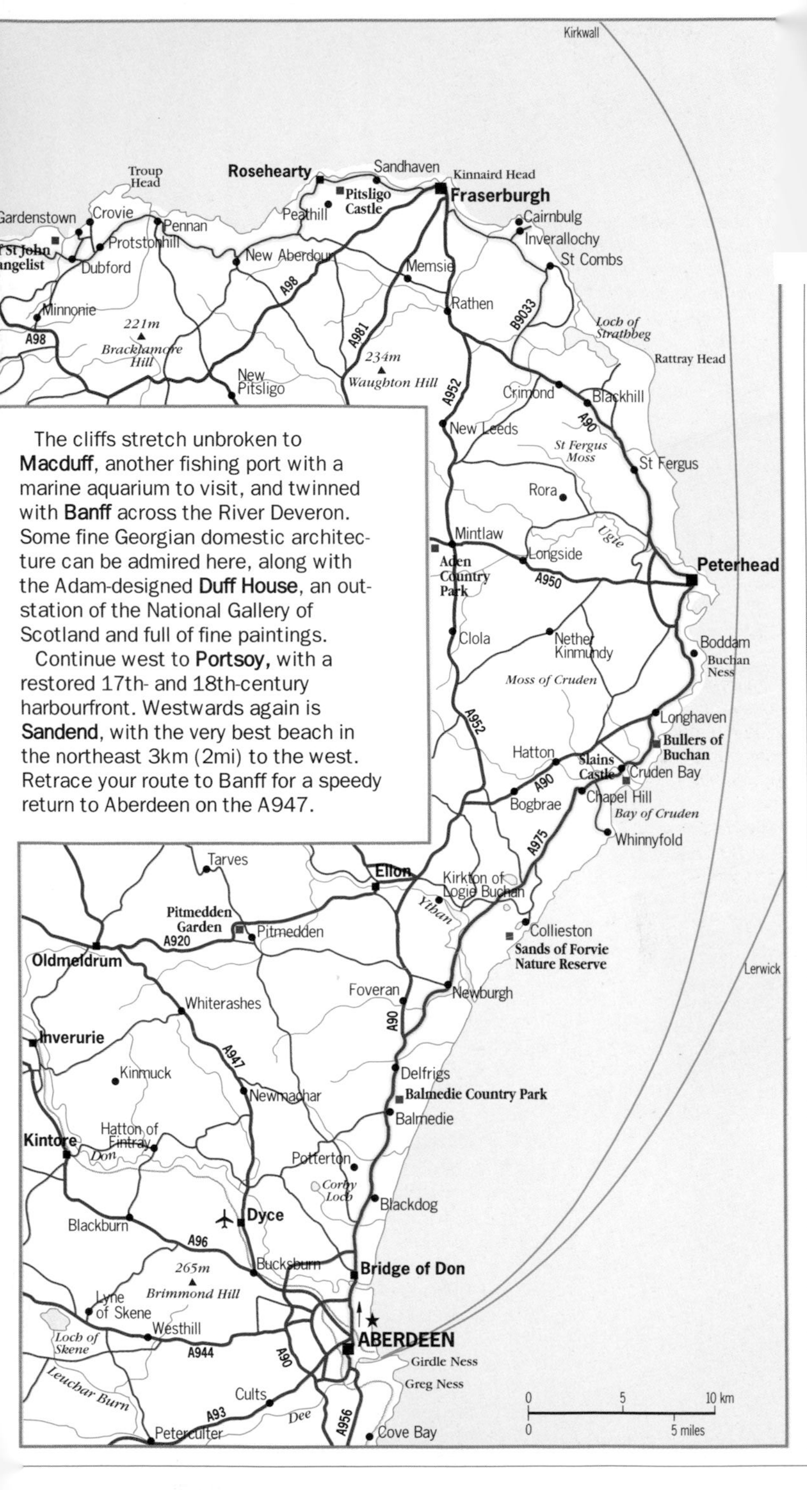

The cliffs stretch unbroken to **Macduff**, another fishing port with a marine aquarium to visit, and twinned with **Banff** across the River Deveron. Some fine Georgian domestic architecture can be admired here, along with the Adam-designed **Duff House**, an out-station of the National Gallery of Scotland and full of fine paintings.

Continue west to **Portsoy,** with a restored 17th- and 18th-century harbourfront. Westwards again is **Sandend**, with the very best beach in the northeast 3km (2mi) to the west. Retrace your route to Banff for a speedy return to Aberdeen on the A947.

Kildrummy Castle, seat of the Earls of Mar; this is the great triple window of the chapel

A TRAITOR'S REWARD
Kildrummy was besieged by the English in 1306. Sir Nigel Bruce (King Robert's brother) held out but was betrayed by Osbarn the smith, who had been promised gold by the besiegers. After the castle fell he got his reward—poured molten down his throat. Or so the story goes.

AN ECCENTRIC BIRD
Among the Leith Hall soldiers was Colonel Alexander Sebastian Leith Hay, who became laird in 1862. He was in the Thin Red Line at Balaclava and also helped crush the Indian Mutiny. He returned home with a white cockatoo named Cocky, which spoke Hindustani and lived for 50 years at Leith Hall. On its death it was given a burial with full military honours.

►► Kildrummy Castle and Gardens *162B2*

Open: Apr–Sep, daily 9.30–6.30. Admission: inexpensive (tel: 01975 571331; www.historic-scotland.gov.uk)

Kildrummy is one of the best-preserved medieval castles in Scotland—though far from complete, as one glance at the shattered walls will confirm. Built to an unusual shield-shape plan and echoing the fortresses at Caernarvon and Harlech in Wales, Kildrummy controlled the routes through Donside to the north. It withstood many sieges and was finally dismantled after its role as Jacobite headquarters in the 1715 rebellion.

Kildrummy Castle Gardens are a separate concern from the castle, though the two make a good combined visit. They occupy the nearby quarry from which the castle rock was cut. In this sheltered bowl are many unusual varieties of rock plant and shrubs, as well as a water garden designed by a Japanese engineer. There is often a chance to buy surplus plants (www.kildrummy-castle-gardens.co.uk).

►► Leith Hall *162B2*

Open: Easter, 12–5; May–Sep, Fri–Tue 12–5; grounds daily 9.30–sunset. Admission: expensive (tel: 01464 831216; www.nts.org.uk)

The archetypal "big hoose," Leith Hall was occupied by the Leiths, later the Leith Hays, for 300 years. They were a military family, and the National Trust for Scotland, who have been here since 1945, have made the most of this with an exhibition within the grand mansion. There are fine walks in the grounds and a pleasant garden.

►►► Macduff Marine Aquarium *162B3*

High Shore, Macduff (tel: 01261 833369; www.macduff-aquarium.org.uk). Open: daily 10–5. Admission: moderate

On the very edge of the sea by the workaday harbour of the undistinguished town of Macduff, this marine display is unique in Scotland. Because the aquarium's 5m (16.5ft) deep, showpiece tank is open topped, daylight filters down through the sea water. The daylight and the surge generator (a wave machine) in the tank allow kelp, the long-fronded brown seaweed, to grow naturally in a replication of a typical Moray Firth kelp reef, complete with its own native fishy community. Although there are other displays in this very family-focused venue, the main tank is a visual delight and is very popular even with the local fishing folk

▶ Stonehaven *162C1*

While Aberdeen's growth has turned many nearby places into dormitories, the heart of Stonehaven has retained its character. Once a fishing settlement, it was extended in 1795 by the local laird who built spacious streets round a main square near the old harbour. Today, there are only a few working boats. The old town's 16th-century Tolbooth, close to the harbour edge, houses the museum (*Open* mid-Apr–mid-Oct, Wed–Mon 1.30–4.30. *Admission free*. Tel: 01771 622807). **Dunnottar Castle▶▶▶** (*Open* Easter–Oct, Mon–Sat 9–6, Sun 2–5; Nov–Easter, Fri–Mon 9–dusk. *Admission moderate*. Tel: 01569 762173; www.dunechtestates.co.uk). A few minutes down the coast, this 14th-century fortress is in a spectacular setting on a rocky headland. It was a stronghold of the Earls Marischal of Scotland. In the wars of the Commonwealth, the Scottish crown jewels were hidden here from Cromwell's army.

THE EARLS MARISCHAL
The title of Marischal originally meant the keeper of the king's mares. The Keith family of Dunnottar were the hereditary Earls Marischal until their extinction in the 18th century.

Stonehaven harbour. This former fishing port also used to have a seaside holiday trade, now diminished, like other east-coast resorts

▶ Tomintoul *162A2*

Near the southern end of the Malt Whisky Trail, Tomintoul ies among the uplands of Moray, with the Cairngorms on he far horizon. It was founded by the Duke of Gordon in 779. The village makes a good base for exploring the lenlivet Estate (part of the Crown Estate), which offers a ariety of outdoor activities amongst the high moors and orests. Tomintoul also has a local museum, part of the ourist Information Centre (*Open* Apr–Oct). It lies on the 939 to Cockbridge, which rises to 600m (2,000ft), giving ccess to the Lecht skiing area, and has gained a certain otoriety as it is usually the first road in Scotland to be locked by snow. However, it is an important link for ourers between Speyside and Deeside.

SCOTTISH HEIGHTS
Tomintoul is the highest village in the Highlands at 354m (1,161ft), though the highest village in Scotland is Wanlockhead (421m/1,381ft) in Dumfries and Galloway.

▶▶▶ REGION HIGHLIGHTS

Cawdor Castle *pages 190–191*
Crarae Garden *page 192*
Fort George *pages 192–193*
Glen Affric *page 194*
Highland Folk Museum (Kingussie) *page 201*
Inveraray *page 200*
Strathspey *page 188*

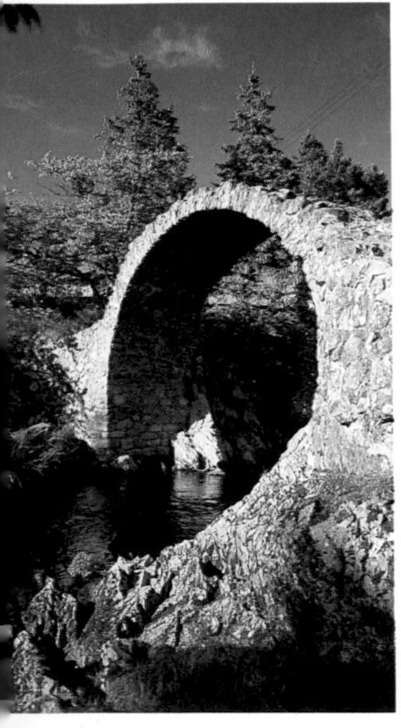

Carrbridge; the arch across the River Dulnain dates from 1715

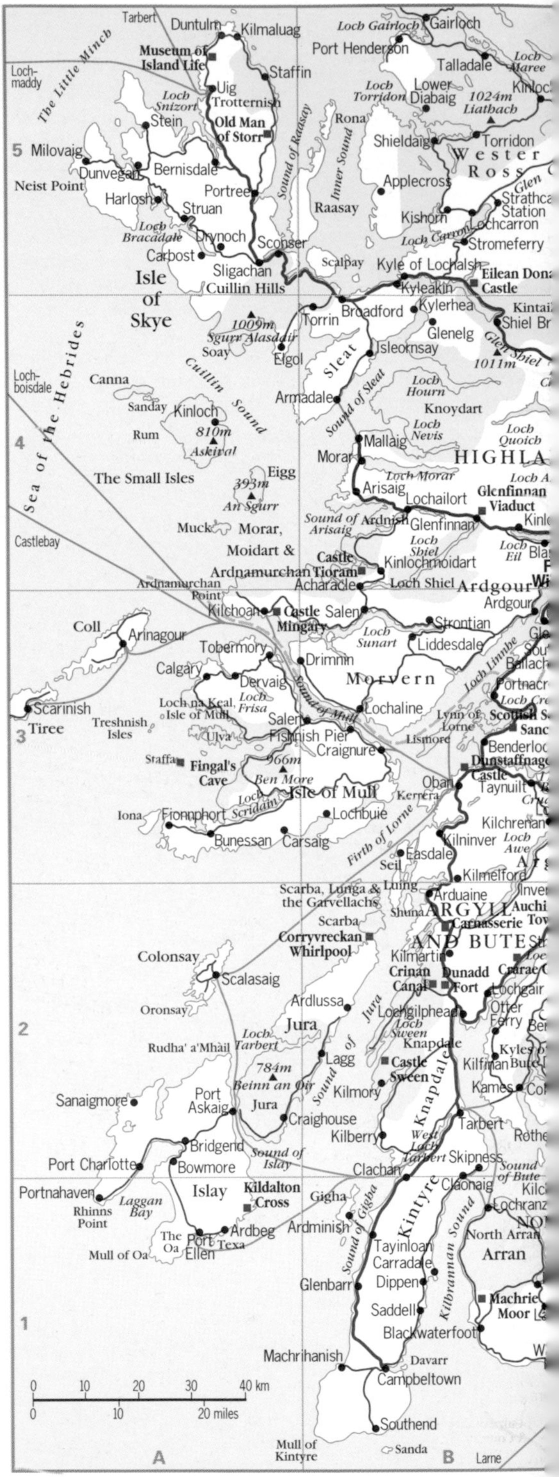

The Great Glen & Western Highlands

THE GREAT GLEN
The wrenching and sliding of the earth's crust formed this coast-to-coast fault line from the searoads of Loch Linnhe to the inner Moray Firth. Granite from Foyers above Loch Ness on its eastern side matches granite around Strontian, over 95km (60mi) away to the west, in the hills of Ardgour.

WESTERN HIGHLAND CONTRASTS
One example of the interplay between loch and high ground which typifies the Western Highlands is the summit of Ben Nevis. Though it is the highest point anywhere in the UK, it is only 8km (5mi) from the salt waters of Loch Linnhe.

THE GREAT GLEN The area surrounding this coast-to-coast fault line that splits the Highlands takes in Scotland's highest mountains and greatest lochs. With the exception of the gentler landscape around Nairn on the inner Moray Firth, and the greenness of the far end of Kintyre, reminiscent of pastoral Ayrshire, most of this terrain is rugged. Though the central Cairngorms have been almost tamed in recent years by ski lifts, which spill visitors all year round onto the fragile arctic plateau, the western Cairngorms remain the province only of the hardy hillwalker. West of the Great Glen, the big glens of Cannich and Affric carry hydroelectric dams but emptiness still lies beyond. Loch Morar, deepest of all in the far west, still leads in to the trackless reaches of the Rough Bounds of Knoydart.

As for the Great Glen itself, its hills just fail to reach truly magnificent proportions: it is large without being impressive. Yet it remains firmly on the touring route of those determined to "do" the Highlands in a day or two and especially of those who hope to find the essence of the Highlands in the busy town of Inverness. Excursions off this main through-route are rewarding, to places such as Glen Roy with its curious Parallel Roads, or to the far reaches of Loch Arkaig and the mysteries of hidden Jacobite treasure. Scotland's newest long-distance pathway, The Great Glen Way (www.greatglenway.com) stretches 117km (73mi) from Fort William to Inverness.

SPEYSIDE This region, among the old pinewoods, is subtly different. The blue shadows on the Cairngorm backdrop change as the sun goes round, first highlighting then casting shadows deep into the Larig Ghru, the ancient mountain pass that links Speyside with Deeside. Adding to the enticements of birch and Scots pine, lochs with ospreys and other unusual birds, long hill passes, and high level excursions, are the commercial developments which range from steam railways to Highland estate safaris.

THE WESTERN HIGHLANDS The Argyll area, taking in Loch Linnhe, is different again. Here is the picture-postcard interplay of sea loch and wooded hillslope. The mountains diminish in height the farther south you travel, yet the landscape still retains a ruggedness, among the drowned valleys of Knapdale for example. Only towards the far end of Kintyre is a sense of the Highlands lost almost entirely.

Most of the main population centres in the area have been involved with generations of visitors. Inverness is a large commercial centre servicing all of the Northern Highlands. Aviemore was a custom-built 1960s development. Redevelopment seems always just around the corner: it is looking seedy and is a definite culture shock for those expecting quaint little cottages on the road north. Fort William is an all but unavoidable natural route centre in the Western

Ben Nevis from Corpach; this view of Britain's highest mountain hints at the great corries and cliffs hidden when looking up from Fort William

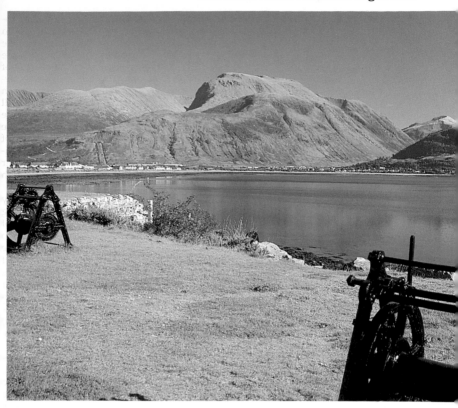

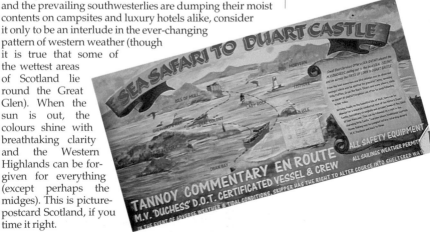

Highlands. It has no pretensions towards the picturesque but is practical in terms of its services. Farther south, Oban is a gateway to the Hebrides and an old-established resort. The often overlooked Campbeltown at the south end of Kintyre is a self-contained working community.

Away from the main towns, there are plenty of smaller places but the essence of this area is definitely rural and rugged, with extensive forestry plantings and a sense of mossy green lushness. When the cloud is down on the hills and the prevailing southwesterlies are dumping their moist contents on campsites and luxury hotels alike, consider it only to be an interlude in the ever-changing pattern of western weather (though it is true that some of the wettest areas of Scotland lie round the Great Glen). When the sun is out, the colours shine with breathtaking clarity and the Western Highlands can be forgiven for everything (except perhaps the midges). This is picture-postcard Scotland, if you time it right.

The true Highland cattle of old were wiry black beasts—unlike the modern cuddly version such as this calf

NEW HEIGHTS
There is now a new way to experience the Cairngorm Mountains. The highest mountain railway in the UK, and the only one in Scotland, opened in 2001. In just 15 minutes, you reach the Ptarmigan station and restaurant and superb views. Open daily (weather permitting) May–Nov, 10–5.30; Dec–Apr (telephone for times). *Admission: expensive*. Tel: 01479 861261; www.cairngormmountain.com.

▶▶▶ Aviemore and Strathspey *185D4*

The transformation of **Aviemore▶** from sleepy Highland railway junction to upmarket St. Moritz-type ski resort never quite worked. Concrete shoeboxes amongst birches failed to appeal to the desired clientele who, unaccountably, still preferred the Alps. Skiing is very popular here, however, although a combination of gale-force winds and the icy upper slopes of the Cairngorms might deter those who just want to pose in fashionable ski gear. **Strathspey▶▶▶** itself is magnificent. Aviemore is a good base with shops and a variety of leisure facilities: ice rink, theatre, cinema, restaurants, discos, amusements, snooker, and so on all within the Aviemore Centre, plus a whole range of activities and places to visit within easy reach.

The innovative **Landmark Forest Heritage Park▶▶▶** at Carrbridge was the first of its kind and portrays many aspects of Scotland, from history to wildlife, by means of audio-visuals and displays. There is also a range of outdoor attractions: mazes, water slides, tree walks and adventure playgrounds (*Open* daily Apr–mid-Jul, 10–6; mid-Jul–Aug, 10–7; Sep–Oct, 10–5.30; Nov–Mar, 10–5. *Admission: expensive*. Tel: 01479 841613; www.landmark-centre.co.uk).

Rothiemurchus Estate▶▶ This working Highland estate, just southeast of Aviemore, offers estate and farm tours by tractor and trailer, Land Rover safari-type excursions, guided walks, a trout farm, fishing lochs, and other activities, including clay-pigeon shooting, walking and cycling trails, pony trekking and a farm shop stocked with estate venison and local cheeses (*Open* visitor centre daily all year, 9.30–5.30. *Admission free*. Tel: 01479 812345; www.rothiemurchus.net).

Highland Wildlife Park Not just today's wildlife, but fauna such as wolves (now extinct in Scotland) can be seen safely fenced off at the Highland Wildlife Park at Kincraig (*Open* Apr–May, Sep–Oct, daily 10–6; Jun–Aug daily 10–7; Nov–Mar daily 10–4. *Admission: moderate*. Tel: 01540 651270; www.highlandwildlifepark.org).

Loch an Eilean▶▶▶ There is a good walk right round this inspiring loch close to Aviemore amid ancient pinewood, a low level option well within the capabilities of

The Great Wood of Caledon—natural pine forest on Speyside

most visitors. Mind your head on the door lintel of the visitor centre beside the loch, which is open daily.

Jack Drake's Alpine Nursery and Gardens►► (*Open Mar–Oct, daily 10–5*. Tel: 01540 651287; www.drakesalpines.com) On the B970 west of Loch an Eilean, this specialist nursery is popular with rock-garden enthusiasts.

►► Boat of Garten *185D4*

Though singling out just one little community from the many in Speyside seems arbitrary, Boat of Garten is typical. It makes a peaceful base for exploring the area, being at a little distance from Aviemore. It has an excellent golf course and a choice of walks through sheltered pinewoods. It is also a steam railway base. Offering the best view (the Cairngorms) of any preserved steam railway line in Britain, the **Strathspey Railway**►►► is pure nostalgia, especially at the original Boat of Garten Station, near the Boat Hotel. There is a small museum here as well. The line runs to Aviemore or Broomhill. It operates most of the main season, but check times (*Admission: expensive*. Tel: 01479 810725; www.strathspeyrailway.co.uk).

Loch Garten►►► here you can spy upon the domestic arrangements of Scotland's most famous pair of ospreys. They get on with the serious business of first catching fish, then feeding it to their offspring, all before the relentless gaze of closed-circuit television cameras, telescopes, and terribly earnest wardens. Ospreys are again becoming almost common in quite a few lochs and rivers hereabouts, though they were extinct in Scotland by the early years of the 20th century, persecuted by gamekeepers guarding fish stocks, and returned only in 1959. The Osprey Centre is open daily (ospreys permitting) in the breeding season (April–August); the reserve opens daily all year (*Admission: inexpensive*. Tel: 01479 821409; www.rspb.org.uk).

BIRD LIFE

Speyside is home to a number of rare bird species, not only the osprey, but the increasingly rare capercaillie. This is like a cross between a large grouse and a very aggressive turkey. It is still found in the old Scots pinewoods, but its habit of failing to spot high deer fences when it is in flight does little for the species' well-being.

Speyside steam trains link Aviemore and Boat of Garten. There are plans to link up eventually to Grantown-on-Spey. Outstanding Cairngorm views are guaranteed

Pause to take in the view of the Cairngorms

A CAIRNGORM GHOST

Few Scottish ghosts are rugged enough for life on top of the Cairngorms plateau, except for one: The Grey Man of Ben Macdhui. He first terrified the life out of a respectable professor who was walking on the plateau in mist when he became aware of something following him, taking one step for every three of his. In 1943, another walker, who happened to be armed, fired his revolver at a "thing" that loomed at him out of the mist. Other tales are told by climbers and local walkers around the fireside—especially after a dram or two.

Skiing in the Cairngorms—big business for Aviemore

►► Cairngorms *185D4*

The Cairngorms contain four of the five highest mountains in Britain, some of the finest hill passes and arguably the best ice, snow, and rock climbing. They represent the country's largest continuous stretch of high ground—an arctic tundra plateau. They are flanked by foothills whose slopes carry Britain's largest surviving fragments of natural pine forest. Now the area is the Cairngorms National Park. Witness the conflict of interest between conservationists and developers by taking a trip on the funicular railway which now permanently disfigures the wild slopes of Cairn Gorm. It offers Britain's highest shopping experience and a restaurant at 1,097m (3,598ft), but you cannot leave the top station, as high numbers of straying people would damage the fragile habitat. There are good views if the clouds stay clear of the tops. (*Open* May–Nov, daily 10–5; Dec–Apr 9–4.30. *Admission: expensive.* Tel 01479 816 336; www.cairngormmountain.com).

► Caledonian Canal *185C4*

The Caledonian Canal, linking east and west coasts, was started in 1803 under the engineer Thomas Telford. It took 19 years to complete and is about 107km (65mi) long. Approximately 72km (45mi) is along the natural passage formed by three lochs, Lochy, Oich and Ness, which lie in the Great Glen fault line. The canal has 29 locks, the most famous being the series of eight near Banavie (3km/2mi north of Fort William) known as Neptune's Staircase. Today its chief use is recreational. One good place for watching canal activity is at Fort Augustus with its series of locks through the centre of the village , and visitor centre.

►►► Cawdor Castle *185D5*

Open: May–early Oct, daily 10–5.30, last admission 5. Admission: moderate (tel: 01667 404401; www.cawdorcastle.com)

Some castles in private hands impress with their opulence, others display stuffy collections while the owner lives elsewhere. Cawdor Castle, the romantic family home of the Earls of Cawdor, does neither of these things, but instead combines the appearance of a fortified stronghold with an air of friendliness. Though it has a legendary association with Shakespeare's *Macbeth*, it post-dates the historical events around which Shakespeare wrote the well-known tragedy. Most of Cawdor is 16th- or 17th-century, though the central tower dates from around 1370, with 15th-century fortifications. Unoccupied for about 100 years after the last Jacobite uprising in 1745, the castle owes much of its charm to its appearance, unaltered since those days.

The family has accumulated a variety of artefacts: portraits, Flemish tapestries and Venetian bed hangings, as well as historical items, including the iron gate or yett from Lochindorb Castle (see page 195), which the 6th Thane of Cawdor was ordered to destroy. But Cawdor is much more about the overall effect than individual display items. Best of all are the room notes. Far from breathlessly tiptoeing past objects, visitors can be heard laughing out loud at the witty captions—a scenario unique in a Scottish castle, which makes it worth visiting for that reason alone. There are also attractive gardens.

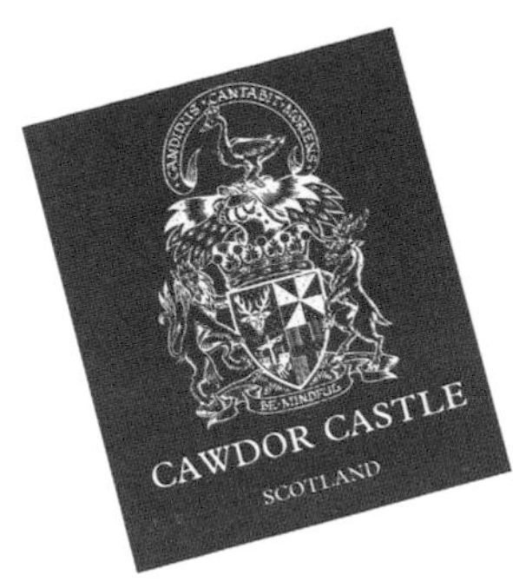

▶ Cowal and the Kyles of Bute *184B2*

Cowal reaches down towards the island of Bute and is bounded by the long, fiord-like sea lochs of Loch Long and Loch Fyne. It is sometimes overlooked but is a most attractive part of Argyll and easy to reach from the south via the Gourock to Dunoon ferry crossing. The Arrochar Alps guard its northern approaches and it has a number of scenically spectacular roads, of which the Rest and Be Thankful, the A83 west of Arrochar, is the best known.

Much of this area is within the **Argyll Forest Park** with its walking and pony trekking routes. There are more exotic trees to see in **Benmore Botanic Garden** (*Open* Mar and Oct daily 10–5; Apr–Sep daily 10–6. *Admission: inexpensive*. Tel: 01369 706261; www.rbge.org.uk). This has some of the largest trees in Scotland and a world-famous rhododendron collection. It is closed in winter.

Cowal's outstretched fingers on either side of Bute form the **Kyles of Bute** (from the Gaelic *caolas*, a strait) These peerless stretches of coastal scenery can be enjoyed from the A886, en route to or from the Bute ferry at Colintraive.

BRODIE CASTLE
After Cawdor, castle enthusiasts can travel eastwards, just into Moray, to enjoy Brodie Castle (see page 177). The long and unbroken line of Brodies (they were here by 1160) has allowed a unique continuity in its acquisitions. Cawdor and Brodie could be fitted into a morning and afternoon.

One of Scotland's most entertaining castles, Cawdor also has attractive gardens and nature trails

ON TOP OF THE MOUNTAIN
A weather observatory operated from 1883 to 1904 on Ben Nevis, surviving the fierce winds and driving snows that so often beset the dangerous summit plateau. There was also a hotel until 1915.

EMPTY THREAT
Do not be unnerved by the stacked powder barrels in the Grand Magazine at Fort George. They are empty replicas. Besides, the building was designed to withstand a direct hit.

▶▶▶ Crarae Garden 184B2

Open: daily 9.30–sunset. Visitor centre Easter–Sep, daily 10–5. Admission: moderate (tel: 01546 886614; www.nts.org.uk)

If there is time for only one Argyll garden, then Crarae should be chosen. All the natural advantages of topography and climate have been used to create this woodland garden on a hillside with a tumbling burn. Snow does not linger, rainfall is copious, and these soft conditions are appreciated by many tender shrubs, acer, and eucryphia, and a range of Himalayan species. Particularly arresting are the large-leaved rhododendrons, including *R. macabeanum*. There is good colour here in spring and autumn too. Be prepared to walk a little way uphill to take it all in—you will see why Crarae has been described as being like a wild corner of some Himalayan gorge.

▶▶ Crinan Canal 184B2

Designed so that ships could avoid the long haul around the Mull of Kintyre, the 14km (9mi) Crinan Canal was

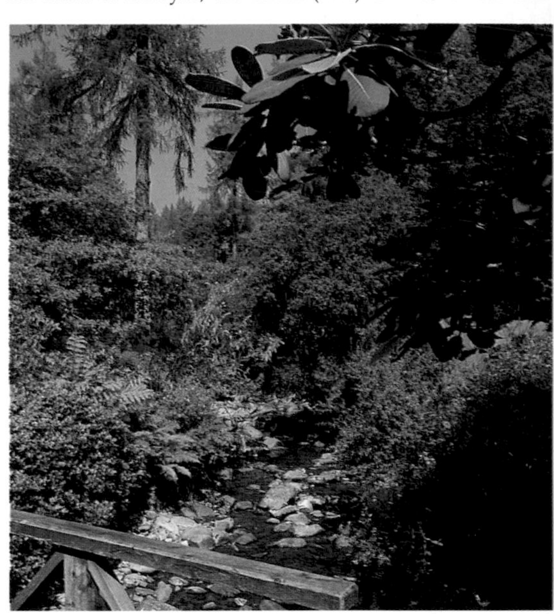

Crarae Garden, of interest throughout the year, but perhaps best in late spring

begun in 1794. After many construction problems and the help of trouble-shooting engineer Thomas Telford, it was pronounced satisfactory in 1817. Once used by the Loch Fyne herring fleet seeking new grounds, the canal is mainly used now by yachts, which can be found at the Crinan end where there is a good hotel and a coffee shop.

▶▶▶ Fort George 185D5

Open: Apr–Sep, daily 9.30–6.30; Oct–Mar, daily 9.30–4.30. Admission: moderate (tel: 01667 462777; www.historic-scotland.gov.uk)

Fort George is one of the most vivid experiences of Scotland's history available today. It is also Europe's finest surviving piece of 18th-century military architecture—a huge Georgian fort on a headland jutting out into the Moray Firth like a vast battleship forever anchored to the land.

It was built in response to the Jacobite rebellion of 1745, to ensure that the Highlands never rose again in revolt. It has never fired a shot in anger. Weapon development soon made it redundant. Yet, oddly, it still has a military presence. You can stroll along the great walls with their sentry boxes and embrasures, noting that the whole

Crinan Canal, west end, at Crinan

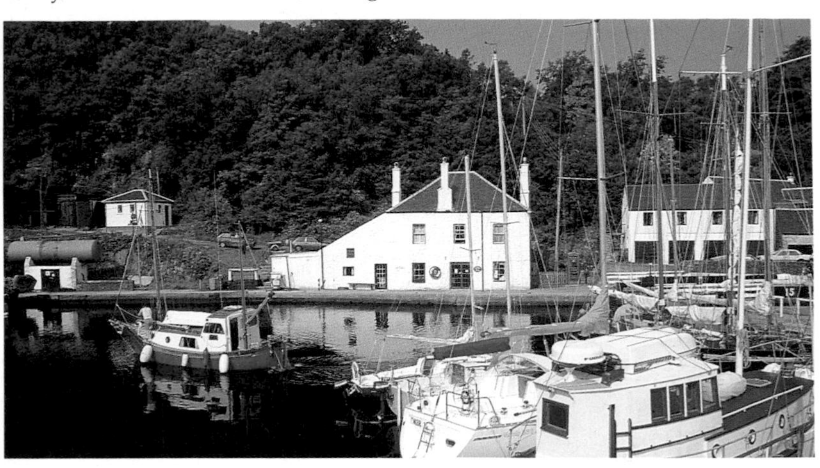

design is in the form of a pentagon with a bastion at each angle. This is the place to learn a whole new military language: ravelin, casemate, counterscarp, firing step, and so on. There is a visitor centre, period rooms of soldiers' quarters, and the regimental museum of the Queen's Own Highlanders.

Perhaps the toughest of the various hill races throughout Scotland, the Ben Nevis race has a summit checkpoint at 1,343m (4,407ft)

▶ Fort William *184B4*

Fort William is famed for its proximity to **Ben Nevis**, though Britain's highest mountain, at 1,343m (4,407ft), hides its best profile from the town itself.

The fort that was founded here in 1690 was named after William, Prince of Orange. It was finally demolished in the 1880s to make way for the railway. Fort William is a natural route centre in Lochaber, all but unavoidable for touring traffic heading for the Great Glen. Like Inverness at the northern end, Fort William is far from picturesque but has an excellent range of services and shops for books, outdoor wear, tartans, tweeds, woollens, and so on.

The West Highland Museum▶▶ has an exhibition on tartan, and touches upon the area's Jacobite connections; there is a fascinating hidden portrait of Prince Charles Edward Stuart (Bonnie Prince Charlie), painted on a cylinder and viewed with a mirror. (*Open* Jun–Sep, Mon–Sat 10–4, also Jul and Aug, Sun 2–5; Oct–May, Mon–Sat 10–4. *Admission: inexpensive*. Tel: 01397 702169; www.westhighlandmuseum.org.uk).

A trip into Glen Nevis is also worthwhile for its spectacular hill scenery. (Look for the signpost from the roundabout at the north end of the town.)

Parallel Roads of Glen Roy▶▶ These curious parallel lines etched on the sides of the glen are the shorelines of an Ice Age loch, dammed by a glacier at the mouth of the glen, which melted in stages, hence the parallel shorelines, the highest being the oldest.

THE GLEN COE MASSACRE

There have been several larger massacres in the bloody history of clan warfare. However, none convulsed Scotland as much as the killing of around 38 members of the MacIan MacDonalds of Glen Coe on 13 February, 1692 by a force of Campbell militia (that is, government troops). The official line was that the clan chief had been late in taking an oath of allegiance to King William (of Orange) so his clan was taught a lesson. Nevertheless, the troops had been billeted with their MacDonald hosts, observing an old Highland custom of hospitality even to bitter enemies. The breaking of this code and the resulting "murder under trust" shocked Scotland. The king had blood on his hands—and, besides, the job was botched.

▶▶▶ Glen Affric *185C5*

Glen Affric has a reputation as one of the most beautiful glens in Scotland—and this even with a hydroelectric dam. To get into the excellent hill and (in some places) natural pinewood scenery, there is a choice of Forestry Commission walks. The best known is around the **Dog Falls**, close to the twisty road up the glen. This trip could also take in the **Aigas Dam Fish Lift▶** on the scenic A831 through Strathglass to the northwest, a facility for viewing migrating salmon (*Open* Jun–Oct, daily 10–3).

▶▶ Glen Coe *185C3*

Glen Coe is probably the most famous glen in Scotland, partly because it carries a main road that allows some of the finest hill scenery in the central Highlands to be viewed with no effort whatsoever. This includes the impressive view of Buchaille Etive Mor guarding the eastern approaches to the glen, and the "Three Sisters," the three long spurs running off Bidean nam Bian, the highest peak in Argyll. Matching these south-side features is the long wall of the Aonach Eagach ridge enclosing Glen Coe to the north. This is the most spectacular ridge-walk on the Scottish mainland—but definitely not for the faint-hearted, the unfit, or the novice.

The National Trust for Scotland is in charge of much of the glen, and has a sensitively built visitor centre (*Open* Mar daily 10–4; Apr–Aug daily 9.30–5.30; Sep–Oct daily 10–5; Nov–Feb, Thu–Sun 10–4. *Admission: inexpensive.* Tel: 01855 811307; www.nts.org.uk). These hills are awesome and high—but certainly not lonely. Also worth exploring is Glen Etive, a road that leads down to the head of a sea loch.

▶▶ Glenfinnan *184B4*

The view down Glenfinnan is a typical Western Highlands landscape, and is an image that is used on everything from picture postcards to place-mats. The rash adventurer, Bonnie Prince Charlie, hardly chose this location for scenery alone when he raised the flag of rebellion in August 1745. However, the subsequent Glenfinnan

A Highlander tops the Glenfinnan Monument rather than Bonnie Prince Charlie

Monument, recalling the escapade, adds interest to the foreground in the view from the main Mallaig road. There is a National Trust for Scotland visitor centre here, which has displays tell-ing the story of the prince's campaign (*Open* Easter–Jun, Sep–Oct daily 10–5; Jul–Aug daily 9.30–5.30; Nov, Sat–Sun 10–4. *Admission: inexpensive.* Tel: 01397 722250; www.nts.org.uk).

Equally photogenic is the **Glenfinnan Viaduct**▶▶▶ on the "Mallaig Extension" of the West Highland Railway of 1901. The engineer Robert MacAlpine ("Concrete Bob") pioneered the use of mass concrete for such large works while building the line. Unlike Bonnie Prince Charlie's excursion here, this brought only benefit to the Western Highlands.

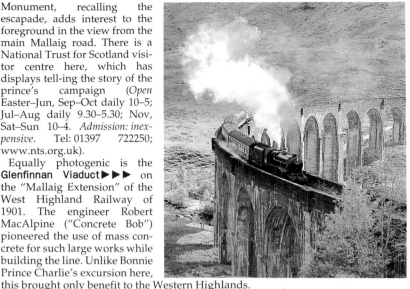

A steam locomotive on the Glenfinnan Viaduct

▶ Grantown-on-Spey *185D5*

James Grant of Castle Grant planned his new town in 1766, intending to get some return on the poor moorland site. Handsome buildings of local silver granite soon sprang up, and local trades such as weaving developed. The town became popular with tourists and is still a handsome place, worth strolling around especially for a complete contrast to Aviemore. It has good shops, if better quality souvenirs and gifts are on your list, a good museum (tel: 01479 872478), and a good café or two.

The **Speyside Heather Centre**▶▶ (*Open* daily 9–6 in summer; 9–5 in winter. *Admission: free; exhibition inexpensive.* Tel: 01479 851359; www.heathercentre.com). Within easy reach of Grantown, this venue will sell you a huge variety of heather species. The displays at its Heather Heritage Centre will also inform you of the many different and remarkable uses heather was put to in the Highland economy of old, ranging from folk remedies to rope-making.

Another excursion north of Grantown-on-Spey leads across the endless moors to lonely Lochindorb Castle, a shattered remnant on an island, once the lair of the Wolf of Badenoch (see page 175).

THE RAILWAY VIADUCT

"Concrete Bob's" railway viaduct at Glenfinnan has 21 spans and is 390m (1,280ft) long. It receives much attention from photographers when it is carrying one of the steam locomotives running a regular summer service between Fort William and Mallaig, especially since it featured in the Harry Potter movie.

THE "LONE ROWAN"

On the way to Glen Coe from the south, on the left-hand side beyond Loch Tulla, look out for the "Lone Rowan" on the approaches to the empty stretches of Rannoch Moor. This single tree grows from a crack on a large boulder. It has survived for years and has become a kind of symbol among conservationists seeking to restore Scotland's natural tree cover.

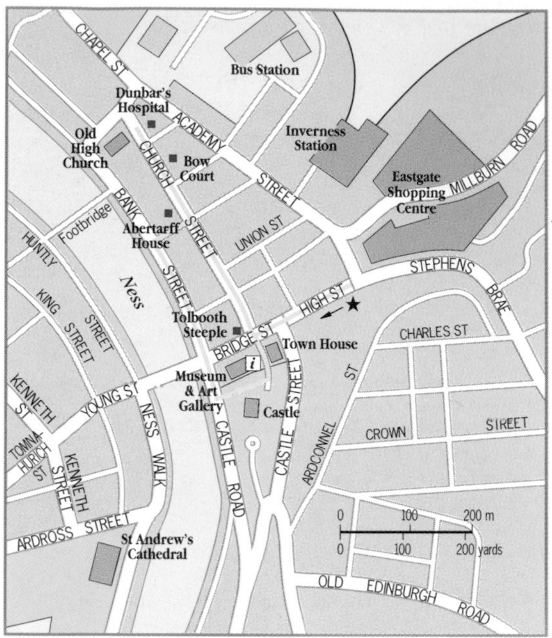

Walk

Around Inverness

Ancient Inverness was regularly burned by marauding clansmen, so little remains. Today, it is a bustling gateway town serving the north of Scotland. Allow 1 hour for this walk.

West along High Street, the **Tolbooth Steeple's** spire, dating from 1791, was damaged and repaired after an earth tremor in 1816. Opposite is Inverness Town House, where in 1921 the then prime minister Lloyd George held the first-ever Cabinet meeting outside London.

Walk up Castle Wynd to **Inverness Castle**. Though its site is older, the present building only dates from 1834–1847 and is the Sheriff Court. Note the nearby statue of Flora MacDonald, helpmate of Bonnie Prince Charlie.

Go down steps and follow the River Ness north to Fraser Street. **Abertarff House**, one of the oldest houses in Inverness, is on Church Street. A little farther down Church Street is the much-restored **Dunbar's Hospital**. Look for the plaque on the side of the nearby **Bow Court**, which dates from the 17th century.

Turning south, the best shopping is on Church Street and in the fine Market Arcade to the east of Church Street. Return to High Street.

Inverness Castle and the River Ness

Culloden was the last major battle on British soil, fought over two and a half centuries ago in order to decide a civil war between the ruling House of Hanover and the Jacobites, who wished to return the exiled House of Stuart—in the guise of Bonnie Prince Charlie—to power. The battle, just to the east of Inverness, accelerated the final demise of a way of life already beginning to disintegrate in the Highlands: The Scottish clan system had become something of an anachronism in an increasingly mercantile age.

Anti-Jacobites Only 5,000–6,000 of the estimated 30,000 fighting men in the Highlands rose in support of the young Stuart prince Charles Edward, known as Bonnie Prince Charlie or the Young Pretender. Anti-Jacobite sentiment prevailed in many parts of Scotland. On his way north from his expedition into England, the prince had no help from Dumfries; and Glasgow was reluctant to supply him with the provisions he demanded. Edinburgh gave the Freedom of the City to the Duke of Cumberland as he took government troops north to confront the Jacobite forces.

THE BATTLE
OF CULLODEN
WAS FOUGHT ON THIS MOOR
16TH APRIL 1746.
THE GRAVES OF THE
GALLANT HIGHLANDERS
WHO FOUGHT FOR
SCOTLAND & PRINCE CHARLIE
ARE MARKED BY THE NAMES

The battle On a sleety day in April 1746, about 5,000 Jacobites, exhausted after marching for an aborted surprise attack on the Hanoverians, faced 9,000 regular soldiers, including 15 infantry regiments. Through a tactical blunder by the prince's Irish adviser, the Highlanders were lined up at perfect shooting range for the superior government artillery.

The Jacobites were blown away in less than an hour. The Highland charge, when it finally came, was ragged and ineffective. The government troops then went on to commit, with their commander's blessing, the worst series of atrocities ever carried out by the British Army.

The episode is graphically described in an excellent audiovisual in the **Culloden Visitor Centre** (*Open* Feb–Mar and Nov–Dec, daily 11–4; Apr–May, Sep–Oct, daily 9–5.30; Jun–Aug 9–6. *Admission: moderate*. Tel: 01463 790607; www.nts.org.uk). This does much to counter the myth that this was a simple Scottish-English conflict. A new state-of-the-art display is due at the end of 2007.

"BUTCHER" CUMBERLAND

The Duke of Cumberland acquired his unsavoury nickname due to the conduct of his army after Culloden. Because the rebels were judged to be beyond the law and also because London was a long way off, no mercy was shown, a state of affairs made easier by the fact that the victims were perceived as being racially different in dress and language. This may explain the slaughter which took place on the road to Inverness where bystanders, including women, who had come to watch, were sabred. Wounded rebels were despatched wherever they were found. Military looting was legalized throughout the Highlands, irrespective of the sympathies of the victims.

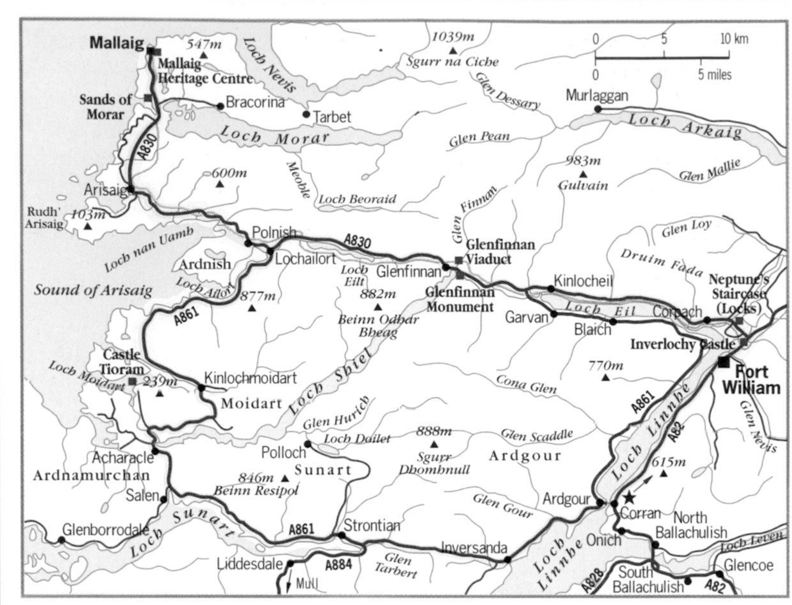

Drive

A loop to the isles

Castle Tioram

You could use part of this drive to reach Skye via the Mallaig to Armadale ferry link, or to make an excursion to the Small Isles from Arisaig—but, if the weather is good, the stupendous island views from Moidart alone make the trip worthwhile. Without the Ardnamurchan option (an extra 64km/40mi return) the drive is 185km (115mi): it can be driven in 3 hours or so, using the Corran ferry, but it is best to allow a whole day.

If approaching from the south, note the Corran Ferry off the A82, useful on the return leg. Go through Fort William to take the A830 along the shores of Loch Eil. You climb away from the sea-weedy levels of Loch Eil to reach the **Glenfinnan Monument** by Loch Shiel. Though the hills on either side of the loch are not especially high, their steeply tilting slopes receding down the loch into a blue haze make them the very distillation of Scottish scenery. The National Trust for Scotland Centre outlines the story of (Bonnie) Prince Charles Edward Stuart's rebellious escapade here.

Rail buffs will doubtless admire the **Glenfinnan Viaduct**. Its 12 spans are 390m (1,280ft) long. Take care, as the train enthusiasts travelling by car are occasionally inclined to chase the locomotive—and it's quite possible that you may be overtaken several times along this particular stretch.

Continue to Lochailort, then keep right on the A830 for Mallaig. Do not expect to have the dazzling **Sands of Morar** all to yourself in high season. You could also drive down for a close-up view of **Loch Morar**. Back on the main road, the approach to the town of **Mallaig** is picturesque, with plenty of interest. Actually being there, at the end of the road (and railway) is, however, something of an anticlimax. The **Mallaig Heritage Centre** displays the history of the port by way of various exhibits and models (*Open* Apr–Jun and Oct, Mon–Sat 11–4; Jul–Sep, Mon–Sat 9.30–4.30, Sun 12.30–4.30; Nov–Mar, Wed–Sat 12–5. *Admission: inexpensive.* Tel: 01687 462085; www.mallaigheritage.org.uk).

Return to take the A861 loop at Lochailort. Here are the classic Scottish views of islands set in ultramarine—over the Sound of Arisaig to Eigg, Muck, and Rum—unless it is raining, which is regrettably very probable. Beyond Kinlochmoidart, **Castle Tioram** is a worthwhile diversion. It was the home of the chief of the MacDonalds of Clan Ranald, who burned it to stop the Campbells getting their hands on it after the 1715 Jacobite rebellion. The castle has a grand setting, on a bracken-covered islet barely attached to the mainland by a sandy beach.

Continue through Acharacle and Salen to Loch Sunart to decide on the Ardnamurchan option. If taking the B8007 across the peninsula to the most westerly point on mainland Scotland at the lighthouse, allow plenty of time as the road is single track and winding. Otherwise continue east to **Strontian**, the community which gave its name to the element strontium, formerly mined nearby. If you go up the road that led to the mining area, you will see a variety of craft businesses on the way.

Continue on the A861 through **Glen Sanda**, joining the faster double track section and, unless returning to Fort William, exit via the Corran Ferry. Alternatively, note the two roads going south into Morven. Both are attractive ways to reach Mull, via the back-door short ferry crossing at Lochaline.

Mallaig harbour

Inveraray Jail with real-life jailor

BRIDGES
Eighteenth-century town planning is seen at its best at Inveraray. The stylishness even extends to its bridges, a notable feature on its northern approaches by the A83. One of at least three good examples is the Garron Bridge of 1747–1749, reminiscent of those seen on willow pattern plates.

Kilmartin grave slabs

▶▶▶ Inveraray *184B2*

Inveraray is one of the most handsome of Scottish towns and owes its appearance to the mighty chiefs of the Clan Campbell. One of them, Archibald, 3rd Duke of Argyll, planned his grand new town in 1743 at a little distance from his castle. Churches and courthouse, bell tower and Georgian facades all stand together in harmony. Sadly, Inveraray is one of the wettest places in the Highlands. However, it has some indoor attractions. These include **Inveraray Castle**, the stately pile of the present duke. There are fine interiors and valuable portraits to admire (*Open* Apr–May, Oct, Mon–Thu and Sat 10–1, 2–5.45, Sun 1–5.45; Jun–Sep Mon–Sat 10–5.45, Sun 1–5.45. *Admission: moderate*. Tel: 01499 302203; www.inveraray-castle.com).

Inveraray Jail▶▶▶ Look out for the live prisoner and jailer in this re-creation of a 19th-century county prison, complete with courtroom and cells. It is more enticing than it sounds (*Open* Apr–Oct, daily 9.30–6; Nov–Mar, daily 10–5, last entry 1 hour before closing. *Admission: moderate*. Tel: 01499 302 381; www.inverarayjail.co.uk).

Auchindrain Township Open Air Museum▶▶▶ This survivor from an earlier age is the last communal tenancy farm township to have survived on its original site in something like its original form. Many of the buildings have been restored and there is an on-site museum (*Open* Apr–Oct, daily 10–5. *Admission: inexpensive*. Tel: 01499 500235; www.auchindrainmuseum.org.uk).

▶▶ Kilmartin and Dunadd *184B2*

Argyll has plenty of early sites and there is a profusion around Kilmartin, a small village on the main Oban–Lochgilphead road. This is the setting for the **Kilmartin House Museum** (*Open* Mar–Oct, daily 10–5.30; Nov–Dec, daily 11–4. *Admission: moderate*. Tel: 01546 510278; www.kilmartin.org). Medieval grave slabs in the local kirkyard, 3,000-year-old cairns, cup and ring markings, burial cists (chests), and stone circles are all interpreted here. The museum also offers the opportunity to listen to Stone Age music and taste wild food. Among other early sites, the **Temple Wood Stone Circles** are close by, and the **Ri Cruin Cairn** farther south is in a group of five cairns in a straight line.

Dating from around AD 500, and dominating the mossy flatland all around, **Dunadd Fort**▶▶ was a stronghold of the first kingdom of the Scots, known as Dalriada, after they arrived from Ireland. Some early walling survives, but the chief point of interest of this hillfort is the carvings: a boar, an outline of a footprint, and a hollowed-out basin can be seen, as well as several lines of inscription in the ancient ogham system of writing (see panel). These features have been linked to the early kingship rituals of the embryonic Scotland. Altogether, it is a mysterious place, with superb views across the levels toward the Crinan Canal. Access at all times.

Shopping choice in Inveraray: For a small loch-side town, the range is fairly wide

OGHAM SCRIPT
Ogham writing as seen at Dunadd and in other early sites is thought to have originated in Ireland. It consists of groups of strokes scored at various angles to a base line. At Dunadd, natural cracks and fissures make up this line.

▶ Kingussie *185D4*

Kingussie (pronounced "kin-*yoo*-see," from the Gaelic for the head of the pinewood) is a typical Speyside tourism community which benefits from year-round tourism. Nearby **Ruthven Barracks**▶, destroyed by retreating Jacobites after Culloden, still dominate the valley floor near Kingussie. They can be visited en route to the Royal Society for the Protection of Birds' **Insh Marshes**▶▶▶, Scotland's largest inland marsh. Goosander and red-breasted merganser breed here; spotted craik and water rail are often heard; and there are wood and common sandpipers in summer, with hen harriers and buzzards all year. In winter 10 percent of the UK population of whooper swans is found here, along with greylag geese and goldeneye.

Highland Folk Museum▶▶▶ Not just a passive show of half-forgotten artefacts, this museum recaptures the past with a series of events: You can smell bannocks toasting or hear a horse being shod on the right day. Costumes, musical instruments, and everyday bits and pieces can be seen, as can reconstructed buildings such as a "black house" from Lewis (*Open* mid-Apr–Aug, Mon–Sat 9–5; Sep–Oct, Mon–Fri 9.30–4. *Admission: inexpensive*. Tel: 01540 661307; www.highlandfolk.com).

Near Southend on the southern tip of the Mull of Kintyre, an area neither Highland nor Lowland in character, but with an ambience all its own

►► Kintyre 184B1

This is the longest peninsula in Scotland, with the Mull of Kintyre at its tip. Kintyre's gateway is Tarbert on the isthmus where there is a heritage centre. Some visitors get no farther, which is a pity, as Kintyre offers splendid sea views from both its east- and west-facing coasts, as well as an unexpectedly Lowland air in places. (The Campbell Dukes of Argyll once settled the area with Lowland farmers.) The raised beaches backed by ancient sea cliffs, typical west-side landscapes, are bright pasture lands, echoing Ayrshire over on the "mainland."

COLUMBA'S FOOTSTEPS
This is the name given to two footprint-shaped impressions on a flat-topped rock near an ancient chapel site. By tradition, this is where Columba first stepped ashore on Scottish soil. As he could still see Ireland, his home, he took to the sea again before ending up on the island of Iona.

With the impressive outlines of Islay, Jura, and Gigha parading along the horizon, the main road leads down to Campbeltown, a substantial town, busy with whisky, creameries, and fishing. It seems a lot farther than 19km (12mi) down the narrow roads to the Mull of Kintyre itself. Facing west, this spot is very romantic at sunset. The best views are from the moorland before the road drops to the lighthouse, which is built well down the steep slope. This trip can also be combined with the loop which goes past **Columba's Footsteps**, on top of a flat-topped rock at Keil, moments from the road (see panel). Return north from Campbeltown by the B842 (on the east side of the peninsula), which is narrow but scenically rewarding.

►► Knapdale 184B2

Knapdale is an area defined by the Crinan Canal to the north and West Loch Tarbert to the south. Without high mountains or overwhelming scenery, Knapdale nevertheless has a special charm. The woods, which drop to the salty tidelines of the sealochs, clothe rugged hills. There are primroses in spring and, later, twining honeysuckle. Extensive plantings supplement the natural oakwoods, and there is some farming (the area was once noted for its beef cattle). There are no large towns; instead the small villages have often grown up round natural anchorages.

The stone walls of **Castle Sween**► overlook the loch of the same name. Possibly dating from the mid-12th century, the historic fortress is one of the oldest in Scotland, and can be viewed at any time. There are also finely carved medieval grave slabs and crosses of the Knapdale School to be viewed at Kilmory and farther south, Kilberry, with the added advantage of a good pub near the latter. Knapdale is a spot for slow tourers. Choose a fine day for the sea views.

▶▶ Loch Awe *184B3*

Loch Awe is Scotland's longest loch. Once it drained southwards, until with the last Ice Age a breach was made in a fault line. The loch now empties by the Pass of Brander westwards to Loch Etive. Loch Awe is most often seen from the A85, the main Perth to Oban road, where its length is not appreciated.

At the **Cruachan Power Station Visitor Centre▶▶▶** there are displays about the impressive hydroelectric project which generates 400MW of electricity by running water from a dam high on Ben Cruachan down into Loch Awe (and pumping it back at off-peak times). Minibuses take visitors 1km (0.5mi) into the mountain to see the turbine hall (*Open* daily 9.30–5. *Admission: moderate*. Tel: 01866 822618; www.visitcruachan.co.uk).

The former 15th-century Campbell stronghold of **Kilchurn Castle▶▶▶** is just a short ferry ride from Loch Awe Pier (tel: 01866 833333). Interpretative boards help identify features in the extensive panorama (*Open* all reasonable times. *Admission free*. Tel: 01838 200393; www.historic-scotland.gov.uk).

Duncan Ban McIntyre Monument▶▶▶ Take the road behind Dalmally for one of the very finest vistas in the Western Highlands. Also worth a look are **Ardanaiseig Gardens▶** (*Open* daily in season) and, farther west by Loch Etive, the **Bonawe Iron Furnace▶** (*Open* Apr–Sep, daily 9.30–6.30. *Admission: inexpensive*. Tel: 01866 822432; www.historic-scotland.gov.uk). Here Historic Scotland look after the well-preserved remains of a charcoal furnace for iron-smelting founded in 1753; a reminder that industry even reached these peaceful Highland shores 250 years ago.

LONG LOCHS
Loch Awe is Scotland's longest loch at 41km (25.4mi), compared with 39km (24.2mi) for Loch Ness and 36km (22.3mi) for Loch Lomond.

"BURNS OF THE HIGHLANDS"
Duncan Ban McIntyre (1724–1812) was a Gaelic gamekeeper turned poet who was born in Glenorchy. He is commemorated by a large granite monument, like a temple, on the old Inveraray road, signposted from Dalmally. It offers superb views towards the ridges of Ben Cruachan and its high neighbours beyond Loch Awe.

Kilchurn Castle on the shores of Loch Awe offers outstanding views from its battlements towards Ben Cruachan and its satellite peaks

AN UNSUCCESSFUL SPEED ATTEMPT

Between Invermoriston and Drumnadrochit on the A82 a cairn recalls the world water speed record attempt by John Cobb. He was killed here in 1952 when his jet-boat hit a mysterious patch of ripples at high speed. Inevitably, this tragedy is linked to the monster phenomenon, as the loch was otherwise calm.

► Loch Ness *185C5*

Loch Ness has a larger volume of water than any other Scottish loch. It is around 250m (825ft) deep in places, and the water in this great glacier-gouged trench is said never to freeze. Because of its mysterious reputation, it is very popular with visitors. Take time to explore the area away from the main loch itself, particularly the big glens to the west around Strathglass and also peaceful Stratherrick eastwards. Though Loch Ness ends up on most people's touring list, like Inverness, Loch Lomond, and the Trossachs, the loch itself can be a mild anticlimax—a big sheet of water, certainly, yet lacking in real grandeur.

The west-bank road, the busy main A82, goes through **Drumnadrochit** with its "Loch Ness 2000" and "Original Loch Ness Monster Visitor Centre" among other enticements. Nearby **Urquhart Castle** was once one of the largest castles in Scotland but was blown up in 1692 lest it fall into Jacobite hands. The castle viewpoint is popular with fast-moving coach parties "doing" Scotland in a day (*Open* Apr–Sep, daily 9.30–6.30; Oct–Mar, daily 9.30–4.30. *Admission: moderate.* Tel: 01456 450551; www.historic-scotland.gov.uk). It is a relief to escape to the gentler and more subtle attractions of the east side road. These include **Loch Tarff**, north of Fort Augustus on the B862, and the superb viewpoint beyond (towards Inverness) with its panorama of the Monadhliath and waves of northern Highland hills. The route here follows the old military road, completed by General Wade's men in 1726. The road runs to Whitebridge, with a handsome preserved Wade bridge, then on to Foyers, where the **Falls of Foyers**►► are worth a visit. (Park beside the post office, but take care with young children on the slippery paths.) Inverfarigaig is lower down. Starting from the Forest Centre, a forest walk leads up to a fine view of the loch.

Although a ruin, Urquhart Castle, on the side of Loch Ness, remains popular in the summer months—perhaps with those hoping to see the loch's famous resident

Scottish folklore has plenty of references to water-spirits which lurk in and around lochs and burns, often with evil intent. The water kelpie is blended with Gaelic each-uisge, *the water horse, and other beasts in a fantastic menagerie of the Celtic imagination.*

The start of the story One quiet week on the *Inverness Courier* in May 1933, there was space for a report which had come from a local correspondent and water bailiff. He had heard of a couple who had seen a strange animal disporting itself in the dark waters of the loch. The couple was thought to be running one of the hotels in Drumnadrochit.

Not *the real thing at Drumnadrochit*

Soon other sightings flooded in. National papers took up the story and "monster mania" hit the headlines. A pre-war AA patrolman reported that he could create pandemonium among the lines of cars parked by the loch merely by pointing over the water. Meanwhile, Inverness Town Council voted to reduce its publicity expenditure substantially for 1934.

The story has refused to go away. It has spawned books, supported a variety of tourism-related businesses both by the loch and in Inverness, and attracted scientists, dedicated amateurs, and hoaxers. It has generated dubious cine film and still photographs, echo soundings, and sincere testimony from dozens of eye-witnesses who have seen something.

There is undoubtedly a strange phenomenon to be witnessed here, whose manifestation is of great importance to the local economy. Its appearance is in inverse proportion to the number of cameras trained on the loch at any given moment. Loch Ness is a very large body of water, prone to mirages in still, calm conditions—ideal visitor and monster-spotting weather.

In the Scottish legal system there is a verdict "not proven." Without enough evidence for a conviction, Nessie has to remain a modern myth—the water kelpie with an excellent publicity machine.

SUNDAY OBSERVANCE

A Free Church minister in Fort Augustus wrote of the 1930s monster craze: "The word 'monster' is really not applicable to the Loch Ness animal, but is truly applicable to those who deliberately sin against the light of law and revelation." He was objecting to visitors going monster-spotting on a Sunday.

SOME EXPLANATIONS

Swimming red deer, diving otters, floating logs or vegetation, cormorants, boats' wakes, seals, and many more everyday things have been suggested as explanations for monster sightings.

ROAD-BUILDING EXPECTATIONS

One explanation often given for the sudden flurry of sightings in the 1930s was the new road which gave better views of the loch. Some even said the beast or beasts had been disturbed by the blasting. Yet General Wade and his men built a military road down the east side of the loch to supersede the first high-level road of 1726. They also blasted out rock above Inverfarigaig and must therefore have created quite a disturbance. Perhaps Wade's forces were too busy keeping a sharp lookout for Jacobites to notice long-necked creatures.

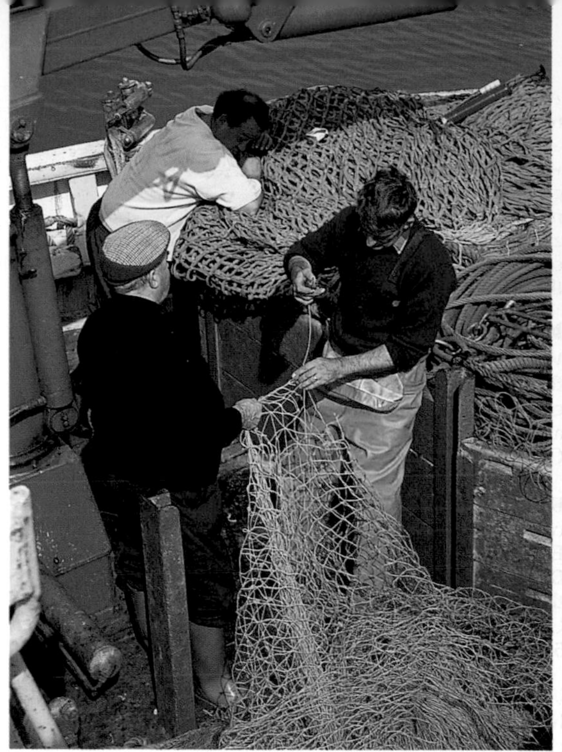

Busy ferry port and yachting haven, Oban's harbour also has room for more traditional commercial fishing activities

TWO CULTURES
It was once the boast of the Stuart monarchs that they had a town in their realm so large that the inhabitants spoke different languages at either end. This was a reference to Nairn, where the Lowland fishers at the sea end of town used the Scots tongue (still heard eastwards along the Moray Firth today). At the landward end of the town, the farmers spoke Gaelic. Thus Nairn has for long been on the dividing line between Highland and Lowland cultures.

THE ATLANTIC BRIDGE
The Clachan Bridge is a single-arched bridge of 1792 linking the island of Seil with the mainland. Seil is one of the so-called "slate islands," recalling an industry which lasted for 200 years until a violent storm in 1881 flooded the quarry workings and closed down the industry overnight. The Clachan Bridge is often called the Atlantic Bridge, because it spans an arm of that ocean. Other bridges on the western seaboard do likewise, but only the Clachan Bridge is so labelled.

►► Nairn *185D5*

More Lowland than Highland, Nairn, with its resort air and famous golf courses, always seems to have had a split personality. The former fisher town by the harbour is separated by the main road from the main shopping streets of a centre once dependent on agricultural activities. Both lie apart from the mansions and hotels of the seaside resort development that benefited from the arrival of the Highland Railway in the mid-19th century.

The **Nairn Museum** is a typical, almost old-fashioned community museum assembled by local people and reflecting their pride in their town's story (*Open* Easter–Oct, Mon–Sat 10–4.30; Nov, Sat 10–4.30, Sun 2–5. *Admission: inexpensive*. Tel: 01667 456791; www.nairnmuseum.co.uk). Thus Nairn Museum reflects on the one event of national importance—the Battle of Culloden—which took place nearby, and displays its battlefield artefacts. Aside from this, the town's story unfolds in the museum around its agriculture and, more prominently, its fishing. Its harbour was built by Thomas Telford in the 1820s, and ushered in about a century of herring fishing activity of varying fortune (like other Moray Firth ports).

Then there are golf courses and beaches backed by dunes, stretching east to Culbin Forest. Fort George, and Cawdor and Brodie castles are also within easy reach.

► Newtonmore *185D4*

Newtonmore is a Speyside community made more peaceful by the A9 bypass. The old Celtic game of shinty (like a suicidal form of hockey) is played here and at nearby Kingussie. The village also has part of the Highland Folk Museum (see page 201) and the **Clan Macpherson Museum►** (*Open*

Apr–Oct, Mon–Sat 10–5, Sun 12–5. *Admission free*. Tel: 01540 673332; www.clan-macpherson.org) with its display of clan artefacts. Within easy reach of Newtonmore, along the A86, west of Laggan, a track leads to the **Corrieyairack Pass▶**, completed by General Wade's men in 1732. This high-level military route from Speyside to the Great Glen, which zig-zags up to about 760m (2,500ft), soon fell into disuse because of the severe Scottish winters. Now it is disintegrating due to the attentions of four-wheel-drive enthusiasts.

▶▶ Oban *184B3*

When the railway arrived in 1880, Oban was described as the new "Charing Cross of the Highlands." The railway company initiated trips to the islands and the sealochs around. Today, the railway is still here, though most of Oban's visitors now come by road rather than rail.

From the east, the A82 passes the **Falls of Lora** at Connel Bridge. This curious turbulence at the mouth of Loch Etive can be seen below the bridge when the tide runs strongly. Even nearer to Oban is the 13th-century **Dunstaffnage Castle**, an old MacDougall stronghold that once controlled the sea-roads of Argyll (*Open* Apr–Sep, daily 9.30–6.30; Oct–Mar, daily 9.30–4.30. *Admission: inexpensive*. Tel: 01631 562465; www.historic-scotland.gov.uk).

Oban is built round a sheltered bay. Unashamedly visitor-orientated, many of the well-built, solid houses have "B&B" signs outside and there is a wide choice of hotels. Oban is both a transit point for the ferry connections and a resort. Within the town is a good choice of commercial attractions with long main-season opening hours, including a distillery and audio-visual shows.

McCaig's Tower▶ is prominent above the harbour. Also called McCaig's Folly, it recalls a local banker who had it built as a family memorial to ease local unemployment. It is open at all times. Both the tower and **Pulpit Hill▶** make excellent viewpoints over this handsome town. There are numerous excursions by boat—on spectacular Loch Etive, for example.

Scottish Sea Life Sanctuary▶▶▶ This is at Barcaldine, 16km (10mi) north of Oban and is a rewarding excursion. Britain's marine life is just as flourishing and exotic as anything in the tropics (*Open* daily 10–5. *Admission: moderate*. Tel: 01631 720386; www.sealsanctuary.co.uk).

EARLY TOWN PLANNING
Oban's promenade might have gone the same way as Fort William's, which had a railway running along it until a new station opened in 1975. However, the local MacDougall lairds of Dunstaffnage forbade the railway to run into Oban via the easy sea-level route. Instead it was forced to turn inland and take on heavy gradients before sneaking into the town by a back-door route. To this day, Oban has a fine and breezy hotel-lined promenade, popular with strollers, without a railway to spoil the sea views.

A World in Miniature—1:12 scale exhibition, at Kilninver, south of Oban

Feeding seals at the Scottish Sea Life Sanctuary, Barcaldine

REGION HIGHLIGHTS

- **Applecross** *page 212*
- **Corrieshalloch Gorge (Ullapool)** *page 225*
- **Cromarty** *page 212*
- **Dornoch** *page 216*
- **Duncansby Head (John o'Groats)** *page 220*
- **Gairloch** *page 217*
- **Kintail** *page 220*
- **Timespan Heritage Centre** *page 224*

The Northern Highlands

THE JOURNEY NORTH From a southern viewpoint, it is easy to assume that Scotland shrinks as you go north. But take care when route planning in this area, as there is still a lot of ground to cover. Inverness to Thurso, for example, is farther than Carlisle to Glasgow and the two-lane highway sections of the A9 come to an end not very far over the Kessock Bridge beyond the Highland capital.

However, this is an area that has seen many road improvements in recent years. Ullapool is no longer a single-track crawl made hazardous by southbound fish lorries. Instead, it is an easy hour from Inverness. Scourie and Laxford Bridge, far north on the western seaboard, are another two places that can be reached without resorting to single-track driving.

All of this means there is more time to look at the scenery, the chief attraction of the north. The eastern side continues to resemble a Lowland farming strip most of the time. Look for the use of lines of Caithness flagstones set on edge as field boundaries, highly characteristic of the sparse wind-honed pastures of the north. Yet the moors with their attendant sense of wildness reach down to the eastern seaboard in places—around Helmsdale, for example. There are also spectacular sea-cliffs.

Destitution Road and the shoulders of An Teallach, near Ullapool

WEATHERBEATEN HILLS
Some mountains are disappearing fast. The popular Stac Polly in Coigach has lost a few pinnacles in recent years and its red sandstone is powdering and strewing great screes down its flanks. Meanwhile, it is said that on Foinaven, a northern peak just below the magic Munro mark (see page 149), you can hear erosion—the gentle tinkle of chips of Cambrian quartzite intermittently falling from its fast-weathering grey rock summits. So visit soon!

Travelling westwards, away from the coastal cultivation, uplands are soon reached—the boggy flows of Caithness, for instance, with their long open vistas ending in blue hills beyond the blocks of alien and controversial conifers. In the far north, the transition westwards into uncultivated landscape is gradual. In the old county of Ross-shire it can be more abrupt. One point that typifies this transition is on the main A832 west of Contin, near the Falls of Rogie (see page 223). Quite suddenly, the last of the Lowland barley, woods, and pasture drops back eastwards and its vivid greenness is replaced, at a single bend, by enveloping Highland pinewoods, grey hills, and a choppy loch.

EMPTY SPACES Beyond, you enter the empty quarter. Settlement in the north is mainly, though not exclusively, coastal. The interior conforms to the pattern of much of Highland Scotland. Generally, it is a network of substantial privately owned estates, with vast areas given over to deer stalking, often bought as an investment by absentee landlords. It is the owners of these exclusive sanctuaries, determined to make their land pay by offering shooting rights, who feel threatened by the increasing numbers of other countryside users, notably hillwalkers intent on "bagging" not a stag, but another Munro.

Fortunately, some of the very best chunks of landscape, such as the Torridons, Kintail, and parts of Coigach, are owned or managed by conservation agencies determined to compromise with all parties.

Beyond the backbone of Scotland in Wester Ross and particularly in Sutherland, the old sandstone peaks sit on their plinth of ancient glacier-scoured rock. It is this spare and empty landscape of a thousand lochans scratched out of the Lewisian gneiss, overlooked by cliffs, rock terraces, and shattered hills that is the essence of the far north.

Summer daylight hours lengthen noticeably hereabouts—it is perfectly possible to read outdoors at 11PM around midsummer (if the midges will let you) and it never seems to get dark. However, the climate does not alter in a uniform way. The far north sometimes has periods of a curious flat calm, especially away from the hills and out on the headlands. Golfers can be enjoying a round at Gairloch in good conditions while climbers in the Torridons are taking compass-bearings and extracting waterproofs from rucksacks. Even at low level, for example walking by Loch Clair, admiring the profile of Liathach in Glen Torridon, you may well experience four seasons within an hour.

It is easy to be hopelessly beguiled by the northwest landscapes, especially in the Torridon hills or, farther north, around Inverpolly. Certainly, the Northern Highlands have attracted lots of permanent newcomers from other parts of the United Kingdom from the 1980s onwards, with a noticeable improvement in eating-out options, compared with 25 years ago. Though many visitors want to make their way north and west, do not forget the gentler attractions of Easter Ross and Caithness with their old-established communities such as Cromarty and Dornoch, just two of the handsome little places on the eastern seaboard.

In this northern region, all roads seem to lead to the "Capital of the Highlands." Inverness is now bypassed but is still a natural route centre, with roads to the north and west leading out like the spokes of a wheel. And though caution is advised when planning touring routes—it may be farther than you think—it is also true that no matter how great the sense of emptiness, of remoteness and spare beauty in these lands of ancient rock, if it all becomes a little too intimidating, then you can always rush back in a few hours to Inverness with its supermarkets, traffic lights, and other comforting signs of civilization…

Durness school children's wallhanging of the Highland Clearances

AN OVERVIEW OF THE NORTH

From the summit of Ben More Assynt, one of Sutherland's Munros (see page 149), on a clear day it is possible to see not only a great swathe of the Northern Highlands but simultaneously Orkney and the Western Isles.

Duncansby Stacks, near John o'Groats, Caithness

Remembering Queen Victoria's Diamond Jubilee, Dingwall

► Achiltibuie and the Summer Isles 208B3

A side-road through Coigach beyond Ullapool offers spectacular views of the impossible crenellations of Stac Polly on the skyline. The single-track road eventually runs through the 5km (3mi) straggle of homesteads which is Achiltibuie. The Summer Isles make up part of the peerless sea views. This bleak group off the mainland of Wester Ross holds a strange fascination for some. Cruises go from Ullapool (tel: 01854 612472) and Achiltibuie (tel: 01854 622315).

►► Applecross 208A1

Access to Applecross used to be easiest by sea, especially when the high-level Bealach-na-Ba was closed by snow. Since the 1970s, the settlement has had a low-level road built from Shieldaig. Applecross is associated with St. Maelrubha, who established a monastery here in AD 673. Only a few fragments of early crosses survive, but the place still has the air of a remote sanctuary.

►►► Cromarty 209C2

Well worth the Black Isle diversion, this is one of the most satisfying of Scottish towns: full of character, a place that has seen its fortunes rise and fall, with herring and coastal trading, and rise again with oil.

Cromarty Courthouse►►► is perhaps the best place to start a tour of the town. Now a visitor centre, it portrays the development of Cromarty into a prosperous 18th-century trading burgh. The house of geologist Hugh Miller is nextdoor. If time permits, take the digital audio tour of the town's fine buildings (*Open* Apr–Oct, daily 10–5. *Admission: inexpensive*. Tel: 01381 600418; www.cromarty-courthouse.org.uk).

► Dingwall 209C2

The former county town of Easter Ross has long been an administrative centre—its name, from the Norse *thing-vollr*, place of assembly, is a reminder that it was an important settlement in 11th-century Viking times. Within easy reach is the little-known **Black Rock Gorge►►** above Evanton. The River Glass runs through a gorge, about 30m (100ft) deep in parts, yet hemmed in by black and mossy rocks only 4m (13ft) apart at their narrowest. The spot has a decidedly sinister atmosphere.

HIGH-LEVEL GROUSE

There are few places in Scotland where you can see ptarmigan from the car, but this sometimes absurdly tame high-altitude grouse makes its home among the frost-shattered boulders on the exposed plateau at the top of the Bealach-na-Ba (Gaelic, meaning the pass of the cattle). This is the spectacular way to Applecross, reaching 626m (2,050ft), with magnificent views to Skye.

FOSSIL FISH

Cromarty-born Hugh Miller (1802–1856) was a pioneering self-taught geologist, who started work as a stonemason. He developed an interest in the fossils he found in the local sandstone quarries, and eventually achieved an international reputation for his discoveries and classification of primitive fishes. His birthplace in Cromarty (National Trust for Scotland) may be visited.

The road to Applecross, towards the Bealach-na-Ba

*Brahan is an estate near Dingwall whose name is now strongly associated with the most famous of Highland prophets, the Brahan Seer. Various stories and legends have become attached to him, and fact and fiction interwoven. The Brahan Seer is thought to have been a certain Coinneach Odhar (the Gaelic for "Brown Kenneth," pronounced "*co-in-yach oar*") who came to work on the estate in the late 17th century.*

His prophecies The Brahan Seer predicted the railways: "Long lines of carriages without horses will run between Inverness and Dingwall and Skye." The rise of Strathpeffer as a spa was likewise noted. Of the well he said: "Uninviting and disagreeable as it now is...the day will come when it shall be under lock and key." Some prophecies are eerie, especially one curious prediction concerning the terrible disaster that would befall the world when the River Ness in Inverness was spanned by five bridges. A fifth bridge was opened on the river a few days before the outbreak of World War II.

The most unsettling of his prophecies has already partly come to pass. In it he saw the 19th-century coming of the sheep and the emptying of the glens of people. Complete fulfilment of the ending has yet to happen: "The deer and other wild animals in the huge wilderness will be exterminated and browned by horrid black rains. The people will then return and take undisturbed possession of the lands of their ancestors." This meaning is still discussed in the Highlands, with oil pollution and nuclear fallout as two unpleasant alternatives.

An unforeseen end It is said that Brown Kenneth came to an unfortunate end when, at an aristocratic gathering to which he had been invited, perhaps as a novelty act, he reported what the husband of Lady Seaforth was doing at the time (being unfaithful while on a visit to Paris). For such an insult in front of her assembled guests, the furious Lady Seaforth had him burned in a tar barrel—or at least that's how the story goes.

BURNED IN A BRAHAN TUB
On the orders of Lady Seaforth, the Brahan Seer was rolled down a hill in a burning tar barrel at Chanonry Point near Fortrose in the Black Isle. A memorial can be seen there to this day. However, this may not have happened to the 17th-century seer but to another Brown Kenneth accused of witchcraft a century earlier. It seems unlikely that someone with a gift for foretelling the future could not have foreseen the consequences of insulting his hostess.

Inverness, where the fifth bridge over the Ness turned out to be "a bridge too far"

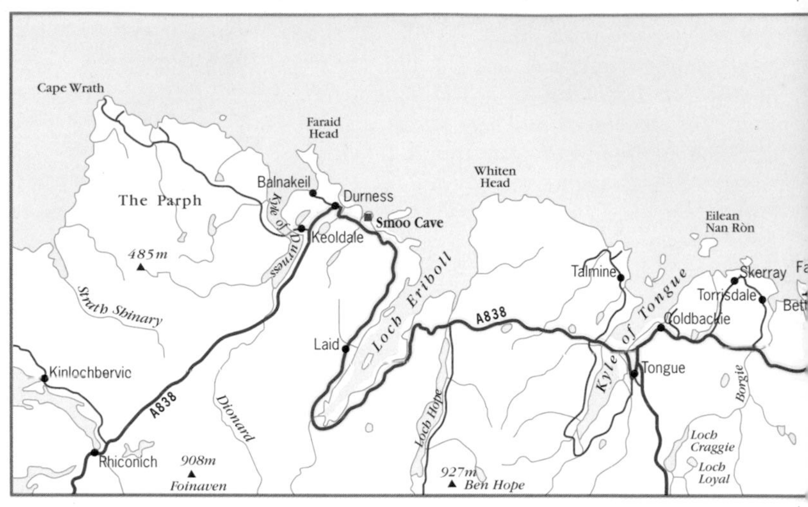

Dunnet Head to Durness along the north coast

Drive

By travelling in an east–west direction on this north coast drive, you can see the flagstone-bordered fields of the edge of Caithness giving way to the moors and mountains of Sutherland. This route (in all 132km/82mi long)

Crossing the Kyle of Durness for the Cape Wrath minibus

could be driven in 2 hours or so, but to get the best from it, stay overnight in the Durness or Tongue area.

Dunnet Head is the most northerly point in Scotland and makes a worthwhile short excursion from Thurso. Heading west from the town, you will see the unmistakable profile of Dounreay, which became the world's first fast reactor to produce commercial electricity, on a site about as far from the Houses of Parliament as it could possibly be. The long process of decommissioning is underway.

At **Melvich**, the landscapes start to become more rugged. If time permits, divert to lighthouse-tipped **Strathy Point**, with the dunes and coastal grasslands en route harbouring some rare plants, notably the tiny Scots primrose in May and June. (The more conspicuous blue among the grass is spring squill.) Back on the main road, **Bettyhill** is a post-clearance settlement. The name refers to Elizabeth, Countess of Sutherland, whose husband ordered the removal of 1,200 people from their dwellings to the coast during the shameful Highland Clearances (see page 38), as the **Strathnaver Museum** relates (tel: 01641 521418). More cheerfully, little coastal loops lead down to empty and beautiful pale sand beaches.

The A836/838 leads on to the **Kyle of Tongue**, with its breathtaking view of spiky Ben Loyal from the causeway which shortens the route round the sea loch. Across the empty moors, with vast and remote seascapes

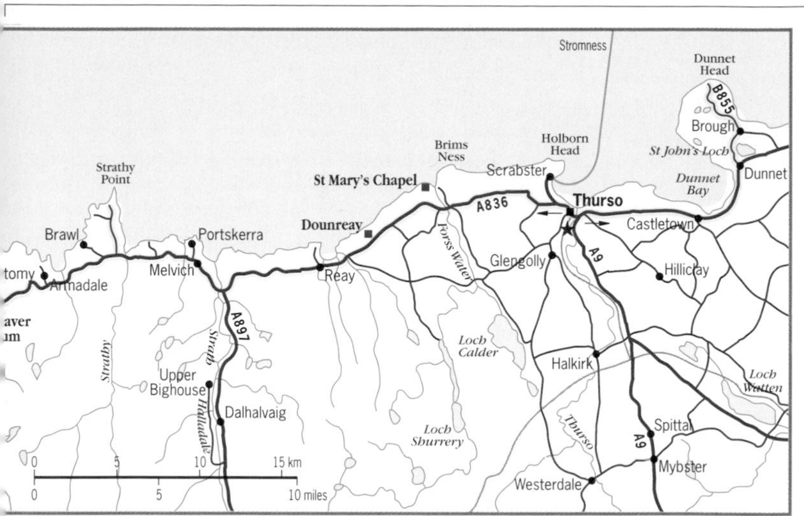

around Whiten Head to the north, lies the next great sea inlet. **Loch Eriboll** was a wartime convoy assembly point, known to mariners as Loch 'orrible. There is a well-preserved prehistoric wheelhouse, among other barely acknowledged sites in the vicinity, just a walk across the moorlands—but you should take a map.

Smoo Cave by Durness is a popular spot, a series of caverns by the shore, cut into the limestone by water action. The other Durness attraction is the excursion to **Cape Wrath**, the northwesternmost tip of mainland Scotland. Note that you cannot take your car. A small ferry crosses the Kyle of Durness and then a minibus goes to the lighthouse (Ferry tel: 01971 511376; minibus tel: 01971 511287). The tallest mainland cliffs are nearby as well, with the whole area carrying a faintly sinister air, thanks partly to the military range that lies between the Kyle and the Cape. A gentler option is puffin-watching at Faraid Head, a very pleasant walk from Durness: Leave the car near the beach at Balnakeil.

Smoo Cave, Durness

THE DESTITUTION ROAD
The roads from Gairloch to Poolewe and northwards were built in a poverty relief scheme following the famine after the failure of the 1840s potato crops. Government boards put up half the cash on the understanding that local landowners would match the funds. The lairds benefited from the improved communications, their estates increasing in value. Instead of wages, the half-starved locals were paid in meal, as both government and landowners wished to avoid a "dependency culture" developing. Part of the A832 is still known as the Destitution Road.

▶▶▶ Dornoch 209C2

Were it not for its northerly location, Dornoch would be better known: a mellow sandstone burgh with a handsome cathedral on its skyline, a picturesque setting by a great sweep of beach, and a famous golf course. The opening of the Dornoch road bridge on the A9 has, however, been of benefit. It is one of the most attractive Scottish towns, also known as the "St. Andrews of the North" because of its reputation for great golf. Though much rebuilt and altered, **Dornoch Cathedral▶** (*Open* daily 9–dusk. *Admission free*. Tel: 01862 810357), dates from the 13th century. As well as just strolling around, admiring how the yellow sandstone sets off the roses in the little gardens, things to do in Dornoch include visiting the Historylinks Museum, behind the Castle Hotel, which tells the story of the town (*Open* Easter–May, Oct, Mon–Fri 10–4; Jun–Sep, daily 10–4. Tel: 01862 811275. *Admission inexpensive*). Another of the peaceful town's delights are its golden beaches to north and south. Ripple-patterned and unpolluted long shoals and banks at the mouth of Dornoch Firth are exposed at low tide.

Between Dornoch and Golspie stands **Beinn a Bhragaidh**, a hill whose top is crowned by a massive statue. This colossus by Sir Francis Chantney is in memory of the first Duke of Sutherland (died 1833), a prime mover in the Highland Clearances, which resulted in mass emigration.

▶ Dunrobin Castle 209C2

Open: Apr, May, 1–15 Oct, Mon–Sat 10.30–4.30, Sun 12–4.30; Jun–Sep, Mon–Sat 10.30–5.30, Sun 12–5.30. Admission: moderate (tel: 01408 633177; www.highlandescape.com/dunrobin

On this sparsely populated and wild coastline, the settlement of Gairloch, with golf course, beaches, and choice of accommodation, is the local equivalent of a resort town

The largest house in the Northern Highlands, Dunrobin started as a 13th-century sandstone keep on a raised beach overlooking the Dornoch Firth. The original keep was progressively enveloped by newer work, the last and most spectacular being the 1835–1850 extensions. These were by Sir Charles Barry, architect of the Houses of Parliament in London, though sadly much of Barry's interior was destroyed by fire in 1915. He gave the pile its present French look with spires and elaborate stonework.

For centuries this has been the seat of the dukes and earls of Sutherland. The 3rd Duke (died 1892) was Western Europe's largest landowner—his holdings included most of the county of Sutherland. Stuffed with the goods acquired by one of the wealthiest families in the land, it has a makeshift air, a series of rooms laid out to impress with displays of uniforms, trophies, medals, endless portraits, tapestries, and such eccentricities as the Duke's own steam-powered fire engine.

The old summer house is a museum containing hunting trophies, from which you gain the impression that the Sutherlands must have kept a squad of taxidermists in work over the years. The attractive gardens below the castle were inspired by Versailles.

Dunrobin Castle, grandest home in the Northern Highlands, is irrevocably associated with the Highland Clearances

GOLFING HISTORY
Many of the priests who came to Dornoch Cathedral had been trained in St. Andrews, where the close-cropped coastal turf was already being used for a curious game with a ball and stick. These religious men were soon exploiting the similar terrain around Dornoch. Thus golf took a very early hold here on the magnificent links, perhaps even as early as the 16th century.

► Fortrose *209C2*

With Avoch and Rosemarkie on either side, Fortrose is an attractive village by the shores of the Moray Firth. The community originally grew around the cathedral, completed in 1485 but now a red sandstone roofless ruin. Avoch, with its fishing heritage, is like the Lowland towns on the south side of the Firth. North of the three villages is Eathie beach, where pioneering 19th-century geologist Hugh Miller (see panel on page 212) made important discoveries about the origin of the local sandstones.

►► Gairloch *208A2*

Gairloch overlooks the safe anchorage of the Gair Loch. Largest of the settlements along this fine stretch of Wester Ross seaboard, Gairloch combines some sea fishing (and processing) activity with tourism, an industry that established itself here in mid-Victorian times. It is a small resort that relies on its own scenic charm. The local sandy beach helps attract families, as does the golf course. Also in the vicinity are **Inverewe Garden** (see page 221) and the beauties of **Loch Maree** (see page 218), as well as **Gairloch Heritage Museum►►** (*Open* Apr–Sep, Mon–Sat 10–5; Oct, Mon–Sat 10–1.30. *Admission: inexpensive.* www.gairlochheritagemuseum.org.uk).

In Fortrose

The mountains of Torridon are exactly to the taste of modern travellers eager to escape from urban pressures. Austere and uncompromising, notched and carved into terraces and ridges, they have a beauty that has made an impact for as long as visitors have made their patient way over the long reaches of Strath Bran to Achnasheen, then the high pass over Glen Docherty.

A TRAIL WITH VIEWS
From a clearly marked parking place by the shore of Loch Maree, a hill path ascends the steep slopes leading on to the flanks of Beinn Eighe. This Scottish National Heritage nature trail is for the well-shod walker, but gives excellent views over Slioch and Loch Maree as height is quickly gained and the pinewoods peter out.

Far from being a long way off across the backbone of Scotland—now that the roads have been improved across the empty middle—the western seaboard and the Torridons are all too accessible. An easy excursion from Inverness will give a feel, though the mountains deserve much more time.

The main mountains Glen Torridon runs from the sea towards the southern end of **Loch Maree**. A single-track road runs through the glen, becoming double-track by the shores of **Loch Torridon**. It is from the southern side of Loch Torridon, on the way to or from Shieldaig, that the best views of **Beinn Alligin** can be obtained. This is the most westerly of Torridon's peaks, a half-horseshoe ridge of red sandstone with a spectacular gash on its southern cliffs, casting a sinister shadow by late afternoon. Its equally lofty companion, **Liathach**, lies east of it. Rising precipitously from sea level, its quartzite-topped sandstone terraces and summit pinnacles are best appreciated from the east, by Loch Clair. Next is **Beinn Eighe**—several kilometres of summits on a quartzite ridge with grey-white rocks cascading down its flanks in long scree slopes. These three mountains are the main performers in the Torridon spectacular.

The National Trust for Scotland owns much of the land by the glen and above Loch Torridon—about 4,330ha (10,700 acres). The visitor centre by the Diabaig road junction is the starting point for ranger-led walks as well as giving an introduction to the unique geology and wildlife of the area. The east end of the glen and much of the west side of Loch Maree was Britain's first National Nature Reserve, now under Scottish Natural Heritage, which operates a visitor centre by the loch (on the A832).

Take your time—but do not hold up the locals!

Single
track
road
Use passing
places
to permit
overtaking

Walks in the area Though much can be seen from the roadside, the Torridons are best explored on foot. All the rules of Scottish mountain walking obviously apply, and even at lower level, the terrain is rough enough to make proper walking boots a necessity. One popular but demanding low-level walk is the "circumnavigation" of the Liathach massif. This demands either two cars, extreme fitness, or a confident approach to hitch-

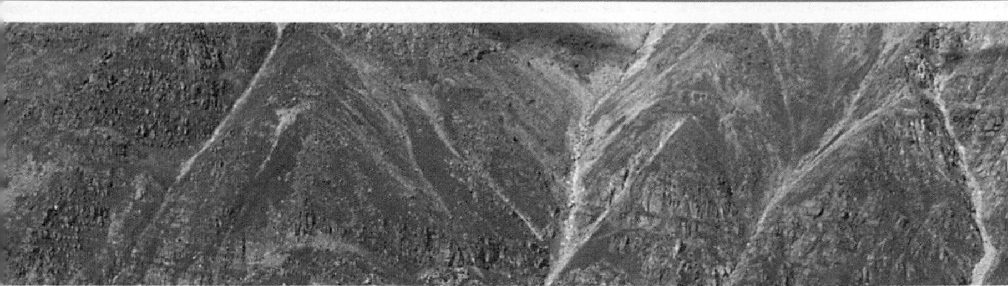

hiking. Start by parking your car either at the waterfall beyond Torridon House on the Diabaig road or in the parking area half-way along Glen Torridon. The off-road section of the walk is 11km (7mi). The views take in the northern slopes and corries of Liathach, and, notably, the less well-known **Beinn Dearg** with its spectacular rock terraces.

Another popular excursion is to view the mighty triple buttresses of **Coire Mhic Fhearchair**. This diverges from the "round Liathach" path to circle into one of the most magnificent corries in the Scottish hills. Alternatively, take advantage of the nature trails on the Loch Maree side, though the mountain trail goes steeply up through the old pines and demands some particularly careful footwork. There are breathtaking views over the loch to Slioch, the peak on its eastern shore.

Fit hillwalkers have many possible excursions. The pinnacles of Liathach are not for the vertigo-prone, though there is a path round them. The **Horns of Alligin**, on Beinn Alligin's eastern end, demand a little bit of hand-work and need great respect. Meanwhile, the long ridge of Beinn Eighe should not be underestimated. If in doubt, stay at low level, explore the shore path by Diabaig, or the route to the headland near Shieldaig, or stroll by Loch Clair, admiring one of Scotland's finest views, with Liathach filling the skyline like an upturned boat.

NORSE PLACE-NAMES

Diabaig is derived from the Norse *deop-vik* (deep bay), while Shieldaig is *sild-vik* (herring bay). Both little villages are in attractive settings and both offer some accommodation, though Kinlochewe at the east end of the glen is a slightly larger centre.

Beinn Eighe from Glen Torridon

Caithness craftsman

SPANIARDS' PEAK
Eilean Donan's destruction by naval gunfire in 1719 came about because of its involvement in the Jacobite rebellion of that year. A force of 300 Spanish soldiers landed nearby to link up with local Jacobites, mainly Mackenzies and Camerons (plus Rob Roy and a few Macgregors). They joined battle in Glen Shiel with government forces, whose superior firepower made retreat or surrender inevitable. The Glen Shiel place-name Sgurr na Spainteach (Spaniards' Peak) recalls the incident.

Kintail sunset

▶ John o'Groats *209D4*

"From Land's End to John o'Groats" is the expression denoting the length of Britain. Yet this is not the most northerly point of mainland Scotland; it's **Dunnet Head▶▶** to the west. The seascapes here are spectacular, notably around **Duncansby Head▶▶▶** with its rock stacks. To the west, the Castle and Gardens of Mey were restored by the late Queen Mother (tel: 01847 851473; www.castleofmey.org.uk)

▶▶▶ Kintail *208A1*

Just how much landscape perceptions have changed is indicated by Dr. Johnson's remark, when travelling hereabouts. He described the main mountains west of the Great Glen as "...matter incapable of form or usefulness, dismissed by nature from her care and disinherited of her favours." Kintail today is highly prized for the elemental qualities that so appalled the doctor. The National Trust for Scotland cares for much of the area, which includes the picturesque **Five Sisters of Kintail▶▶▶**. These five peaks are all Munros (see page 149), as indeed are many others farther east up Glen Shiel. Also within the National Trust for Scotland sphere are the spectacular **Falls of Glomach▶▶**, tumbling 113m (370ft) in remote Glen Elchaig, accessible only by an 8km (5mi) path over rough country—treat it as a hillwalk and dress accordingly.

The best-known low-level landmark is **Eilean Donan Castle▶** on its islet on Loch Duich. This was wrecked in 1719 (see panel) and rebuilt between 1913 and 1932. It includes a memorial to the Clan Macrae, whose seat it was, and there's an excellent visitor centre and café (*Open* Mar, Nov 10–4.30; Apr–Oct 10–6. *Admission moderate*).

A dead-end minor road heads off from the end of Glen Shiel to Glenelg. This route is worth exploring, to view not only Skye and Knoydart but also the best preserved brochs (see panel page 229) on the Scottish mainland. **Dun Telve** stands over 9m (30ft) high. Also nearby are the ruins of the **Bernera Barracks**, originally built around 1722 to control Jacobite activities (see pages 34–35).

Inverewe Garden is on the same latitude as Labrador, but has a cool and temperate climate because it is favoured by the lapping waters of the North Atlantic Drift. The western seas blunt the keen edge of the winter frosts, and extensive shelter belts create the micro-climate beloved of rhododendrons, mahonia, and other lovers of dappled shade and moisture. Plants from cool temperate zones all over the world can be found here.

History Until 1862, the garden site was a windy, bare headland with only the island of Lewis between it and Northern Canada. But Osgood Mackenzie, whose father and grandfather had been lairds of Gairloch, started his lifetime's work to create a garden in this unpromising landscape. Some of the first trees were planted, not by digging a hole in soil (since often there was none), but by carving out solid rock.

Osgood Mackenzie died in 1922, with the now maturing garden appreciated by temperate eucalyptus trees from Tasmania, species of rhododendrons from the Himalayas, and pernettyas, olearias, nothofagus, and other southern hemisphere plants that found this Highland home compatible with the Patagonian plains or the high forests of the Andes. By 1952 the garden was in the care of the National Trust for Scotland.

The garden today Inverewe is a late garden, which can mean that you might add a month to six weeks on to flowering times quoted in the gardening manuals—particularly in the early months. This cautious start also means that there is a running together of late spring—and early summer—flowering plants into a more continuous display than in many southern gardens. Its most attractive feature is the sense of different "rooms" within the overall structure—turn a corner to reinvigorated plantings and geographically linked species, a deliberate management policy in which the team of gardeners is given comparatively free rein within their own patches.

EARTH MOVING

Osgood Mackenzie's hard work in creating Inverewe did not only involve excavating holes in solid rock for trees. Soil by the basket load had to be moved in as even the thin blanket of peat that had originally overlaid the rock had been stripped off for fuel by previous crofting tenants.

OPENING TIMES

Open daily Easter–Oct 9.30–9; Nov–Mar 9.30–4. Guided walks: May–Sep, Mon–Fri at 1.30. *Admission: expensive* (tel: 01445 781200; www.nts.org.uk).

Inverewe Gardens; a tribute to its determined founder, Osgood Mackenzie, as well as a reminder of the winter warming effect of the North Atlantic Drift on the western seaboard of Scotland

Guillemots, razorbills, and kittiwakes on Handa's cliffs

AN UNSIGHTLY SCAR
When a proposal was made to put a deep-water oil-rig platform site near Drumbuie, the National Trust for Scotland, who owns land nearby, fought long and hard for an alternative site. The yard was eventually built near Kishorn, arguably a more conspicuous spot, with its breathtaking mountain backdrop. In the boom years it had a workforce of 4,000 and was the birthplace of the largest mobile structure ever built, the Ninian Central rig.

▶ Lochcarron *208A1*

Glen Carron seems mostly empty: Its soaring hills are clothed with forestry. The blueness of Loch Carron, on the western seaboard, is almost a relief after the unpeopled wildness. The village of Lochcarron is a long ribbon of dwellings, shops, guest-houses, hotels, and so on, without a real focal point (it even boasts a golf course). Across the loch, beyond the road and the railway with its avalanche shelter, is one of Scotland's larger virtually uninhabited areas. With the Applecross Hills and the Torridons to the north, Lochcarron is ideal for exploring wild country. The A896 northwards passes through Kishorn and then opens up breathtaking views of the series of corries on the Applecross hills. Also nearby is the **Rassal Ash Wood▶** nature reserve (administered by Scottish Natural Heritage), where fenced grazing "exclosures" show a rich woodland fauna, contrasting with the over-grazed moors around the reserve.

▶▶ Lochinver *208B3*

Lochinver is the largest centre in Assynt, and a busy little fishing port. Seen from across the sea loch, the blunt bows of Suilven (731m/2,398ft) rise end on in the rough lands behind the village, as a reminder of the eye-catching Assynt landscapes. Though far north on the map, Lochinver is served all the way by roads that allow two cars to pass, and also offers magnificent touring options on (single-track) loops to both north and south. The B869 goes round via Stoer and Drumbeg, giving fine views of **Quinag**. From this road at Stoer, there are unclassified roads leading out to the Stoer peninsula with its scattered crofts. Park near the lighthouse for a clifftop walk to see the rock stack, the **Old Man of Stoer▶▶**. (It is farther than you think.)

For equally spectacular coastal scenery, a longer excursion (by car) goes via the Kylesku Bridge and on beyond Scourie to Tarbet. This Royal Society for the Protection of Birds reserve has impressive seabird colonies—including puffins—on awesome cliffs, as well as skuas in the interior which alarmingly dive-bomb intruders near their nest sites. Southwards, there is more wildlife interest to be found by taking the unclassified road leading towards the **Inverpolly National Nature Reserve▶▶** (look out for wild cat and golden eagles). There is an information centre at Knockan Cliff, close by the A835.

▶▶ Plockton *208A1*

Too impossibly neat to be true, Plockton was a fishing settlement but now has a number of holiday properties. Complete with rambling roses and hardy palm trees, the neatly painted coastal village makes the most of its sheltered east-facing position—unusual in Wester Ross—and turns its back on the prevailing westerly winds. Other points of interest on the Lochalsh peninsula include the **Lochalsh Woodland Garden▶**, a National Trust for Scotland woodland garden with sheltered walks by the lochside (open throughout the year). Many of the trees are over 100 years old, but the garden is still being developed.

▶▶ Strathpeffer *208B2*

The mineral springs in this spa town were described in print by 1772. The first pump room was built in 1819. The local lairds gave the town their blessing and further development took place, assisted by the arrival of the railway which conveyed a regular clientele to the spa to take the sulphurous waters. The great Victorian heyday lives on in the town's confident and solid architecture. The waters can still be sampled. Though the railway has gone the station is now an attractively converted craft and gift complex with a small **Highland Museum of Childhood▶** (*Open* Apr–Jun and Sep–Oct Mon–Sat 10–5, Sun 2–5; Jul–Aug, Mon–Fri 10–7, Sat–Sun 2–5. *Admission: inexpensive*. Tel: 01997 421031).

Nearby are a number of points of interest, including the vitrified walling of the fortified hilltop of **Knock Farril** (as yet unexcavated) which can be reached on foot from Strathpeffer. **Strathconon** is also worth exploring, as this glen often offers good views of red deer. The **Falls of Rogie** are signposted from the main road west of Contin and also make an enjoyable stroll.

Plockton, arguably Wester Ross' prettiest village

Inspiration by Loch Carron

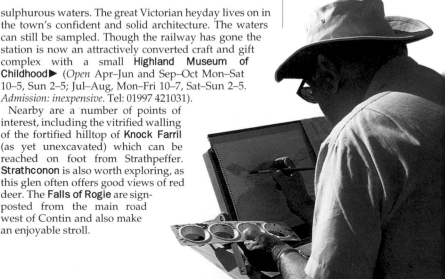

THE BATTLE OF STROME PIER

Sabbatarianism is still quite strong in certain parts of the Highlands and in May 1883 it resulted in a bizarre incident. East coast fishermen started landing herring at Strome Pier for rail shipment seven days a week. The west coast fishermen opposed the Sunday activity. Along with the locals, they seized the pier, thus preventing the loading of fish on to the trains bound for the London market. The protestors fought off six local constables and the loading crews. Matters escalated. The War Office in London was informed. Only a large police presence and a troop train on standby the following Sunday ensured that religious beliefs did not stand in the way of commerce.

Though the fishing industry was vital to Wick, no harbour existed here before about 1803. Until then the 200 or so boats that sailed for herring had only the river mouth for shelter

AN UNSAFE SANCTUARY
Tain may have been a shrine and sanctuary of St. Duthac, but that did not stop it being violated. In 1306, the wife and daughter of King Robert I (the Bruce) fled the tightening English siege of Kildrummy (see page 182) to find sanctuary at Tain. This proved no obstacle to the local Earl of Ross (who supported Balliol, not Bruce). He snatched them from the sanctuary and made them prisoners. In the next century, a MacNeil warrior pursued his foes to the chapel and set fire to it.

▶ Tain *209C2*

Some say Malcolm Canmore granted Tain's first charter in the 11th century. The little town has a fine tolbooth and steeple. The ruins of nearby **St. Duthac's Chapel** (built 1065–1256) mark the site of the birthplace of St. Duthac, an early missionary to the Picts. Tain was a place of pilgrimage for centuries, the chapel a sanctuary and shrine. **St. Duthus Church▶** was built in 1360 and served many pilgrims, as told in the **"Tain through Time" Pilgrimage Visitor Centre▶** and museum (*Open* Apr–Jun, Sep–Oct, Mon–Sat 10–5; Jul–Aug, Mon–Sat 10–6. *Admission: inexpensive.* Tel: 01862 894089; www.tainmuseum.org.uk).

▶▶ Timespan Heritage and Arts Centre *209C3*

Open: Easter–Oct, Mon–Sat 10–5, Sun 12–5. Admission: moderate (tel: 01431 821327; www.timespan.org.uk)

Timespan, in Helmsdale, is the work of a local group of enthusiasts who wanted to preserve the area's heritage, and knew how to acquire funding. The centre portrays many aspects of life in the Highlands of old, from neolithic and Pictish times up to the Clearances, with a mix of tableaux, artefacts, and audio-visuals. It also has a fascinating account of the "gold rush" in the nearby Strath of Kildonan which took place in 1869. What makes Timespan different is the thought-provoking way the exhibits tell the story. There is one jarring note: The centre has a bizarre shrine to the novelist Barbara Cartland, who had property nearby. The Centre also holds monthly exhibitions of local art.

Farther up the Strath is the site of the gold rush town. At **Baile an Or** "gold town," 13km (8mi) to the northwest, it is still possible to pan for gold, using equipment hired from a craft shop in Helmsdale. Do not expect to be able to subsidize your trip this way!

Whaligoe Steps near Ulbster, south of Wick—not for the vertigo-prone

▶▶ Ullapool *208B2*

In contrast to many older settlements with obscure origins, Ullapool can be dated precisely. The abundant herring in Loch Broom inspired the founding of a fishing station and village there soon after the formation of the British Fisheries Society in 1786. This society paid for the infrastructure of curing sheds, storehouses, a pier, inn, and even a school and some of the dwelling houses. All was laid out on a regular grid plan and mostly completed by 1792. However, it soon became clear that the herring were not a reliable harvest. Ullapool's fortunes rose and fell, and many turned to the land for a living. Overall Ullapool has maintained a strong fishing connection, rising into prominence in the 1980s with the arrival of the Eastern Bloc "klondykers"—vessels buying fish direct for on-board processing.

An excellent museum in the town, plus a number of shops and a pottery factory provide diversion for the strolling tourists, as this is one of the largest centres on this stretch of seaboard. Ullapool also has an important ferry link with Stornoway in the Outer Hebrides.

Corrieshalloch Gorge▶▶▶ On the A835 south of Ullapool this is just one of the area's many scenic attractions. Meltwater from a glacier at the end of the last Ice Age cut a 60m (200ft) deep gorge, into which the **Falls of Measach** now plunge, half hidden by trees and lush greenery. (Closed in 2006 for restoration.).

▶ Wick *209D3*

The workaday, east-wind flavoured town of Wick made a big contribution to the development of fishing. **Wick Heritage Museum**▶▶, with its wide-ranging displays of fishing artefacts, recalls the time when herring brought prosperity to the town in spite of a dangerous and inadequate harbour (*Open* Apr–Oct, Mon–Sat 10–5, last admission 3.45. *Admission inexpensive.* Tel: 01955 605393; www.caithness.org).

North of the town, a pleasant walk along the coastal grazings from the signposted parking area soon leads to **Castles Girnigoe** and **Sinclair**, perched on the cliffs above Sinclair's Bay. These adjacent gloomily ruined strong-holds were the works of the Sinclair Earls of Caithness and can be visited any time—but take care, as their situation is exposed.

CHEAP FOOD
Before slavery was abolished, Wick herring, salted in barrels and exported, was used as a source of cheap food for plantation slaves.

ALONG THE A99
Diversions off the A99 near Wick include trips to Whaligoe Steps, where a dizzying set of steps leads down the cliff to a former fishing station, and, inland from Whaligoe, to the Grey Cairns of Camster, neolithic burial cairns of the area's first farmers. Nearby is the Hill o' Many Stanes: 200 stones arranged in 22 rows, dating from the early Bronze Age. Their purpose is a mystery.

On the Stornoway to Ullapool ferry

REGION HIGHLIGHTS

Inner Hebrides

Torosay Castle (Mull) *page 236*

Islands of the Clyde

Mount Stuart House (Bute) *page 231*

Orkney

North Hoy Nature Reserve (Hoy) *page 240*

Mainland *pages 238–239*

Shetland

Lerwick *pages 244–245*

Mainland *pages 242–243*

Hermaness National Nature Reserve (Unst) *page 246*

Skye and the Western Isles

Blackhouse at Arnol *page 250*

Traigh Luskentyre (Harris) *pages 248–249*

Skye *pages 252–254*

Cladach Chairinis, North Uist, with Eaval beyond

The CalMac ferry doing the Ardrossan–Brodick (Arran) run

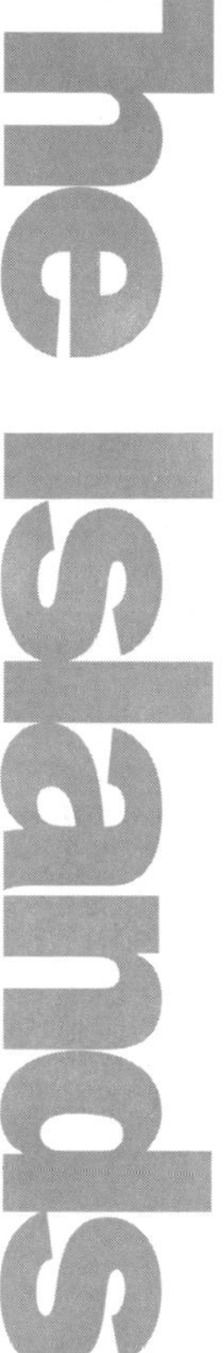

THE ISLANDS Scotland's western seaboard is about 416km (260mi) in a straight line, but if you count all the indentations and island shores it is around 3,200km (2,000mi) long. On such a complicated rocky coast, even counting islands can be difficult (it all depends on the definition) but it is usually said that Scotland has 790, of which 130 are inhabited.

Apart from the outliers like North Rona or St. Kilda, the island clusters fall into natural groupings: the islands of the Clyde, which lie within the estuary between the mainland and the Kintyre peninsula; the Inner Hebrides, comprising the main islands of the western seaboard between Kintyre and Skye; the Outer Hebrides, now usually called, somewhat confusingly, the Western Isles, and stretching in a long line from the Butt of Lewis to Barra and beyond; and finally Orkney and Shetland, utterly different in culture and outlook from anything western.

THE CLYDE ISLANDS Access has much to do with character. The Clyde islands were for generations an easy-to-reach holiday playground for the workforce of the Glasgow conurbation and, no matter how much the local authorities try to change this image, just a little of earlier days still hangs around. A 1950s air clings on in the occasional café in Arran or Bute—that is part of their charm. **Arran** is sometimes labelled "Scotland in miniature" because of its scenic attractions. The granites of the Goatfell ridges (the principal hill complex) have enticed generations of outdoor enthusiasts.

FAIR ISLE
Sometimes the P&O ferry between Lerwick and Aberdeen sails close to Fair Isle to give passengers a glimpse of this isolated island midway between Orkney and Shetland. It is called the remotest inhabited island in the UK, and has outstanding coastal scenery, bird colonies, and a bird observatory, as well as the George Waterston Memorial Centre, displaying the island's folklore and history (*Open* May–Sep, Mon and Fri PM, Wed AM only, telephone to check times. *Admission free*. Tel: 01595 760244). A ferry runs from Grutness, Sumburgh.

MENDELSSOHN AND THE HEBRIDES
The basalt columns carved by the sea into caves on the island of Staffa, west of Mull, inspired the composer Mendelssohn to write his overture *The Hebrides*, or *Fingal's Cave*. This little island has recorded a series of famous literary visitors: Scott, Tennyson, Keats, and Wordsworth, as well as the artist Turner, all came to admire the soaring cathedral-like symmetry. It can be visited from Iona or from Mull.

Bute, meanwhile, still echoes the old days of traditional holidays, with its seafront mansions built by wealthy industrialists in Victorian times. It is now a very peaceful place, with an attractive rural hinterland to which the spectacular Victorian Gothic Mount Stuart House provides an unusual contrast.

THE INNER HEBRIDES Islay and Jura are often grouped together because of their proximity and ferry connections (the Jura ferry leaves from Islay). Yet they are completely different in character. Because of its farming and whisky, **Islay**, at least in part, still has a sense of a community held together without recourse to too many twee craftware ventures earnestly worked by urban refugees—the characteristic feature of all too many parts of the west.

Jura is simply empty. Not literally devoid of people, perhaps, but there are few other places where depopulation has been quite so spectacular. The island has been divided up into a few sporting estates. Some come to the island because of its connection with George Orwell's *Nineteen Eighty Four*, which was written at Barnhill, a remote house well up the east coast. Neither this spot nor the famous but seldom seen Whirlpool of Corrievreckan, a tidal conflict at the tip of Jura, is accessible by ordinary car.

Mull is particularly famed for its wildlife, and boasts the only other island Munro apart from Skye: Ben More. There is also some highly attractive coastline. Like Skye, Mull has proved a magnet for a new breed of resident, eager to escape the pressure of life in the south of the UK.

As for smaller islands, **Colonsay** is the very distillation of Hebridean charm. With only 22km (14mi) of roads it is hardly worth bringing a car. Colonsay is popular both as the ultimate in relaxing Scottish hideaways and as a good place for birdwatchers, with its excellent variety of habitats. These include sand, cliff, machair, moor, and garden, and its own rather stunted woodland. **Oronsay**, its companion to the south, with an interesting ruined priory, is a separate island only at high tide—take your wellington boots for the walk. **Coll** and **Tiree** are also interesting Hebridean destinations, with machair and long beaches.

The so-called Small Isles—**Rum**, **Eigg**, **Muck**, and **Canna**—also offer a true island experience, very definitely away from it all, with Rum the best for scenery.

Orkney tractor

SKYE AND THE WESTERN ISLES Skye, strictly part of the Inner Hebrides, is the most scenically spectacular island of the western seaboard, with glorious mountain landscapes. It is therefore very popular. However, the main ridge of the Cuillins (with the possible exception of Bruach na Frithe) is not a place for the inexperienced climber. The ascent of many of the Cuillins peaks demands rock-climbing skills or, at the very least, a good head for heights.

One of the ways in which the **Outer Hebrides (Western Isles)** differs from most of the mainland is in

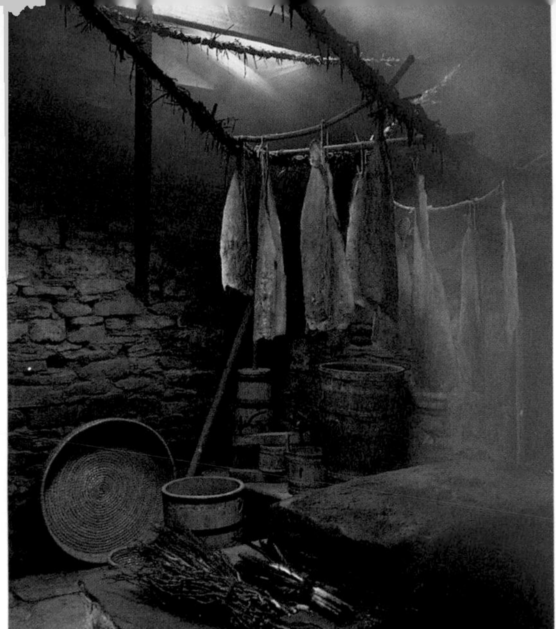

SCOTTISH BROCHS
These are circular defensive structures, dry-stone walled and double skinned, of which the Broch of Mousa is the best preserved. There are about 400 of them scattered in Shetland, Orkney, Caithness, and Sutherland and farther down the western seaboard. Brochs are presumed to have been built for defensive purposes around the 1st century BC to 3rd century AD, probably against sea-borne raiders in the turbulent Celtic world of the time.

Kirbuster Farm Museum, Kirbuster, Orkney

their deeply felt Sabbatarianism. Once widespread in the west, the setting aside of Sunday for almost exclusively religious pursuits has retreated to a stronghold here. All too easy for outsiders to dismiss as curiously joyless, the staunch faith must be a source of strength for those who choose to live among the bleak landscapes of the north end of the island. Visitors should respect it.

The lower end of the island chain is Catholic with a more relaxed community to be found there. Beaches receding to infinity, corncrake-haunted hayfields, and outhouses tied down to escape the wind are just a few of the far Hebridean images—as is the very real sense of a rhythm of life attached to tide and ferry times.

ORKNEY AND SHETLAND Orkney and Shetland look to their Scandinavian heritage. **Orkney** also looks farther back, to a time when the climate was warmer and the ancient peoples who farmed here left more prehistoric monuments than anywhere else in Britain. These include Skara Brae, an ancient settlement where, amid the Stone Age furniture, an idea of the life of these shadowy ancestors of ancestors can be gained.

Most northerly of all, from the average Briton's point of view, **Shetland** is almost like having a foreign holiday without leaving Britain. It is known for its awesome seascapes—Esha Ness on Mainland, for example—and brochs (see panel).

Do not let the sea be any kind of barrier to visiting these islands. Access by the main ferry gateways—Oban, Mallaig, Ullapool, Scrabster, Aberdeen, and others—is straightforward. All of Scotland's main islands are viable communities, with reliable car-ferry links and, in the case of the Outer Hebrides, Islay, Orkney, and Shetland, with good air services as well. And if you want the island experience but do not like ferry travel, then the new bridge to Skye is the answer.

Trimming hoofs on Shetland; on the poor pastures and brown moors of the islands only the hardy sheep survive

HUTTON'S UNCONFORMITY
A rough 10-minute walk over the sheep-cropped, raised beach beyond the north shore of Loch Ranza takes you to Hutton's Unconformity. In 1787, the geologist James Hutton noticed a change in the angle of the rocks, where 600-million-year-old grey-green Cambrian schist dips and is overlain by the sprightly young red Devonian sandstone, a good 200 million years its junior. This observation helped Hutton work out his theories about the age of the earth.

Islands of the Clyde

►► Arran *230A1*

Arran has long enjoyed a reputation as an island for outdoor-lovers and walkers. The Highland Boundary Fault runs through the island: Arran's southern end is accordingly less hilly. Its largest township is Brodick, with a frontage spaciously set back from promenade and beach.

Brodick Castle and Country Park►► is Arran's most famous attraction. On the north side of Brodick Bay and in the care of the National Trust for Scotland, the former seat of the Dukes of Hamilton displays furniture, paintings, silver, and sporting trophies, but the real attraction is the rhododendrons, particularly in late spring and early summer. There is also a walled garden (*Open* Easter–Sep daily 11–4.30; last entry 4; Oct daily 11–3.30. Reception Easter–Oct daily 10–4.30; Nov–Dec, Fri–Sun 10–3.30; Country Park, daily. *Admission: moderate.* Tel: 01770 302202; www.nts.org.uk).

Much of the settlement on Arran is clustered round the coast: pottery and crafts at **Corrie**, with its mountain backdrop; even better views at **Mid Sannox** with its bay of ground-down granite. **Lochranza**, where Loch Ranza spills in shallows up the flat-bottomed glacial glen, is yet another focus of craft activity. Here too is **Lochranza Castle** where Robert the Bruce is said to have first landed in 1307 at the start of the independence campaign. Look out for the "**Twelve Apostles**" at Catacol—a row of former fishermen's houses, identical except for differing window shapes, in order to be identified from offshore.

The Arran tapestry, Brodick, displays aspects of island life

Evening calm on Bute

On the west side, around **Machrie Moor**, are atmospheric standing stones, chambered cairns, and hut circles. On the east shore, **Lamlash** has a cheerful air and views to Holy Island (now a religious settlement) and a sobering boulder memorial to the Highland Clearances.

▶ Bute *230B3*

The waterfront resort of **Rothesay** contrasts with the brackeny woodland found on the rest of this peaceful island. The resort was popular in the heyday of the steamer network on the Clyde, a story told at the **Bute Museum** in Rothesay (*Open* Apr–Sep, Mon–Sat 10.30–4.30, Sun 2.30–4.30; Oct–Mar, Tue–Sat 2.30–4.30. *Admission: inexpensive.* Tel: 01700 505067; www.butemuseum.org).

Rothesay Castle▶▶ This fortress in the town centre is built round a circular courtyard. The Norse assailed it in 1230, breaching the wall (*Open* Apr–Sep, daily 9.30–6.30; Oct–Mar, Sat–Wed 9.30–4.30. *Admission: inexpensive.* Tel: 01700 502691; www.historic-scotland.gov.uk).

Just outside Rothesay is **Mount Stuart House▶▶▶**, ancestral home of the Marquesses of Bute. A splendid Victorian Gothic palace, it has plenty to admire inside, from the Marble Hall's galleries, stained glass, and astronomical painted vault, to outstanding furniture, paintings, and tapestries (*Open* gardens May–Sep, daily 10–6; house May–Sep, Sun–Fri 11–5, Sat 10–2.30. *Admission: moderate.* Tel: 01700 503877; www.mountstuart.com).

Bute has beaches and interesting walks up the west coast overlooking the Kyles of Bute. There are also ancient hill forts and faint echoes of neolithic folk, but the most peaceful place has to be **St. Blane's Chapel**, a 6th-century religious foundation with a 12th-century ruined chapel.

MEDICAL SUPPLIES
The soft and mossy woods of Bute once provided an unusual harvest. During World War I, cotton wool became scarce and sphagnum moss, with its antiseptic and absorbent properties, was used instead for dressing wounds. It was gathered from the Balnakeilly Woods, dried, sorted, and packed for hospitals and field units.

THE CUMBRAES
Often overlooked, these are the smallest of the main Clyde islands. Like Arran they are fondly regarded by many visitors, who come for the beaches, sailing, cycling, gentle walks, and traditional entertainment. Great Cumbrae and its even smaller neighbour are only a few minutes off Largs on the Ayrshire coast, to which they are linked by ferry.

Cart decoration, Arran & Argyll Transport Museum, Brodick

CHOUGHS
These very rare crows (pronounced "chuffs") make their home on Colonsay and Islay. From a distance, they look black, in common with most of their cousins. If you observe choughs closely as they poke about for insects in old cowpats, you may glimpse their bright red beaks and feet. In flight they look like square and ragged-winged jet-black jackdaws. Their survival, research shows, seems to be dependent on the overwintering of cattle outside. Hence the cowpats.

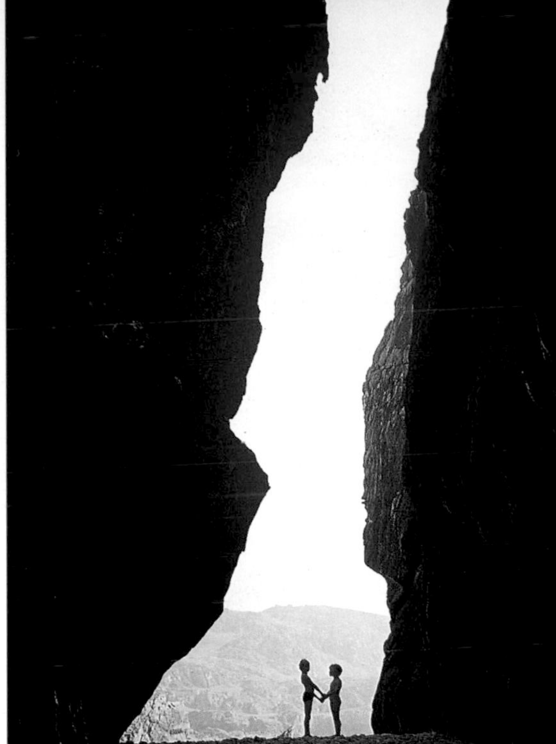

Spectacular coastal scenery on Colonsay, an island which offers coastline and sandy beaches and dunes

JURA
Jura has one road, one distillery, one hotel, six sporting estates, and 6,000 red deer—outnumbering the people by at least 30 to one. Jura's human population was cleared to make the island into a deer forest and sheep walk. It is a haunting kind of place, with a few traces of the vanished villages—the faint shapes of the "lazy-beds" (cultivated strips) still show through the heather. Otherwise, especially near the road end, the bracken and yellow flag-irises, mossy woods, and strands of seaweed crisping on the salty grass form idyllic pictures of summer on the Hebrides.

The Inner Hebrides

► Coll and Tiree *233A4/A3*

Coll and Tiree duck low on the Hebridean horizon to let the Atlantic weather systems pass over, thus boasting good sunshine records. Tiree looks friendlier in cream and green, while Coll is rockier, with more acid moorland. Tiree has long been famed for its fertile, sandy soil, and the crofting way of life is still followed, more so than in Coll with its cattle rearing. Both islands were cleared, at least in part, with Ayrshire dairy farmers the new tenants in Coll in the 1850s. In Tiree the clearances were less severe: even today its population, around 750, is five times that of Coll. Long beaches with crashing Atlantic surf are popular with surfers. Tiree has reliable conditions almost all year. Visit these islands if wide skies, open seas, wild flowers, and a pace of life governed by the tide and the ferry is your idea of Hebridean bliss.

►► Colonsay *233B2*

Two hours from Oban lies 13km (8mi) long Colonsay, its grey rock rubbing through threadbare moorland. If you only have time for one Hebridean island, this is the one to choose. Colonsay's farms raise sheep and cattle, the rabbit-cropped coastal strip is shadowed by hunting buzzards, while wild goats browse round the edges of protected patches of unusual Hebridean natural woodlands of oak, hazel, and willow. Bird habitats include gleaming sandy beaches and extensive tidal sandflats as well as impressive sea-cliffs and a loch. Colonsay's most famous (and scarcest) bird is the chough (see panel).

Lord Strathcona's family owns Colonsay, residing at Colonsay House. The extensive **Woodland Gardens** of this rambling pink mansion, with their tender rhododendrons, thickets of rampant escallonia, and many much rarer species, are open to the public all year.

▶▶ Gigha *233C1*

Tucked out of the weather off Kintyre, 8km (5mi) long Gigha has a mild climate. Its main attraction is **Achamore Gardens**. These 130ha (325-acre) gardens were originally created by Sir James Horlick in 1944, who saw the place as ideal for exotic shrubs. Within the wooded windbreaks he created one of Scotland's finest woodland gardens. There are thickets of camellias, azaleas hoary with lichen, heather banks, and damp places as well as a superb viewpoint revealing Jura's spectacular profile. The gardens are open all year and it is possible to visit them by ferry from the mainland in a long morning or afternoon (*Open* all year, dawn–dusk. *Admission: inexpensive*. Tel: 01583 505254; www.gigha.org.uk).

ORONSAY

Oronsay is separated from Colonsay at low tide by 2km (1mi) of sand flats, a splashy cockle-strewn haunt of plover. Bring wellington boots to visit Oronsay Priory, an abandoned 14th-century Augustinian foundation with impressive grave slabs and a magnificent early 16th-century cross. Make sure you keep an eye on the tide to avoid being cut off.

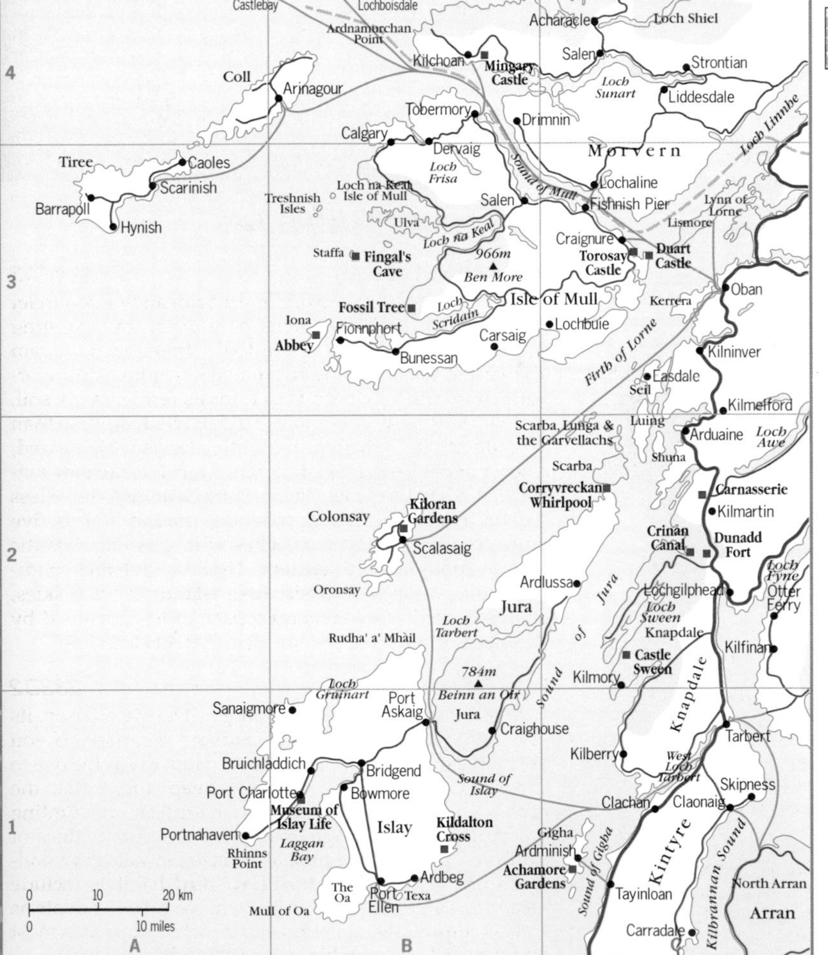

Drive

Around Islay

(www.isle-of-islay.com)

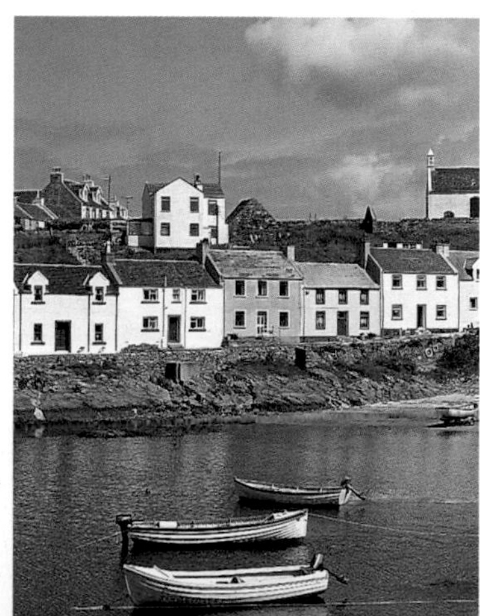

Islay has a quite different feel from the rest of the Hebridean islands. In the western half in particular, it is a place of farms, rather than crofts, and a number of distilleries provide work for the local community. For both the 91km (56mi) round trip from Bowmore and the southern excursion via Mull of Oa (84km/ 52mi) make sure you allow plenty of time for short walks and sea views.

Bowmore is a tidy little town which gives its name to the whisky made in the distillery (founded 1779) by the shore. The dominating parish church of 1767 was built to an unusual circular design so that the devil could not find a corner to hide in.

Take the A846 north out of Bowmore to Bridgend, then the A847 to skirt the sand flats at the head of

Portnahaven, Islay

Loch Indaal, following its shores to **Bruichladdich**, a village with a distillery and another malt whisky name. Continuing south for a few minutes you reach **Port Charlotte.** On the right of the road, in a converted church, is the **Museum of Islay Life** (*Open* Apr–Oct, Mon–Sat 10–5, Sun 2–5. *Admission inexpensive.* Tel: 01496 850358).

Return north to take the B8018 turning, then take a minor road that ends close to **Machir Bay** with its superb sandy beach. The nearby derelict church of **Kilchoman** has some interesting grave-slabs and two late medieval crosses. Circle **Loch Gorm**, which has fine seascapes at Saligo Bay beyond the former war-time camp.

Return east, turning right on to the B8018, then left on the B8017. Take a left for **Kilnave**, where the chapel is associated with the massacre of Maclean clansman after a skirmish with the Macdonalds in 1598. In the graveyard is an 8th-century cross.

The Royal Society for the Protection of Birds have several farms here, including **Aoradh Farm**, a visitor centre (*Open* daily. *Admission: donation* . Tel: 01496 850505; www.rspb.org.uk) with information on their nature reserve. The low-lying lands are still farmed, providing a wintering ground for barnacle and white-fronted geese around the dunes and beaches of **Loch Gruinart**. Drive up its east shore and park before a gate, where the road deteriorates. Walk as far as the headland—Killinallan Point—before returning to Bowmore.

The Paps of Jura from the northern part of the Mull of Kintyre. Jura, the fourth largest island of the Inner Hebrides (45km/28mi long) is sparsely populated

To the south of the island is the southern peninsula of **The Oa**, a region of caves, cliffs, and smuggling tales. At the tip, the **Mull of Oa**, a monument recalls 650 men who lost their lives when the troopships *Tuscania* and *Otranto* went down nearby in 1918. Farther east near Ardmore Point is the highly wrought 8th-century **Kildalton Cross**, carved from a single slab of epidiorite rock.

En route for the Jura ferry take in the **Islay Woollen Mill** (*Open* Mon–Sat 10–5. *Admission free*. Tel: 01496 810563; www.islaywoollenmill.co.uk) and, a little farther, **Loch Finlaggan**, the former power base of the Macdonalds, the Lords of the Isles. Their story is told in a small visitor centre (tel: 01496 850273) overlooking the loch with its little island on which their headquarters stood.

The magnificent Kildalton Cross

ACCESS TO IONA
This is via the well-used A849 on Mull through Bunessan to a long parking area opposite the houses of Fionnphort. The ferry service is frequent in summer and takes only a few minutes.

►► Mull 233B3

Eilean Moula, Isle of Mull, is an island of great beauty. It has a history of emigration and eviction. Today it is known for its wildlife—including sea eagles—and for its links with a popular children's TV programme, **Balamory**.

You can take the ferry from Oban to Craignure, though it is more interesting to use the short (summer-only) ferry crossing from Lochaline to Fishnish. Both ferries are within easy reach of Torosay and Duart castles.

Torosay Castle, Mull

SUNKEN TREASURE
After England's defeat of the Spanish Armada, several vessels were driven into northern waters. The *San Juan de Sicilia* put into Tobermory for supplies. Rumours spread that it was carrying £300,000 in gold. Donald Maclean of Duart sneaked on board and fired the ship's magazine, though how this would have helped him acquire a fortune is unclear. The ship blew up and sank with the loss of over 300 lives. Since then, every so often, salvage attempts have been made but with little success.

Torosay Castle►►► Scottish baronial-style Torosay (*Open* Easter–Oct daily 10.30–5; gardens summer daily 9–7, winter dawn–dusk. *Admission: moderate*. Tel: 01680 812421; www.torosay.com) is full of interest and humour. The energetic can walk along the shore from Torosay to **Duart Castle►**, otherwise reached off the A849. This historic Maclean seat was restored by Sir Fitzroy Maclean in 1911 (*Open* Apr–Oct, Sun–Thu 11–4. *Admission: inexpensive*. Tel: 01680 812319; www.duartcastle.com).

Tobermory is the largest settlement, and, like Ullapool was founded as a fishing station. Its gradual decline was hastened by the arrival of the railhead at Oban, which took away fish traffic. However, the brightly painted crescent of mainly 18th-century buildings gives Tobermory a faintly Mediterranean air. A museum and a distillery stand on the waterfront, both opening weekdays all season.

In Torosay Castle Gardens, Mull

Mull's attractions tend to the ruggedly scenic. Near the tip of the dramatic cliff ramparts of Ardmeanach is **The Burg►**, with its fossil tree reached by a rough walk. There is more coastal spectacle at Carsaig, where a very rough path leads west, below lava cliffs, to the impressive **Carsaig Arches►►**.

Even from the road, there is plenty of dramatic scenery, notably on the west coast loops. North of Loch Scridain, the B8035 breaches stepped cliffs and drops to the shore with fine views of the island of Ulva. This is a remote stretch with unnervingly fresh-looking rock splinters strewn on it.

Isle of Mull Weavers

St. Ninian, the first named missionary to Scotland, is said to have built a church at Whithorn in Galloway around AD *397 (see* *page 120**), but it is the tiny island of Iona that is called the cradle of Scottish Christianity, because of its association with St. Columba.*

Foundation of the monastery The fiery and argumentative Irish monk Columba chose Iona for the setting up of a monastery in AD 563 because it was the first place he reached from which Ireland could not be seen—or so the tale is told. The word of St. Columba's church was spread widely among the northern Picts, these early missionaries being regarded as some kind of superior "medicine men." Such was the importance of this religious communitythat it eventually became the burial place of the kings of Scotland.

It also suffered dreadful atrocities during repeated Norse sackings which finally caused the evacuation of the community to Kells in Ireland. Even after this it was not abandoned entirely and many monks were martyred here. It became a Benedictine foundation around 1203, finally falling into ruin by the Reformation. Restoration work began at the turn of the last century, the Iona Community was founded in 1938, and today the restored buildings are a spiritual centre under the jurisdiction of the Church of Scotland.

Iona today Today the ambience within the complex is a curious mix of the ancient and the earnest, but beyond the restored cloisters the most mystifying aspect of all is the little island's ability to absorb its visitors and still feel peaceful. Most people only make the short walk from the ferry pier via the nunnery to the abbey. They miss the beautiful white shell beaches and the machair with its undisturbed rich insect and bird life beyond the bare rocks and the thin pasture of the interior. The best place to see the shape of the island is from the top of the low (and oddly-named) hill Dun I (see panel).

A LITERARY LOCATION
From Dun I (a low hill), look for Erraid island, lying close inshore to the south, and difficult to see separately from Mull. Robert Louis Stevenson came from a famous lighthouse engineering family and knew the area well, as there was a shore base and quarry on Erraid in 1867 for the building of the Dhu Heartach lighthouse, on an outlying tooth of rock 18km (11km) to the southwest. In *Kidnapped*, Stevenson set the wreck of the brig *Covenant* on the reefs offshore, the treacherous Torran Rocks.

The 15th-century MacLean's Cross, Iona

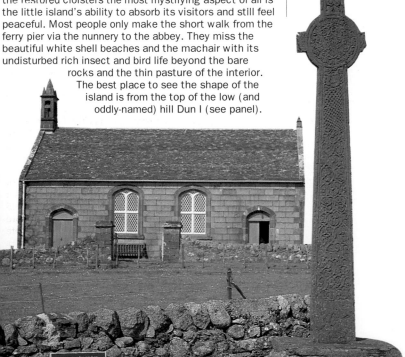

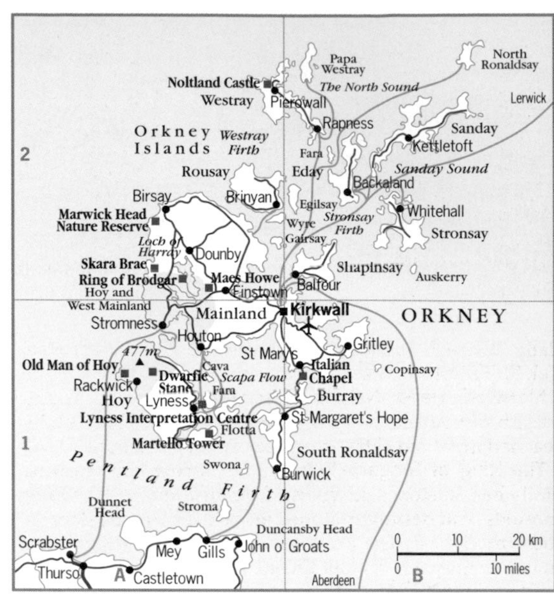

KITCHENER'S MEMORIAL
The huge bird colonies of Marwick Head are below the clifftop memorial to Lord Kitchener. He was on his way to Russia in 1916 aboard HMS *Hampshire* when it hit a mine and sank, with the loss of the warlord and most of the ship's crew.

TICKET BARGAIN
Buy a Historic Scotland joint ticket to all Orkney's prehistoric sites, and save money. It is valid until you have seen them all.

Stromness garage

Orkney

►► Mainland *238A2*

Orkney is an ancient archipelago of gently contoured islands, with place-names identifiable from the rich Norse heritage of the Viking sagas. It has the greatest concentration of prehistoric sites anywhere in Western Europe. Mainland is the largest island and quite a lot of visitors never venture beyond it. **Kirkwall** is the largest town and island capital, built by a natural harbour. This early Christian settlement took its name from the Old Norse *kirkjuvagr*, "church bay," and has several attractions.

Bishop's Palace►► and the **Earl Patrick's Palace** The Bishop's Palace dates originally from the mid-12th century as accommodation close to the then new cathedral. Earl Patrick's Palace, Scotland's finest example of French Renaissance architecture was built in 1600 for Patrick Stewart, ruler of the islands, executed for treason soon after (*Open* Apr–Sep, daily 9.30–6.30. *Admission: inexpensive*. Tel: 01856 871918; www.historic-scotland.gov.uk).

St. Magnus Cathedral►►► This magnificent church's harmonious proportions belie its smallness. Founded in 1137 by Earl Rognvald Kolsson and dedicated to his uncle, St. Magnus, the red sandstone structure took three centuries to complete. Visit any day.

Tankerness House►► A 16th-century merchant-laird's mansion that is now a museum of Orkney life from prehistoric times to the present (*Open* Apr–Sep, Mon–Sat 10.30–5; Oct–Mar, Mon–Sat 10.30–12.30, 1.30–5, also Sun 2–5 May–Sep. *Admission: inexpensive*. Tel: 01856 873191).

Maes Howe►►► Off the A965 13km (8mi) from Kirkwall, this huge burial chamber dates from around 2500 BC and has workmanship unsurpassed in Western Europe. It was almost 3,500 years old when Vikings scratched graffiti on the walls (*Open* Apr–Sep, daily 9.30–6.30; Oct–Mar,

Taking the air in Kirkwall

daily 9.30–4.30. *Admission: inexpensive, booking essential.* Tel: 01856 761606; www.historic-scotland.gov.uk).

Marwick Head Nature Reserve▶▶ Orkney has a wealth of wildlife, notably seabird colonies. These easily reached great red cliffs are stacked with guillemots.

The Ring of Brogar▶▶▶ Orkney's best-known stone circle has 36 stones surviving from around AD 60. Other mounds and standing stones all add to the mystery of these monoliths. The **Stenness Standing Stones** are also in the vicinity (*Open* at all times).

Skara Brae▶▶▶ At this unforgettable prehistoric site, 5,000-year-old stone dressers, beds, and cupboards have survived as fitments to the snug circular dwellings built before the Egyptian pyramids; (*Open* Apr–Sep, daily 9.30–6.30; Oct–Mar, daily 9.30–4.30. *Admission: moderate.* Tel: 01856 841815; www.historic-scotland.gov.uk). **Skaill House**, near Skara Brae, is the finest 17th-century mansion in Orkney (*Open* Apr–Sep, 9.30–6.30. *Admission: inexpensive.* Tel: 01856 841501; www.skaillhouse.com). Joint ticket with Skara Brae.

Stromness is the main ferry port for mainland Scotland connections. In the 18th century, whalers, traders, and round-the-world explorers stopped off here. Today, with its fishing fleet, boatyards, narrow lanes, and old traders' houses, it has a period feel. Visit **Stromness Museum** (*Open* May–Sep, Mon–Sat 10–5, Sun 10.30–5; Oct–Apr, Mon–Sat 10–5. *Admission: inexpensive.* Tel: 01856 850025) for excellent background on the town's fascinating history.

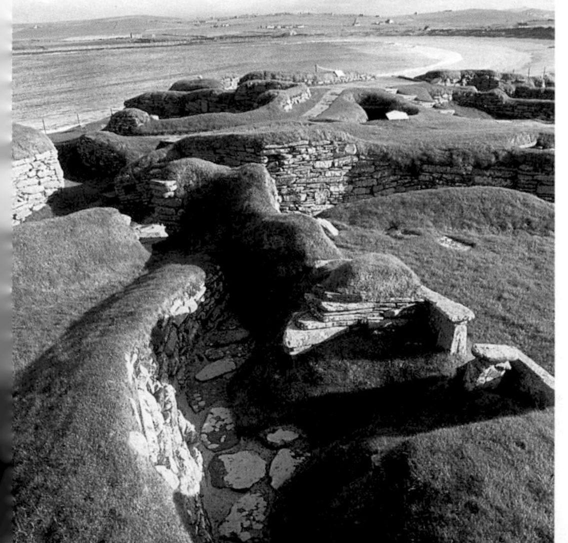

Skara Brae on Mainland Orkney is perhaps the most spectacular of the island's prehistoric sites. This extraordinary slice of Stone Age life lay buried beneath the sands until a storm revealed it in 1850

VIKING INSCRIPTIONS
The party of Vikings who came into the Maes Howe tomb in the winter of 1153 not only contributed to one of the largest surviving collections of runic inscriptions, but also executed some fine animal drawings on a buttress. These include the Maes Howe Dragon (though some say it looks like a lion), which has inspired artists and jewellery designers ever since its rediscovery in 1861.

A FAMOUS MARINER
Captain Bligh (of later *Mutiny on the Bounty* fame) was one of many well-known mariners who called at Stromness. This was in 1780 when he was with the *Discovery* and *Resolution*, returning home from the South Seas after Captain Cook's death. He dined at the Whitehouse of 1680, which can still be seen today.

A SCUTTLED FLEET
It was off the islands of Cava and Flotta that the interned German High Seas Fleet scuttled itself on Midsummer Day in 1919. In doing so, they not only created a massive amount of scrap metal that was salvaged for years after, but they also became what is now rated as Britain's best amateur diving site, as not all of the German ships were cut up.

►► Hoy 238A1

Hoy, the second largest island in the group, is the exception to Orkney's prevailing low-lying greenness, its north and west being high and craggy. Here the red sandstone has weathered into almost Highland scenery, with a west coast of spectacular natural beauty, glimpsed from the ferry en route to Stromness. With the most northerly natural woodland in Britain, glacial features such as small corries at comparatively low levels, and U-shaped valleys, plus an arctic-alpine flora (and mountain hares), Hoy has a very distinct character.

Many of Orkney's landscape features come together at St. Margaret's Hope, South Ronaldsay: the prevailing greenness of the pasture, the sturdy, grey-slated dwellings, and the ever-present sea

The eerily deserted **Lyness Naval Base** on the east coast was the shore base which serviced the key anchorage for the Royal Navy in two world wars. The former Pump House is now the **Lyness Interpretation Centre** (*Open* all year, Mon–Fri 9–4.30, also mid-May–Sep, Sat and Sun 10.30–4. *Admission: free.* Tel: 01856 791300; www.scapaflow.co.uk). Here, too, is the cemetery as an inevitable epilogue to warfare, with sailors' graves from many famous ships, including HMS *Hampshire*, mined and sunk in 1916; HMS *Vanguard*, accidentally blown up off Flotta in 1916; and HMS *Royal Oak*, torpedoed at anchor here in 1939. Also nearby are the Martello Towers, first built between 1813 and 1815 as protection for Baltic-bound British convoys against American privateers.

A road leads west to **Rackwick**, a crofting township coming back to life after a period of decline. This is one of the most attractive parts of Orkney, amid the heathery hills with steep cliffs nearby. From here a footpath leads to the **Old Man of Hoy**, a spectacular sea stack.

North Hoy Nature Reserve►►► This area takes in the Old Man of Hoy and is noted not only for its seabird colonies, but also species such as the great skua, which breed on the island. It is administered by the Royal Society for the Protection of Birds.

Dwarfie Stane► Yet another curiosity, reached on foot from the Rackwick Road, is the so-called Dwarfie Stane, the only rock-cut tomb in Britain. Quite why its 3rd millennium BC excavators should have bothered to chip away at this natural block of red sandstone in its windy valley is a mystery. The tomb has been empty since recorded time.

A WALK ON HOY
Naturalists who want to explore the rugged Hoy hinterland can reach Rackwick on foot by a well-marked track that goes round the north side of Ward Hill, the highest point on Orkney at 479m (1,571ft). Look out for great skuas bathing at the Sandy Loch on the way.

▶ South Ronaldsay *238B1*

Though strictly speaking a separate island, this can be easily visited from Mainland by the road link over the Churchill Causeway, formed by lines of tipped concrete blocks. Sir Winston Churchill ordered its construction during World War II in order to close off the eastern arm of the Scapa Flow anchorage after a German U-boat slipped in and torpedoed HMS *Royal Oak* with great loss of life. Rusty shipwrecks, previously scuttled as part of the navy defences, still line part of the route, adding a surreal quality to the scene.

Italian Chapel▶▶ Starting with a Nissen hut, Italian POWs in 1943 built this extraordinary *trompe l'oeil* building (even the windows are painted on), creating an intricate embellishment with only scrap metal, cement, and other scrounged bits and pieces. Years after World War II had ended, the Italian labour of love began to fall into decay. By this time the local Orcadians had become so fond of it that they used the Italian media to find the original builders, who then returned to Orkney to restore it. It stands on Lamb Holm, half-way along the Churchill Causeway, and is open at all times.

The road continues to **St. Margaret's Hope,** grey houses tucked next to a seaweedy harbour and on to Burwick on the southern tip.

OTHER ORKNEY ISLANDS Among the farther-flung Orkney islands are **Papa Westray**, where two 5,000-year-old dwellings (believed to be the oldest houses in Europe) can be seen at Knap of Howar; **Sanday**, where a tomb of the Maes Howe type—and many other remains—suggests that this was a burial place of great importance in the 2nd millennium BC; and **Westray**, with its ancient church and **Noltland Castle**, a very impressive 16th-century Z-plan edifice, guarding the natural harbour at Pierowall. These and almost all of the other northern outliers of Orkney are well served by the inter-island plane and ferry network from Kirkwall.

VICTORIAN TOURISTS
The Dwarfie Stane is mentioned in Sir Walter Scott's *The Pirate* as the favourite dwelling of Trolld, a dwarf of Norse legend. By Victorian times, the spot was visited regularly, as can be gauged by the surviving graffiti. This includes an inscription in Persian, carved in 1850 by a certain Major William Mouncey. He was an ex-Afghanistan and Persian spy of eccentric habits, including adopting Persian costume and spending several nights inside the tomb.

The Old Man of Hoy, a spectacular sandstone sea stack

Many-layered Jarlshof, near Sumburgh Head on the southern tip of Shetland

SUMBURGH HEAD
With its cluster of attractions, South Mainland alone needs a couple of trips from Lerwick, particularly if you are interested in the birdlife. Though there are plenty of other places to see puffins, the Sumburgh Head colony is particularly convenient. Park before the wall that marks the lighthouse area, go through the gap in the wall, and walk up the road to the first hair-pin bend. Look over the cliff to the right for the puffins.

Shetland

With its ever-changing seascapes, its Norse heritage, and the sheer challenge of its ocean-girt northerly setting, Shetland confounds any stereotypes of tartans and glinting lochs. Nowhere is more than 8km (5mi) from the sea, thanks to the voes and (smaller) geos, the long fingers of sea that find their way far inland. The ocean is a glittering or grim backdrop to every view, and has historically made Shetland into a surprisingly cosmopolitan place.

The islands themselves are subtly different, with a prevailing inland landscape of crofts and small fields or eroded peatland vegetation, and virtually no trees. The biggest island, Mainland, has the island "capital" Lerwick, the only town of any size, and also some excellent seascapes and nature interest as well as historic sites.

▶▶▶ Mainland *243A2*

Esha Ness▶▶▶ Here the sea has hammered away at the cliffs and quarried out awesome rock features: the Holes of Scraada, the Heads of Grocken, and the Grind of the Navir. South of the B9078, **The Drongs**, sea stacks in the bay, resemble a Norse galley under sail. North of Ronas Voe, the scoured hump of Ronas Hill can be seen. Though only 453m (1,486ft) high, its exposed northerly situation has created a low altitude arctic environment, with a variety of interesting arctic and alpine plants on its boulder fields.

Close to Sumburgh Airport, the major archaeological

A fairly quiet day at Esha Ness

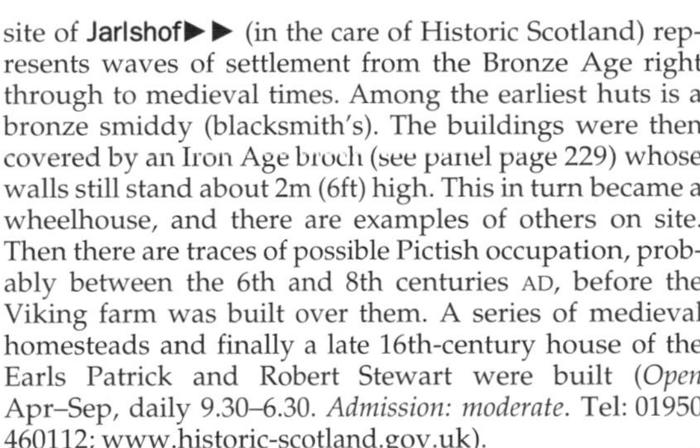

site of **Jarlshof▶▶** (in the care of Historic Scotland) represents waves of settlement from the Bronze Age right through to medieval times. Among the earliest huts is a bronze smiddy (blacksmith's). The buildings were then covered by an Iron Age broch (see panel page 229) whose walls still stand about 2m (6ft) high. This in turn became a wheelhouse, and there are examples of others on site. Then there are traces of possible Pictish occupation, probably between the 6th and 8th centuries AD, before the Viking farm was built over them. A series of medieval homesteads and finally a late 16th-century house of the Earls Patrick and Robert Stewart were built (*Open* Apr–Sep, daily 9.30–6.30. *Admission: moderate.* Tel: 01950 460112; www.historic-scotland.gov.uk).

Nearby look for puffins and otters on **Sumburgh Head** and bonxies (great skuas) loafing around the Loch of Spiggie before their next spot of air piracy. Also within easy reach is **St. Ninian's Isle**, where a treasure was discovered in 1951 near a historic chapel site. St. Ninian's Isle is a tombolo—an island joined to Mainland by a spit of dazzling cream sand.

The **Shetland Croft House Museum▶▶▶**, a 19th-century thatched building, is typical of the style of croft house once found on the islands (*Open* mid-Apr–Sep, daily 10–1 and 2–5. *Admission: free.* Tel: 01950 460557; www.shetland-museum.org.uk/crofthouse). It gives an excellent insight into rural life in Shetland. Walk down to the fascinating "click mill"—a miniaturized horizontal water-mill powered by a tiny burn.

Explanatory panels at the Jarlshof site help unravel the complex pattern of settlement

MAVIS GRIND

Mavis Grind is the appealing name given to a point on the A970, west of Brae, where Mainland all but splits in two, except for a narrow rocky waist that carries the road. It is said to be the only place in Scotland where it is possible to throw a stone from the North Sea to the Atlantic, though it still needs a strong arm.

▶ Lerwick 243B1

This is by far the largest town in Shetland. No settlement existed here before the 17th century, as the area was not considered very fertile. The Norsemen named the area *leir vik*—mud bay—but muddy or not, the sheltered stretch of water between modern Lerwick and the island of Bressay was a safe anchorage for enterprising Dutch fishermen. Lerwick started as a fishing season trading post, then in the Anglo-Dutch wars of the mid-17th century, it became a permanent town, built around Fort Charlotte, whose walls still survive. Now it has around 8,000 people, one third of the total Shetland population.

Today, the centre of Lerwick is full of character, especially the waterfront, with the older buildings hard against the sea still retaining their "lodberries" built out over the water. These were shops-cum-houses-cum-storage-areas with their own private loading and unloading areas.

The main commercial street is flagged and at least partly for pedestrians only, with as good a range of shops as anywhere else in Scotland. There are also fine and sturdy Victorian buildings as well as the housing boom on the edge of town prompted by the oil developments. The brand new **Shetland Museum** on Hays Dock (*Open* from early 2007. Tel: 01595 695057; www.shetland-museum.org.uk) covers the main Shetland themes of folk life, shipping, art, and archaeology.

Once solitary on the edge of a boggy loch, now with lots of new housing nearby, **Clickhimin Broch▶▶** has the complication of being a broch (late-prehistoric circular defensive structure) built within an Iron Age fort. Open at any time, it makes an extremely good preamble to an excursion to Mousa Broch.

Eerie **Mousa Broch▶▶▶** is the most complete example of a broch anywhere in Scotland, with 12m (40ft) walls. As it is on the island of Mousa, the visit involves taking a boat, which runs daily in summer—check with Skara Brae (tel: 01856 841815), or call Mousa Boat Trips (tel: 01950 431367; www.mousaboattrips.co.uk).

A NORSE LEGEND
The Orkneyinga Saga tells how Mousa Broch, or Moseyjarborg, already a thousand years old, was used as a refuge in 1153 by a wayward Orkney earl who had abducted the woman of his dreams (a rival earl's mother, hence the complications).

Lerwick and its harbour; always busy with ferries, fishing boats, and oil-supply vessels

Exclusive knitwear labels, Lerwick Museum

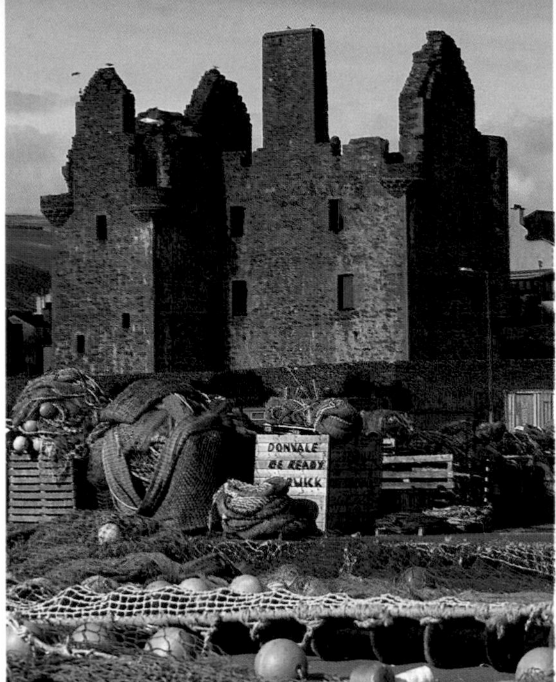

THE SHETLAND BUS
This was the name given to the small craft that maintained the highly dangerous sea connection from Shetland to Norway during World War II. It was used by the Norwegian Resistance for taking in saboteurs and taking out refugees.

Scalloway Castle adds a sense of drama to the skyline of the little town

Another very worthwhile Lerwick excursion is across the nearby island of Bressay to visit the nature reserve of **Noss▶▶▶**, a much smaller island looked after by Scottish Natural Heritage. Though its vertiginous seabird colonies are not for the faint-hearted, the massed puffins and rapier-beaked gannets provide spectacle on a grand scale. Take the regular Lerwick–Bressay ferry, then walk, cycle, drive, or take a taxi 5km (3mi) across Bressay for a small boat crossing to Noss, and walk all round the island.

Scalloway▶▶ The second biggest settlement on Mainland (and in all of Shetland) is older than Lerwick. It lies in a more fertile area on the west coast and was the original main town. Dominating the roofs of the town are the ruins of **Scalloway Castle**. After the demise of Norse power, Shetland gradually came under the sway of a particularly predatory breed of Scottish baron, of which Earl Patrick Stewart was a typical specimen. As the displays within the castle tell, he used forced labour from the surrounding area to build his fortress in 1600. He was executed in Edinburgh in 1615, the castle thereafter gradually falling into ruin. The key-keeper lives nearby and access is at any reasonable time.

Also nearby is the locally run **Scalloway Museum**, which, among other maritime matters, tells the story of the Shetland Bus (see panel) which used Scalloway as a base (*Open* May–Sep, Mon 9.30–11.30, Tue–Fri 10–12, 2–4.30, Sat 10–12.30, 2–4.30. The museum can be visited at other times; tel: 01595 880783/880666). Access to the lesser islands of Trondra and East and West Burra is by the B9074, also near Scalloway. All are linked to Mainland by bridges; the road eventually ends at Papil. At the road end, walk through a little gate to find another fine beach, with views to distant Foula framed by rocky headlands.

By the Town House, Lerwick

CURIOUS ENCLOSURES
First-time visitors to "the bonnie isle" of Whalsay are often puzzled by the small circular stone-built enclosures that dot the landscape. The locals will inform you that they are "planticruives" (variously spelt). They were used to grow winter fodder of the brassica variety. The round wall kept the sheep out and provided shelter. The structure was usually covered with net to keep out birds.

FOULA
Foula (from a Norse word for bird island) offers spectacular coastal scenery even by Shetland standards. The Kame on the west coast is a sheer 365m (1,197ft) cliff, the second highest in Britain. (Only the cliff by Conachair on St. Kilda is higher at 430m/1,411ft.) Foula is 43km (27mi) west of Scalloway.

A variation on the theme of a boathouse at Gutcher, Yell

►► Unst 243B3

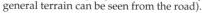

Thanks to cheap prebookable inter-island ferries, getting up to Unst is not a problem. It is worth going, if only to see the United Kingdom's most northerly just about everything, from post office to lighthouse.

Muness Castle► Scotland's most northerly stone castle was built on low ground by the sea for yet another tyrannous Shetland laird, Lawrence Bruce, half-brother to Scalloway Castle's Earl Patrick Stewart. Muness shares approximately the same building date as Scalloway (1598) and the same architect, Adam Crawford. He created a handsome yet functional oblong fortress flanked by two towers on the diagonal, though the second floor and roof are now missing. His client's invocation in verse carved above the main entrance—"To help and not to hurt his work always"—did not impress the French privateers who burned the building within 30 years of its completion. Access is at all reasonable times, via a keykeeper, and the building can also be seen from the road.

Hermaness National Nature Reserve►►► At the other end of Unst from Muness, this is the very end of the United Kingdom. However, the RAF community at Baltasound and the conspicuous radar station on top of Saxa Ford, one of the twin headlands on top of Unst, give the area a slightly sinister ambience. To make the most of the headland, climb the 200m (660ft) high Hermaness Hill. Strong shoes are advised on the rough moorland path. There is a good hilltop view of Muckle Flugga with its lighthouse. Take care if investigating the puffin-hollowed cliffs and gannet-plastered stacks on the west side as the grassy edges slope away treacherously. Look out too for dive-bombing great and arctic skuas breeding on the moor and keep on the path.

Other features of Unst to note are the most northerly post office at **Haroldswick,** as well as a number of broch sites and other prehistoric places; also, for the botanist, the **Keen of Hamar**, a low, domed hill near Baltasound with plant species from the arctic tundra (Scottish National Heritage permit access only—though the general terrain can be seen from the road).

Clickhimin Broch, Lerwick

► Whalsay *243B2*

The Hanseatic League, the trading confederation of European cities that flourished until the 17th century, was important for Shetland. The most vivid reminder of those sea-trading days can be seen at Symbister on the island of Whalsay. The **Bremen Böd** (booth) is a curious little building by the harbourside, a restored Hanseatic storage and trading booth, possibly dating from the 17th century. The key-keeper is nearby, so visiting is possible at reasonable times. Otherwise, Whalsay is an island for bird lovers, with several rarities recorded on migration here. It is also a wealthy island, as it is the home of many of the successful local skippers.

► Yell *243B2*

Yell is a dark brown stepping stone between Mainland and Unst. It has more peat than any other part of Shetland, and this is widely cut for fuel. The **Old Haa of Burravoe** is a 17th-century house (or hall) built by the local laird on the best spot to keep an eye on shipping entering Burra Voe. It has been restored as a local museum with extras such as genealogy, crafts, and a good cup of tea (*Open* late Apr–Sep, Tue–Thu, Sat 10–4, Sun 2–5. Tel: 01957 722339).

Up at the north end of Yell, it's worth tracking down the **Gloup Fishermen's Memorial** in a field behind one of the crofts. Gloup Voe is long and narrow, and once had a large fishing community; it was devastated in July 1881 by the loss of 58 men from ten "sixerenes," the island's native six-oared craft.

VIKING QUARRIES
Among the variety of rock types in Shetland is steatite or soapstone, a soft, easily worked rock extensively used by the Vikings for making a variety of vessels including lamps. One source was near Clibberswick, east of Haroldswick on Unst, where traces of quarrying can still be seen. Sometimes the vessels were formed while still attached to the living rock. They were chiselled into shape, upside down, then removed and hollowed out.

THE WHITE WIFE
On the way up Yell by the B9081, look towards the sea edge for the White Wife near Otterswick and Queyon. She was the figurehead of the German sail training ship *Bohus* and now looks over the waters in which her ship was wrecked. The Old Haa at Burravoe has a copy of her, as well as details of the drama.

Skye and the Western Isles

► Barra 251A1

The sea-going Macneil clan owned Barra for centuries, and often practised piracy. One chief sold the island to pay debts in 1838, and part of it was bought back in 1937 by the 45th chief, an American architect, who restored **Kisimul Castle** (also known as Kiessimul)► in Castlebay (*Open* Apr–Sep, daily 9.30–6.30. *Admission: moderate*. Tel: 01871 810313; www.historic-scotland.gov.uk). Castlebay itself was once a thriving fishing port.

As well as the open shell-sand beaches, one of which achieved fame as the island's landing strip, and the rough inland walking, other points of interest on Barra include **Kilbarr Church**, a ruinous medieval church dedicated to the saint who gave his name to the island.

► Benbecula 251A2

Benbecula, joined to the Uists by causeways, is patterned and interlaced with inland waters. It presents great sweeps of sand to the Atlantic, with flowery machair beyond and attendant crofts. To the west, a missile range points into the ocean. To the east there is much rough bogland. The highest point, Rueval, is barely 120m (393ft) above sea level and overlooks endless peaty lochans, beloved of fishermen.

►► Harris 251B3

Harris has austere rocky landscapes, except for some western machair and the highest hill in the Outer Hebrides, **Clisham**, at almost 800m (2,600ft). The "border" between Lewis and Harris runs east from Kinlochresort. Traditionally, the Macleods of Lewis held the island of their name, while Harris was under the sway of the Macleods of Dunvegan in Skye. Walking, fishing, birdwatching, and visiting beaches are the main activities. **St. Clement's Church**►► at Rodel, on the southern tip,

GEARRANAN
On the exposed Atlantic coast of Lewis, Gearrannan, a traditional blackhouse village gradually abandoned during the first half of the 20th century, has had its croft houses and lands restored in the 1990s, to create an authentic settlement. Modern facilities have now been built into them for the enjoyment of today's visitors wishing to sample life on the edge of Scotland.

LEVERBURGH
One odd chapter in Harris's story is encountered at Leverburgh, near Rodel, which recalls the efforts of one of Britain's most successful industrialists, the soap magnate Lord Leverhume, to spend some of his riches turning a tiny fishing village into a major fish processing port. He owned most of Lewis and Harris at the time.

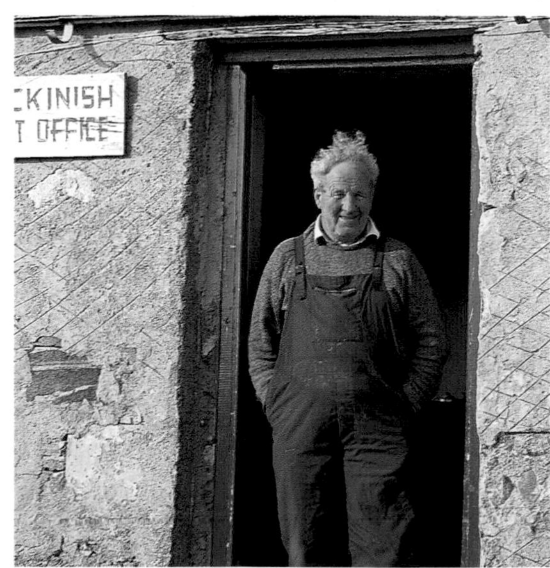

Stockinish post office and postmaster, on Harris

is a cruciform church built around 1500 by the 8th chief of the Macleods, sometimes known as Alasdair Crotach, who died 20 years after the construction of his magnificent tomb within the church. Visit it at any reasonable time.

If visiting Rodel from Tarbert, take in the endless empty sands of **Traigh Luskentyre▶▶▶** and loop back towards Tarbert from Rodel by the east coast road,

enjoying the wild and remote bouldery country. The small island of Taransay lies off the coast. Made famous by the year-long British TV series, *Castaway 2000*, where a group of people from various backgrounds and with minimal materials had to build homes, cultivate food and care for livestock; you can rent a cottage or take a day trip there (www.visit-taransay.com). Another very twisty drive along the B887, northwest of Tarbert towards uninhabited Scarp, passes the former whaling station at **Bunavoneadar** (which was abandoned in 1930—look for the sentinel chimney stack beside the road), and **Amhuinnsuidhe Castle** with its "no stopping" notices. This grand structure was built by the then owners of Harris, the earls of Dunmore, in the 1860s.

Kisimul (Kiessimul) Castle and Castlebay, Barra

Above East Loch Tarbert, Harris

ERISKAY
This island between Barra and South Uist was the place where Bonnie Prince Charlie first landed on Scottish soil. Its other claim to fame is that the SS *Politician* was wrecked there in 1941 while carrying 20,000 cases of whisky. The subsequent events inspired Compton Mackenzie's *Whisky Galore*.

Calanais Standing Stones

▶ Lewis *251B4*

Most of Lewis's townships are close to the coast, forming a narrow green strip between the ocean and the inland brown sea of endless lochan-dotted peatlands. This initially unpromising landscape has a long history of settlement dating from neolithic and Norse times.

Calanais Standing Stones▶▶▶ This is the most famous of the prehistoric sites, possibly dating from 3000 BC. It is a cruciform setting: 19 monoliths form an avenue running north–south from a circle of 13 other stones, with outliers adding to the inexplicable design (Free access to stones. Visitor Centre *open*: summer only. *Admission: inexpensive*. Tel: 01851 621422).

Dun Carloway Broch▶ A fairly well-preserved structure visible from the main A858. The walling stands in part over 9m (30ft) high. View any time.

Blackhouse at Arnol▶▶▶ This once typical local dwelling is in the care of Historic Scotland. The byre is under the same roof (*Open* Apr–Sep, Mon–Sat 9.30–6.30; Oct–Mar, Mon–Sat 9.30–4.30. *Admission: moderate*. Tel: 01851 710395; www.historic-scotland.gov.uk)

Calanais, Carloway, and Arnol are all on the west coast. It is worth continuing northeast on the main road, the A857, all the way to Port of Ness to see the **Butt of Lewis** and its lighthouse. Though the cliffs are not spectacularly high, the ambience is wild and windswept. There are streams of gannets, other seabirds, skuas, and sometimes dolphins or whales can be seen.

Lewis also offers good seascapes on the way to Great Bernera, an island joined to the "mainland" by a causeway: There are plenty of diving gannets and terns off the little beach at the road end at **Bosta**. Arguably the finest beach on Lewis is on the east coast: **Tràigh Mhór** (literally in Gaelic "big beach") can be seen near at the Tolsta road-end.

Stornoway, the main administrative centre for the Western Isles, is not overtly picturesque and is very hushed on Sundays, but it has a fine asset in the **An Lanntair Art Centre** with its changing exhibitions and concert venue

SCOTLAND'S OLDEST UNIVERSITY

Some historians maintain that the Teampuill na Trionaid (Trinity Temple) on North Uist is Scotland's oldest university. This monastery and college founded in the early 13th century lies in ruins, ransacked in the Reformation, its valuable books said to have been cast into the sea. A number of other historical sites are near this former seat of learning.

LORD LEVERHUME

Perhaps Lewis's owner, Lord Leverhume, with his English public school background and wealth, failed to understand the Gaelic mind. He became deeply involved in post-World War I politics on the island, in a complex confrontation with land raiders—ex-servicemen returning from war and eager to acquire crofts. Yet many on Lewis supported his vision of an industrialized island society. He eventually turned his attentions to Harris, his grand dream for Lewis unfulfilled.

An abandoned croft at Barvas, Lewis

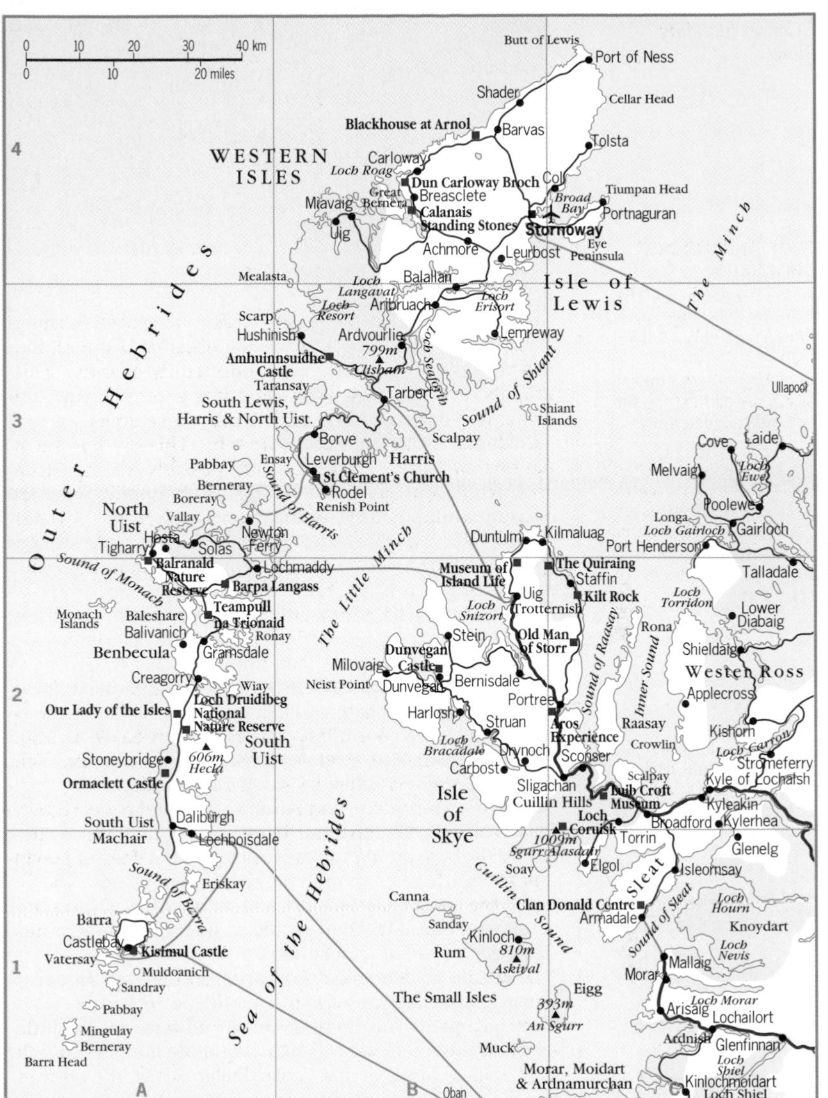

(*Open* Mon–Sat, 10am–1am. *Admission free*. Tel: 01851 703307; www.lanntair.com).

► North and South Uist *251A2*

These are classic Hebridean islands of shell-sand and peaty lochans, golden beaches with crashing Atlantic surf and a rocky, wild, and forbidding easterly coast. All of this provides a varied habitat for wildlife, hence the importance of the RSPB's **Balranald Nature Reserve** on North Uist. There is a reception cottage for information on what to see on the reserve, which is open daily.

On South Uist **Loch Druidibeg** is another wildlife area under the care of Scottish Natural Heritage and noted for its breeding greylag geese, among many other species. Check with the warden's office for visiting details.

THE TALLEST MONOLITH

The Calanais stones may be tall, but tallest of all on the islands is the Clach an Trushal, a solitary monolith standing by the township of Ballantrushal (between Barvas and Shader) on the A857 (north of the junction with the A858). This grey, grizzled, lichen-covered tooth reaches a height of around 6m (20ft).

Pony trekking at Sligachan, Skye

Roadside shrine on the predominantly Catholic island of South Uist

FAILTE GU SGIRE
AN EILEIN SGITHEANAICH
AGUS LOCHAILLSE
WELCOME TO
SKYE & LOCHALSH

A Gaelic welcome on a Skye road sign

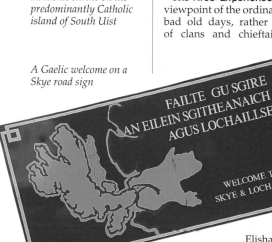

▶▶▶ Skye *251B2*

Superlatives and Skye scenery go together. The big hill masses catch southwesterly weather systems, so it does rain a lot here, but when it is clear, the hills make the heart ache. Skye is unforgettable. Though there is a Mallaig–Armadale ferry link, most people arrive via the Skye Bridge near Kyle of Lochalsh, which replaced the ferry to Kyleakin. The Bright Water Visitor Centre at Kyleakin (*Open* Easter–Oct) is a great introduction to local wildlife. The road runs through Broadford, a well-resourced little community strung along Broadford Bay, with the austere slopes of the Red Cuillin beyond, as a foretaste of the craggier (Black) Cuillin to come. (There is definitely a sense of expectation along this road!). Finally, towards Sligachan, the jagged tops gradually reveal themselves, with the tooth of Sgurr nan Gilean especially prominent.

The **Cuillins** are also distantly in view from the "capital" of Skye itself. Picturesque (depending on the angle of view), **Portree** has quite good shops and services.

The **Aros Experience**▶▶▶ tells Skye's story from the viewpoint of the ordinary folk who lived there in the fairly bad old days, rather than dwelling upon heroic tales of clans and chieftains. It also has an art gallery, exhibitions, a restaurant, play facilities and woodland walks, plus a summer video link to nesting sea eagles (*Open* daily Easter–Oct 9–6; Nov–Easter 10–5. Tel: 01478 613649; www.aros.co.uk).

The most interesting of Skye's scenic road loops is the **Trotternish** peninsula. Beyond the curious rock form of the **Old Man of Storr**▶▶, a popular stop is the **Kilt Rock**▶▶ at Elishader. Seen from the viewing platform, the cliff edge has alternate bandings of sedimentary rock with dolerite, giving the strong impression of kilt pleats. Much of the coastline around here is spectacular, including the 90m (300ft) seaward vertical drop of the **Mealt Falls**.

Beyond the impressive **Quiraing▶▶▶** with its rock towers and pinnacles, and round the top of the peninsula, the **Museum of Island Life▶▶** by the main road at Kilmuir portrays crofting life as it was lived in a self-contained township. Flora Macdonald's grave is nearby (*Open* Easter–Oct, Mon–Sat 9.30–5. *Admission: inexpensive*. Tel: 01470 552206; www.skyemuseum.co.uk).

Though there are other places with Jacobite associations to track down on your way round Trotternish, **Dunvegan Castle▶** is the big attraction in the northern half of Skye. For 700 years the chiefs of the Clan Macleod have inhabited this rock above the sea loch, and between the 19th-century front entrance and the 14th-century keep there is plenty of historic lumber to enjoy. Among the relics is the Fairy Flag. All true Macleods believe this ancient cloth has the power to save the clan one more time if waved in battle (*Open* mid-Mar–Oct, daily 10–5; Nov–mid-Mar 11–4. *Admission: moderate*. Tel: 01470 521206; www.dunvegancastle.com).

The Sleat peninsula is sometimes overlooked by visitors heading for Trotternish and the Cuillins, unless they are travelling from the ferry port at Armadale. The area's principal attraction in this centre is a restored portion of **Armadale Castle▶**. It tells the story of the MacDonalds when they held sway over the western seaboard and beyond as the Lords of the Isles. Around the castle are gardens and nature trails (*Open* Apr–Oct, daily 9.30–5.30, last entry 5. *Admission: inexpensive*. Tel: 01471 844305).

The Small Isles▶▶ This is the collective name for Muck, Eigg, Rum, and Canna. Accommodation is very limited on all of them, so they are usually visited on a day-trip from either Arisaig or Mallaig. The most spectacular is Rum, which is entirely in the care of Scottish Natural Heritage. Red deer are studied here and there are large numbers of breeding burrow-nesting shearwaters.

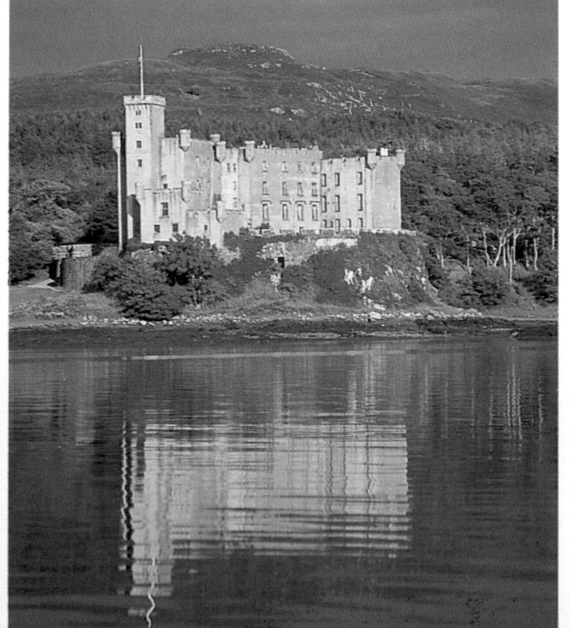

A VIEW OF THE CUILLINS...
The B8083 runs to Elgol and offers a close view of the Cuillins. Hardy walkers can get into the interior via a rough track which leads to Camasunary. This starts some 6km (4mi) from Elgol itself. There is also a coastal path from Elgol.

...AND ANOTHER CUILLINS VIEWPOINT
Follow the minor road, off the B8009 near Drynoch, into Glen Brittle. Park your car right at the end of the road by Loch Brittle and follow the obvious track that rises on to rough moorland for a closer view of the Cuillin ridges. Strong footwear is advised, otherwise enjoy the roadside views, especially from where the road descends into Glen Brittle.

Dunvegan Castle is on the itinerary of most visitors to Skye. It offers a wide range of historic artefacts with Clan Macleod connections

Skye's 80km (50mi) length is the distilled essence of Scottish scenery. In geological terms it has a greater area of basaltic plateau than anywhere else in the UK. It also has what some writers claim to be the finest view: the view of the Cuillin Hills from Elgol. Sir Walter Scott was inspired by it, so was the painter J.M.W. Turner who was one of many artists who journeyed here.

SKYE MARBLE
Among the many geological complexities of Skye, the island even has its own marble. This grey-, green-, and white-striped rock is not only found in lamp bases and paperweights in souvenir shops, but is also exported for decorative, building and agricultural purposes from the Torrin Quarry on Loch Slapin (visible from the Elgol road). The marble has come about by "thermal metamorphism" millions of years ago—limestone in contact with igneous rocks in their molten state has been converted and hardened into the attractive stone found here today.

Sgurr nan Gillean from the Old Bridge at Sligachan

South of the island Skye starts off gently enough, from a visitor's point of view, with the **Sleat** peninsula. Even the bulky granite flanks of the **Red Hills** (sometimes known as the Red Cuillin) give no hint of the spectacle just around the corner. Then the pinkish granite gives way to dark toothed gabbro, and the **Cuillins** reveal themselves at Sligachan with the spire of Sgurr nan Gillean, well over the 914m (3,000ft) contour. More than 20 of its companions also reach this magic Munro mark (see page 149), the highest being Sgurr Alasdair at 1,009m (3,310ft), on a spiky arête which eventually tumbles into **Loch Scavaig** in the west. Complicated volcanic geology has been further notched and splintered by more recent glaciation.

The Trotternish peninsula Yet even with the Cuillins, Skye has not finished with scenic spectacle. Most of the north of the island is basalt plateau, the ancient lavas suddenly ending in a long line of slipping cliffs, again the most spectacular of their kind in Britain. The **Old Man of Storr** on the horizon is a 49m (161ft) pinnacle adrift from its parent cliff. It stands insecurely on a jumbled complication of clays and limestones unable to support the weight of the lava-plateau above. The infinitesimally slow rotational slippage of great slabs of lava cliff has also created the extraordinary rockforms of the **Quiraing**, into whose confines only sure-footed walkers should venture. Skye is unbeatable—when the sun shines.

Travel Facts

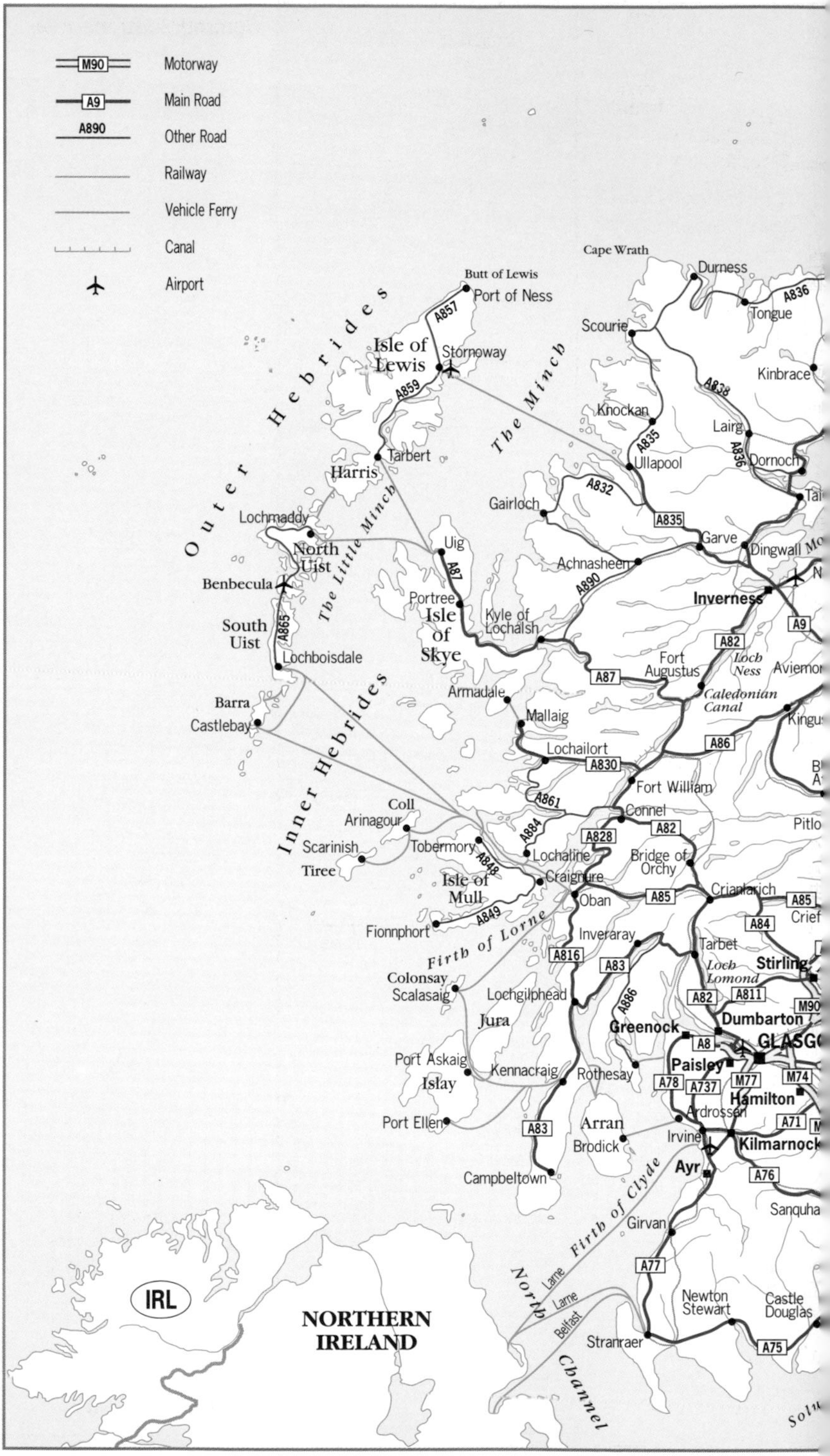

M90 Motorway
A9 Main Road
A890 Other Road
Railway
Vehicle Ferry
Canal
Airport

Cape Wrath
Durness
Butt of Lewis
Port of Ness
A836
Tongue
Scourie
A857
Isle of Lewis
Stornoway
Kinbrace
Outer Hebrides
The Minch
A859
A838
Knockan
Lairg
A835
A836
Tarbert
Ullapool
Dornoch
Harris
A832
Tain
Gairloch
A835
Lochmaddy
The Little Minch
Garve
Dingwall
North Uist
Uig
Achnasheen
Benbecula
A87
A890
Inverness
Portree
South Uist
A865
Isle of Skye
Kyle of Lochalsh
A9
A82
Lochboisdale
Fort Augustus
Loch Ness
Aviemore
A87
Armadale
Caledonian Canal
Barra
Castlebay
Mallaig
Kingussie
Inner Hebrides
A86
Lochailort
A830
Fort William
A861
Coll
Arinagour
Connel
A82
Pitlochry
A884
A828
Scarinish
Tobermory
Lochaline
Bridge of Orchy
Tiree
A848
Craignure
Isle of Mull
Oban
A85
Crianlarich
A85
A849
A84
Crieff
Fionnphort
Inveraray
Firth of Lorne
Tarbet
A816
A83
Loch Lomond
Stirling
Colonsay
Scalasaig
Lochgilphead
A886
A82
A811
M90
Jura
Dumbarton
Greenock
A8
GLASGOW
Port Askaig
Paisley
Islay
Kennacraig
Rothesay
A78
A737
M77
M74
Hamilton
Ardrossan
Port Ellen
Arran
A71
A83
Brodick
Irvine
Kilmarnock
Ayr
Campbeltown
A76
Firth of Clyde
Sanquhar
Girvan
A77
North Channel
Larne
Larne
Belfast
IRL
Newton Stewart
Castle Douglas
NORTHERN IRELAND
Stranraer
A75
Solway

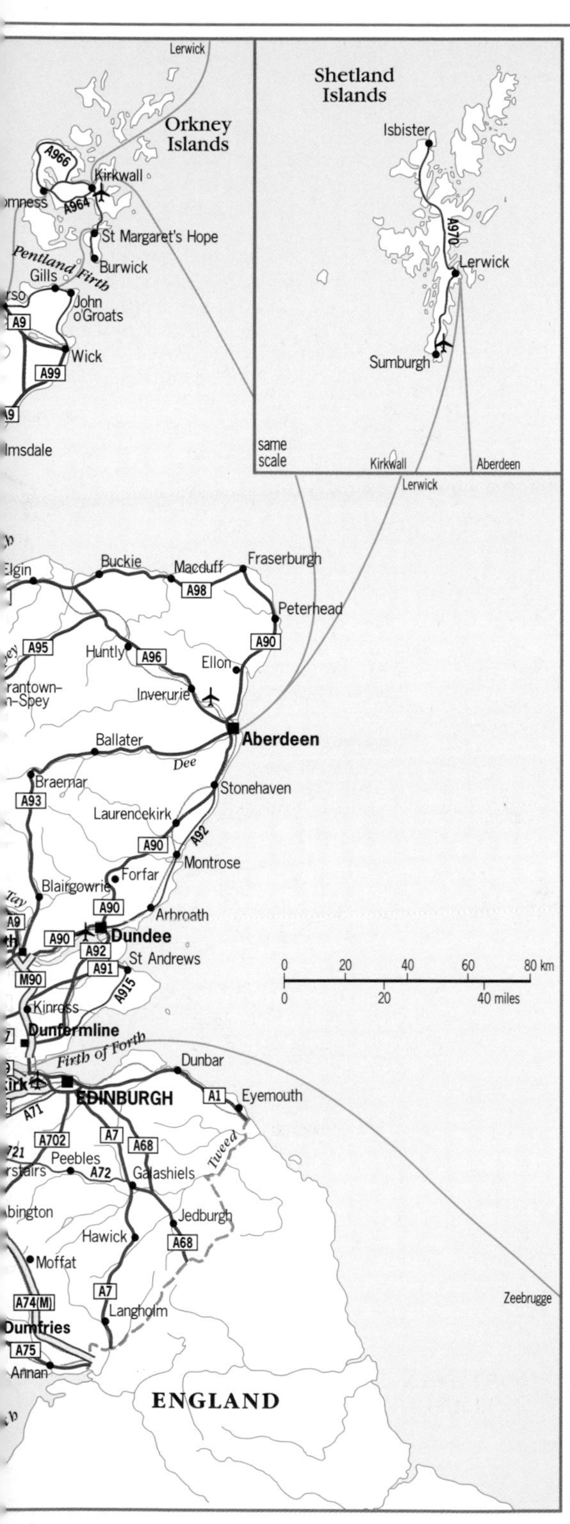

Communications map

In all, Scotland has about 790 offshore islands, most of which are uninhabited. Ferry routes between larger islands, and between them and the mainland, are shown on this map, as are other communication routes

Arriving

By air

Scheduled transatlantic flights use Glasgow airport, though additionally there are chartered flights that use Edinburgh airport. There are direct overnight services to Glasgow from Newark and Chicago, with journey times of 6 hours 30 minutes and 7 hours 30 minutes respectively. Visitors flying from San Francisco can travel either via Chicago or Toronto. Transatlantic visitors can also fly to London, Frankfurt or Amsterdam and connect with a wide choice of flights to Scotland. Some carriers offer fly-drive deals; check with your travel agent.

You can fly direct from London to **Edinburgh**, **Glasgow**, **Aberdeen**, and **Inverness**. There are also Scottish connections from other English airports. Main operators within Scotland include British Airways and Loganair. Ryanair operate daily scheduled flights from Dublin, Frankfurt, London, Stansted, Brussels, and Paris into Glasgow Prestwick International. Flybe, Easyjet, and ScotAirways also operate flights to Scotland from the rest of the UK.

Aberdeen, Edinburgh and Glasgow airports have information desks and left-luggage facilities.

By sea

From Europe Superfast Ferries operate a service from Zeebrugge to Rosyth, just north of Edinburgh. There are also frequent ferry services from the Continent to the north of England within easy reach of the Scottish Border. A variety of Scandinavian connections exist to **Aberdeen** and **Newcastle**, within 90 minutes of the border, and **Hull**, 3–4 hours away, has ferries to Rotterdam and Zeebrugge.

From Northern Ireland there are frequent regular sailings from **Larne** to **Stranraer** and **Cairnryan**. Full details are available from Stena Line or from P&O appointed travel agents. There is also a SeaCat service from **Belfast** to **Stranraer** and **Troon**.

By train

Rail services connect the main cities of Scotland with the south. Fast electrified routes run from **London King's Cross** to **Edinburgh Waverley** and between **London Euston** and **Glasgow Central**. Some King's Cross services also run to Glasgow Central. In addition there are some (non-electrified) through services from London to Aberdeen and Inverness. The fastest journey time between Edinburgh and London is just under 4 hours, with many services taking around 4.5 hours including stops. The fastest direct service between London Euston and Glasgow Central takes 5–5.5 hours; services linking Glasgow and King's Cross take about the same time.

Rail services also connect main English cities and towns with Scottish destinations. Overnight travel by sleeper services is available. For further information contact the National Rail Enquiry Service (tel: 08457 484950; www.nationalrail.co.uk)

By bus

There are a number of companies in the UK operating express services to Scotland. They offer direct services, many of which run daily throughout the year, to a variety of destinations. Overnight travel is available on most major routes.

Many services offer facilities such as steward or hostess service with hot and cold drinks and light refreshments, toilet and washroom facilities, air-conditioning, and seating in smoking or non-smoking areas.

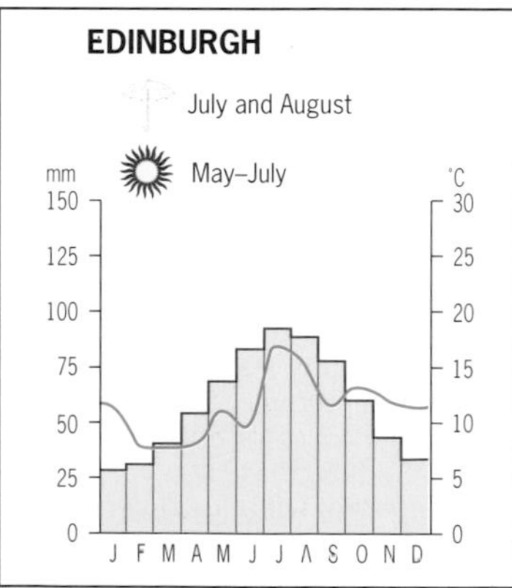

Further details on all services and ticket prices can be obtained from appointed travel agents or main city bus stations.

By car
Many travellers from the south use the M6 motorway, which becomes the M74 and A74 north of the Border. Using this route to Glasgow, and then taking the M80 and M/A90 north, it is possible to reach as far north as Aberdeen by motorway or dual carriageway all the way from London or even Exeter.

Alternatively, the M1, A1(M), and A1 is the main route on the eastern half of the country, though it is not possible as yet to reach Edinburgh, the capital, without encountering

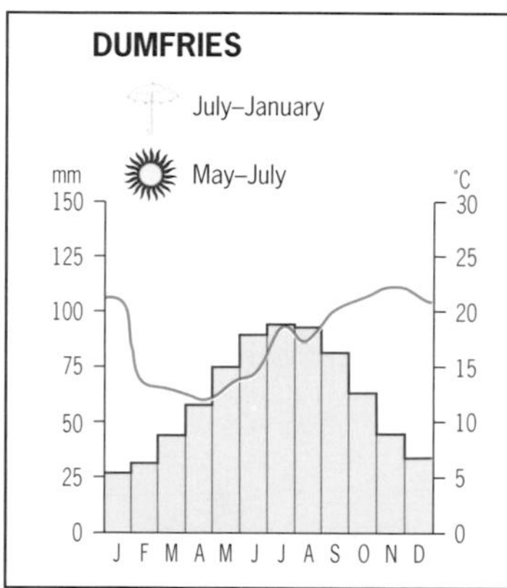

some single carriageway stretches of the A1 north of the Border. Allow seven or eight hours to reach Edinburgh comfortably from London, including stops and keeping reasonable average speeds.

Customs
There are no border checkpoints between England and Scotland. Transatlantic visitors flying direct to Glasgow will find the standard UK regulations apply with regard to quantities of duty-free cigarettes, alcohol, and perfume. There are higher allowances for duty-paid goods bought in the EU.

The import of wildlife souvenirs sourced from rare or endangered species may be either illegal or

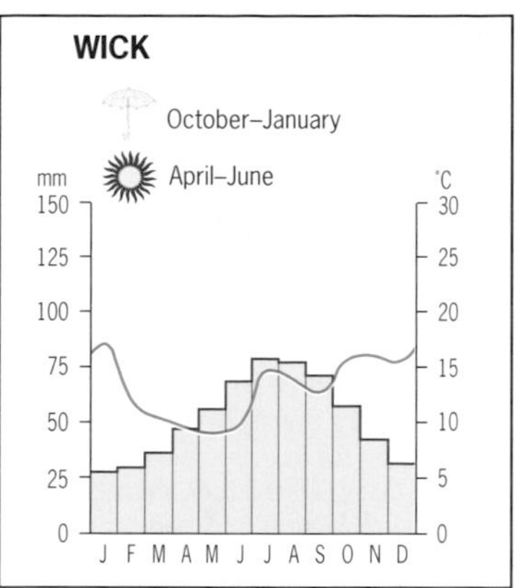

require a special permit. Before purchase you should check your home country's regulations.

When to go
Most Scots would say that May and June are the best months. Peak holiday season is July and August, when there is less accommodation choice in some of the smaller places in the west. Festival time in Edinburgh (late August to early September) is very busy. Scotland's indigenous biting insect, the midge, is active from late May to mid-September on the west coast and the islands. Though an irritation, it poses no serious threat.

In terms of visitor attractions, most properties belonging to the National Trust for Scotland (see address page 269) are closed by the beginning of November and open again at Easter. However, the grounds of many of these properties stay open throughout the year. Many Historic Scotland properties are open throughout the year, though some opening times are quirky, with Thursday afternoon and all-day Friday closing between October and March. Many privately owned castles also close between November and March.

Most municipal museums and art galleries stay open in the winter, as do some nature reserve visitor centres, plus a number of other attractions. Cromarty Court House (see page 212) and The Museum of Scottish Lighthouses (see page 177) are just two places of interest in the north open year-round (remember winter daylight hours are short).

Rainfall, Edinburgh
Average rainfall in mm

	Jan	Feb	Mar	Apr	May	Jun	Jul	Aug	Sep	Oct	Nov	Dec
mm	57	42	51	41	51	51	57	65	67	65	63	58

Essentials

Climate
The Scots say that Scotland does not have a climate: it only has weather. Scotland's position on the edge of Europe, surrounded by sea on three sides, means that the weather is varied—though plenty of east-coast places have less rain than Rome.

The east coast of Scotland tends to be cool and dry, the west coast milder and wetter. Remember also that only a short distance can make a great deal of difference to the weather. The occasional outbreak of haar (summer sea mist) along the east coast is usually a sign of brilliant sunshine only a little way inland. Most important, if you do meet rain, with Scotland's ever-changing weather patterns, the chances are that it will not last for long. See also **When to go** on page 259.

Hours of daylight
There are longer summer daylight hours in the north of Scotland—up to an hour's difference on Midsummer Day (24 June) depending on how far north from Edinburgh you go.

Public holidays
In Scotland, "bank holidays" apply only to banks and some other financial and commercial offices, although in England and Wales they are general public holidays. **Christmas Day**, **Boxing Day** (26 December), and **New Year's Day** (and **2 January**) are usually taken by everyone.

In place of the general holidays in England, Scottish towns and cities normally have a spring and autumn holiday. The actual dates when these local holidays occur varies from place to place but they are

almost invariably on a Monday. In general, all visitor-orientated places including restaurants, remain open but a local holiday in a small town means that local businesses and many shops will be shut for the whole day.

Time differences
Scotland observes the same time as the rest of the UK. Between the end of October and the end of March, Greenwich Mean Time operates: Thus at 12 noon in Edinburgh it is 8–10PM in Australia, 4–8.30AM in Canada, 12 noon in Eire, midnight in New Zealand and 4–7AM in the USA. From the end of March to the end of October, British Summer Time operates (one hour ahead).

Visas and vaccinations
Scotland's visa requirements are identical to those of the rest of the UK. All foreign visitors will need a full passport. Those visitors from the European Union, the US, Japan, much of South America, and most Commonwealth countries do not need a visa for stays of up to six months, but there are exceptions. If there is any doubt, contact the British Embassy before travelling.

No special vaccinations are required for holidays in the UK.

Money and banking
English currency is accepted in Scotland and signs to this effect can be still be seen decorating the till of the occasional Highland shop.

There are four major banks in Scotland: Bank of Scotland, Royal Bank of Scotland, Clydesdale Bank, and Lloyds TSB Scotland. Only the Royal Bank of Scotland still prints pound notes; £1 coins are much more common.

The opening hours of Scottish banks are approximately 9.15–4.45, with some closing later on Thursdays. A very few banks open on Saturday mornings.

In Scotland generally, banks do not necessarily give the best exchange rates for foreign currency. It is also possible to change money in airports, larger rail stations, travel agents, and some of the larger hotels (if you are a resident). Travellers' cheques can be used in some shops, and can be cashed in banks.

Several major English banks have branches in Edinburgh, Glasgow, and Aberdeen. There are also several foreign banks in Edinburgh and Glasgow. For details of these check the local telephone book or ask at the local Tourist Information Centre.

Credit cards Most larger shops, stores, hotels, and restaurants in Scotland will accept the majority of British and international credit cards, such as MasterCard, Visa, and Diners Club. Debit cards and cheques are also widely accepted, but it is advisable to carry some cash in case of difficulty. Many smaller accommodation establishments, such as bed and breakfasts, are unlikely to accept any form of credit card. American Express has offices in Glasgow, Edinburgh, and Aberdeen.

Above: near Aberfeldy in Tayside
Left: the weather closes in

Driving

Car rental
Scotland has a selection of car rental firms. Both national and local companies offer competitive rates. Major operators can often arrange in advance for a car to be available at your destination. Some hotels also offer this service. It is advisable to contact several companies in order to compare the rates. Away from the main cities and in northern Scotland, the choice decreases and may be restricted. There are car rental companies at the major airports in Scotland.

A familiar sight—a Caledonian MacBrayne (CalMac) ferry

Alamo tel: 0870 400 4562;
www.alamo.co.uk
Aberdeen, Dundee, Edinburgh, Glasgow, Prestwick, Hamilton, Inverness, Stirling

Arnold Clark The biggest Scottish car rental company, with a large number of branches and good local knowledge. Check www.arnoldclarkrental.co.uk for a list of all their branches, or tel: 0845 607450

Avistel: 0870 6060 100;
www.avis.co.uk
Aberdeen, Edinburgh, Glasgow, Inverness, Oban, Prestwick, Stirling

Budget tel: 08701 539170;
www.budget.co.uk
Aberdeen, Edinburgh, Glasgow, Inverness

Europcar BCR tel: 0845 722 2525;
www.europcar.co.uk
Aberdeen, Edinburgh, Glasgow, Prestwick, Inverness, Orkney, Shetland

Hertz tel: 08708 448844;
www.hertz.co.uk
Aberdeen, Dundee, Edinburgh, Fraserburgh, Glasgow, Inverness, Perth, Prestwick, Stranraer

Car rental companies can, in many instances, arrange for your rental car to be available at a ferry terminal.

Driving in Scotland
Driving in Scotland, like the rest of the UK, is on the left side of the road. Some British driving terms may be unfamiliar to visitors from the US. These include petrol (gas), car park (parking lot), motorway (freeway), dual carriageway (divided highway), roundabout (traffic circle), and overtaking (passing).

You may never turn on a red light anywhere in Britain; wait for green. In urban areas, if you park in a marked bus lane you could get a ticket.

Compared to America's freeways, British motorways have very few access points (junctions) and opportunities for fuel, meals, and restrooms. Look for "Services."

Scotland's roads include an efficient motorway network in central Scotland, with good roads to key places farther north such as Aberdeen—a dual carriageway, now the A90(M)—and Inverness (partly dual carriageway via the A9).

Radio Scotland (FM 92.4–94.7MHz/ MW 810kHz) broadcasts details of road conditions throughout the day, as do Scotland's local radio stations.

Insurance Visitors bringing their own cars from overseas will require appropriate insurance and should carry their car registration documents.

Driving licence Any holder of an overseas driving licence may for a period

Rush hour in the Highlands

of up to one year drive a motor vehicle in Britain, but only for a class of vehicle which the original licence authorizes.

Speed limits On motorways and dual carriageways the speed limit is 70mph/112kph; on single carriageways it is 60mph/96kph; in built-up areas, 30mph/48kph unless otherwise signposted.

Drinking and driving The police in Scotland strongly advise against drinking alcohol and driving afterwards. This advice applies to citizens of Britain and overseas visitors alike. Anyone caught driving with more than the legal limit of alcohol in their bloodstream by the police is subject to prosecution.

Motorway breakdowns If you break down on the motorway, you can stop your car on the hard shoulder. Free emergency telephones are positioned at regular intervals (approximately every kilometre or half mile) on the hard shoulder. The hard shoulder is for emergency use only, however—you must never use it simply to stop for a rest.

Accidents If you are involved in a road traffic accident, you should stop and stay a the scene to give your registration number, name and address and insurance company to the other vehicle owner or the police.

Single-track roads In some of the more remote areas of Scotland there are still some single-track roads, where there is not enough room for two cars to pass. When two cars approach from opposite directions, the car that first reaches a passing place should pull in or stop opposite to allow safe passage. It is an offence to hold up a following vehicle and not give way. It should also be noted that passing places are not to be used as parking places.

Parking Parking is difficult in Scotland's cities and you are advised not to take chances. Traffic wardens are vigilant, fines for parking offences are high, and you could have your car impounded.

There are usually coin-operated meters for individual parking spaces or else ticket-issuing machines. There are also parking areas run by the local authority or National Car Parks (NCP). These can be the best option, saving you the time and frustration of looking for a space on the street.

An unusual—and comprehensive—cast-iron milepost in Fife

Public transportation

By train

Scotland has a reasonable internal network, with fast connections to the four main Scottish cities and points between. In addition, there are 260km (160mi) of track north of Inverness and also west coast railheads such as Mallaig and Kyle of Lochalsh, with superb scenery on the way. For information about tickets, check with your travel agent, main rail station, or the nearest Tourist Information Centre in Scotland, or contact the National Rail Enquiry Service (tel: 08457 484950).

Glasgow Central Station

Most rail services are efficient and, if you avoid rush hours, are not overcrowded. There are differences in pricing between the many companies that operate different lines.

There are two levels of rail travel. First class is more costly but you are guaranteed a seat and the price includes complementary newspapers and drinks. Second (standard) class is also comfortable, and you can reserve a seat if you buy your ticket in advance. Sleeping compartments can be reserved with First ScotRail on some of their overnight services (tel: 08457 550033).

Allow plenty of time if you need to change trains to continue your journey.

Your journey could be delayed due to engineering work which is usually undertaken at weekends and during national holidays. You can check if you will be affected at relevant stations or in advance by contacting National Rail Enquiries (see above).

For train times and information about fares call the 24-hour National Rail Enquiry Service on 0845 7484950. Their leaflet, *Map and Guide to Using the National Rail Network*, is available at rail stations.

Most stations display timetables, and you should note that services run differently on weekends.

First ScotRail is the largest train operator in Scotland. It also operates the overnight sleeper linking Scotland's major cities with London (tel: 08457 550033; www.firstscotrail.com). The website has information about the facilities available at all stations, such as parking, refreshments and access for people with disabilities.

Railbus offers onward links to non-rail destinations (tel: 08457 550033).

Tickets can be bought at most rail stations from the counter or from a machine.

Always have a valid ticket before boarding a train, unless your journey starts from a station without a ticket office, in which case you can buy your ticket on the train. Ticket inspectors operate on most trains and you must be able to produce your ticket.

Children under five years travel free and between five and 15 years, ticket are half price, but there are exceptions to this, so always check.

The Britrail Pass gives unlimited rail travel for non-UK residents but can only be purchased overseas (www.britrail.com).

By bus

A network of operators covers the smaller towns and rural areas of Scotland. Local Tourist Information Centres carry full details and timetables. Alternatively, for further information on getting around by bus contact Traveline, tel: 0870 608 2608; www.travelinescotland.com

Postbus Many remote areas are served by Postbuses, small minibuses delivering mail which also have seats for fare-paying passengers. Space on these buses, however, is limited, so do not plan an entire or a tight itinerary round the Postbus network, especially if you have a lot of luggage. There are over 130 rural routes throughout Scotland; timetables are available from: www.postbus.royalmail.com.

By ferry

Ferries are a major means of transportation on the western seaboard and also around Orkney and Shetland. Ferries will carry cars, caravans, foot passengers, bicycles and freight. They vary in size and in frequency and since bad weather can affect sailings, always check whether your planned journey is affected.

Information about ticket prices and timetables is available from the ferry companies listed on this page.

When reserving tickets, you will be asked about the planned number of passengers and the make andsize of your vehicle.

An Island Rover ticket is available from Caledonian MacBrayne (see below). It lasts 8 or 15 days and offers a considerable saving.

Caledonian MacBrayne Ltd (CalMac) operate the majority of ferry services on the River Clyde and west coast of Scotland, sailing to 22 islands. Most ferries carry vehicles, although some (to the Small Isles, for instance) only convey passengers. On many services, it is advisable to make advance vehicle reservations, especially during the summer and at other peak times. Caledonian MacBrayne offer flexible tickets which make island touring easier. Caledonian MacBrayne Ltd., The Ferry Terminal, Gourock, Renfrewshire PA19 1QP, tel: 01475 650100, fax: 01475 635235. Reservations: tel: 08705 650000, www.calmac.co.uk.

Northlink Ferries sail regularly to Orkney and Shetland from Aberdeen and Scrabster (near Thurso). The main Orkney crossing is from Scrabster to Stromness. There are also some sailings between Orkney and Shetland, but these are not as frequent as the ferries to and from the Scottish mainland. Book in advance for cars on all sailings and also for passengers from Aberdeen to Lerwick. Information is available from: Northlink Orkney & Shetland Ferries Ltd., Kiln Corner, Ayre Road, Kirkwall, Orkney KW15 1QX, tel: 01856 885500, fax: 01856 879588. Reservations: tel: 0845 6000449, www.northlinkferries.co.uk.

Western Ferries operate ferries between the mainland towns of Gourock and Dunoon. Information is available from: Western Ferries (Clyde) Ltd., Hunters Quay, Dunoon, Argyll PA23 8HJ, tel: 01369 704452, fax: 01369 706020, www.western-ferries.co.uk.

From May to September a ferry service for foot passengers only operates between John o'Groats and Burwick, Orkney. Contact the ferry office at John o'Groats, Caithness KW1 4YR, tel: 01955 611353.

Kirkwall Harbour

Orkney Ferries operate services between the various Orkney islands: Orkney Ferries Shipping Co. Ltd., Head Office, Shore Street, Kirkwall KW15 1LG, tel: 01856 872044: www.orkneyferries.co.uk.

The **Shetland Islands Council** operate ferry services within the Shetland Isles: Information is available from Ferry Services, Port Administration Building, Sella Ness, Shetland ZE2 9QR, tel: 01806 244219; www.shetland.gov.uk/ferries.

Media and communications

The media Scotland has its own indigenous media, at both the quality and tabloid ends of the market. *The Scotsman,* based in Edinburgh, aspires to the crown as Scotland's national newspaper, though challenged by its Glasgow-based competitor, *The Herald*. Both are exceeded in circulation by the unashamedly regional, if not parochial, Aberdeen-based *Press and Journal*. (It is said that the P&J headlined the *Titanic's* sinking with "North-East Man Drowns at Sea"). All of these have their evening equivalents. Scotland's other popular daily is the tabloid *Daily Record*.

The Sunday Post is a top selling Scottish institution peddling its own unique brand of homespun, Conservative, family-orientated journalism, while *The Herald's* Sunday paper *The Sunday Herald* and *Scotland on Sunday* from the same stable as *The Scotsman*, are the heavyweights that see off *The Sunday Times* north of the Border. Scotland also has many local weekly newspapers worth dipping into to see what entertainment is on offer in your chosen holiday locality. *The List* is excellent for both Glasgow and Edinburgh listings. There is also a reasonably widespread circulation and availability of quality and tabloid newspapers printed in England, partly servicing the many English people in Scotland.

The Scotsman, *voice of Edinburgh*

Scotland's television choice is essentially what is broadcast from south of the Border, with home-based material slotted in as appropriate. Both BBC1 and BBC2 have Scottish opt-ins, including, on BBC1, substantial Scottish news coverage and the all-important weather forecasts. The commercial television networks north of the Border include Border Television, the influential STV (Scottish Television), based in Glasgow, and Grampian Television from Aberdeen. One curious anomaly of the 1990s is the availability of funding for the making of Gaelic programmes, which both the BBC and independents beam out not just to the Gaels but to chunks of Scotland where the language has not been spoken since the 13th century, such as the northeast, and even Orkney and Shetland, where it has never been spoken.

BBC Radio Scotland has a loyal following. Though also on FM, its medium-wave transmissions can easily be found by locating Radio 4 on long-wave and pressing the medium-wave button (not guaranteed to work on all radios!). Radio Scotland is very useful for *Scottish* weather forecasts. Otherwise, the station broadcasts a broadly based mix of news, discussion, travel, magazine format, and music shows. There are also various commercial radio stations, some of which are good, some of which are startlingly amateurish.

Post offices

Post offices in reasonably sized Scottish towns were formerly instantly recognizable and housed in distinguished, often handsome, buildings. However, recently they have become heavily disguised as chemists or grocers, for example, and

Some old style red phone kiosks survive in Scotland

are much harder to identify. Look for the sign "Post Office," in yellow lettering on red. Beware of the tendency for small post offices to shut on half days and also on local holidays, which means making a journey to the nearest large town if postal services are required urgently. Otherwise, all post offices open for "conventional" shop hours, from approximately 9AM to 5PM and also on Saturday mornings. Most of the smaller post offices close for an hour at lunch time.

Telephones

Telephones are standard throughout the whole of the UK. Modern payphone equipment usually means that the amount of money inserted is shown on a display which "counts down" throughout the conversation. Some phones accept the commonly used credit cards. Fax machines are often available at hotels in Scotland, as well as at printing, photocopying, and internet access in larger towns.

Language guide

English-speakers will be able to understand just about anyone north of the Border unless people are using a particularly dense form of Scots. Scots speakers frequently "modulate" almost unconsciously into some form of "standard English" when they are dealing with non-Scots. As for the Gaels, they all speak English anyway, so there should be absolutely no problem.

Scottish post offices come in all shapes and sizes

Emergencies

In general, Scotland is an extremely safe destination, though the police would certainly advise using common sense.

Thefts from cars (and of cars) do occur, especially in the main cities, in crowded parking areas, and at popular beauty spots. It is not a good idea to keep valuable material of any sort in an unattended vehicle. If this is unavoidable then cover your belongings or lock them out of sight.

As for personal safety, again, use common sense. You are probably perfectly safe late at night in any Scottish city centre, but from time to time, incidents—muggings and worse—do occur, often alcohol-related.

One Scottish activity which all too often requires emergency action by the authorities is hillwalking. It must be strongly emphasized that Scotland's hills are rugged and should be treated with respect. Snow can occur above 900m (3,000ft) in any month, and hill conditions can change very rapidly. Proper water- and windproof clothing and equipment and—most importantly—properly soled hillwalking boots (definitely not with a cut-away heel) should be worn. **Always** take a map and compass, and know how to use them. The police also advise leaving word, for example, with your hotel, about your proposed route and estimated time of return. Though there are some obvious security implications, it is also advisable to leave a similar note displayed on or in your car.

Embassies and consulates

As Scotland is part of the UK, the chief foreign embassies are located in London. However, a number of representatives for other nations have consular offices within Scotland and these can be found in the *Yellow Pages*.
They include:

The US Consulate General
3 Regent Terrace
Edinburgh
tel: 0131 556 8315,
www.usembassy.org.uk/scotland/

Australian Consulate
69 George Street
Edinburgh, EH2 2JG
tel: 0131 624 3333;
www.australia.org.uk

Emergency telephone numbers

As in the rest of the UK, dial **999** to summon police, fire, and ambulance services, as well as coastguard and mountain rescue. These calls are free from all phones, including public payphones.

Lost property

The police operate an efficient lost property service, as do both the railways and major bus operators. Broadly speaking, the Scots are fairly honest and if an item is left behind in a restaurant or other establishment it is always worth going back or making enquiries by phone.

Health

Medical insurance If you fall ill in Scotland, unless you are a UK or EU (European Union) citizen, you are eligible only for free emergency treatment at National Health Service Accident and Emergency departments of hospitals. If you are hospitalized even from an Accident and Emergency department or referred to an out-patient clinic, you will be asked to pay. Therefore you are strongly advised to take out adequate insurance cover before travelling to Scotland. Your travel agent will advise.

Pharmacies Except in remote rural areas, where some doctors do their own dispensing, you must take a doctor's prescription to a pharmacy. These part-prescribing, part-retail businesses have normal shop hours plus a rota system whereby one pharmacy in a given area stays open to cover half-day closings and other holidays. In cities, there is usually a pharmacy staying open at other times to deal with urgent prescriptions. In all cases, a notice usually prominently displayed on the shop door will tell you where you can get the prescribed medication. In an emergency, police can contact a pharmacist and request him or her to attend.

Other information

Camping and caravanning
There are over 400 licensed and recognized camping and caravan parks in Scotland. All area tourist boards carry listings of parks within their own area while VisitScotland produces a comprehensive annual guide called *Scotland: The Official Where to Stay Caravan and Camping*. This is available both direct from VisitScotland (address on page 272) and from bookshops.

Caravanning is popular in Scotland. Any roads that are unsuitable for towed caravans are clearly marked. Towing a caravan on single track roads demands extra vigilance and care should be taken to ensure that following traffic is not held up. Please note that most local authorities do not permit overnight parking of caravans in laybys and other parking areas, and in places barriers prevent their entry.

So-called "wild camping" is still fairly popular in Scotland. In fact, Scotland is recognized as one of the last areas of the UK where camping away from official parks is still possible. It is always polite and in your own interests to seek out permission from the landowner first if intending to camp in the countryside.

Self-catering
The main single source of listings of self-catering properties is VisitScotland's *Scotland: The Official Where to Stay Self-Catering* guide, published annually and available direct from VisitScotland (address on page 272) or from bookshops. There are also a number of agencies specializing in self-catering property rental.

Visitors with disabilities
A comprehensive bank of information is available from Capability Scotland. Their database includes information on hotels, camping and caravanning, sports and leisure facilities, guest-houses, and so on. A holiday directory is also published, covering the whole of Scotland. Contact Capability Scotland at: 11 Ellersly Road, Edinburgh, EH12 6HY. (tel: 0131 313 5510, fax: 0131 346 1681, www.capability-scotland.org.uk.

Opening times
Opening times are given within the text for all main attractions and tourist sights. Information on opening times has been provided for guidance only. We have tried to ensure accuracy, but things frequently do change and we would advise readers to check locally before planning a trip to avoid any possible disappointment.

Scotland's supermarkets and DIY stores often open on Sundays even in quite small towns, and in the main cities shopping malls may also be open. In popular tourist areas most shops will open daily. Beware the local half-day closing, usually a Wednesday or Thursday, on which many little shops and small businesses in small towns close.

Evening opening for shopping is usually confined to Thursdays in the cities, though, certainly in Edinburgh, bookshops in particular are tending to open late in the evening. In addition, many superstores stay open most nights till around 8PM.

Conservation bodies
Historic Scotland
Longmore House,
Salisbury Place,
Edinburgh
EH9 1SH
(tel: 0131 668 8800,
www.historic-scotland.gov.uk).

The government agency that is responsible for the preservation of a huge range of monuments from standing stones to castles and industrial buildings.
Many of its properties have standard opening hours: Apr–Sep, daily 9.30–6.30; Oct–Mar, Mon– Sat 9:30–4.30, Sun 2–4.30.

National Trust for Scotland,
28 Charlotte Square,
Edinburgh
EH2 4ET
(tel: 0131 243 9300,
www.nts.org.uk).

The leading charitable organization that cares for castles and other grand properties, as well as a smaller range of humbler places, and also wild land of high landscape value.

Other information

Scottish Natural Heritage, 12 Hope Terrace, Edinburgh EH9 2AS (tel: 0131 447 4784, fax: 0131 446 2277, www.snh.org.uk). The main government agency with responsibility for environmental matters and nature conservation, it operates nature reserves in some of Scotland's finest unspoilt places.

Royal Society for the Protection of Birds, Dunedin House, 25 Ravelston Terrace, Edinburgh EH4 3TP (tel: 0131 311 6500; www.rspb.org.uk). The leading charitable body in the preservation of habitat suitable for birdlife, this operates a number of nature reserves of high ornithological interest.

Scottish Wildlife Trust, Cramond House, 16 Cramond Glebe Road, Edinburgh EH4 6NS (tel: 0131 312 7765, fax: 0131 312 8705, www.swt.org.uk). Scotland's own charitable conservation agency, concerned with the preservation of habitat for all kinds of wildlife, operates a number of nature reserves.

Places of worship

Scotland recognizes many religions. The most widespread is the (Presbyterian) Church of Scotland.

Dunblane Cathedral, a historic setting for Sunday worship

Roman Catholics, Episcopalians, Baptists, and Free Presbyterians are also represented as well as a variety of non-denominational "chapels" and other sects.

Because of liberal Sunday drinking laws and shopping hours, Sabbath observance is fairly low-key, with the notable exception of Lewis and Harris and also Skye. The local press usually carries church notices with times of worship. Tourist Information Centres will also help.

Toilets

Public toilet provision in Scotland is fairly good but does seem to vary in standard between local authorities. Some are free; some attended toilets require a small fee.

Photography

With its spectacular scenery, Scotland is a great place for photography. Because it is a popular hobby, even quite small towns often have photography businesses where a wide range of film can be obtained and disks printed. Pharmacists and other shops, particularly in tourist areas, also carry stocks of film.

Electricity

Voltage is 240V 50Hz AC, as in the rest of the UK. If you need a voltage adaptor it is best to buy one before you leave home. Almost all accommodation in Scotland has 3 square pin sockets for 3, 5 and 13amp fused plugs.

Etiquette: dealing with the Scots

Preconceived images can make it easy to see the Scots as being more "different" than they actually are. Certainly, the Scots can be defined as an ethnic minority within the United Kingdom, but they differ from the other groups in quite subtle ways. However, the Scots have an intense dislike of being labelled English.

Also to be noted is the curious double meaning of the word "national," which within the Scottish media can mean either Scottish or UK-wide British, depending on the context. Radio Scotland, for instance, announces itself as "The National Network." Many of the subtle distinctions that mark out the Scots are linguistic, and in everyday speech there are opportunities for misunderstanding.

A number of minor points of etiquette apply to food and drink. Do not be surprised to be given biscuits and home-bakes if invited into someone's house for coffee or tea, no matter what the hour of the day. When ordering beer in Scottish pubs listen out for the local words "export," "heavy," and "special," rather than the English word "bitter," which is virtually absent north of the Border. And finally, if your host offers you a dram (a glass of whisky) and suggests malt whisky rather than an everyday blend, only add water, if anything, to it. Ginger or other soft drinks will be at least an irritation, if not an insult.

However, no one is going to mind if you put sugar instead of salt in your porridge; nobody is going to arrest you for wearing the "wrong" tartan (there is no such thing); and hardly anyone will even notice if you get the words of "Auld Lang Syne" wrong at the end of the ceilidh. (Most Scots do as well.)

Please note. For reasons quite unknown, the Scots do not like to be "Scotch" and much prefer "Scottish." See also below.

Scotch a word for whisky never used by Scots people.

Scotch broth broth made with a meat stock, plenty of vegetables, and lots of barley to give it a glutinous texture.

Scotch egg a boiled egg in sausage meat and breadcrumbs.

Scotch mist a characteristic western weather condition of relentlessly damp misery, created to test cheap summer anoraks.

Scotch bluebell *Campanula rotundifolia*, called the harebell south of the border, and common on Scottish heaths.

Scotch thistle the national emblem of Scotland, sometimes called the cotton thistle, though not a native plant.

Scotch verdict "not proven," a peculiarity of Scotland's legal system.

CONVERSION CHARTS

FROM	TO	MULTIPLY BY
Inches	Centimetres	2.54
Centimetres	Inches	0.3937
Feet	Metres	0.3048
Metres	Feet	3.2810
Yards	Metres	0.9144
Metres	Yards	1.0940
Miles	Kilometres	1.6090
Kilometres	Miles	0.6214
Acres	Hectares	0.4047
Hectares	Acres	2.4710
Gallons	Litres	4.5460
Litres	Gallons	0.2200
Ounces	Grams	28.35
Grams	Ounces	0.0353
Pounds	Grams	453.6
Grams	Pounds	0.0022
Pounds	Kilograms	0.4536
Kilograms	Pounds	2.205
Tons	Tonnes	1.0160
Tonnes	Tons	0.9842

MEN'S SUITS

UK	36	38	40	42	44	46	48
Rest of Europe	46	48	50	52	54	56	58
US	36	38	40	42	44	46	48

DRESS SIZES

UK	8	10	12	14	16	18
France	36	38	40	42	44	46
Italy	38	40	42	44	46	48
Rest of Europe	34	36	38	40	42	44
US	6	8	10	12	14	16

MEN'S SHIRTS

UK	14	14.5	15	15.5	16	16.5	17
Rest of Europe	36	37	38	39/40	41	42	43
US	14	14.5	15	15.5	16	16.5	17

MEN'S SHOES

UK	7	7.5	8.5	9.5	10.5	11
Rest of Europe	41	42	43	44	45	46
US	8	8.5	9.5	10.5	11.5	12

WOMEN'S SHOES

UK	4.5	5	5.5	6	6.5	7
Rest of Europe	38	38	39	39	40	41
US	6	6.5	7	7.5	8	8.5

Tourist Information Centres

Tourism in Scotland is in the control of VisitScotland, 23 Ravelston Terrace, Edinburgh EH4 3EU, tel: 0845 2255 121, fax: 0131 315 4545, www.VisitScotland.com.

All telephone calls are now centralized. If you call Visit Scotland they will be able to help you with all queries. In exceptional circumstances, when specialized knowledge is needed, they will direct you to the appropriate local tourist office. The majority of Tourist Information Offices throughout Scotland are now walk-in centres only and cannot be contacted by telephone or fax. They still offer the full range of local advice, and brochures and leaflets.

In Scotland there is an integrated network of TICs. The main offices are:

- Edinburgh and Scotland Information Centre, Waverley Market, 3 Princes Street, Edinburgh EH2 2QP tel: 0845 2255 121
- Greater Glasgow and Clyde Valley Tourist Board, 11 George Square, Glasgow G2 1DY tel: 0141 204 4400

The South

- Ayr: 22 Sandgate, Ayr KA7 1BW
- Jedburgh: Murray's Green, TD8 6BE
- Linlithgow: Burgh Halls, The Cross, EH49 7AH
- Peebles: High Street, EH45 8AG

Central Scotland

- Dundee : 21 Castle Street, DD1 3AA
- Perth West Mill Street, PH1 5QP
- St. Andrews: 70 Market Street, KY16 9NU
- Stirling: The Esplanade, FK8 1EH

The Northeast

- Aberdeen: 23 Union Street, AB11 5BP
- Elgin: 17 High Street, IV30 1EG

Great Glen and Western Highlands

- Aviemore: Grampian Road, Inverness-shire PH22 1PP
- Fort William: Cameron Square, Inverness-shire, PH33 6AJ
- Inverness: Castle Wynd, IV2 3BJ
- Oban: Argyll Square, Argyll PA34 4AR

The Northern Highlands

- Dornoch: The Square, Sutherland IV25 3SD
- Thurso: Riverside, KW14 8BU
- Ullapool: Argyle Street, IV26 2UB

The Islands

- Orkney: 6 Broad Street, Kirkwall KW15 1DH
- Shetland: Market Cross, Lerwick ZE1 0LU
- Skye: Bayfield House, Bayfield Road, Portree IV51 9EL
- Stornoway: 26 Cromwell Street, Lewis HS1 2DD

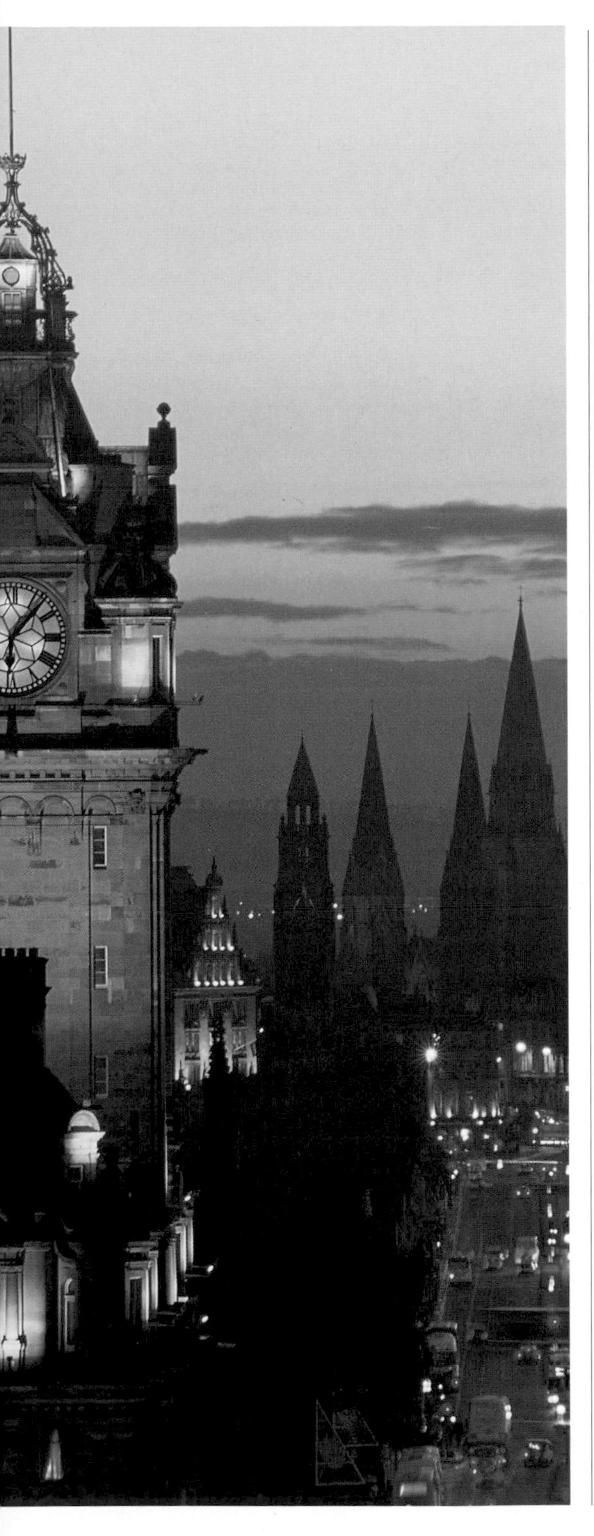

Hotels & Restaurants

HOTELS

Finding good accommodation is not a problem. Off-season rates vary, and may be negotiable.

As a rough guide in this listing £££ is over £100 per person for bed and breakfast; ££ is between £50 and £100; and £ is under £50.

Full listings of inspected and graded hotels, guesthouses and bed-and-breakfast establishments across Britain and Ireland can be found and booked at the AA's Internet site: www.theAA.com/hotels.

EDINBURGH

Balmoral Hotel (£££)
1 Princes Street, Edinburgh EH2 2EQ tel: 0131 556 2414 www.roccofortehotels.com
£23 million bought a total refurbishment of this landmark hotel in the early 1990s. Roman-style health spa. 188 rooms.

The Bonham (£££)
35 Drumsheugh Gardens, Edinburgh EH3 7RN tel: 0131 226 6050 www.thebonham.com
A Georgian town house on the edge of the city's New Town. Striking bedrooms. 48 rooms.

The Carlton Hotel (£££)
North Bridge, Edinburgh EH1 1SD tel: 0131 472 3000 fax: 0131 556 2691 www.paramount-hotels.co.uk
Close to the Royal Mile, the Carlton has 189 rooms and extensive leisure facilities. Popular with visitors and the business trade.

Channings (££)
15 South Learmonth Gardens, Edinburgh EH4 1EZ tel: 0131 315 2226 or 0131 332 3232 www.channings.co.uk
A superbly stylish conversion of five Edwardian terraced town houses. A place for comfort and indulgence. 41 rooms.

Edinburgh Marriott Hotel (£££)
111 Glasgow Road, Edinburgh EH12 8NF tel: 0131 334 9191 or 0870 400 7293 www.marriott.co.uk
Modern hotel on western outskirts, 245 bedrooms. Leisure centre with pool.

George Inter-Continental (£££)
19–21 George Street, Edinburgh EH2 2PB tel: 0131 225 1251 www.edinburgh.interconti.com
Supremely convenient, luxury standard in elegant surroundings, 195 rooms.

The Howard (£££)
34 Great King Street, Edinburgh EH3 6QH tel: 0131 557 3500 fax: 0131 557 6515 www.thehoward.com
Ideal central location amid New Town refinement. Very comfortable. 18 rooms.

Malmaison (£££)
1 Tower Place, Leith, Edinburgh EH6 7DB tel: 0131 468 5000 www.malmaison.com
Elegantly converted from a former seamen's mission, close to the waterfront. Striking decor. Rooms have CD players and minibars. 10 minutes from the city centre. 101 rooms.

Norton House (£££)
Ingliston, Edinburgh EH28 8LX tel: 0131 333 1275 fax: 0131 333 5305 www.handpicked.co.uk
In 22ha (55 acres) of parkland setting on the western outskirts of the city, a country house hotel close to airport and motorway system. 47 rooms.

Open Arms Hotel (££–£££)
Dirleton, East Lothian EH39 5EG tel: 01620 850241 www.openarmshotel.com
Old-established, much-loved, comfortable hotel in attractive village, easy access to Edinburgh. 10 rooms.

The Prestonfield Hotel (£££)
Prestonfield Road, Edinburgh EH16 5UT tel: 0131 225 7800 www.prestonfield.com
Opulence and luxury are the bywords of this lavishly restored mansion house, located near the Royal Commonwealth Pool, with 24 rooms and a top restaurant.

The Roxburghe (£££)
38 Charlotte Square, Edinburgh EH2 4HG tel: 0131 240 5500 www.macdonald-hotels.co.uk
Right in the heart of the New Town, with 197 well-equipped bedrooms and a choice of restaurants. Indoor heated pool and gym, dance studio, and spa treatments.

The Scotsman Hotel (£££)
20 North Bridge, Edinburgh EH1 1YT tel: 0131 556 5565 www.thescotsmanhotel.co.uk
Stylish modern hotel in the former headquarters of *The Scotsman* newspaper, superbly equipped, with stainless steel swimming pool. 69 luxurious rooms.

Sheraton Grand Hotel and Spa (£££)
1 Festival Square, Edinburgh EH3 9SR tel: 0131 229 9131 www.starwood.co.uk
This opulent and stylish hotel adds a subtly Scottish stamp to Sheraton quality without resorting to clichés. Outdoor hydropool.

GLASGOW

Beardmore Hotel (£££)
Beardmore Street, Clydebank, West Dumbartonshire G81 4SA tel: 0141 951 6000
Stylish modern hotel on the banks of the River Clyde, with 166 rooms, complimentary therapies, a solarium and indoor pool. Innovative contemporary cooking in the restaurant.

De Vere Cameron House (£££)
Balloch G83 8QZ tel: 01389 755565 www.devereonline.co.uk
Top-quality hotel on banks of Loch Lomond, a 30-minute drive from city centre. 96 luxurious bedrooms. Sports facilities include 9-hole golf.

Glasgow Marriott (£££)
500 Argyle Street, Glasgow G3 8RR tel: 0870 400 7230 fax: 0870 400 7330 www.marriott.co.uk
Close to the Kingston Bridge and SEC, modern 300-bed hotel with sports facilities including gym and heated indoor pool.

Holiday Inn (££–£££)
161 West Nile Street, Glasgow G1 2RL tel: 0141 352 8300 www.higlasgow.com
Central city hotel with 113 modern bedrooms. Parking nearby.

Malmaison (£££)
278 West George Street, Glasgow G2 4LL
tel: 0141 572 1000
www.malmaison.com
Style-conscious hotel with 72 rooms (CD players, minibars) and good French cuisine in brasserie restaurant. Small gym.

One Devonshire Gardens (£££)
1 Devonshire Gardens, Glasgow G12 0UX
tel: 0141 339 2001 fax: 0141 337 1663
www.onedevonshiregardens.com
Adjoining elegantly furnished town houses. Very high reputation in all departments, 35 rooms, several with four-poster beds.

Premier Travel Inn (Glasgow City Centre) (££)
Montrose House, 187 George Street, Glasgow G1 1YU tel: 0870 238 3320
www.premiertravelinn.co.uk
Modern building with accommodation in spacious, en suite bedrooms. Great for families. No restaurant. 254 rooms.

The Radisson SAS Glasgow (££)
301 Argyle Street, Glasgow G2 8DL
tel: 0141 204 3333
www.radisson.com
Set in the heart of the city centre, opposite Central Station, this modern hotel offers every facility, including Jacuzzi, sauna, indoor pool and 247 comfortable, stylish bedrooms.

THE SOUTH

Ayr

Piersland House Hotel (£££)
Craigend Road, Troon, Ayrshire KA10 6HD
tel: 01292 314747
www.piersland.co.uk
Fine Edwardian mansion with 30 rooms (including one with four-poster bed), originally built for whisky firm owner.

Savoy Park Hotel (££)
16 Racecourse Road, Ayr KA7 2UT
tel: 01292 26112
www.savoypark.com
Well-established, traditional hotel offering baronial style and elegance, with the feel of a Highland shooting lodge. Convenient for racegoers. 15 rooms.

Dalbeattie

Balcary Bay Hotel (££)
Auchencairn DG7 1QZ
tel: 01556 640217/640311
www.balcary-bay-hotel.co.uk
Waterside hotel dating from 1625 with 1.25ha (3 acres) of lovely gardens and 20 well-equipped bedrooms.

Dumfries

Cairndale Hotel and Leisure Club (£££)
English Street, Dumfries DG1 2DF
tel: 01387 254111 fax: 01387 250555
www.cairndalehotel.co.uk
Within walking distance of the town centre, each of the 91 rooms in this hotel have tea- and coffee-making equipment and satelite TV. Leisure facilities include a heated indoor pool, sauna, Jacuzzi, and steam room.

Gatehouse-of-Fleet

Cally Palace Hotel (££)
Gatehouse-of-Fleet, Kirkcudbrightshire DG7 2DL
tel: 01557 814341 www.callypalace.co.uk
Georgian mansion set in a large forested estate. Extensive leisure facilities. 55 rooms, one with four-poster. Indoor heated pool and 18-hole golf course.

Kelso

Cross Keys (££)
36–37 The Square, Kelso TD5 7HL
tel: 01573 223303
www.cross-keys-hotel.co.uk
Former coaching inn in town centre. 27 rooms, café bar and restaurant.

Ednam House Hotel (££)
Bridge Street, Kelso TD5 7HT
tel: 01573 224168
www.ednamhouse.com
Tradionally run Georgian mansion beside the River Tweed, with 30 rooms and choice of public areas.

The Roxburghe Hotel & Golf Course (£££)
Heiton, Kelso, Roxburghshire TD5 8JZ
tel: 01573 450331
www.roxburghe.net
Formerly called Sunlaws House, this luxurious country house is of the highest standard, owned by the Duke of Roxburghe. 22 rooms, five with four-poster beds.

Melrose

Burt's Hotel (££)
Market Square, Melrose, Roxburghshire TD6 9PL tel: 01896 822285
www.burtshotel.co.uk
Friendly, family-run hotel of the kind that generates a loyal local clientele. Ideally placed for Border touring. 20 rooms, all non-smoking.

Moffat

Moffat House Hotel (££)
High Street, Moffat, Dumfriesshire DG10 9HL
tel: 01683 220039
www.moffathouse.co.uk
An elegant, 20-room Adam house, near town centre, well placed for north-bound travellers and Border explorers.

Newton Stewart

Kirroughtree House (££–£££)
Minnigaff, Newton Stewart DG8 6AN
tel: 01671 402141
www.kirroughtreehouse.co.uk
A 17th-century mansion house set high above Wigtown Bay. Elegant interior decoration, which includes antiques, and stunning views. 17 rooms, one with four-poster.

North Berwick

Greywalls (£££)
Muirfield, Gullane, East Lothian EH31 2EG
tel: 01620 842144 www.greywalls.co.uk
Architecturally exciting house by Edward Lutyens, adjacent to some of Scotland's best golf. 23 rooms.

Portpatrick

Fernhill Hotel (££)
Heugh Road, Portpatrick DG9 8TD
tel: 01776 810220 www.fernhillhotel.co.uk
Family-run, elevated position on coastal site, excellent service. 36 rooms. Golf nearby.

Peebles

Cringletie House Hotel (£££)
Edinburgh Road, Eddleston EH45 8PL
tel: 01721 725750 www.cringletie.com
Plenty of personal and professional attention in rural, family-run, 14-room baronial mansion.

Park Hotel (££)
Innerleithen Road, Peebles EH45 8BA
tel: 01721 720451 www.parkpeebles.co.uk
24-room hotel with valley views; guests can use leisure facilities of sister hotel, the Hydro.

St Boswells

Dryburgh Abbey Hotel (££–£££)
St. Boswells TD6 0RQ tel: 01835 822261
www.dryburgh.co.uk
Stone-built mansion set beside Dryburgh Abbey ruins. Spacious, with 38 rooms and pool.

Stranraer

North West Castle Hotel (££)
Stranraer, Wigtownshire DG9 8EH
tel: 01776 704413
www.northwestcastle.co.uk
Excellent range of leisure facilities at this former home of Arctic explorer. 72 rooms. Curling rink in winter.

Strathaven

Strathaven Hotel (££)
Hamilton Road, Strathaven, Lanarkshire
ML10 6SZ tel: 01357 521778
www.strathavenhotel.com
Adam fireplace and stairway feature in this refurbished house, 22 rooms, making ideal base for Glasgow.

Turnberry

Malin Court Hotel (££)
Turnberry KA26 9PB tel: 01655 331457
www.malincourt.co.uk
Eighteen rooms, including nine family rooms in this comfortable, low-built complex, with great views over the Firth of Clyde and the famous golf course.

The Westin Turnberry Resort (£££)
Turnberry KA26 9LT tel: 01655 331000
www.westin.com/turnberry
Famous golfing hotel with spa, leisure suite, and every comfort. 221 rooms.

CENTRAL SCOTLAND

Blair Atholl

Atholl Arms Hotel (£–££)
Old North Road, Blair Atholl, Perthshire PH18 5SG tel: 01796 481205
www.athollarmshotel.co.uk
Convenient for both Blair Castle and the local railway station, this traditional inn has a baronial dining room, friendly staff and just 30 bedrooms. Fishing and shooting can be arranged.

Blairgowrie

Kinloch House Hotel (£££)
by Blairgowrie, Perthshire PH10 6SG
tel: 01250 884237 www.kinlochhouse.com
Mid-19th-century oak-panelled country house with 18 rooms, fine antiques (and 130+ malt whiskies). Heated indoor pool.

Callander

Roman Camp Country House Hotel (£££)
Callander, Perthshire FK17 8BG tel: 01877 330003 www.roman-camp-hotel.co.uk
Beautiful riverside site for this charming 17th-century house, like a small château. 14 rooms. Fishing nearby.

Dunblane

Cromlix House Hotel (£££)
Kinbuck, Dunblane, Stirling FK15 9JT
tel: 01786 822125
www.cromlixhouse.com
Sweeping gardens and a magnificent estate surround this imposing old mansion, with falconry and archery as optional extras. 14 rooms.

Dundee

Apex City Quay Hotel & Spa (££–£££)
1 West Victoria Dock Road, Dundee DD1 3JP
tel: 01382 202404
www.apexhotels.co.uk
Part of Dundee's regenerated heart, this smart and comfortable 153-bedroom hotel is purpose-built. Indoor pool and sauna.

Premier Travel Inn Dundee Centre (££)
Discovery Quay, Riverside Drive, Dundee DD1 4XA tel: 08701 977079
www.premiertravelinn.com
High-quality, modern budget accommodation in the middle of Dundee's top attractions, with family restaurant close by. 40 rooms.

East Neuk Villages

Old Manor Hotel (£££)
Leven Road, Lundin Links KY86 6AJ
tel: 01333 320368
www.oldmanorhotel.co.uk
On village outskirts with sea views. 24 rooms with modern furnishings. Golf nearby. Choice of restaurants.

Glamis

Castleton House Hotel (£££)
Castleton of Eassie, by Glamis, Angus DD8 1SJ
tel: 01307 840340
www.castletonglamis.co.uk
Splendid Victorian house hotel boasting its very own moat, as well as top-notch food in the conservatory restaurant. Putting green, and just 6 bedrooms.

Kirkcaldy

Dunnikier House Hotel (££)
Dunnikier Park, Kirkcaldy, Fife KY1 3LP
tel: 01592 268393
www.dunnikier-house-hotel.co.uk
Enjoy comfort and good food in this imposing 18th-century former manor house. Park views, and right by golf course. 15 rooms.

Perthshire

The Gleneagles Hotel (£££)
Auchterarder, Perthshire PH3 1NF
tel: 01764 662231
www.gleneagles.com
Arguably Scotland's best-known hotel, with the ambience of an ocean-going liner. Your every need is catered for; you will never need to step outside the hotel grounds. 269 bedrooms, 11 with four-posters. Superb leisure facilities.

Green Hotel (££)
2 The Muirs, Kinross, Perthshire KY13 8AS tel: 01577 863467
www.green-hotel.com
A 46-room independent hotel, with an excellent range of leisure facilities including its own golf courses, heated indoor pool, and gym.

Huntingtower Hotel (££–£££)
Crieff Road, Perth PH1 3JT
tel: 01738 583771
www.huntingtowerhotel.co.uk
Smart Edwardian country house in idyllic rural setting, just west of the city, with prices including a skilfully prepared dinner in the Oak Room restaurant. 34 rooms.

Pitlochry

Knockendarroch House Hotel (££)
Higher Oakfield, Pitlochry, Perthshire PH16 5HT
tel: 01796 473473
www.knockendarroch.co.uk
Victorian mansion, 12 rooms, of considerable charm and style.

Pine Trees Hotel (££)
Strathview Terrace, Pitlochry PH16 5QR
tel: 01796 472121
www.pinetreeshotel.co.uk
With marble staircase and ornate plasterwork, this 20-room mansion set in 4ha (10 acres) of secluded grounds, offers high standards in all areas.

St. Andrews

The Old Course Hotel (£££)
Old Station Road, St. Andrews KY16 9SP
tel: 01334 474371
www.oldcoursehotel.kohler.com
Superb setting beside the 17th hole of the famous championship course. 146 rooms. Gymnasium and indoor pool. Excellent restaurants.

Rufflets Country House (£££)
Strathkinness Low Road, St. Andrews KY16 9TX tel: 01334 472594
www.rufflets.co.uk
Country house in its own grounds; garden provides fresh produce for restaurant. 24 rooms.

Russell Hotel (££)
26 The Scores, St. Andrews KY16 9AS
tel: 01334 473447
www.russellhotelstandrews.co.uk
Family-run hotel with 10 rooms, close to Old Course on seafront.

St. Andrews Golf Hotel (£££)
40 The Scores, St. Andrews KY16 9AS
tel: 01334 472611
www.standrews-golf.co.uk
Close to the Old Course, large Victorian terraced building with high standards throughout. 21 rooms, and a choice of bars.

Stirling

Stirling Highland Hotel (££–£££)
Spittal Street, Stirling FK8 1DU
tel: 01786 272727
www.paramount-hotels.co.uk
Fascinating conversion of former high school, full of character and very comfortable. 96 rooms.

Travelodge (£)
Pirnhall Roundabout, Snabhead, Stirling FK7 8EU tel: 08700 850950
www.travelodge.co.uk
Good-value, modern accommodation at the M9/M80 intersection, ideal for families and well located for exploring the area. 37 spacious rooms.

THE NORTHEAST

Aberdeen

Ardoe House Hotel (££–£££)
South Deeside Road, Blairs, Aberdeen AB12 5PY tel: 01224 860600
www.macdonald-hotels.co.uk
Well-equipped baronial mansion in a superb position high above the River Dee, with countryside views. Spa and leisure club. 109 bedrooms.

Atholl Hotel (££)
54 King's Gate, Aberdeen AB15 4YN
tel: 01224 323505
www.atholl-aberdeen.co.uk
Handsome building in residential area, close to city centre. Personally-run establishment, friendly staff. 34 rooms which all have ADSL Internet access.

Craighaar Hotel (££)
Waterton Road, Bucksburn, Aberdeen AB21 9HS tel: 01224 712275
www.craighaarhotel.com
Behind a plain exterior there is plenty of design flair and a high standard of comfort. 55 rooms. Convenient for the airport.

Marcliffe at Pitfodels (£££)
North Deeside Road, Pitfodels, Aberdeen AB15 9YA tel: 01224 861000
www.marcliffe.com
Luxury hotel run by proprietors with plenty of experience of local hotel scene. 42 rooms. Spa and putting green available.

Maryculter House Hotel (££)
South Deeside Road, Maryculter AB12 5GB
tel: 01224 732124
www.maryculterhousehotel.com
To the south of Aberdeen, this ancient mansion is now a comfortable hotel, with open fires and cocktail bar. Fishing available. 23 rooms.

Ballater

Darroch Learg (££)
Braemar Road, Ballater AB35 5UX tel: 013397 55443
www.darrochlearg.co.uk
Country house in-town hotel, with Deeside views, 17 rooms and conservatory restaurant.

Banchory

Raemoir House Hotel (££)
Raemoir, by Banchory AB31 4ED
www.raemoir.com
A beautiful 18th-century mansion is the setting, with tapestries on the walls, open fires and

antiques. 20 bedrooms, shooting and deer stalking by arrangement.

Tor-na-Coille (££)
Banchory AB31 4AB tel: 01330 822242
www.tornacoille.com
Relish the period charm of this historic house, set in tree-studded grounds and opposite a golf course. Facilities include a squash court. 22 rooms.

Banff

Banff Springs Hotel (££)
Golden Knowes Road, Banff AB45 2JE
tel: 01261 812881 fax: 01261 815546
www.banffspringshotel.co.uk
A modern business and leisure hotel with 31 rooms. Sea views and gymnasium.

Craigellachie

Craigellachie Hotel (££)
Craigellachie, Banffshire AB38 9SR
tel: 01340 881204 fax: 01340 881253
www.craigellachie.com
Imposing fishing and shooting hotel with excellent food and 25 well-appointed rooms.

Cullen

The Seafield Hotel (££)
Seafield Street, Cullen AB56 4SG
tel: 01542 840791
www.theseafieldhotel.com
Originally built as a coaching inn in the appealing fishing town of Cullen, this comfortable old hotel features a carved wooden fireplace in the lounge bar. Cycling and quad biking available. 19 rooms.

THE GREAT GLEN & HIGHLANDS

Appin

Airds Hotel (£££)
Port Appin, Argyll PA38 4DF
tel: 01631 730236 www.airds-hotel.com
Stylish but relaxed family-run hotel, originally a ferry inn, with superb views over Loch Linnhe. 12 rooms. Fine dining.

Boat of Garten

The Boat Hotel (££–£££)
Boat of Garten, PH24 3BH
tel: 01479 831258, fax: 01479 831414
www.boathotel.co.uk
Stylish, smart hotel with warmth and charm. Excellent food. Steam railway close by.

Dunoon

Royal Marine Hotel (££)
Hunters Quay, Dunoon PA23 8HJ
tel: 01369 705810
www.rmhotel.co.uk
Great views over the Firth of Clyde from this welcoming, privately owned hotel. Bar and café-bar as well as formal dining. 31 rooms.

Fort William

Inverlochy Castle Hotel (£££)
Torlundy, by Fort William, Inverness-shire PH33 6SN tel: 01397 702177
www.inverlochycastlehotel.com
The by-word for luxury country house-style accommodation in Scotland. 17 rooms.

Kilcamb Lodge Hotel (££)
Strontian, Argyll PH36 4HY tel: 01967 402257
www.kilcamblodge.co.uk
Sturdy Georgian house with private shoreline on Loch Sunart. 12 rooms.

Letterfinlay Lodge Hotel (££)
Letterfinlay PH34 4DZ tel: 01397 712622
www.letterfinlaylodgehotel.com
Family-run hotel with 13 rooms, 20km (12mi) north of Fort William on A82. Views over Loch Lochy.

Moorings Hotel (££)
Banavie, Fort William, Inverness-shire PH33 7LY
tel: 01397 772797
www.moorings-fortwilliam.co.uk
Canal-side location with panoramic mountain views. Ideal touring base. 28 rooms.

Grantown-on-Spey

Culdearn House (££)
Woodlands Terrace, Grantown-on-Spey PH26 3JU tel: 01479 872106
www.culdearn.com
Small hotel where genuine hospitality and good food are part of the appeal.7 rooms, no children under 12.

Muckrach Lodge (££)
Dulnain Bridge PH26 3LY tel: 01479 851257
www.muckrach.co.uk
A former sporting lodge, set at the foot of the mighty Cairngorm Mountains, with a roaring log fire in the bary. Excellent restaurant, and bistro option. 14 rooms, all non-smoking.

Inverness

Bunchrew House (£££)
Bunchrew, Inverness IV3 8TA
tel: 01463 234917
www.bunchrew-inverness.co.uk
A 17th-century mansion set on the shores of Beauly Firth, popular with sporting, business, and leisure guests. 16 luxurious bedrooms, including four family bedrooms and two with four-poster beds.

Premier Travel Inn (££)
Millburn Road, Inverness IV2 3QX
tel: 08701 977141 fax: 01463 717826
www.premiertravelinn.com
Modern hotel with 39 spacious rooms. Good for families.

Lochgilphead

Cairnbaan Hotel (££)
Crinan Canal, Cairnbaan, by Lochgilphead PA31 8SJ tel: 01546 603668
www.cairnbaan.com
Watch the bustle of the water traffic at the lock here in summer, and tuck into fresh seafood in the pleasant restaurant. 12 rooms.

Oban

Ardanaiseig Hotel (£££)
Kilchrennan, by Loch Awe, Argyll PA35 1HE
tel: 01866 833333
www.ardanaiseig.com
Superb country house in romantic setting with outstanding garden.

Falls of Lora Hotel (£–££)
Connel, by Oban PA37 1PB tel: 01631 710483
www.fallsoflora.com
A popular hotel, with restaurant and bistro bar. 30 rooms, ranging from luxury to basic.
Isle of Eriska (£££)
Ledaig, by Oban, Argyll PA37 1SD
tel: 01631 720371
www.eriska-hotel.co.uk
Family-owned baronial mansion offering the highest standards of comfort. 17 rooms
Manor House Hotel (£££)
Gallanach Road, Oban PA34 4LS
tel: 01631 562087 www.manorhouseoban.com
Set in Georgian mansion, close to centre. 11 rooms with sea views. Excellent restaurant.

Onich

Onich Hotel (£–£££)
Onich PH33 6RY tel: 01855 821214
www.onich-fortwilliam.co.uk
Find this modern hotel on the shores of Loch Linnhe, just north of Ballachulish, its gardens extending down to the waterside. 25 rooms. Facilities include a games room.

THE NORTHERN HIGHLANDS

Dornoch

Burghfield House (£–££)
Dornoch, Sutherland IV25 3HN
tel: 01862 810212
www.burghfieldhouse.com
Victorian mansion in extensive gardens, with antiques. 14 rooms, plus 15 annexe rooms.

Gairloch

Myrtle Bank Hotel (£)
Low Road, Gairloch IV21 2BS
tel: 01445 712004
www.myrtlebankhotel.co.uk
Friendly, family-run hotel with seafront location and views to the Isle of Skye. Superb sunset views from the restaurant. 12 rooms.

Invergordon

Kincraig House Hotel (££)
Invergordon IV18 0LF tel: 01349 852587
www.kincraig-house-hotel.co.uk
Crow-stepped gables, a tower and friendly hospitality are all part of the appeal of this picturesque, white-painted mansion house overlooking the Cromarty Forth. 15 rooms.

Lochinver

Inver Lodge Hotel (££)
Lochinver, Sutherland IV27 4LU
tel: 01571 844496
www.inverlodge.com
Modern hotel with wide coastal views, 20 rooms with good facilities. Solarium and sauna.

Scourie

Eddrachilles Hotel (££)
Badcall Bay, Scourie IV27 4TH
tel: 01971 502080 www.eddrachilles.com
Spectacular island-studded views. 11 well-equipped bedrooms.

Tain

Glenmorangie Highland Home at Cadboll (£££)
Cadboll, Fearn IV20, 1XP
tel: 01862 871671
www.glenmorangieplc.co.uk
Meals are served in dinner-party style at this remarkable, historic Highland home-from-home. Top-quality hospitality and facilities, including beauty treatments and husky sled tours. 9 rooms. No children under 14.

Torridons

Loch Torridon Country House Hotel (£££)
Torridon, by Achnasheen, Wester Ross
IV22 2EY tel: 01445 791242
www.lochtorridonhotel.com
Delightful hotel with very high standards and an excellent reputation. 19 bedrooms, all non-smoking.
Tigh an Eilean Hotel (£££)
Shieldaig, by Strathcarron, Wester Ross
IV54 8XN tel: 01520 755251
email: tighaneilanhotel@shieldaig.fsnet.co.uk
Welcoming hotel, 11 rooms. Good seafood.

THE ISLANDS

Arran

Auchrannie Country House Hotel (££)
Brodick, Arran KA27
www.auchrannie.co.uk
Previously home to a dowager duchess, a 28-bedroom hotel with luxurious add-on leisure facilities, including indoor pool and gym.
Kilmichael Country House Hotel (£££)
Glen Cloy, Brodick KA27 8BY
tel: 01770 302219
www.kilmichael.com
Delightful small mansion close to Brodick, with flowers, books and excellent food. Seven rooms. No children under 12.

Harris

Scarista House (£££)
Scarista, Isle of Harris HS3 3HX
tel: 01859 550238
www.scaristahouse.com
Elegance and comfort in this hotel which has a high reputation for its cuisine. Five rooms.

Mull

Highland Cottage Hotel (££–£££)
Breadalbane Street, Tobermory PA75 6PD
tel: 01688 302030
www.highlandcottage.co.uk
Sitting high above Tobermory, the island's capital, this gem of a place offers natural and unassuming hospitality and just 6 rooms. It can be found opposite the fire station.
Tobermory Hotel (£–££)
53 Main Street, Tobermory PA75 6NT
tel: 01688 302091 fax: 01688 302254
www.thetobermoryhotel.com
Some of the 16 rooms at this pink facaded, waterfront hotel have harbour views.

Shetland (Mainland)
Lerwick Hotel (££)
15 South Road, Lerwick ZE1 0RB
tel: 01595 692166
www.shetlandhotels.com
Recently refurbished hotel, near town centre with 34 rooms, and a restaurant with sea views.
Shetland Hotel (££)
Holmsgarth Road, Lerwick ZE1 0PW
tel: 01595 695515 www.shetlandhotels.com
Modern 64-roomed hotel conveniently located for the ferry.

Skye
Bosville Hotel (££)
Bosville Terrace, Portree, isle of Skye IV51 9DG
tel: 01478 612846
www.macleodhotels.co.uk
Admire the views over the harbour from this handsome, stylish hotel, with its excellent restaurant, and leisure-club facilities. 25 rooms.

RESTAURANTS

It is possible to eat very well in Scotland, though locals sometimes argue that the best produce is sent south to market. Scotland's cities are notably cosmopolitan in their offerings.

As a rough guide in this listing, £££ is over £30 per person for a three-course meal excluding drinks, ££ is between £30 and £20, and £ is under £20.

EDINBURGH

The Atrium (££)
10 Cambridge Street, Edinburgh EH1 2ED
tel: 0131 228 8882
Fresh Scottish produce, with a strongly theatrical element. Popular with locals.
La Garrigue (£–££)
31 Jeffrey Street, Edinburgh EH1 1DH
tel: 0131 557 3032
www.lagarrigue.co.uk
Rustic and informal French dining, with cool blue walls, wooden floor and handsome wooden furniture to match. Hearty menu—try the cassoulet for gutsy flavours.
Haldanes (£–££)
39A Albany Street, Edinburgh EH1 3QY
tel: 0131 556 8407
www.haldanesrestaurant.com
A tranquil oasis in the heart of this busy city, Haldanes offers a top-notch, modern Scottish menu of the freshest ingredients, served in the basements of three Georgian town houses.
Henderson's Salad Table and Wine Bar (£)
94 Hanover Street, Edinburgh EH2 1DR
tel: 0131 225 1231
www.hendersonsofedinburgh.co.uk
A New Town institution for more than 40 years, Henderson's is a favourite vegetarian restaurant, with deli attached. Steps lead down to a basement restaurant, where the décor may be limited but the wholefood is superb.
Malmaison Brasserie (££)
1 Tower Place, Leith, Edinburgh EH6 7DB
tel: 0131 468 5001
www.malmaison.co,uk
Chic brasserie food in a docklands setting.
Martin's (££)
70 Rose Street, North Lane, Edinburgh EH2 3DX
tel: 0131 225 3106
Tucked well away in a city-centre service lane but in the top-flight. Simply one of the very best anywhere in Scotland. Modern British cuisine.
No. 1 The Restaurant (£££)
Balmoral Hotel, 1 Princes Street, Edinburgh EH2 2EQ tel: 0131 557 6727
www.thebalmoralhotel.com
Deep red décor and top quality modern Scottish cuisine, served in supreme style.
Vintner's Rooms (££)
The Vaults, 87 Giles Street, Leith, Edinburgh EH6 6BZ tel: 0131 554 6767
A restaurant and wine bar of high repute, housed in a 17th-century building in Edinburgh's port. Serves French cuisine in modern style.
The Witchery by the Castle (££)
Castle Hill, Edinburgh EH1 2NF
tel: 0131 225 5613
www.thewitchery.com
Two atmospheric candlelit rooms in which to savour the latest cooking trends and a huge choice of wines. Situated by the gates of Edinburgh Castle.

GLASGOW

The Buttery (£££)
652 Argyle Street, Glasgow G3 8UF
tel: 0141 221 8188
An old-established restaurant with famously polite, unobtrusive service and great food. Traditional Scottish cooking with a modern twist.
Cafe Ostra (£)
The Italian Centre, 15 John Street, Glasgow G1 1HP tel: 0141 552 4433
www.cafeostra.com
Laid-back seafood bistro in the Italian centre that caters for a friendly mix of students, shoppers and businesspeople. Sample salmon and leek quiche, or perhaps fish soup with crab, ginger and herb oil, to a jazz soundtrack.
Ètain (££–££)
Princes Square, Glasgow G1 3JX
tel 0141 225 5630
www.etain-restaurant.co.uk
This Conran-styled restaurant is on the top floor of a glass-fronted building in the heart of the city, serving top-quality Scottish food with a strong French twist. Poached Loch Fyne oysters with champagne sabayon could be just the starter.
Gamba (£–££)
225a West George Street, Glasgow G2 2ND
tel: 0141 572 0899
Basement restaurant with a Mediterranean feel. Scottish seafood is a speciality.
Malmaison Café Bar and Brasserie (£)
278 West George Street, Glasgow G2 4LL
tel: 0141 572 1001
www.malmaison.co.uk
British favourites mix with classic French dishes in this booth-lined basement restaurant.

Stravaigin (£–££)
30 Gibson Street, Glasgow G12 8NX
tel: 0141 334 2665
www.stravaigan.com
Cheerful basement restaurant serving excellently prepared dishes from around the world including Hanoi, Chile, and Mexico, using Scottish ingredients. Situated next to Glasgow University.

Ubiquitous Chip (££–£££)
12 Ashton Lane, Glasgow G12 8SJ
tel: 0141 334 5007
www.ubiquitouschip.co.uk
A sophisticated interpretation of Scotland's larder is guaranteed at "the Chip"; the discriminating Glaswegian's restaurant choice in the West End.

THE SOUTH & FIFE

Anstruther
Cellar Restaurant (££–£££)
24 East Green, Anstruther, Fife KY10 3AA
tel: 01333 310378
Probably one of the best seafood restaurants in Scotland. Don't miss it if visiting Fife.

Ayr
Fouters Bistro Restaurant (££)
2A Academy Street, Ayr KA7 1HS
tel: 01292 261391
www.fouters.co.uk
A highly regarded establishment taking full advantage of Ayrshire's own produce. Exciting food, and interesting ambience in these old bank vaults.

Dalry
Braidwoods Restaurant (££)
Drumcastle Mill Cottage, Dalry, Ayrshire KA24 4LN tel: 01294 833544
Locally caught seafood, and the best lamb feature on their ever-changing menu.

Elie
Sangsters Resaurant (£–£££)
51 High Street, Elie, Fife KY9 1BZ
tel: 01333 331001
www.sangsters.co.uk
Relaxed and friendly restaurant on the main street of this little coastal town, with funky cutlery and big plates. The set lunch is particularly good value, but keep space for desserts such as lemon and blueberry moulee.

Gullane
La Potinière (£££)
Main Street, Gullane EH31 2AA
tel: 01620 843214
www.la-potiniere.co.uk
Near-legendary restaurant in this popular golfing resort, transcending fashion to go its own sophisticated way.

Open Arms Hotel (££)
Dirleton, East Lothian EH39 5EG
tel: 01620 850241
www.openarmshotel.com
Food with plenty of panache provided by very experienced hoteliers.

Linlithgow
Champany Inn (££–£££)
Linlithgow EH49 7LU
tel: 01506 834532
www.champany.com
Legendary restaurant famous for its menu devoted to first-class Aberdeen Angus beef.

Portpatrick
Knockinaam Lodge (£££)
Portpatrick, Galloway DG9 9AD
tel: 01776 810471
www.kockinaamlodge.com
A place of pilgrimage for foodies in the far west;- serves basically modern French and highly inventive cuisine.

Swinton
Wheatsheaf Restaurant with Rooms (££)
Main Street, Swinton TD11 3JJ
tel: 01890 860257
The menu at this country inn features carefully cooked seasonal produce.

Troon
Lochgreen House Hotel (££–£££)
Monktonhill Road, Southwood, Troon, Ayrshire KA10 7EN tel: 01292 313343
www.costleyhotels.co.uk
Top-notch dining in this luxurious country house hotel. The four-course dinner menu gives a French twist to locally sourced ingredients, including Ayrshire lamb.

CENTRAL SCOTLAND

Arbroath
Gordon's Restaurant (££)
Homewood House, Main Street, Inverkeilor, by Arbroath, Angus DD11 5RN
tel: 01241 830364
www.gordonsrestaurant.co.uk
Cosy village restaurant, decorated in cottage style.

Blairgowrie
Kinloch House Hotel (££–£££)
Blairgowrie PH10 6SG tel: 01250 884237
www.kinlochhouse.com
The fruit and vegetables from the 19th-century walled garden of this country house are married to the very best Scottish meats and seafood. A special dining experience.

Callander
Roman Camp Country House Hotel (£££)
Callander, Perthshire FK17 8BG
tel: 01877 330003
www.roman-camp-hotel.co.uk
Cooking with Scottish flair at the restaurant of this old country house by the river.

Carnoustie
11 Park Avenue (££)
11 Park Avenue, Carnoustie DD7 7JA
tel: 01241 853336
www.11parkavenue.co.uk
Unpretentious town-centre restaurant offering good, simply cooked food.

Crieff
The Bank Restaurant (££)
32 High Street, Crieff PH7 3BS
tel: 01764 656575
www.thebankrestaurant.co.uk
Housed in a former bank, the food here is fresh and simple, with French influences.

Killiecrankie
Killiecrankie House Hotel (£££)
Killiecrankie, Pitlochry PH16 5LG
tel: 01796 473220
www.killiecrankiehotel.co.uk
Great atmosphere and cuisine proving that modern trends do penetrate far beyond the big cities.

Luss
Colquhoun's (££)
Luss, Argyll G83 8PA
tel: 01436 860201
www.loch-lomond.co.uk
Quality food is served in undisturbed scenic surroundings in the Lodge on Loch Lomond Hotel.

Perth
Let's Eat (£)
77–79 Kinnoull Street, Perth PH1 5EZ
tel: 01738 643377
www.letseatperth.co.uk
Modern bistro in the heart of Perth occupying the site of a former theatre. Simple, quality food, and a great atmosphere, thanks to warm colours and shelves of cookbooks.

THE NORTHEAST

Aberdeen
Ardoe House Hotel (£££)
South Deeside Road, Blairs, Aberdeen AB12 5YP tel: 01224 867355
Country-house-style panelled dining room in a baronial mansion, featuring a menu of game, seafood and excellent puddings.
Maryculter House Hotel (££)
South Deeside Road, Aberdeen AB12 5GB
tel: 01224 732124
www.maryculterhousehotel.com
Popular hotel on the banks of the River Dee that puts the emphasis on prime Scottish produce.
The Silver Darling (££–£££)
Pocra Quay, North Pier, Aberdeen AB11 5DQ
tel: 01224 576229
Romantic seafood restaurant with stunning views over the harbour, in a former customs house, with a conservatory. Fish is freshly caught, the cooking style French. Look for dolphins in the bay, too.

Ballater
Balgonie House Hotel (££–£££)
Braemar Place, Ballater AB35 5NQ
tel: 013397 55482
www.balgonie-hotel.co.uk
Local salmon and seafood fresh from the east coast feature on the French-influenced menu at Balgonie House, a secluded mansion popular with country sports enthusiasts.
Darroch Learg Hotel (£££)
Braemar Road, Ballater AB35 5UX
tel: 013397 55443
www.darrochlearg.co.uk
A Victorian mansion on Royal Deeside with a set-price or taster menu offering Scottish produce cooked with great flair.

Craigellachie
Craigellachie Hotel (£££)
Craigellachie, AB38 9SR
tel: 01340 881204
www.craigellachie.com
Fine dining in the heart of Speyside at this impressive Victorian hotel, in the centre of the village. The décor is traditional, with hunting artefacts and log fires, the food locally sourced, including Craigellachie smoked salmon.

Elgin
Mansion House Hotel (££–£££)
The Haugh, Elgin IV30 1AW
tel: 01343 548811
Candlelit dining room in a baronial mansion, where the cooking is based on the best Scottish produce.

Montrose
Best Western Links Hotel (££)
Mid Links, Montrose, Angus DD10 8RL
tel: 01674 671000
www.linkshotel.co.uk
For an exciting menu in a trendy, Parisian-style bistro, look no further than this newly refurbished Edwardian hotel, where daring menus are matched by accomplished cooking. Also a popular jazz venue.

Stonehaven
The Tolbooth (££)
Old Pier Road, Stonehaven AB3 2JU
tel: 01569 762287
www.tolboothrestaurant.co.uk
The modern, Scottish cuisine revolves around availability, with fish dominating the menu. It's popular with both visitors and locals. Closed Sun and Mon.

THE GREAT GLEN & WESTERN HIGHLANDS

Arduaine
Loch Melfort Hotel (££)
Arduaine, by Oban PA34 4XG
tel: 01852 200233
www.lochmelfort.co.uk
Set beside Arduaine Gardens and with sea views, a hotel restaurant emphasizing seafood.

Fort William
Inverlochy Castle House (££–£££)
Torlundy, by Fort William PH33 6SN
tel: 01397 702117
www.inverlochycastlehotel.com
With Ben Nevis providing the backdrop, this splendid castle, on the edge of a loch, is the setting for lavish dining on the best of Scottish cuisine. Notable wine list, too.

Inverness

Culloden House Hotel (£££)
Culloden IV2 7BZ tel: 01463 790461
www.cullodenhouse.co.uk
The modern set-price dinner menu remains loyal to traditional Scottish roots.

Rocpool (££)
1 Ness Walk, Inverness IV3 5NE
tel: 01463 717274
A lively, cosmopolitan air prevails at this modern, Mediterranean-themed restaurant overlooking the river. The cooking takes in Pacific Rim and Italian influences, for a truly international feel. Advance booking advised.

Kingussie

The Cross (£££)
Tweed Mill Brae, Ardbroilach Road, Kingussie, Inverness-shire PH21 1LB tel: 01540 661166
www.thecross.co.uk
A mill conversion full of character, but do not be distracted from the top-quality food.

Nairn

The Boath House (£££)
Auldearn, by Nairn IV12 5TE
tel: 01667 454896
www.boath-house.com
Stunning food and effortless service are the main attractions at this small country house hotel. The menu reflects Scottish and French influences, including fresh produce from the hotel's own walled garden. Fixed price lunch and dinner.

Oban

Airds Hotel (£££)
Port Appin, Argyll PA38 4DF tel: 01631 730236 www.airds-hotel.com
This elegant hotel, housed in a former ferry inn, offers creative food with great finesse.

Isle of Eriska Hotel (£££)
Isle of Eriska, Ledaig, by Oban, Argyll PA37 1SD
tel: 01631 720371
www.eriska-hotel.co.uk
An island setting for a hotel dining room with a daily changing, six-course menu, ably supported by Scottish game, fish, and seafood.

THE NORTHERN HIGHLANDS

Achiltibuie

The Summer Isles Hotel (£££)
Achiltibuie IV26 2YG
tel: 01854 622282
www.summerisleshotel.co.uk
Dinner at this remote, peaceful gem of a hotel is a special experience, with stunning sunset views across to the rugged islands of the Hebrides. The fixed-price, five-course menu is based on the best local produce. Closed Oct–Easter.

Dornoch

2 Quail Restaurant (£££)
Inistore House, Castle Street, Dornoch IV25 3SN tel: 01862 811811
www.2quail.com
Offering a limited number of dishes that are all part of a three-course set meal. Charming, friendly service and intimate dining, with just four tables. Closed Sunday and Monday.

Dundonnell

Dundonnell Hotel (££)
Dundonnell IV23 2QS tel: 01854 633204
www.dundonnellhotel.com
Highland hospitality beside Little Loch Broom, where the chef excels at fish and seafood.

Lochinver

The Albannach (£££)
Baddidarrach, by Lochinver IV27 4LP
tel: 01571 844407
www.thealbannach.co.uk
The daily-changing, five-course menu combines French techniques with Scottish flavours, making the most of locally caught fish, deer from the nearby forest, and lamb and beef from Moray's farms. Closed mid-Nov to mid-Mar.

Tongue

Ben Loyal Hotel (££)
Main Street, Tongue IV27 4XE tel: 01847 611216 www.benloyal.co.uk
A family-run hotel offering ambitious British cooking, including Thai-spiced langoustines, with poached peach pavlova for dessert.

THE ISLANDS

Arran

Auchrannie Country House Hotel (££–£££)
Brodick, Isle of Arran KA27 8BZ
tel: 01770 302234
www.auchrannie.co.uk
Enjoy fine dining in the Garden restaurant of this popular resort hotel in the island's capital. Modern Scottish dishes might include truffle-crusted loin of venison, followed by raspberry and Drambuie brûlée.

Mull

Druimard Country House Hotel (£££)
Dervaig, Isle of Mull PA75 6QW
tel: 01688 400345
www.druimard.co.uk
Enjoy potted wild salmon with oatcakes, game terrine, and iced cranachan at this personally run small hotel.

Orkney

Creel Restaurant (££)
Front Road, St Margaret's Hope, South Ronaldsay, Orkney KW17 2SL
tel: 01856 831311
www.thecreel.co.uk
A very popular restaurant working wonders with seafood, as well as Orkney beef and lamb.

Skye

Cuillin Hills Hotel (£££)
Portree, Isle of Skye IV51 9QU
tel: 01478 612003
www.cuillinhotel-skye.co.uk
Smart hotel offering a menu based on fresh local produce. Some traditional favourites and Highland specialities.

Index

285

286

T

U

W

Y

Picture Credits

The Automobile Association would like to thank the following photographers, libraries and associations for their assistance in the preparation of this book.

ABERDEEN UNIVERSITY LIBRARY 42–43 Embarking at Broomielaw, Glasgow MARY EVANS PICTURE LIBRARY 25 19th-century shipbuilding, 28 Bannockburn, 30–31 execution warrant, 34–35 Battle of Prestonpans, 38/39 Crofters of Lewis, 41 Andrew Carnegie, 56b Stevenson sketch, 104–105 Robert Burns, 197a Culloden D. HARDLEY 110 Culzean Castle, 120 Logan Gardens, 202 Mull of Kintyre, 231a Rothesay Harbour, 232 Colonsay, 234 Islay, 235a Ferry to Jura, 235b Kildalton Cross GLASGOW SCIENCE CENTRE 79a HULTON DEUTSCH COLLECTION LTD 42b building of the *Queen Mary*, 205a Loch Ness Monster NATIONAL GALLERY OF SCOTLAND 33 Earl of Seafield PICTURES COLOUR LIBRARY 139 ROYAL GEOGRAPHICAL SOCIETY 37a map SCONE PALACE 150 Scone Palace SCOTTISH PARLIAMENTARY CORPORATE BODY 2005 21a New debating chambers, Holyrood SPECTRUM COLOUR LIBRARY 39 Dunrobin Castle

The remaining photographs are held in the Automobile Association's own library (AA PHOTO LIBRARY) and were taken by: M. ADLEMAN 38, M. ALEXANDER, 18–19, 23b, 40b, 76, 77, 78a, 78b, 81a, 81b, 82a, 82b, 83b, 83c, 86a, 86b, 87a, 87b, 90, 91, 94, 97, 98, 99, 100a, 100b, 101, 102, 106a, 106b, 107, 112a, 112b, 113a, 113b. 114a, 115, 118a, 124, 125a, 125b, 127a, A. BAKER 17a, 131, 147a, 154, 155a, 155b, 155c, 172–173, 190b ,J. BEAZLEY 5c, 9, 35a, 108b, 109a, 109b, 114b, 116, 117, 118b, 121a, 121b, 122a, 122b, 128b, 192, 193a, 196, 200b, 213b, 216, 221a, 221b, P.&G. BOWATER 169b, J. CARNIE 2, 10a, 10b, 14, 15, 20b, 31, 34, 130, 138, 151c, 184, 189, 190, 191, 195a, 199, 200a, 204, 205b, 212a, 213a, 226, 230, 231b, D. CORRANCE 20a, 23a, 48a, 49, 50, 51a, 51b, 55, 59a, 64, 67, 111, 119, 127b, 129a, 129b, S. L. DAY 11a, 13b, 18, 19, 21b, 22a, 22b, 24a, 29a, 29b, 35b, 128a, 132/133, 135a, 135b, 135c, 136, 137, 139, 140, 141b, 142a, 142b, 143a, 143b, 144a, 144b, 145a, 145b, 147b, 148, 149, 151a, 151b, 152, 153a, 153b, 156, 157, 158, 159a, 159b, 160–161, 160, 161, 167b, 186, 187a, 187b, 188a, 193b, 194, 195b, 198, 203, 206, 207a, 207b, 260, 261b, 263a, 263b, 266a, 270, E. ELLINGTON 5a, 7, 16–17, 26b, 163, 164, 165a, 166, 167a, 168, 170b, 174, 175a, 176a, 176b, 177a, 177b, 179, 182a, 210, 211a, 212b, 214, 215, 217a, 217b, 218–219, 218, 220a, 223a, 223b, 224b, 227, 228, 229a, 229b, 238, 239a, 239b, 240a, 240b, 242a, 242b, 243, 244a, 244b, 245a, 245b, 246, 247a, 247b, 262, 265, 267a. R. G. ELLIOTT 6–7, 64–65, 68, 69, 70b, 95b, 96, 220b, 225, 226–227, 236a, 236b, 236c, 237a, 237b, 248, 249a, 249b, 250a, 252b, 252c, 254a, 254b, 255, 267b, 273, S. GIBSON PHOTOGRAPHY 43, 79b, 80, 83a, 85a, 88a, 88b, 89a, 92, 93a, 93b, 95a, 108a, 264, D. HARDLEY 27, 146, 219, A. J. HOPKINS 188b, 222, R. JOHNSON 241, S. KING 148–149, CAMERON LEES 60b. S.&O. MATHEWS 126, K. PATERSON 3, 8, 11b, 12a, 12b, 13a, 16, 17b, 32a, 32b, 36a, 37b, 44, 46, 47, 48b, 52a, 52b, 53, 54a, 54b, 56a, 56b, 57, 58, 59b, 60a, 61a, 61b, 62, 63a, 63b, 65, 66, 70a, 71, 72a, 72b, 73, 74a, 74b, 75a, 75b, 136, 141a, 261a, 266b, D. ROBERTSON 5b, P. SHARPE 84, 103a, 103b, 105, 170a, 201, M. TAYLOR 171a, 171b, 171c, 178, 180, 211b, 224a, R. WEIR 4, 24a, 134, 165b, 169a, 172, 173, 175b, 183, 197b, 252a, 253, S. WHITEHORNE 123a.

Contributors

Original copy editor: Barbara Fuller   Revision verifier: Ann F. Stonehouse